Walden Pond

Walden Pond
A History

W. BARKSDALE MAYNARD

OXFORD
UNIVERSITY PRESS

OXFORD
UNIVERSITY PRESS

Oxford New York
Auckland Bangkok Buenos Aires Cape Town Chennai
Dar es Salaam Delhi Hong Kong Istanbul Karachi Kolkata
Kuala Lumpur Madrid Melbourne Mexico City Mumbai Nairobi
São Paulo Shanghai Taipei Tokyo Toronto

First published by Oxford University Press, Inc., 2004
198 Madison Avenue, New York, New York 10016
www.oup.com

First published as an Oxford University Press paperback, 2005
ISBN-13: 978-0-19-518137-1
ISBN-10: 0-19-518137-9

Oxford is a registered trademark of Oxford University Press

The Library of Congress has catalogued the cloth edition as follows:
Maynard, W. Barksdale (William Barksdale)
Walden Pond: a history / W. Barksdale Maynard.
p. cm.
Includes bibliographical references and index.
ISBN-13: 978-0-19-516841-9 ISBN-10: 0-19-516841-0
1. Walden Pond (Middlesex County, Mass.)—History.
2. Thoreau, Henry David, 1817–1862—Homes and haunts—Massachusetts—
Walden Pond (Middlesex County).
I. Title.

F72.M7M56 2003
974.4'4—dc21 2003051867

1 3 5 7 9 8 6 4 2
Printed in the United States of America
on acid-free paper

Contents

❧

List of Maps

Preface and Acknowledgments

❧

One rainy August afternoon in 1986, I stepped inside the Thoreau Lyceum, a warmly lit and cluttered enclave that offered a cheerful welcome to a college student on a pilgrimage. It was my first visit to Concord, and to my delight a young man offered to take the afternoon off and show me around Walden Pond. I remember standing beside the cairn in the rain, then climbing the hill behind it to see the moldering stumps of white pines that Thoreau had supposedly planted in his former beanfield.

That memorable visit raised more questions than it answered, however. Here before Thoreau's door was a sizable marsh hardly mentioned in *Walden*. Thoreau had lived on Emerson's land, but nobody seemed exactly sure where the boundaries of that property lay. And if the beanfield had been behind Thoreau's house, far from Walden Road, how could the *agricola laboriosus* have overheard bypassers' conversations, as he said he had? Small questions, it would seem, but suggestive of how much remained mysterious about the places Thoreau cherished. The more I read about him, the more it seemed that the scholarly emphasis had long been on his ideas and his life story, not on the landscapes from which he drew inspiration, places that it might be possible to revisit today, if only they could be identified.

A decade passed before I visited Walden again, with Susan Matsen, who encouraged me to renew my youthful interest in Thoreau and undertake research toward the present book. I soon learned that I was not alone in my curiosity about Thoreau Country, past and present. Photographer Herbert Gleason drew an indispensable map a century ago. J. Walter Brain, Tom Blanding, Richard O'Connor, Ray Angelo, and others have explored Concord minutely seeking to match Thoreau's journal accounts to the contemporary environment. More casual explorations have been taken every summer by Thoreau Society members in Concord for their annual gathering. Walden Pond has always been a chief focus of these visits, and back in 1970, Pulitzer Prize-winning naturalist Edwin Way Teale urged Walter Harding of the Society, "Why don't you write a book on the most famous pond in the world, a book that will contain *everything* about Walden?" The busy Harding never produced that volume. Surely the need for it only grew greater, though, with the conservation battles that erupted over Walden Woods not long after my initial visit. Now that the dust has settled, the time seems right for a detailed study of the pond and its surroundings, one that will build on the extensive research that has been carried out by many talented scholars and enthusiasts.[1]

Walden Pond: A History is the first book-length account of this famous place since Thoreau's *Walden* was published 150 years ago, and it is meant to provide context for that earlier classic. There is much that *Walden* is deliberately vague about. What role did Emerson play in Thoreau's intellectual development and his decision to build a rustic house? What experiences did Thoreau have in Walden Woods in the seven years it took for his book to be completed and published? I have tried to address these questions and others, hoping that readers will want to reread *Walden*, perhaps with a fuller understanding of its roots in the literary and landscape setting of Concord. The maps attempt to update—for Walden Woods, at least—Gleason's now-venerable one from the 1906 journal edition. I hope they will be helpful to readers of *Walden* who desire a visual and geographical framework in which to understand the phenomena Thoreau describes.

Much has happened at Walden Pond since Thoreau last visited its shores six generations ago. In the second half of the book, I have tried to interweave two connected stories, ever-increasing touristic visitation and the growth of Thoreau's literary fame. With their depiction of noise, crowds, and environmental crisis, these chapters may disillusion those who cherish *Walden* and love to hear the pond's water "in the deep heart's core." But Walden and surrounding woods have proven surprisingly resilient, are being managed with increasing skillfulness, and retain considerable beauty even in the overdeveloped twenty-first century. Visit early in the morning—or in rainy weather, as I did that August afternoon—and you can still have a Thoreau-like experience.

Research for *Walden Pond: A History* was undertaken in 2001-02 and was facilitated by a series of stays at the Thoreau Institute at Walden Woods. I wish to thank Don Henley, Kathi Anderson, Helen Bowdoin, Jeff Cramer, and the entire staff for their hospitality and assistance. Much of my research was done in Special Collections, Concord Free Public Library, where Leslie P. Wilson and Joyce Woodman were unfailingly helpful. Denise Morrissey and Steve Carlin patiently answered my many questions at Walden Pond State Reservation.

All whom I met in Concord and Lincoln showed great warmth in welcoming an outsider recklessly trespassing onto the geographic and intellectual territory they know so well. Thanks to Peter Alden, Ronald Bosco, Debra Kang Dean, Malcolm Ferguson, Tom Harris, Joe Lenox, John Hanson Mitchell, David Sibley, Richard Smith, Lucille Stott, Edna Toska, Joe Wheeler, and David Wood. Thanks too to all the Thoreauvians I met at three annual gatherings of the Thoreau Society. Elsewhere in the United States, I wish to thank Ray Angelo, David Barto, Anthony Bianculli, Jack Borden, Phyllis Cole, John Colman, Randall Conrad, Charles Cook, Jacqueline Davison, Dave Ganoe, Ron Hoag, Hugh Howard, William Howarth, Donald Linebaugh, John McPhee, Nedda Moqtaderi, Wes Mott, John Paoletti, Sandra Petrulionis, Dale Schwie, Charles Seib, Laura Dassow Walls, Stuart Weinreb, Richard Winslow, and Ann Zwinger.

The scholarly literature on Thoreau is vast, and I have constantly been aware of my debt to other researchers. Especially valuable were the vast amounts of primary material published over the years by Walter Harding and Kenneth Cameron. Thoreau expert Brad Dean has been a model of scholarly mentoring. Tom Blanding annotated my manuscript extensively. Ed Schofield sent thick research files from his extensive personal collections and offered great encouragement. In addition to the last three, a remarkable group of people read all or part of the manuscript or examined the maps. They were Kathi Anderson, Ken Bassett, Helen Bowdoin (who kindly passed my draft on to many others), J. Walter Brain, Brian Donahue, Steve Ells, Jayne Gordon, Michael Kellett, Vidar Jorgensen, Richard O'Connor, and anonymous readers. Those who know Thoreau Country will appreciate what an illustrious group this represents, and I am grateful for the many comments that all these readers made. Far from jealously guarding their domain, they showed great generosity in sharing knowledge acquired through years of research and exploration. Thanks also to readers Katherine Maynard, Mims Zabriskie, and Pauline Pelletier.

Concerning the contentious issues of the 1990s, I have tried to incorporate reviewers' divergent perspectives within the framework of a brief chapter, recognizing that the results will satisfy no one completely. The fact that a person reviewed the manuscript in no way implies that he or she endorsed my final conclusions. Any factual errors are entirely my responsibility, and I hope that readers will inform me of them.

The maps, redrawn from my originals by Barbara Stein, attempt to show woods and woodlots near Walden in 1850, based on historical sources, including the writings of Thoreau and the maps of John G. Hales (1830), H. F. Walling (1852), and Albert E. Wood (1895). Richard O'Connor provided additional details. Advocates for conservation of Thoreau Country stress that Walden Woods is not confined to the wooded outlines of 1850 or any other calendar year, but represents an ecological region as defined by potential natural vegetation, geology, and other factors. My maps do not intend to show "Walden Woods" as it is currently understood, but instead the approximate extent of non-agricultural land at a specific time in history.

I am grateful to Susan Ferber and the staff of Oxford University Press for their great skill in bringing the book to publication. As with my previous book, *Architecture in the United States, 1800–1850*, this one would not have been possible without the assistance of my parents, George and Isabel Maynard of Birmingham, Alabama. Susan Matsen, too, has helped make this book a reality by her constant love, support, and good ideas, not to mention her extraordinary patience with the stringencies of what Emerson called the "life of labor and study."

Walden Pond

I

❧

In Morning Time

❧

At five A.M. the power shuts off to an electromagnetic gate, which automatically unlocks. With the cessation of current and the click of the latch, another day begins at Walden Pond State Reservation, fifteen miles west of Boston. This system, like everything at Walden, is a compromise—it allows fishermen to drive down a steep road and unload their boats into the water, but never quite as early as they would like. Sometimes they complain and ask for 4:30, but in the end they accept the limitations that are imposed, as must all users of the park. The gate discourages nocturnal mischief makers, and in the hours of darkness it divides the pond from the larger world of traffic and noise that rushes by on Route 126. In a larger sense, it divides nature from culture, past from present, ideal from reality; as Thoreau said of his nearby beanfield, it is "the connecting link between wild and cultivated" spheres. Because this is Walden Pond, the gate with its electromagnetic lock is as awesome a symbol as the Gates of Paradise or of Elysium, for one inclined to see things that way.[1]

It is right to begin in the morning, as fishermen's boats splash into the water and the first streaks of dawn glow ruddy over Pine Hill at the east end. "All memorable events, I should say, transpire in morning time and in a morning atmosphere," Thoreau declared. He used the word *morning* nearly a hundred times in *Walden*. It was his

Famed for trout.
A. H. Kleinberg of
Arlington caught rainbow
trout in Walden, April 1944.
From Williams, "Walden,
Then and Now."

private hour, powerfully symbolic of the renewal in both nature and the human spirit that lay at the heart of his transcendentalist creed. Each morning the world was reborn; each morning the mind of the philosopher, refreshed, could look clearly into the heart of things. It is right, too, to begin with the fishermen, because they were here at the start—Walden's day begins with them, and so did Walden's history. First on the scene, always, are fishermen.[2]

Thoreau knew them well and admired the fact that they spent mornings in nature. "Such is oftenest the young man's introduction to the forest, and the most original part of himself. He goes thither at first as a hunter and fisher, until at last, if he has the seeds of a better life in him, he distinguishes his proper objects, as a poet or naturalist it may be, and leaves the gun and fish-pole behind." Thoreau had followed this progression, for he had once been that young fisherman at Walden. But as an adult, whenever he tried fishing, he wished he hadn't; he felt a certain loss of self-respect, as if he were wasting time and violating his principles as a transcendentalist and philosopher-vegetarian: "It is a faint intimation, yet so are the first streaks of morning."[3]

Few fishermen have been converted by Thoreau's preaching. In early hours they troll the waters of Walden from boats or stand along the stony shoreline. In winter, they cut holes in the ice. Smallmouth and largemouth bass, perch, and shiners swim these waters, along with pumpkinseed, bluegill, chain pickerel, and brown bullhead in the warmer parts and rainbow smelt in the colder. The public is cautioned against regularly eating any of these, especially the bass, owing to high levels of mercury in the area's ponds and rivers. In spring and fall, thousands of fingerling trout are dumped in, making Walden one of the finest trout ponds in New England, yielding annual-record rainbow and brown trout, some as heavy as ten pounds and more than two feet long, the largest taken in winter through the ice. Those days are blessed compared to summer, when the fishing is abruptly spoiled in midmorning with the arrival of that other, ancient denizen of Walden waters: the swimmer.[4]

The diehards are here earliest, and they and the fishermen glower at each other. Fishermen fume when swimmers breaststroke between line and boat. Swimmers fret about lures and hooks the fishermen strew. Walden attracts Olympic-quality swimmers with expensive wetsuits who swing muscular arms on Red Cross Beach before slipping beneath the waves. Others are less athletic but come constantly in a quasi-religious ritual. Over the years, their numbers have included some famous intellectuals. The expatriate German Bauhaus architect Walter Gropius was one. Another was psychologist B. F. Skinner. Landscape historian Frederick Turner liked to skinny-dip off the railroad embankment in summer. Today's regulars divide themselves into select enclaves, shunning the crowds at the east end on what they dismissively label "Dirty Diaper Beach." On Swimmer's Point, as some now call it, at the mouth of Thoreau's Cove an intellectual coterie gathers daily to swim and talk geopolitics, ignoring the tourists who stream by on their obligatory trek to Thoreau's housesite.[5]

On Red Cross Beach, an octogenarian spreads his towel on his usual sandy spot beneath the birches. Thoreau called this "the fireside," the warmest corner in winter, and this swimmer is among a dedicated few who brave the waters into January. His memories of Walden go back far, to when he first visited at age eight. His parents had gone "promenading" and dancing in their youth at the Lake Walden amusement park on the west shore, and they told of how the locomotive would stop there in winter so that ice could be taken to fancy Boston hotels for the drinks. He spent childhood summers on this beach and now smiles to recall rafts so crowded they would sink, the first lifeguard tower he had ever seen, people going down the tin slides four at a time—the metal so hot it burned. Bathhouses were separated by sex, as was swimming. His mother allowed him to hitchhike here in summer from "Ahlington," as he calls the Boston suburb of Arlington, with one stipulation—that he only climb into a "nice" car.

One senses, as he arranges his towel, that Walden is his private paradise, and yet he shares it with thousands in summertime. The place has long been a beloved swimming hole for greater Boston, and swimmers account for many of the seven hundred thousand annual visitors. A count of monthly attendance in 1994-96 showed ten thousand people coming in each of the sparsest months, December and January, and more than one hundred thousand in July. Attendance on a hot Saturday or Sunday can reach eight, ten, perhaps even fifteen thousand—notwithstanding the "official" limit of one thousand users at any one time, enforced by periodic closures of the parking lot. Many have learned to park elsewhere and trudge in. Such hefty visitation makes this fragile park, for its size, one of the most intensively used in the United States. It attracts not Concordians so much as residents of Boston's near-suburbs, from Malden to Waltham. On Main and Red Cross Beaches, Hispanic, Eastern European, and Asian tongues are heard as often as English. "Body to body, beach towel to beach towel, the blankets stripe the edges of the sacred shore," observed historian Jane Holtz Kay. By late morning the scent of suntan lotion wafts up and over Walden Road. "I went to Walden Pond the other day and laid my towel down on the little beach," one urbanite recalled. "If all the residents in my building were to sit on the throw rug beneath my dining room table we would have more personal space."[6]

Undeniably, Walden Pond is rather ordinary, just "the average mean of New England nature," as a 1905 visitor said, or, to Kay more recently, "pleasant if unspectacular." It is one of 1100 Massachusetts lakes. Even Thoreau admitted that "the scenery of Walden is on a humble scale." As for any uniqueness, he wrote that nearby White Pond was "just like" it—and, in fact, "since the wood-cutters, and the railroad, and I myself have profaned Walden, perhaps the most attractive, if not the most beautiful, of all our lakes, the gem of the woods, is White Pond." Walden Pond is not even the only Walden Pond in the state; there is one in the town of Lynn, north of Boston. Walden can lay claim to just one superlative, that of being the deepest lake in Massachusetts. With an average depth of forty feet, a 102-foot, seven-story office building could be fully dunked in the middle of the pond.[7]

From the reservation parking lot a paved road leads steeply down the east bank, to the lakeside path that sees tourists stepping over the bikini-clad by noontime. At the foot of the road a young man in a business suit talks loudly into his cellphone: "Mom, it's really a *lake!*" His reaction is common. Anne McGrath, longtime curator of the Thoreau Lyceum in Concord, said that "about ninety percent of visitors think of Walden as a little pool of sacred water deep in primeval woods" and are shocked by the reality. "I was seated by the shore of a small pond," said Thoreau, which does nothing to prepare us for a truly sizable body of water—61.5 acres, as big as forty-seven football fields.[8]

"Pond" was once common New England usage for even the largest lakes. Still today, of the nine biggest natural lakes in Massachusetts, seven are called "pond." The smallest of these, Monponsett Pond, is more than twelve times larger than Walden. In the late nineteenth century, many New England ponds were rechristened "lake." And if it weren't for Thoreau's book, people might well call it "Lake Walden" today, as that name flourished during the heyday of the picnic grounds. Some early-twentieth-century visitors complained about the abandonment of Thoreau's title for the pond—"If it were not for Thoreau, it would not matter what anybody called it"—and when in 1922 the place became a park meant to safeguard a famous transcendentalist landscape, it was called Walden Pond once again, and always will be.[9]

One comes to Walden seeking nature and Thoreau, but as often as not it is people who arrest the attention. Fanatical, get-out-of-my-way joggers on the encircling path. Bespectacled professors pondering deep mysteries. Overprotective mothers snatching toddlers from the aquatic dangers of Main Beach. Preening teenyboppers arrayed on the griddle at Red Cross, with a busload of foreign tourists trundling amongst them in evident confusion. A photographer who comes at the exact same hour every morning to record water and sky from a fixed location, showing nature's kaleidoscopic moods. Hikers for whom Walden Woods is just one stretch of the Bay Circuit Trail; they are aware, as most visitors are not, that the pond lies, in Thoreau's words, "in the midst of an extensive wood" between Concord and Lincoln, a wood linked to other woods now that the Massachusetts forests have regenerated on a vast scale.[10]

"Many a traveller" visited Thoreau at Walden, and these are their descendants. Thoreau's own house was always unlocked, and friends and strangers stopped by anytime: "One man proposed a book in which visitors should write their names, as at the White Mountains; but alas! I have too good a memory to make that necessary." His memory would not suffice today, as the guestbook for 1999 alone shows signatures from every state and ninety-one foreign countries. Entries from summer 2001 reveal that among the crowds of tourists ticking off obligatory Boston sites are, in fact, some dedicated Thoreauvians. "Reading an 1883 edition of *Walden*," one writes. An Austrian says, "I'm on a transcendentalist pilgrimage." One couple reports, "Trying our best to live deliberately." Such visitors can quote favorite passages from memory: "To suck all the marrow out of life." "Drive life into a corner." "In wildness is the preservation of the world." "Wherever I sat, there I might live." "Keep your accounts on a thumbnail."[11]

For many of these passionate visitors, Walden fulfills an old yearning: "I can't believe I'm finally here!" "Now I understand." For a couple from Delaware, "It took over forty years but we are not too late!" But others carp about high parking fees or, until it was recently closed, the Concord Landfill that loomed over the reservation's northeastern treeline. A Minnesotan writes, "So sad to see Thoreau's solitary spot commercialized." "Walden deformed and scarred by tourists, progress, capitalism." "Thoreau is rolling over in his grave." "I wonder what fraction of the many that visit understand even a little of this place's significance." Some, however, are pleasantly surprised: "Nicer than in the '60s." "Much better preserved than I would have thought." "Heard there were condos around the pond now. Glad I heard wrong."

For all the changes that Walden has suffered since Thoreau's day, guestbook comments suggest that it retains considerable capacity to

Transcendentalist dreamer. N. C. Wyeth's 1942 vision of Thoreau beside his beanfield, *Walden Pond Revisited*. Collection of the Brandywine River Museum, Bequest of Carolyn Wyeth, 1996.

uplift. A traveler from England "sat & wrote & sketched for three hours. How can one not be inspired here?" Standing inside the replica, some seem ready to change their lives: "I want to live deliberately." "We long for this life." "Makes me rethink my lifestyle." "It's amazing what we can do without." "Let's start throwing out our cell phones now!" Pond and house can be very personal places, even for those who have never seen them before: "Henry D., I'm home."

These devotees know the story well—how Henry David Thoreau lived the simple life by the pond's northwestern cove in a tiny house of his own construction for two years, two months, and two days. He was twenty-seven years old when he moved in on July 4, 1845. Here he wrote his first book, *A Week on the Concord and Merrimack Rivers*. It was a commercial flop of legendary proportions. But here too he wrote the initial version of the work that gained him, and the environs, fame and immortality. Several drafts later,

Walden was published, in 1854. It received more than sixty favorable reviews, but only after Thoreau's premature death would it be widely read, thanks to the aggressive promotion of his works by Emerson and other friends. A third event of significance occurred while Thoreau lived at Walden: in protest against slavery and the Mexican War he refused to pay the poll tax and spent a night in Concord Jail. "Civil Disobedience," which influenced Gandhi and Martin Luther King, was published in 1849. Thoreau's house was sold shortly after he left the pond. The farmer who ultimately acquired it moved it north of the village and used it for corn storage before demolishing it in 1868. A memorial to Thoreau was established at his Walden housesite ten years after he died: at the cairn visiting admirers add a stone, so that it grows steadily larger, along with his fame.

The idea of Walden Pond has swept the world: birthplace of the modern environmental movement, symbol of simplicity taken up in deliberate antithesis to chaotic and destructive modernity. But for some historians, attention to the *place* has been anathema, arguing as they do that Thoreau's *Walden* finds its meaning as a philosophical discourse, not a descriptive account of a lake in the woods. A visitor in 1912 concluded "that the spirit of Thoreau is still in his books, and not in any place." And scholar Raymond Adams told an audience, "Walden is not significant as a *place* at all. . . . It is significant only because the word *Walden* suggests some thoughts a man had once. Where he had them doesn't really matter." This may explain why, with all the historical books written on Thoreau, none has been forthcoming on the pond itself.[12]

Thanks to Thoreau, Walden Pond—both place and idea—is a household phrase. It is a staple of magazine cartoons and has lent its name to the commune of aging hippies in *Doonesbury*. The pond has served as a backdrop in movies, novels, and a surprising number of paperback murder mysteries. There are today at least ten populated places in the United States named Walden, and six cemeteries, all presumably tranquil. (But oddly enough, Walden, Ontario, is an anagram for three towns that merged—Waters, Lively, and Denison.) Even a site on the moon has been named Walden. Walden Ponds are to be found in Maine, Pennsylvania, New Jersey, Wisconsin, Minnesota, Iowa, and Colorado. With its connotations of privacy, placidity, and repose, one finds Walden apartments in Wisconsin and Delaware; Walden Pond apartments in Washington State; Walden Pond condominiums in Michigan; Walden Pond housing tracts in Alabama, North Carolina, Indiana, and Illinois, and one called Walden Park in Georgia; a Walden Pond low-income housing project in Florida. The Forest at Walden Pond, near St. Louis, boasts "huge lots, panoramic views, thickly wooded homesites and exceptional floor plans," and its "Thoreau" model home, with four bedrooms and two-and-a-half baths, starts at $224,700. In Lynchburg, Virginia, "Walden Pond Apartment Homes is just minutes from River Ridge Mall, Wal-Mart, Target, Food Lion, CVS Pharmacy, the Plaza Shopping Center and much more! . . . Comprised of buildings 1400 to 2400, Thoreau's Cove is nearest the pond, gazebo, picnic area and a tot lot. . . . If you have your own washer and dryer, consider Thoreau's Cove."[13]

Walden offers a pleasing and evocative name with which to appeal to consumers: Walden Kayaks; Camp Walden in Michigan; Walden University on the Internet; the vast bookstore chain Waldenbooks, which sued little Walden Pond Books in Oakland, California, for trademark violation. Rock musician Don Henley's Walden Woods Project has used Walden's extraordinary emotional appeal to raise money for land conservation near the pond. That six-letter word truly resonates.[14]

On any given day—even as fishermen, swimmers, joggers, and tourists vie for control of the real Walden Pond—English teachers across America grapple with *Walden* the work of literature. It is perhaps surprising how often the book is assigned in high schools, given the difficulties it presents: it is one of the most densely packed of texts, every sentence weighted. Moreover, Thoreau was immensely learned and refers often to obscure sources in the classics and Eastern religion. The results can be beautiful and moving but are far from easy, especially since, as Joyce Carol Oates has written, the author is "the supreme poet of doubleness, of evasion and mystery." One teacher remarks. "It's not easy to dispel his stereotype as a curmudgeon and hermit, or else a nature-gazing cloud-head." Some students grow hostile: "The things this dude said made absolutely no sense [and] we get to see what neurosis plagued his diseased mind. . . . Pages upon pages of vivid description about scenery, the little fighting ants, the whippor-whill, the squirrels under the floor-boards. . . . What do we care about his pests in nature? I mean, how much can you really say about ice melting?"[15]

And yet some teachers succeed in making *Walden* come alive, sometimes by making it tangible. At a high school in Sudbury, Massachusetts, students built a full-scale replica of Thoreau's house. At an elementary school in Pennsylvania, a janitor helped fifth-graders create a $500 Walden Pond in their classroom out of wood, plastic, and tile and stock it with goldfish. It is "about the size of a plastic swimming pool. . . . Like Thoreau . . . the children sit by the pond and read poetry." Not to be outdone, Concord-Carlisle High School, almost in sight of the actual Walden Pond, built a plastic-lined, five-foot-deep, sixty-foot-long copy in a courtyard, with a house replica beside it, and a woodshed. The science teacher in charge brought in mallards, turtles, fish, and frogs. He even a planted a beanfield in which he released a live (and, as it turned out, pregnant) woodchuck.[16]

❦

By the noon hour at the real Walden Pond, if the weather is fair and warm, the place becomes inhospitable for the lover of nature and solitude. This is nothing new; a visitor of 1910 said, "To come to Walden at mid-day . . . is not at first to be impressed." On the crowded beach, one faces what Edwin Way Teale once called the "paradox" of Walden: wild, yet not wild; in some ways improved since Thoreau's time, yet markedly worsened. For ornithologist Kate Tryon, riding her bicycle to Walden in 1895, "It is a charming place, and it isn't." Ninety-eight years later, another cyclist agrees: "Walden Pond was somewhat better and a lot worse from what I expected." A first-timer in 2001 said, "I have always wanted to visit and had images of what I thought it would be like. It almost lived up to my expectations."[17]

Some forays are downright crushing—likeliest those in midsummer. For Robert Whitcomb, "Thoreau was the only god of my late adolescence," but his 1931 encounter with Walden brought only "the disappointment of the modern reality." Walden Pond "is no longer a refuge of the spirit," concluded another disappointed pilgrim in 1945.

Like Coney Island. Main Beach is thronged in summer. July 11, 1948, from the Roland Wells Robbins Collection of the Thoreau Society. Courtesy of the Thoreau Society, Lincoln, Mass., and the Thoreau Institute at Walden Woods.

More recently, the *Boston Globe* numbered the park seventeenth on its list of the fifty most "overrated" things in the region. A birdwatcher stopped by in 1995, only to record in disgust, "What a waste. That place is trafficked by huge crowds. . . . We saw one ring-billed gull and that was it." Over the years a few Thoreauvians have actually refrained from visiting the pond, fearing dashed hopes. One wrote in 1949, "Now it is probably a resort with hotdog stands, chute-the-chutes, popcorn whistles, noisy bathers and squalling babies"—not far off the mark. One more recently allowed himself a quick visit to Thoreau's housesite; "Then I hurried away, meaning not to profane his woods any longer than necessary with my presence."[18]

But surely this paints too bleak a picture of conditions at the pond. On a quiet winter's day, the snow-covered landscape near Wyman Meadow, a marshy extension of Thoreau's Cove, seems unchanged from Thoreau's time, and one can almost imagine that the naturalist will come sauntering down a woodland path. And early in the morning, before the crowds, Thoreau's Cove is green, intimate, and beautiful—still today, as a visitor found it in April 1869, "one of the quietest and most picturesque spots about the pond." One of the great American places, the cove deserves to be contemplated, not merely passed by in a rush to get to the house site. The play of sun and shade, the reflections of foliage, the drifting clouds all form a scene constantly changing. Birds bathe along its beaches and fish swim in its quiet waters. No wonder that Emerson bought property embracing the head of the cove, that Thoreau chose to live beside it, that Ellery Channing brought his sketchbook, and that Concord's early photographers set up their tripods here.[19]

"My cove" played a prominent role in the Walden experiment. Filling his water pail here in the morning, Thoreau startled a loon; kneeling at the shore, he drank from a dipper; and here he swam: "I get up early and bathe in the pond—that is one of the best things I do." "After sitting still in my house or working in my field in the forenoon, I usually bathed again in the pond swimming across one of its coves for a stint." Beside the cove he kept a boat for fishing: "Sometimes, when I pushed off my boat in the morning, I disturbed a great mud-turtle" hiding underneath.[20]

Pilgrims have come for generations to see, as one wrote in the 1890s, "the beautiful and secluded cove where Emerson and Thoreau kept a boat, and where the shining ones often came to bathe in this limpid water. Ablution here seems to have been a sort of transcendent baptism, and many a visitor, eminent in art, thought, or letters, has boasted that he walked and talked with Emerson in Walden woods and bathed with him in Walden water." A pilgrim of 1910 "sat there on his shore" and watched the "path of golden light" formed by the moon on the cove, just as Thoreau had described. Nearby was "the beach where he took his morning swim," and "he who would know Thoreau's Walden will do well to bathe in it." As early as May 1858 a disciple put "heels in the water . . . at Thoreau's dipping place." In 2001 a visitor on a round-the-world trip was told by a Thoreau devotee, "You can't come to Walden Pond without touching the water. He was right . . . the water here did feel different. But maybe it was just the residue from a thousand unwashed bodies."[21]

Those bodies aside, there is still beauty to be discovered at Walden. And there is something inspiring about the dogged persistence of wildness here even as the modern world has surrounded the reservation on all sides, just beyond the electromagnetic gate. Concord author Margaret Sidney said in 1888, "It is a sweet dream of Life's possibilities in the midst of dull leaden actualities." And however disappointing the reality may sometimes be, the idea persists and thrives. Kay has written, "If *Walden* is the Koran of conservation, Walden, zipcode 01742, is its embodiment. No parallel tract or body of water or place has so captivated the human imagination or so taught us how to relate to the natural world from which we spring. Nowhere else is there a literary memorial and monument of such breathtaking consequence. In a world devoid of symbols and a landscape almost uniformly for sale, Walden is an international shrine."[22]

How did an ordinary pond come to have such extraordinary meanings? What is this remarkable place with such power to delight and disappoint, inspire and alarm? Who made it famous, who spoiled it, who has fought to bring it back? These are the subjects of our story, which begins nearly two hundred years ago, through the eyes of a little boy.

2

Visited at All Seasons

(1821–1834)

One day a family rode fifteen miles or so out from Boston to picnic in the woods. Just south of Concord village, their carriage rattled down a narrow, rutted road through a forest. Suddenly a broad sheet of water appeared through the trees. The year was 1821, and four-year-old Henry Thoreau caught his first glimpse of Walden Pond.[1]

His parents, John and Cynthia Thoreau, loved the out-of-doors and had often roamed the woods when they lived in Concord, where Henry had been born. In later years a villager recalled that "one of the Thoreau children came very near seeing the light for the first time, on Nashawtuc hill," just north of town. After they moved to Boston, the Thoreaus found Walden a welcome respite from urban life. Henry would fondly recall, "When I was four years old, as I well remember, I was brought from Boston to this my native town, through these very woods and this field, to the pond. It is now one of the oldest scenes stamped on my memory."[2]

In 1823 the Thoreaus moved back to Concord, and shortly afterward they brought Henry to the pond to boil a kettle of chowder on a sandbar that projected one hundred feet into the water, which was, in its mysterious, periodic fluctuations, then very low. As the seven-year-old splashed and frolicked in the refreshing coolness of the cove, his parents could not have imagined that he would someday gain fame for building a house within sight of where they sat and for

Elusive sandbar. It began to reappear during drought in 1918. Looking west; Thoreau's Cove at right. Herbert W. Gleason, "The Sand-Bar," April 24, 1918, courtesy Concord Free Public Library.

hoeing beans in a field beside the road leading down to the pond's shore.

These childhood memories of what seemed primeval forest left an indelible impression on Thoreau—"That woodland vision for a long time made the drapery of my dreams." Henry developed a fascination with Indians, once writing his brother John a letter in the guise of Tahatawan, sachem of the tribe that lived near the Musketaquid, later Concord, River. He loved to imagine the days when Tahatawan paddled his canoe on Walden. Henry later unearthed arrowheads while hoeing his beanfield, proof "that an extinct nation had anciently dwelt here and planted corn and beans," exactly as he did. Modern-day archaeology has confirmed that little groups of Indian hunters, as early as eight thousand years ago, camped for a few nights at a time on sandy rises in Walden Woods, chipping stone tools.[3]

"When I first paddled a boat on Walden it was completely surrounded by thick & lofty pine woods, and in some of its coves grape vines had run over the trees & formed bowers under which a boat could pass. The hills which form its shores are so steep & the woods on them were then so high, that as you looked down the pond from west to east—it looked like an amphitheater—for some kind of forest spectacle." Nostalgia aside, the place showed unmistakable signs of disturbance even in the 1820s. The pines on the shore had sprung up to replace earlier forests of the seventeenth and eighteenth centuries, lost to the ax. Studies of old pollen layers in deep Walden mud show that these forests had been largely comprised of pitch pine and white oak. Wood was cheap back then, and whole logs had been left to rot in the water. From a boat, young Henry peered down at these wrecks of the forest strewing the sandy bottom. Walden had been "a place of eagles once," he romantically supposed, but no longer. Woodcutters were felling trees on the south hill in the early 1820s. Despite these disturbances, the beautiful place would move Thoreau profoundly with suggestions of antiquity: "Perhaps on that spring morning when Adam and Eve were driven out of Eden Walden Pond was already in existence." When he lived there he would call it "a place of pines—of forest scenes and events visited by successive nations of men all of whom have successively fathomed it—And still its water is green & pellucid . . . While the nations pass away." His wishful dreams of Walden's unspoiled past echoed Wordsworth on the Lake District in England, who had tried in Romantic imagination to "recall to this region of lakes the native pine-forests" once "haunted by eagles."[4]

Thoreau would make Walden Pond famous, but it was far from unknown to locals in his day—indeed, it had always been popular and useful. Concord was founded nearly two hundred years before by settlers eager to exploit its rich meadow hay. The sterile, sandy uplands south of town were disappointingly infertile but provided bountiful cordwood. They were immediately divided into small woodlots that were passed down in families through the generations. Several of these lots touched the pond shore. Thoreau's future beanfield was acquired by the Minotts, early Concord settlers who came originally from the English town of Saffron Walden, England. Some have thought that this was the origin of the name "Walden Pond"—but digging through old town records one evening, Thoreau found a reference to "Wallden Pond" from 1653, before the Minotts arrived. Environmental historian Brian Donahue is among several recent scholars who hold that "the name derived from the once-wooded upland Weald in Kent (home of many Concord settlers), or more generally from the fact that Walden means 'in the woods.'"[5]

The pond occupied what an historian in 1835 called "Walden woods," a province of sandy "light-soil land" poor for agriculture, an enclave completely surrounded by meadow, pasture, and cropland. Thoreau subtitled his book *Life in the Woods*, but he was never far from civilization: he could hear cattle lowing in farmyards beyond the edge of the forest. Still, he could fairly say he lived "in the midst of an extensive wood between [Concord] and Lincoln." In Concord there were four "great uninhabited tract[s]," one being "the Walden Woods," and it is in this larger, semiwild context that Walden Pond itself must be understood.[6]

The term Walden Woods was rescued from obscurity in the late 1980s by local historians and conservationists waging a David-and-Goliath fight to protect the area from development. Seeking an emotionally resonant descriptor for this threatened place, they demonstrated that Concordians had long used the phrase "Walden Woods" to refer to various sections of the forest between Fair Haven Bay and Flint's Pond. "Shaken by the unrelenting intensity" of a lawyer for the developers who tried to get him to deny under oath that Walden Woods ever existed, Edmund A. Schofield realized the need to define the ecosystem as precisely as possible, using a variety of historical and scientific sources. Extensive research convinced him that Walden Woods could be readily outlined on a map, based on unique characteristics that distinguished it from the rest of the Concord-Lincoln environment. Its 4.2 square miles, Schofield said, occupy the region overlain by sandy deposits from Glacial Lake Sudbury; are fast draining and prone to drought; get fire-swept and were, until lately, thereby kept in a condition of pine and oak, in contrast to the more diverse forests surrounding them; were relatively sterile and sparsely farmed, consisting instead of small woodlots, collectively mapped in 1895 as "Walden Woods"; and preserved a distinctive, wildish character for centuries, as described by many observers. The outlines of Walden Woods as drawn by Schofield and his conservationist colleagues, though not without their critics, have gained widespread acceptance and today form the cornerstone of the efforts of Don Henley's Walden Woods Project.[7]

Walden was not the only pond in Walden Woods. Nearby lay Goose Pond, described in 1835 as "one of a number of small ponds, in a tract of land peculiarly broken into ridges and vales, which in

Seen from Pine Hill, 1906. Thoreau: "The shore is composed of a belt of smooth rounded white stones like paving stones a rod or two in width." No round-the-pond path is yet visible. Gleason, "Overlooking Walden Pond toward Mt. Wachusett, from Pine Hill," April 28, 1906, courtesy Concord Free Public Library.

some seasons are nearly dry," as Goose Pond became in a 2002 drought. Thoreau took pains to situate the various bodies of water accurately in his chapter "The Ponds": Walden, though lacking a visible inlet or outlet, was evidently linked to Flint's Pond to the east and Fair Haven Bay to the west by chains of small ponds. These, plus the more distant White Pond, together comprised "my lake country."[8]

Thoreau's remarks about Walden's relationship to the adjacent chains of ponds and to an ancient flow of water show remarkable intuition about local geology. We now know Walden Pond and its near neighbors (though not Flint's Pond) are "kettles" formed by the melting of huge blocks of ice left behind when the glacier retreated fifteen thousand years ago. As the Walden block slowly dwindled over a period of some two hundred years, it towered like a monolith in the midst of a frigid lake of glacial meltwater, Lake Sudbury, which was oriented southwest along the line of the chain of ponds, in an ancient, fault-formed valley in the bedrock. Into this lake the melting glacier that overlay Concord to the north dumped the thick deposits of sand and gravel one sees today all around Walden Pond. Once the thawing ice block disappeared, it left its irregular outline forever preserved in the contours of the pond shore.[9]

But Thoreau and his contemporaries did not know about Concord's history of glaciation, as the pioneering theories of Emerson's friend Louis Agassiz at Harvard were slow to gain acceptance. Emerson thought Concord's hills had been uplifted by volcanic force and that its stones were shaped by some "fiery inundation of the world." As for the formation of the pond, he supposed that "here once the Deluge ploughed, / Laid the terraces, one by one." Actually, these explanations were not so far from the truth. His beloved hill, Emerson's Cliff, is an outcrop of Andover granite formed in the fiery heat of the Earth's crust some 450 million years ago and later shaped by the glacier into classic drumlin shape, hump-backed on the north, craggy on the south. Plateau-like outwash deposits from the postglacial deluge overlie its base.[10]

There was disagreement in Thoreau's day as to whether Walden's water flowed out by subterranean channels. One winter, ice cutters showed him "a 'leach hole,' through which the pond leaked out under a hill into a neighboring meadow," probably at Little Cove on the southwest shore. He was skeptical, but a 2001 study showed that Walden does in fact leach on a vast scale. With its porous cushion of sand and gravel, it is a "flow-through lake" that takes in 55 percent of its water underground from the Goose Pond-Pine Hill areas to the east and seeps out 74 percent to the west—leaking constantly into the groundwater in a wide arc from Thoreau's house site all the way around the west end of the pond to Deep Cove. The Leach Hole vicinity is only a tiny part of this tremendous subsurface flow. Between evaporation and seepage, Walden entirely replaces its 3.2 million cubic meters of water every five years.[11]

All of this has just been discovered. In earlier generations there was lively speculation and puzzlement about Walden's unpredictable hydrologic cycles, its waters experiencing a "rise and fall extending through a long series of years." "Five years elapse from flood to ebb," Emerson wrote. Thoreau's journal records the pond's behavior: very high in 1850–52, dropping in 1853–54, very low in 1858, higher in 1859, very low again in 1860. It did not rise rapidly after rain, nor shrink immediately during a drought, as nearby ponds did. This mystified Thoreau, who wrote during the dry summer of 1854 that the shore at Flint's was "so exposed that you can walk round—which I have not known possible for several years—& and the outlet is dry. . . . But Walden is not affected by the drought." One baffled commentator wrote in 1885, "The pond rises and falls, but it is impossible to tell what laws govern it, as it is often higher in a drought."[12]

Like other observers, Thoreau supposed that the "water shed by the surrounding hills is insignificant in amount" and could not possibly keep the large pond filled, and therefore Walden must be fed by secret springs. Even today one still hears talk of Walden and White Ponds' being "fed by the same spring." But Eugene H. Walker has studied long-term records of Walden's height, which, he discovered, "rises and falls through seasons and years almost exactly in agreement with changes in local ground-water level. It is like a very large well surrounded by water-saturated sand and gravel." The hills have no streams because rainwater, on hitting the earth, instantly disappears into the deep sand. Walden responds to droughts only after long delay, in union with the local watertable. And there are no springs.[13]

Walden's hydrological distinctiveness was recognized early. "There is enough that is singular about this pond, to warrant a stranger in going a little distance to view it," said a newspaper account in 1821. "Its banks are very bold, and decorated on all sides with evergreens and other forest trees—its waters are pure—no weeds or grass grow on its borders, no stream runs into it, or issues from it, and it is found to be highest in the driest time." Some thought it bottomless, the pond being renowned for "the remarkable depth of the water, which has never been fathomed." Others guessed that there had been no fish when the first settlers arrived, for how, they wondered, would they have gotten into this high, landlocked pool? But fish have ways of getting into remote places, and in time fishermen stocked the pond, too. Thoreau, casting for his supper in 1845, could recall that at least two centuries' worth of anglers had preceded him. In 1821 the pond was noted for its pike and pickerel. The species he found when he lived there included pickerel, perch, pouts, shiners, chivens or roach, breams, trout, and eels, many of which must have been deliberate releases. Piscatorially as in all else, Walden was no wilderness tarn; it was a fishing hole for Concord and Middlesex County, its fish populations periodically enhanced for recreational pleasure.[14]

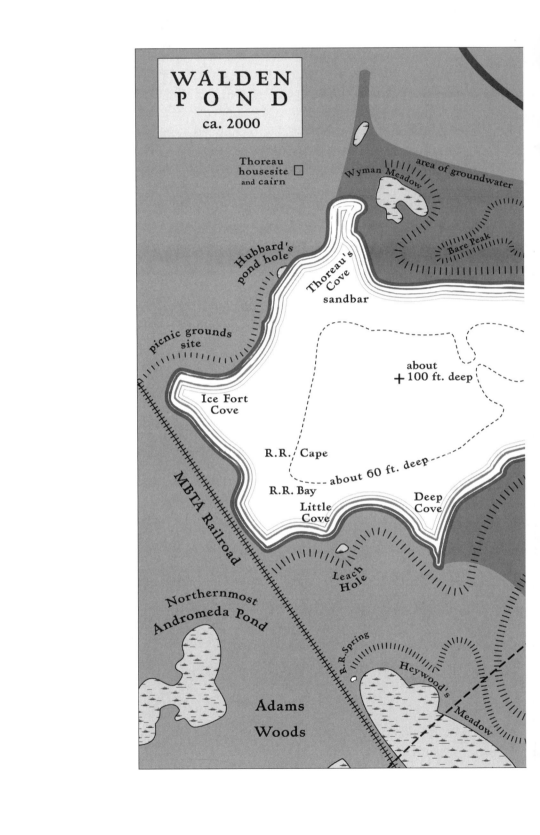

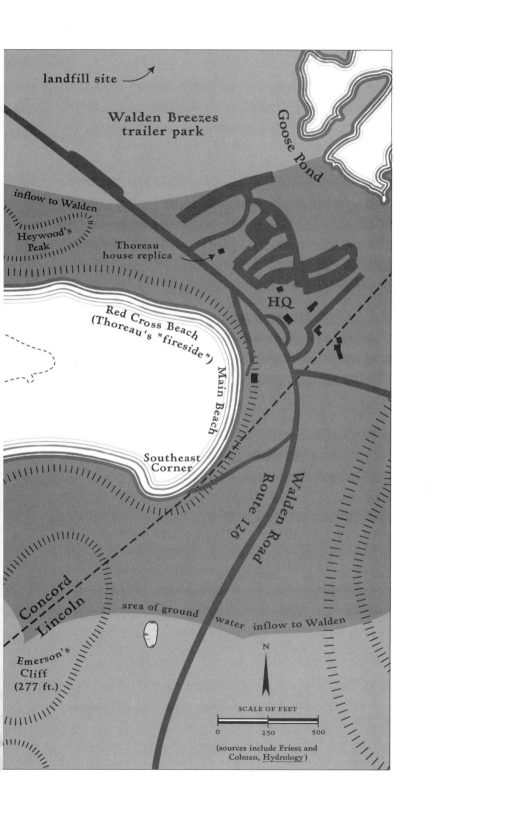

landfill site

Walden Breezes
trailer park

Goose Pond

inflow to Walden

Heywood's
Peak

Thoreau
house replica

HQ

Red Cross Beach
(Thoreau's "fireside")

Main Beach

Southeast
Corner

Route 126

Walden Road

Concord
Lincoln

area of ground water inflow to Walden

Emerson's
Cliff
(277 ft.)

N

SCALE OF FEET

0   250   500

(sources include Friesz and
Colman, Hydrology)

From aloft, 1940s. Thoreau could walk to Walden from the village (upper left) in half an hour. Courtesy Concord Free Public Library.

Concord resident Horace Hosmer recalled in 1891, "For one hundred years, certain, Walden has been visited at all seasons of the year by hunters, sportsmen, boys, wood choppers, and land owners. Before I was born, men would leave the tavern in the village, and go for a swim across the pond on a bet, *even at midnight.* The shoemakers of Bedford (five miles distant) used to fish for pouts and stay nearly all night while Henry was in College. Acton people know all the fishing ground in Concord and parties go every winter to fish through the ice . . . and have needed no guide to Walden." The pond was popular for other reasons, too: "Walking was a very common exercise and enjoyment for the young men and women of the village. In summer afternoons walking parties to [Fair] Haven Hill and also to Walden Pond were very frequent." The 1829–38 diary of George Moore, a student at a local school, provides evidence of this kind of constant use. He enjoyed walking in Walden Woods, bathing in the pond, and catching "a pretty good '*mess.*'" "Went to Waldron pond on a fishing excursion. Had a pleasant company—caught an abundance of fish—partook of a nice chowder—and returned well satisfied with the day's enjoyment."[15]

Moore and other visitors found no primeval forest, but wood-lots regularly thinned, as they had been for twenty decades. They lay on either side of much-traveled Walden Road, along which there were signs of present and former habitation. As Thoreau affectionately describes in *Walden*, a string of little houses had been occupied by freed slaves, loners, outcasts, and drunkards—all were banished or fled to the farthest fringes of town. This is a venerable tradition; during the last two decades of the twentieth century a hermit lived under a warren of plastic tarps in the woods just off Walden Road.

Of the cellar holes Thoreau lists, the farthest from the village and nearest the pond—across the road from the high east bank—was squatter John Wyman's place. A potter who furnished Concordians with earthenware before the Revolution, Wyman had hunted foxes with Thoreau's friend George Minott, who recalled his fearlessness in striding across the pond when it was frozen just two inches thick. Contributing to folklorish associations of Walden with Native Americans, John's son Tommy terrified local children with tales of how "an Indian doctor dwelt in a hidden recess near the pond and would seize children and cut up their livers to make medicines." Tommy bought the eleven acres of what came to be known as the "Wyman lot," which Emerson would acquire and where Thoreau would hoe beans. Tommy Wyman felled the trees along the carriage road where the Thoreaus had descended to the pond shore.[16]

On that lot, "by the very corner" of the beanfield, bricks from Zilpha White's chimney littered the oak copse where Thoreau sought midmorning shade. He called this former slave who died in 1820 a "colored woman of fame" who busied herself with spinning linen and "making the walden woods ring with her shrill singing—a loud shrill remarkable voice." He knew about her from Minott, who fished in Howard's (later Heywood's) Meadow in the days before the railroad bisected it. Minott and friends would hand her part of their catch as they went by. English soldiers on parole during the War of 1812 set fire to Zilpha's house when she was away, killing her cat, dog, and hens in the conflagration.[17]

Nearby, east of Walden Road, lay a half-obliterated cellar hole concealed from the traveler by a fringe of pines, where smooth

Walden Road climbs Brister's Hill, linking village and pond. Looking northwest. Alfred Winslow Hosmer, ca. 1890, from Hosmer's extra-illustrated copy of the 2d edition of Salt, *Life of Henry David Thoreau,* courtesy Concord Free Public Library.

sumac and early-blooming goldenrod thrived. Here had lived the slave Cato Ingraham, a Guinea Negro, who died in 1805. Duncan Ingraham, a famously wealthy Concord gentleman of the eighteenth century—sea captain, Surinam merchant, slave trader—had owned Cato, then built a house on his extensive holdings in Walden Woods and granted him permission to live there. Years later, in 1797, Ingraham's acres were deeded to John Richardson, who harvested nuts from walnut trees Cato had planted.[18]

Still more cellar holes lay hidden along Walden Road closer to the village, starting with that of Brister, east of the road, and Stratton, on the west. Brister's Hill was named for the former—Bristol or Brister Freeman, a Negro, who lived with his family on the brow of the hill and who was recalled as "a very passionate man [who] often got into quarrels with the boys who loved to insult and plague him." He died in 1822 at age seventy-eight, but his apple trees lingered into Thoreau's day. At the foot of the hill a shortcut climbed through Laurel Glen to Walden, a much-used route. "This is a path which somebody travels every half-day, at least," said Thoreau, who once surveyed the Stratton lot, which lay at the opening to this shortcut. He noted that a 1777 deed mentioned only a cellar hole even then: "For so long, at least, it has been a mere dent in the earth there, to which, from time to time, dead horses or hogs were drawn from the village and cast in. These are our Ninevehs and Babylons. I approach such a cellar-hole as [archaeologist of the Near East] Layard the scene of his labors, and I do not fail to find there relics as interesting to me as his winged bulls." In *Walden* he writes, "There was a dead horse in the hollow by the path to my house, which compelled me sometimes to go round & out of my way"—evidence of how Walden Road and Woods served as dumping grounds for all things unwanted. Somewhere not far from here, too, was "the tin-hole near Brister's," or "Callitriche Pool, where the tin is cast. We have waste places—pools and brooks, etc.,—where to cast tin, iron, slag, crockery, etc." It is no surprise, then, that a series of Concord town dumps would later be located on Walden Road, the last and largest only closing in the 1990s.[19]

Of all the fascinating ruins, John C. Breed's cellar hole, east of the road and still visible today, was one of the newest. Breed, a barber and drunkard, was found dead in the road in 1824. Thoreau was among the young men of the town who raced out to the old house when it burned in May 1841; there was talk, briefly, of throwing a nearby frog pond on it. That pond, Stow's Cold Pool, was called into service in 1894, when a fire in Walden Woods threatened the house of William Chisholm on the corner of Thoreau and Walden Streets, narrowly saved by the fire engine drawing water from this "mud hole." Breed's place stood "just on the edge of the wood," at the boundary between the "rural" and the "sylvan," to use Thoreau's three divisions of the Concord landscape (the third being "villageous"). Long before Thoreau's day, this area had been a wild corner of town: "Where Breeds house stood—tradition says a tavern once stood, the well the same and all a swamp between the woods & town & [a] road made on logs." Once a woman returning from Lincoln with a watermelon was overcome by fear in dark "Walden Woods, which had a rather bad reputation for goblins and so on in those days," and dropped her cargo, which "lay in a dozen pieces in the middle of the Walden road." Before its rehabilitation by the transcendentalists, Walden Woods lurked in the popular imagination as a place of mystery, with a hint of disrepute and fearsomeness.[20]

Nonetheless, the woods and pond were beloved to the town's outdoorsmen—among them, young Henry Thoreau's parents, who "were seen year after year . . . at Walden." Henry, his brother John, and their friend Benjamin Hosmer delighted in exploring the countryside during their childhood in the 1820s and early 1830s, Mrs. Thoreau recalling "that when the boys came racing in leaving the doors open behind them she knew what was coming. 'Ben has come mother, and we want some luncheon and are going to Walden, or Fairhaven Cliffs, or Lincoln and shall not be home till dark.'" Even on trips home from college, Thoreau doubtless continued his favorite activities at Walden, including paddling in his rowboat to the middle "and lying on my back across the seats, in a summer forenoon, dreaming awake, until I was aroused by the boat touching the sand, and I arose to see what shore my fates had impelled me to." Perhaps it was with John that he would come "in dark summer nights, with a companion, and [make] a fire close to the water's edge, which we thought attracted the fishes." He recalled, "we caught pouts with a bunch of worms strung on a thread; and when we had done, far in the night, threw the burning brands high into the air like skyrockets, which, coming down into the pond, were quenched with a loud hissing." Walden for the young brothers was a place of pleasure and delight, but it was about to become something far more significant for them and, in time, for everyone.[21]

3

✣

Intellectual Grove

(1835–1844)

❧

The transformation of Walden Pond into a place more than merely physical—into a spiritual and poetical realm at the center of an "intellectual grove" (to borrow a term from Amos Bronson Alcott)— began not with Thoreau but with his friend and mentor Ralph Waldo Emerson. A tireless advocate for American letters, Emerson gathered a circle of writers around him in Concord, and together they discovered and promoted Walden and its surrounding woods as, in essence, an American analogue to England's Lake District. As literary scholar Joseph Moldenhauer has argued, the Concord transcendentalists owed an enormous debt to Wordsworth, Emerson regarding him "as a seminal genius of the modern age, one who had given due dignity to nature and reunited it with the human mind." Emerson sought Wordsworth out at his English lakeside cottage, Rydal Mount, in 1833 and 1848 and followed the great master's example when he refashioned the Walden environs into a serviceably poetic landscape.[1]

In September 1835, Emerson, a thirty-two-year-old minister, moved with his new wife into a big frame house on Lexington Turnpike, bought for $3500. He had chosen Concord, population two thousand and an ancestral seat of the Emerson family, for its suburban location—his house, standing right on the highway, was close enough to Boston that he could travel in to give a lecture, but

"Bush" in Emerson's day. He landscaped the yard with horse chestnuts and conifers, embowering the house in foliage. His study was at the front right corner, downstairs. Stereoview, 1875, courtesy Concord Free Public Library.

far enough into the country that nature lay at his door. He explained his rationale in words that hint at Thoreau's decision to move to Walden Pond ten years later: "Being a lover of solitude I went to live in the country seventeen miles from Boston."[2]

That same year Emerson met thirty-six-year-old Alcott, a self-taught schoolteacher in Boston who kept a copious journal recording transcendentalist speculations. He loaned the volume to Emerson, who admired its "perfectly simple and elegant utterance" and the author's "hearty faith and study by night and by day." The exchange of ideas between these two men gave vital shape to the developing transcendentalist creed. In October, Alcott and George P. Bradford rode three hours from Boston to Emerson's house, where, with Waldo and his like-minded brother Charles, they reveled in what Alcott called "very interesting conversation . . . of an intellectual and spiritual character. On most subjects there was striking conformity of taste and opinion." The interaction of these seekers began to make Emerson's study a crucial center for the emerging transcendentalist circle.[3]

Whereas the front of Emerson's house faced the turnpike, the rear looked to Walden Woods on the horizon. From the kitchen garden at the back door Waldo could gaze south across little Mill Brook (then meadowy) to Walden Road where it turned on its way out of the village and crossed fields toward tree-clad Brister's Hill and the woods beyond. From his study the pond was only half-an-hour's walk, and this beautiful place immediately became a favorite destination for meditative strolls. "I study the art of solitude," he wrote during his first summer at the house, and from the garden he could hear the woods summoning him. In an intellectual sense, his house proved to lie midway between the competing forces of civilization and nature, society and solitude, the "thought-destroying air of the town" and "the murmur of my woods" teaching "melodious lessons of a higher Right." Upon rising from his desk he could make a quick foray into either. In autumn 1835 came what may be his first reference to Walden Pond, as he took an afternoon walk with Charles: "We came to a little pond in the bosom of the hills, with echoing shores." At this early date the environs were unfamiliar enough that he feared getting lost in the darkening woods.[4]

Charles Emerson died suddenly the following May, plunging his brother into despair at the loss of his closest friend. Walden Woods offered solace to the grieving philosopher. He associated the place with Charles, the companion who had inspired him to a deeper love of nature: "We shall think of him when the June birds return. The birds he loved & discriminated & showed them us." Now during repeated woodland walks he meditated on the relationship of mankind to the natural environment and formulated his great essay, *Nature*, which biographer Robert Richardson calls "Emerson's open letter to the world on behalf of Charles." Their strolls had not been limited to Walden Woods; Emerson recalled the origins of "a rude dirge which was composed or rather hummed by me one afternoon . . . as I walked in the woods & on the narrow plain through which our Concord River flows, not far from my grandfather's house [the Old Manse], and remembered my brothers Edward & Charles, to who as to me this place was in boyhood & youth all 'the country' which we knew." But of all the verdant locales near Concord, including Sleepy Hollow, Beck Stow's Swamp, and Estabrook, Walden Woods drew Emerson most regularly. Charles's life—and death—heightened Waldo's appreciation of that scenic landscape.[5]

Emerson was to be found in late May 1836 "in the wood" musing on "the three aspects of Natural Beauty." In June he equated lofty thoughts with the forest—"I seem to walk into woods by

Among the pines. Trees transplanted from Walden Woods sheltered Emerson's "Bush" from the village. Looking southeast, ca. 1900, courtesy Concord Free Public Library.

known ways & to hear wood birds & see pines & birches." He asked himself, "What learned I this morning in the woods, the oracular woods? Wise are they the ancient nymphs. Pleasing sober melancholy truth say those untamable savages the pines." After a walk in a lashing storm, "I love the wood god. I love the mighty PAN." Even when busy in town he found Walden Woods inspiring, hovering always at his southern limit of sight: "I gladly pay the rent of my house because I therewith get the horizon & the woods which I pay no rent for."[6]

Emerson's Wordsworthian walks and meditations both in Walden Woods and beside the blue pond were not idle sauntering. He was hard at work on what would prove to be his greatest achievement. In August, "I went to Walden Pond this evening a little before sunset, and in the tranquil landscape I behold somewhat as beautiful as my own nature," a line that made its way into *Nature*, the first proofs of which arrived two weeks later. This essay was to stand as a landmark in the development of American literature and environmental thought, as the perceptive Alcott recognized: "I have just finished reading *Nature*. . . . Nature becomes a transparent emblem of the soul. Psyche animates and fills the earth and external things. The book is small . . . but it is a gem throughout. I deem it the harbinger of an order of works given to the elucidation and establishment of the Spiritual."[7]

After penning this manifesto of transcendentalism, Emerson turned to new projects, always retaining his intimate connection to Walden Woods, a connection that seemed preordained, even in the felicitous similarity between the names Walden and Waldo. A "brilliant & warm" October day "led me out this morn into the wood & to Goose Pond," where he thought over his coming course of lectures, the first principle of which was the complex "relation between man & nature." In November he revisited Goose Pond, and he dug forest hemlocks to plant in his yard at home, part of the continuing process by which his town life and woods life grew intertwined. In December he stood on the shore of Walden and played the "ice-harp": "I threw a stone upon the ice which rebounded with a shrill sound. . . . I was so taken with the music that I threw down my stick & spent twenty minutes in throwing stones single or in handfuls on this crystal drum." Modern visitors do the same, and the cumulative effect in recent decades has been to denude the shoreline of its once-distinctive fringe of round white stones, which Emerson doubtless would have deplored.[8]

In his frequent walks in Walden Woods, Waldo participated in a habit long popular in England—what is sometimes called "peripatetic," the art of strolling for pleasure and instruction. Walking was not merely exercise, but mental endeavor, as Wordsworth suggested in *Guide to the Lakes*: "In preparing this Manual, it was the Author's principal wish to furnish a Guide or Companion for the *Minds* of Persons of taste, and feeling for landscape." The invention of rural Concord and Walden Woods as American fields for sauntering, rich in beauty and poetical inspiration, was a deliberate emulation of English habit, and when Emerson and later Thoreau stressed how perfect Concord was for walking, they recalled Wordsworth's praise for the Lake District, where "the interesting walks are inexhaustible." Thoreau was, of course, to become the greatest walker of them all and the most eloquent exponent of American peripatetic. This "peripatetic philosopher," as Alcott called him, would find in Emerson's example a high intellectual rationale for the sauntering habit he naturally enjoyed, but he was always aware of British precedent, too, opening an early lecture draft of his famous essay "Walking" with "Wordsworth on a pedestrian tour through Scotland."[9]

With the general rise in American affluence and increase in leisure time, Bostonians looked to their suburban lakes as sources of pleasure and recreation. As in England, attentiveness to nature and landscape design was a mark of intellectual refinement. Architect A. J. Downing praised the Perkins estate, "Pine Bank," on Jamaica Pond, where the shore was "richly fringed with trees, which conceal here and there a pretty cottage." On a visit in the 1830s, Harriet Martineau was charmed: "If I lived in Massachusetts, my residence during the hot months should be beside one of its ponds." It may have been during the summer at the end of his senior year at Harvard—1837—that Thoreau spent six weeks living in a shanty on the shores of Flint's Pond with his roommate from Lincoln, Charles Stearns Wheeler. To William Ellery Channing, Thoreau's friend and first biographer, it seemed likely that this experience helped inspire the Walden experiment. It is true that, in *Walden*, Thoreau's attention keeps turning to the needs of "poor students." He gives advice, as well, to "whoever camps for a week in summer by the shore of a pond," which suggests that many young men may have done so beside Massachusetts's numerous lakes.[10]

Wheeler's home was just a half-mile from Flint's, and he lived pondside during several college vacations between 1836 and 1842. A cousin recalled of the cabin, "Wheeler and one or more of his college chums used to sleep in it (but had their meals at the house) in vacation. . . . I remember [Thoreau's] coming to the house and begging some yeast of my Aunt Julia." Channing said years later, "Stearns Wheeler built a 'shanty' on Flint's Pond for the purpose of economy, for purchasing Greek books and going abroad to study. Whether Mr. Thoreau assisted him to build this shanty I cannot say, but I think he may have; also that he spent six weeks with him there. As Mr. Thoreau was not too original and inventive to follow the example of others, if good to him, it is very probably this undertaking of Stearns Wheeler [that] suggested his own experiment on Walden. I believe I visited this shanty with Mr. Thoreau. It was very plain, with bunks of straw, and built in the Irish manner." Legend has it that Thoreau wanted to build his own house on Flint's Pond instead of Walden, but the Flints refused him permission—hence his attack on the "skin-flint" in *Walden*.[11]

Emerson's Walden walks grew fewer in 1837. He was busy with lecturing, preaching, and getting his home in order, digging in the garden as a yellowthroat chanted "Extacy! Extacy!" But in August, "After raffling all day in Plutarch's Morals . . . I sallied out this fine afternoon through the woods to Walden Water. . . . I came to the blackberry vines. . . . The pond was all blue & beautiful in the bosom of the woods." In October, "A lovely afternoon and I went to Walden Water & read Goethe on the bank." The pond was richly alive: "The waterflies were full of happiness. The frogs that start from the shore as fast as you walk along, a yard ahead of you, are a meritorious beastie."[12]

This year the lives of the two worshipers of nature, twenty-year-old Thoreau and thirty-four-year-old Emerson, at last intersected. Emerson was keeping a journal that recorded his "wood life," one meant to "smell of pines & resound with hum of insects," so one of the first questions he seems to have asked Thoreau was, "Do you keep a journal?" Thoreau—smitten with *Nature* even before he came under Emerson's spell in Concord—went home and promptly wrote the first of more than two million words that comprise his vast life's work. Among his entries in 1837–39 were accounts of Walden and environs: wood ducks at Goose Pond; bluebirds arriving from over Walden Woods; drifting in a boat on a sultry day. In a poem the pond becomes a face with pebbled lips and a thousand-year-old source of truth. He had fallen deeply under Emerson's sway, unconsciously imitating the older man to the point that the sound of their voices in conversation could hardly be distinguished. James Russell Lowell quipped that Henry was even "getting up a nose like Emerson's."[13]

For Emerson and the intellectual circle who clustered in his parlor—now including Thoreau—Walden Pond was confirmed as a sacred, symbolic locus, the New World equivalent of the Pierian Spring beloved of the Muses, its surrounding woods a place of inspiration akin to those in classic myth and to Plato's groves of Academe near Athens. Thoreau joined the rarefied circle eagerly. But at the same time, this scrappy and self-reliant young man sought to claim a distinct identity within the coterie as the only native Concordian

Rydal Water, heart of England's Lake District. Wordsworth lived beside this poetical precursor to America's Walden Pond. From *Black's Picturesque Guide to the English Lakes*, facing p. 54, University of Delaware Library.

among them, one proud of his almost Indian-like knowledge of the local landscape. One of his first journal entries tells how he discovered with uncanny premonition an arrowhead. He would repeatedly stress in *Walden* his long-term connection with the pond, thanks to those early childhood visits. He said that throughout college, "heart and soul I have been far away among the scenes of my boyhood . . . scouring the woods and exploring the lakes and streams of my native village. . . . My spirit yearned for the sympathy of my old and almost forgotten friend, Nature." For his mentor Emerson, as for Wordsworth, the poet's earliest responses would have been the purest and most authentic, and Thoreau knew there was real transcendentalist status conferred by these youthful memories. One recalls, too, his thoughts beside Walden of the value of "leading a simple epic country life—in these days of confusion and turmoil— That is what Wordsworth has done—Retaining the tastes and the innocence of his youth."[14]

The Harvard-educated Thoreau was steeped in the classics and knew that his rooted connection to place linked him to the so-called primitive races, Greeks and Native Americans among them, that he admired through literature. He aspired to exemplify the homegrown fortitude of classical philosophers in the modern world, "to live a primitive and frontier life, though in the midst of an outward civilization. . . . Is it impossible to combine the hardiness of these savages with the intellectualness of the civilized man?" Gradually, over a period of years, his poetical mind would turn to an experiment at Walden, that timeless place, where he could attempt "a life of simplicity, independence, magnanimity, and trust" and "to solve some of the problems of life, not only theoretically, but practically." From the start he was the most pragmatic, rooted member of the transcendentalist circle, a role this Concord native assiduously cultivated in order to differentiate himself from his more famous peers.[15]

But for all his assertions of independence, still his ideas largely derived from Emerson, who had spent childhood summers in Concord and cherished those memories of his own. In Emerson's writings, a return to the woods is frequently equated with a rediscovery of youth. He freely shared his thoughts with Thoreau, who absorbed them eagerly and repeated them. Are the following words, one might ask, Thoreau's or Emerson's?

> Something of the physical perfection of the heroic age is exhibited by the Indian in the woods, but without the ardent temperament, and without the taste of the Greek. We feel that he stands in stricter relations with Nature than other persons, and possesses a portion of her majesty. Like the moose and bison which he hunts, he belongs to the order of the world. He is part of the morning and evening, of forest and mountain, and is provided for as the ravens are. It was a just remark of Talleyrand that to go from the American coast one or two thousand miles into the wilderness was like going back one or two thousand years in time. You pass in both from the extreme of civilization to the extreme of barbarism.

In its celebration of primitivism and the antique, this could be *Walden*, but in fact is the conclusion of a lecture Emerson gave at the Mercantile Library in Baltimore on January 10, 1843, and several times later—well in advance of his disciple's Walden experiment. Apparently Thoreau learned much from his older friend—although scholar Tom Blanding points out that Thoreau's ideas about the "natural man" and a woodland retreat were deep-seated and may have in fact inspired Emerson. What Henry gained from Waldo, he argues, was "confirmation and clarification of the nature of spiritual experiences he had already had."[16]

Emerson did not mind being echoed by his followers. His passion was the cultivation of American poets on American soil, drawing inspiration from the inexhaustible riches of American nature. Years later he wrote to his friend Caroline Sturgis, then living in Italy, of the contrast between her poetical "land of wine & oil" and this pragmatic "land of meal." Nonetheless, "Italy cannot excel the banks of glory which sun & mist paint in these very days on the forest by lake & river. But the Muses are as reticent, as nature is flamboyant, & no fire-eyed child has yet been born." He hoped that Thoreau would be that child, one who could answer his plea for "hearing the Choral Hymns of a new Age & adequate to nature"; "Why can we not breed a lyric man as exquisite as Tennyson[?] . . . Is all this granite & forest & prairie & superfoetation of millions to no richer result?" Perhaps nature's profligacy itself was to blame, as he often thought in Walden Woods: "As soon as we walk out of doors, Nature transcends all poets so far, that . . . we lose the lust of performance."[17]

Bronson Alcott spent three days with Emerson in June 1838, describing the philosopher's methods during his most fecund intellectual moment. "He gives his days to observation of nature, walking much, and recording his thought, when suggested, in his common places, ready for use in his lectures. There, he also sees his friends, and whatsoever of life or light shall chance come from interview with these, supplies matter, also, for the diary. Hence the freshness of all his descourses, taken as these are from life and nature." At Emerson's suggestion, Thoreau would follow a similar course, with identical emphasis on the immediacy and vividness of ideas born in the woods—although, in time, the young pragmatist's entries would become more botanical than purely philosophical.[18]

As Alcott indicated, Emerson continued to walk frequently to Walden. Of his countless outings of the 1830s and 1840s, only a handful are recorded in his journals, but he says in 1846 that "for years" he had walked there "once or twice in a week at all seasons."

Emerson. Here at forty-four, in 1847. He gave this daguerreotype portrait to his literary friend Thomas Carlyle in England. Courtesy Concord Free Public Library.

In May 1838 he praised his little boy Waldo as being "as handsome as Walden pond at sunrise." He took the visiting George P. Bradford there in early September. In November, "my brave Henry Thoreau walked with me to Walden this P.M." The younger man heatedly complained that landowners wouldn't let him cut across their fences but insisted that he stay in the road, thereby depriving him of his birthright in nature. Emerson defended property rights as a necessary evil but urged Thoreau to write up his argument. Thoreau declined, so Emerson did it for him, working their exchange into his January lecture in Boston, "The Protest."[19]

By 1839, the year John and Henry Thoreau took their memorable trip on the Concord and Merrimack Rivers, the subject of the latter's first book, Emerson's fame had spread far, thanks to his great published essays, including *Nature* (1836), "The American Scholar" (1837), and "The Divinity School Address" (1838). "These I deem first fruits of a new literature," Alcott said. "They are indigenous. Like a plant uprooted from its native soil, the earth yet cleaves to the roots. Nature and the Soul are conjoined. The images are American." Emerson labored on a book of essays, from which a walk in the woods was a relief; in November he wrote, "I flee to the secretest hemlock shade in Walden Woods to recover my selfrespect." This may have been near Deep Cove on the cool, shady south shore, where hemlocks flourished. Alcott understood perfectly, having written this year in heroic terms that we think of as quintessentially "Thoreauvian,"

> I need the influences of Nature. The city does not whet my appetites and faculties. Life is got at too great an expenditure of labour. I know not how much I lose by this artificial style of living. The morning, at Lynn, I walked out before breakfasting and had a vivid experience of the bald ugliness of life in cities when thus contrasted with the fresh grace of existence amidst the scenes of nature. I felt guilty before the fair sun, genial earth, and invigorating air, and confessed to them. The light, blithe season of my boyhood and youth revived in my mind, and I seemed breathing the air of my native hills once more, treading their summits and morning's dawn, and looking again into the dignified manhood of my being, enjoying the foretaste of noble thoughts and magnanimous deeds.[20]

Alcott left no doubt as to the source of these attitudes: Emerson. The day before a trip to Concord in April, he wrote, "My thought, I perceive, is quick with the doctrine of Nature. A cosmogony is growing in me. A few days with my friend will be quite opportune. His tastes are sylvan. He haunts the groves, delights in the freedom of the fields and the song of birds. He is a true son of Old Pan. I shall learn, perchance, of him the secret by which the wood-god veils the features of Psyche from the profaning gaze of mortals." The next day, "I think I could sit under the ministry of Emerson. . . . We had some conversation after dinner on high themes: the genesis of Nature, the dependence of the elements of the corporeal and physical world on the Soul, etc. Afterward, a walk to E's favorite haunts."[21]

Alcott would later look back in gratitude on these lofty transcendentalist experiences indoors and out, in study, parlor, and Walden Woods: "My week's intercourse with Emerson has done me good. . . . He lives to see and write. He looks abroad on Nature and life and sketches their features with his pen. He sits in the theatre of Nature and draws the players and scenes. He is an observer, an eye, an ear, a pen." Happy to be back in Concord in August, "I had an agreeable walk amidst Emerson's sylvan haunts this morning, discoursing with him on the great questions of the time," Emerson arguing "the supremacy of the scholar's pen" and Alcott "the omnipotence of the prophet's spoken over the written word." Alcott's journal shows how indispensable Walden Woods had become for Emerson's daily ritual of walking and meditating, an intellectual grove of inspiration for the philosopher.[22]

The dreamy poet Jones Very visited Emerson in April 1840 and walked with him to Goose Pond, Emerson recalling, "I sat on the bank of the Drop or God's Pond & saw the amplitude of the little water, what space what verge the little scudding fleets of ripples found to scatter & spread from side to side & take so much time to cross the pond, & saw how the water seemed made for the wind, & the wind for the water, dear playfellows for each other,—I said to my companion, I declare this world is so beautiful that I can hardly believe it exists." "At Walden Pond, the waves were larger and the whole lake in pretty uproar." Very too had undergone the now-customary transcendentalist baptism into the woods and waters of Walden.[23]

Spiritual as it increasingly seemed, Walden remained earthy and profane, too. As Emerson walked through its surrounding woods, he desired to name their features to his liking: "Let us call Goose Pond The Drop, or God's Pond; Henry Thoreau says 'No; that will shock the people: call it Satan's Pond & they will like it, or still better, Tom Wyman's Pond.'" Perhaps "God's Pond" referred to the similarity of its outline to Aleph, א, the Hebrew letter symbolizing God. In September 1840, Emerson spoke humorously of the contrast between highly sociable utopias (of which Brook Farm would become the most famous) and the life that hermitlike Wyman lived: "Will there not after so many *social* ages be now & here one *lonely* age? Tom Wyman at Walden Pond will be the saint & pattern of the time." It is an intriguing forecast of Thoreau's tenancy there.[24]

In October Waldo wrote a friend, "In these beautiful days which are now passing, go into the forest & the leaves hang silent & sympathetic, inobtrusive & related, like the thoughts which they so hospitably enshrine. Could they tell their sense, they would become the thoughts we have." By now, Walden had been a leitmotif in Emerson's mind for six autumns. Its meanings struck him as profound, but they were difficult to communicate to friends in town, as he confided to his journal:

> I knew a man who learned that his modes of living were false & mean by looking at the hill covered with wood which formed the shore of a small but beautiful lake which he visited in his almost daily walk. He returned to his gossips & told them his schemes of reform and they contradicted & chided & laughed & cried with vexation & contempt and shook his confidence in his plans. But when he went to the woods & saw the mist floating over the trees on the headland which rose out of the water, instantly his faith revived. But when he came to his house he could not find any words to show his friends in what manner the beautiful shores of the lake proved the wisdom of his economy. He could not show them the least connexion between the two things. When he once tried to speak of the bold shore, they stared as if he were insane. Yet whenever he went to the place & beheld the landscape his faith was confirmed.

Probably the only person who fully understood this Walden vision of "economy," "self help," and "modes of living [not] false & mean" was Thoreau. It would eventually be Thoreau who would do what Emerson, the family man, could not—go "to the woods" to undertake an extended philosophical and practical experiment.[25]

Like Emerson, the Thoreau brothers were making regular use of Walden Woods. Henry and John taught school in town, and "if the weather permitted John took his scholars to walk on Saturdays and gave them a running lesson in Botany, Geology, Natural History &c, at Walden, Fairhaven, the boiling springs." In January 1840, Thoreau, twenty-two, looked forward to spring, inviting his sister, Helen, to go "roaming with me in the woods, or climbing the Fair Haven cliffs,—or else, in my boat on Walden, let the water kiss your hand, or gaze at your image in the wave." He basked in the sun on the Walden shore and, with one of his students, caught frogs at Goose Pond. Inspired by English place-poems and peripatetic writings, in December he drew up accounts of winter walks around Concord, hoping to publish them in the transcendentalists' new journal, *The Dial*. On the fourth of the month he recalled a view of the opposite shore on a hazy fall afternoon. Days later, snow lay on the ice, and fishermen dropped lines to catch pickerel: "I am as much moved and elevated when I consider men fishing on Walden Pond in the winter, as when I read the exploits of Alexander in history." "Its history is in the lapse of its waves, in the rounded pebbles on its shore, and the pines which have grown on its brink. It has its precessions and recessions, its cycles and epicycles"—linking its risings and fallings with the great patterns of human history. In these December meditations he first hinted at the grand transcendentalist themes he would take up in earnest in *Walden*. Along the way, they would form part of "A Winter Walk," finished in 1843.

Thoreau's way of seeing the Concord landscape was strongly shaped by the Picturesque, an English aesthetic approach popularized around 1800 by the writings of Wordsworth, William Gilpin, and others. It may be simply defined as Romanticism applied to tangible things, with emphasis on roughness, irregularity, variety, primitivism, and the ancient. Natural beauty is a starting point, but the Picturesque favored a spice of boldness and mystery, as Thoreau found in the Walden shoreline. The Picturesque as disseminated in poetry, prose, and art showed strong interest in architecture, especially the rough and rustic cottage, as seen in Thoreau's descriptions of his Walden house and the nearby cellar holes. It was strongly evident in spring 1841, too, as he first turned his attention to having a home. He was nearly twenty-four and had never lived independently; now the idea consumed him, as ideas often did. It was, as he later described in *Walden*, that "certain season of our life [when] we are accustomed to consider every spot as the possible site of a house. I have thus surveyed the country on every side within a dozen miles. . . . Wherever I sat, there I might live." In February he bought the Hollowell Farm on Sudbury River, only to have the owner immediately take it back. Historian Brian Donahue believes the story may be more allegorical than factual; nonetheless, Thoreau did long for a rustic home: "I should prefer that my farm be bounded by a river."[26]

His praise of Hollowell is one of Thoreau's clearest expressions of English Picturesque philosophy and of the explicitly literary and

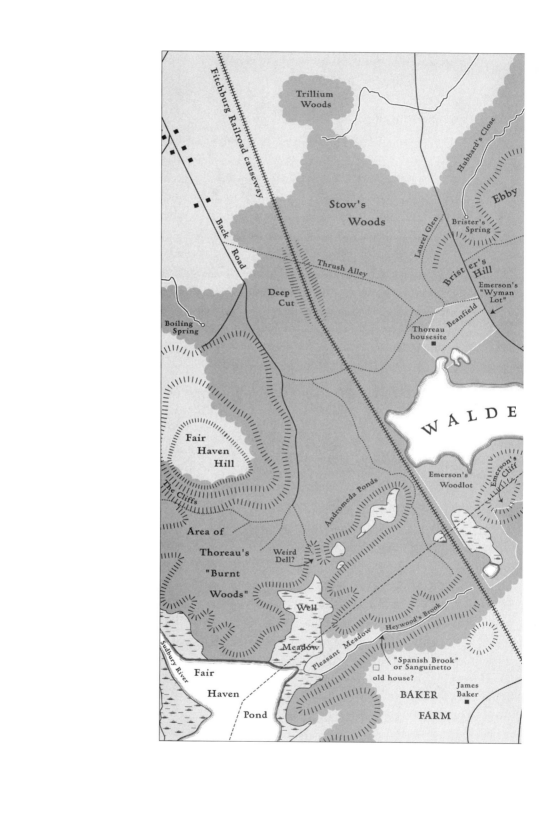

Trillium
Woods

Fitchburg Railroad causeway

Back Road

Stow's
Woods

Hubbard's Close

Ebby

Laurel Glen

Brister's
Spring

Brister's
Hill

Thrush Alley

Deep
Cut

Emerson's
"Wyman
Lot"

Beanfield

Boiling
Spring

Thoreau
housesite

W A L D E

Fair
Haven
Hill

Emerson's
Woodlot

Emerson's
Cliff

The Cliffs

Andromeda Ponds

Area of

Thoreau's

"Burnt

Woods"

Weird
Dell?

Well

Sudbury River

Meadow

Heywood's Brook

Pleasant Meadow

Fair

Haven

Pond

"Spanish Brook"
or Sanguinetto
old house?

BAKER

James
Baker

FARM

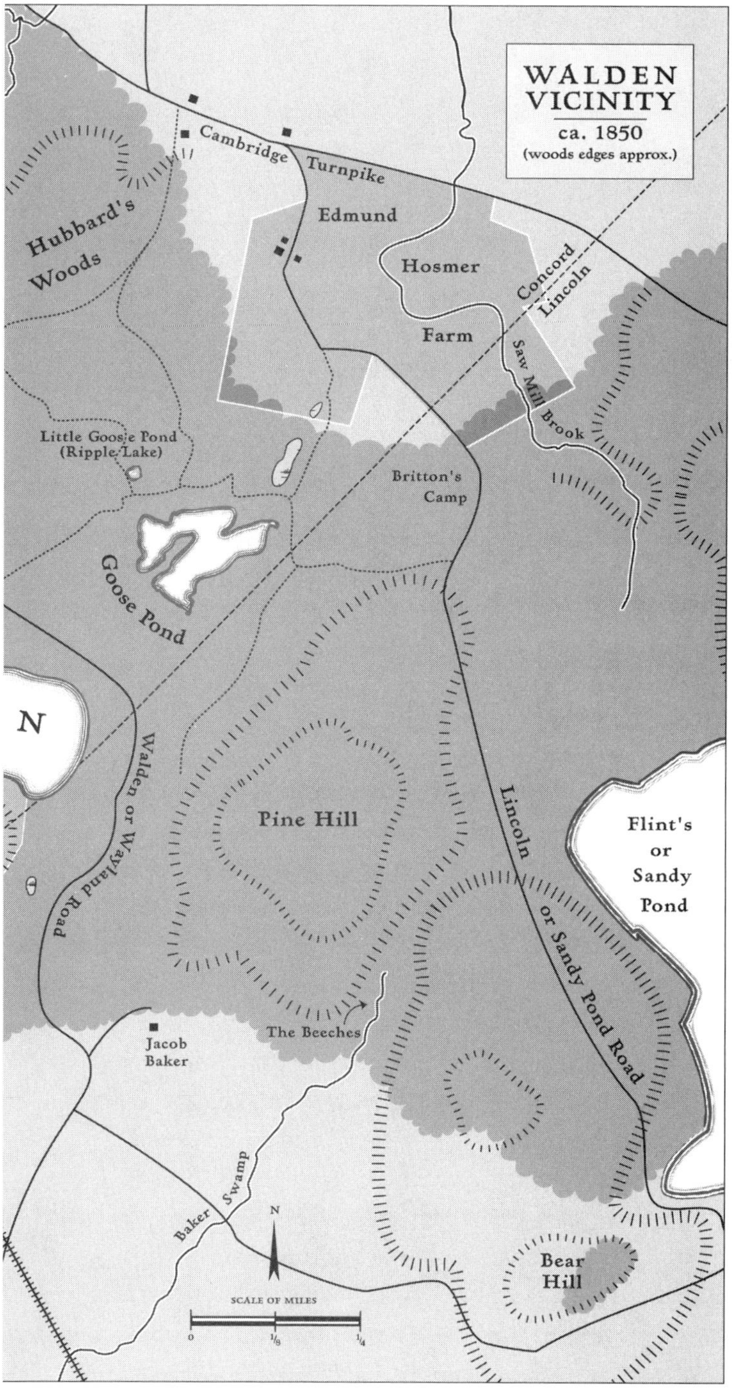

WALDEN
VICINITY
ca. 1850
(woods edges approx.)

Hubbard's
Woods

Cambridge Turnpike

Edmund

Hosmer

Concord
Lincoln

Farm

Saw Mill Brook

Little Goose Pond
(Ripple Lake)

Britton's
Camp

Goose Pond

N

Pine Hill

Walden or Wayland Road

Lincoln or Sandy Pond Road

Flint's
or
Sandy
Pond

Jacob
Baker

The Beeches

Baker Swamp

N

Bear
Hill

SCALE OF MILES

0   1/8   1/4

Pastoral Baker Farm, celebrated in *Walden*. Agriculture surrounded Walden Woods on all sides. Looking northwest toward Fair Haven Bay. Gleason, "Cows in Pasture at Baker Farm," June 20, 1903, courtesy Concord Free Public Library.

poetical basis of his environmentalism. It is important in explaining his decision to move to Walden, where he uses similar language in describing his retirement, "a mile from any neighbor." Hollowell was inspiring for its Picturesque values, falling into the category that Wordsworth described as "COTTAGES . . . scattered over the valleys, and under the hill-sides, and on the rocks; and, even to this day, in the more retired dales, without any intrusion of more assuming buildings." They were "a production of Nature," seeming more to have "grown than to have been erected." And they were "rough and uneven" with walls "the colour of the native rock" and covered with "lichens, mosses, ferns, and flowers," the whole screened by "a cluster of embowering sycamores for summer shade." The deeply Wordsworthian nature of Thoreau's responses surely results from the fact that, as Robert Sattelmeyer has shown, he had just begun an ambitious project, the compilation of an anthology of English poetry, which he worked on for several years (1841–44) and may have intended as his first book-length publication. Although that volume never appeared, Thoreau's immersion in place-poetry bore fruit in the place-prose of *Walden*.[27]

Channing was even more conventionally poetical and Picturesque than his friend Thoreau. One senses his influence in Thoreau's April 1853 lament against improvement along Corner Road, one of their favorite walks, south of Hollowell Farm. "The main charm about the corner road, just beyond [Hubbard's] bridge, to me has been in the little grove of locusts—sallows & birches &c which has sprung up on the bank as you rise the hill. Yesterday I saw a man who is building a house nearby cutting them down—I asked him if he was going to cut them all. He said he was—I said If I were in his place I would not have them cut for a hundred dollars—that they were the chief attraction of the place." Worse still, "Wm Wheeler has raised a new staring house beyond the Corner bridge & so done irreparable injury to a large section of country for walkers. It obliges us to take still more steps after weary ones—to reach the secluded fields & woods." So concerned was Channing with Picturesque sensibilities, he suggested "that we petition him to put his house out of sight."[28]

In his search for the perfect Picturesque situation, Thoreau never considered living in town. Rather, he would be a Wordsworthian cottager dwelling in retired simplicity in some scenic corner of the landscape. After Hollowell fell through, he explored other possibilities, as Channing listed: "Henry did buy the Hallowell place, and thought to buy Weird Dell [at Well Meadow Field], and one side of Fairhaven Hill, that of the orchard. He also thought of the Cliff Hill, and the Baker Farm." All were in the district west of Walden Pond, and some would have given him considerably more solitude than he had at Walden, which refutes the idea that living absolutely hermit-like was his top priority.[29]

In April 1841, Thoreau said impatiently, "I only ask a clean seat. I will build my lodge on the southern slope of some hill." His language recalls a passage in "A Winter Walk" in which he visits a "deserted woodman's hut" somewhere in Walden Woods: "Here man has lived under this south hillside, and it seems a civilized and public spot." His mind was already formulating an experiment that would combine a rustic but well-built dwelling and a deliberate exercise in emulating the life of the ancient philosophers, one that at the same time linked him to the "Former Inhabitants" of the Wordsworthian cottages (subsequently cellar holes) on Walden Road. And yet the real life of a farmer would be hard work, a friend writing, "Henry will have to take care that he don't hurt himself seasoning—a very common occurrence. When he gets settled on his farm—I should like to look in upon him."[30]

His move toward a life close to nature proved abortive, however. Unable to find an affordable tract of land, and having lost his teaching job when the local school shut its doors on April 1, the young writer accepted Emerson's offer of financial help. On the twenty-sixth Thoreau moved into Emerson's household as handyman, gardener, and manager of the estate. Waldo referred to him as one of the family and needed his help, as he himself by June had "quite deserted my books, and do hoe corn & wheel a wheelbarrow whole days together. I . . . doubt not to reap a better harvest from it than peas lettuce apples & pears." Thoreau too exerted himself strenuously in planting pear trees and grape vines and chopping and sawing wood. In polite circumstances at Bush, as Emerson called the place, it did not take him long to grumble that "life in gardens and parlors is unpalatable to me," but his employer generously allowed him ample time for his own activities—reading, writing, and going out "to saunter."[31]

That first summer at Emerson's was an exciting time, intellectually, for young Thoreau, as he ranged through his mentor's library. He was reading seventeenth-century poetry at midnight in May when alarm bells signaled that Breed's house was on fire at the foot of Brister's Hill. He jumped Mill Brook and sprinted there ahead of the fire engines. Emerson pointed him to Oriental literature as appropriate for the coming steamy months. The *Laws of Menu* in particular were about to set Thoreau's mind ablaze with the spirit of independence and high-mindedness that would later be felt on almost every page of *Walden*. Henry would escape at night to the barn to read and write, enjoying a bit of the rustic solitude he had hoped for at Hollowell Farm and would eventually experience in his Walden house: "The sublime sentences of Menu carry us back to a time—when purification—and sacrifice—and self devotion—had a place in the faith of men, and were not as a superstition." And the place that most embodied those values of ancientness and wisdom was Walden Pond and Woods, to which he would walk in summer with the *Laws of Menu* filling his mind.[32]

On the night of May 27, 1841, he sat in his boat on Walden playing his flute and seeming to charm the perch that lazily swam beneath him, finding that, to the transcendentalist imagination, "Concord nights are stranger than the Arabian nights." He would later write this experience into *Walden* as if it had happened during the time he lived there. *Dial* editor Margaret Fuller, then visiting the Emersons, went rowing with Thoreau one moonlit evening. She wrote her brother Richard, "He is three and twenty, has been through college and kept a school, is very fond of the classics and an earnest thinker, yet intends being a farmer. . . . He has a boat which he made himself, and rows me out on the pond." Mesmerizing to Thoreau during these visits was his continuing Hindu reading: "That title—The Laws of Menu . . . comes to me with such a volume of sound as if it had swept unobstructed over the plains of Hindostan, and when my eye rests on yonder birches—or the sun in the water— or the shadows of the trees—it seems to signify the laws of them all." As Walden and Menu grew exhilaratingly intertwined, Henry came naturally to see the pond as "the oriental asiatic valley of my world," its plateaulike south shore (later Emerson's woodlot) stretching infinitely toward "the steppes of Tartary." Emerson shared his disciple's swelling enthusiasm for the place; a year earlier he had himself been reading the Vedas avidly for "primeval inspiration. . . . It is of no use to put away the book: if I trust myself in the woods or in a boat upon the pond Nature makes a Bramin of me presently." In summer 1841 he spoke of his own series of "Walden or Waldonian poems" and wrote figuratively to Fuller, "You know I was baptized in Walden Pond."[33]

In October, Fuller wrote Thoreau, "Let me know whether you go to the lonely hut, and write me about Shakespeare, if you read him there." By now Henry's scheme for woodsy retirement was common knowledge. He wrote decisively on December 24, "I want to go soon and live away by the pond where I shall hear only the wind whispering among the reeds." This statement places his favored house site precisely, for only at Wyman Meadow do reeds grow at Walden: he had chosen the cove where he would move in

1845. Next day, "I don't want to feel as if my life were a sojourn any longer. . . . It is time now that I begin to live." On January 3, 1842, "I would have my house a bower fit to entertain" nature. And on March 15, grieving for his brother John, who died from lockjaw in January, he tucked a small book in his pocket and walked out the twisting Walden Road past the Poor House on his way to the pond. Stopping at Brister's "Cold Spring" he wrote, "I hear nothing but a phoebe, and the wind, and the rattling of a chaise in the wood. For a few years I stay here—not knowing—taking my own life by degrees—and then I go. I hear a spring bubbling near—where I drank out of a can in my earliest youth. The birds—the squirrels— the alders—the pines—they seem serene and in their places—I wonder if my life looks as serene to them too." Again Walden Woods promised a fertile transcendentalist return to childhood memories, a reconnection with deep and primal values. Many modern interpreters would add that it also promised a source of refuge from the pain of John's death—although this likely has been overemphasized. Many months were still to pass, however, before the Walden experiment became reality.[34]

Emerson continued to introduce others to the delights of Walden in 1842. Nathaniel Hawthorne and his bride had recently moved to Concord's Old Manse, and with houseguest George Hillard the Salem writer "set out for a walk to Walden Pond, calling by the way at Mr. Emerson's, to obtain his guidance or directions." Emerson accompanied them. Hawthorne wrote, "The pond itself was beautiful and refreshing to my soul. . . . Farther within its depths, you perceive a bottom of pure white sand, sparkling through the transparent water, which, methought, was the very purest liquid in the world. After Mr. Emerson left us, Hillard and I bathed in the pond."[35]

Margaret Fuller lived with the Emersons in late summer 1842: "Waldo & I went to walk to Walden pond, as usual, & staid till near sunset on the water's brink beneath the pines. It was a very lovely afternoon, great happy clouds floating, a light breeze rippling the water to our feet." A few days later she was there with her brother: "Richard and I spent the afternoon at Walden, & got a great bunch of flowers, a fine thunder shower gloomed gradual up, & turned the lake inky black, but no rain came till sunset." Another "calm bright afternoon" she walked with William Ellery Channing, her poet brother-in-law who would move to Concord the following April and become Thoreau's lifelong friend and walking companion. Today, she said, "He was full of whimsies. . . . At Walden we sat down among the bushes, & there E[llery] was amusing me with his fancies of possible life upon the lake, & had just built his cottage, where he wrote verses from eight in the morning till four in the afternoon, summoning his attendant who hovered during the day on the edge of the wood by notes graduated on a key bugle to express his wants,—when Waldo dashed through the trees, and came down close to us." This extraordinarily prescient conversation shows Channing already thinking, however casually, of Walden Pond as the ideal literary retreat *for himself*—he who would encourage Thoreau strongly in March 1845 to "build yourself a hut" there and "begin the grand process of devouring yourself alive."[36]

This urge to flee to nature had taken sturdy root among the intimates of the Emerson circle, forming one of what the visiting Swedish novelist Fredrika Bremer would call "attempts by unusual ways to escape from the torment of common life." She noted that Channing had "built himself a hut on the western prairies, and lived there as a hermit," in Illinois in 1839–40. Describing her own frontier experiences in *Summer on the Lakes in 1843*, Fuller would praise a certain "double log cabin" as perfect for "the poet, the sportsman, the naturalist." Here "all kinds of wild sports, experiments, and the studies of natural history" could take place. She anticipated *Walden* when she wrote, "Then, with a very little money, a ducal estate may be purchased, and by a very little more, and moderate labor, a family be maintained upon it with raiment, food and shelter. The luxurious and minute comforts of a city life are not yet to be had without effort disproportionate to their value. . . . Cannot these be given up once for all?"[37]

Surely Thoreau's ideas and attitudes, however individualistic they have been held to be, cannot be understood without this larger intellectual context. On January 17, 1843, Emerson gave two lectures on "New England" in Baltimore. Their belated publication in 2001 allows us to see that a great many of the ideas in *Walden* were already part of Emerson's thinking. He spoke of the heroic age, the "Indian in the woods," and the Greek, and of how entering the wilderness takes one back two thousand years in time, going from civilization to barbarism. He argued "against the spirit of commerce in New England," in praise of "whatever goes to separate a man," remarking that society shows "despondency," sadness, and anxiety (compare Thoreau's "quiet desperation"). "Heroic farming" was rare, as most farmers were degraded, and he excoriated "Irish laborers . . . low and semi-barbarous." He critiqued village life. And, finally, he mentioned his enjoyment in watching the colorful stream of commerce passing before his door (compare Thoreau on the railroad). Readers of *Walden* will find all of these themes familiar, broached by Emerson two years before Thoreau moved to the pond and fully eleven before Thoreau published his masterpiece.[38]

Even as Walden Pond rose to prominence among the transcendentalists, the site was about to see great changes, in the form of the Boston-to-Fitchburg railroad. In the 1840s the juggernauts of technology and affluence were inescapable and astonishing, stoking the growing reaction that was transcendentalism. The Baltimore and Ohio, America's first real railroad line, was underway in Maryland in 1830; Boston followed almost immediately in constructing two of its own in 1831–35. For a time Concord was spared, but in 1843 a thousand Irish workmen and their families arrived. The men were paid fifty cents a day for their labor, "dark to dark"—up to sixteen hours straight, to the horror of liberal-minded Concordians. But Emerson was not much troubled, writing of the railroad, "it will be American power & beauty, when it is done."[39]

Undulating topography required the excavation of deep cuts in the sand-gravel hills and the building of earthen causeways across valleys. Digging cuts in summer 1843 involved "the blowing of rocks, explosions all day, & now & then a painful accident." Emerson wrote in June, "The town is full of Irish & the woods of engineers with theodolite & red flag singing out their feet & inches to each other from station to station." He marveled at the labor that went into extending the "bold mole" across wide fields between Walden Woods and the depot site at the western edge of Concord village. This causeway would eventually become one of Thoreau's favorite walking routes to the pond, but at the moment he was gloomy about news of the construction, which reached him during a brief period in which he worked as a tutor on Staten Island. He wrote his

Locomotive cloud. Fitchburg Railroad sliced along the western shore in 1843. Looking southwest from Thoreau's Cove. Gleason, "Northwest cove of Walden, ice breaking up (train in distance)," March 31, 1920, courtesy Concord Free Public Library.

mother, "I should have liked to be in Walden woods with you, but not with the railroad."[40]

The Irish suddenly filling those woods were a picturesque and surprising sight on the cart paths, and, as it happened, their numbers hinted at the great unruly crowds of visitors to come in a later era. Emerson wrote with surprise, "I walked this P.M. in the woods, but there too the snow banks were sprinkled with tobacco juice." These workers inhabited shantytowns along the tracks, several of them near Walden, along which the railroad cruelly impinged. One community clung to a hillside by Railroad Spring at Heywood's Meadow. Concord ladies sent their daughters "to the farthest corner of Walden Pond" to offer a little education for the ragged children there. Another shantytown stood at what Thoreau would eventually call Ice Fort Cove, and a third at Deep Cut. When Hawthorne "took a solitary walk to Walden Pond" in October 1843, he came upon the thriving shantytown at the future Ice Fort Cove:

In a small and secluded dell, that opens upon the most beautiful cove of the whole lake, there is a little hamlet of huts or shanties, inhabited by the Irish people who are at work upon the rail-road. There are three or four of these habitations, the very rudest, I should imagine, that civilized men ever made for themselves, constructed of rough boards, with protruding ends. Against some of them the earth is heaped up to the roof, or nearly so. . . . These huts are placed beneath the trees. . . . To be sure, it is a torment to see the great, high, ugly embankment of the rail-road, which is here protruding itself into the lake, or along its margin, in close vicinity to this picturesque little hamlet. I have seldom seen anything more beautiful than the cove, on the border of which the huts are situated; and the more I looked, the lovelier it grew.[41]

The first trains ran in June 1844 at what seemed an astonishing speed, a mile in under two minutes. Railroad construction had torn a swath through the middle of Walden Woods, locomotives would soon devour much of the woods' timber, and flying sparks would routinely ignite fires along the right-of-way. One more casualty was the cold and bubbly Boiling Spring, beloved of farmers and berry parties traversing the main path from Back Road to sunny pastures on Fair Haven Hill and for transcendentalists on their way to the inspiring heights of the Cliffs. Unfortunately, Boiling Spring was purchased by David Loring, local manufacturer of lead pipe, to feed the locomotives' steam engines. The spring, Thoreau wrote, was "much deepened and enlarged and more or less covered," provided with a "Spring house," and altogether "turned into a tank for the Iron Horse to drink at." Now it no longer bubbled up, but ran "more or less copiously through the gravel on the upper side, sometimes from under a rock in a considerable stream and with a tinkling sound," still however with a "crystalline or Walden-Pond-like look." In *Walden*, he would condemn "that devilish Iron Horse, whose ear-rending neigh is heard throughout the town" for muddying the Boiling Spring.[42]

His anger simultaneously paralleled that of Wordsworth in England on hearing of the projected Kendal and Windermere Railway. In autumn 1844 the famous poet fulminated in the *Morning*

Thoreau's "bloated pest." This 1843 engine of Fitchburg Railroad was likely one of those that he saw passing Walden. Recently discovered photograph, collection of Anthony J. Bianculli.

Post, "Is then no nook of English ground secure / From rash assault? . . . Baffle the threat, bright Scene." Now in his last years, he "lamented the probable intrusion of a railway with its scarifications, its intersections, its noisy machinery, its smoke" along the wooded margins of the lakes, the enemy " 'Utilitarianism,' serving as a mask for cupidity." Likewise for Thoreau, it was the railroad more than anything else that threatened to change the character of Concord and Walden. By the early 1850s there was, he said, hardly a place in Massachusetts out of range of the locomotive whistle, to the fatal destruction of "pastoral life." That shrill sound instantly suburbanized the landscape. Even before Thoreau moved to the pond, there were men who gave Walden's beauty only a glimpse over the top of their newspapers while commuting daily to Boston by train.[43]

※

One wishes to follow Thoreau's thinking closely in 1843 and 1844 as he moved ever closer to the final Walden decision, but unfortunately he later scissored the relevant journals to pieces in the composition of his published works, including *Walden*. Perhaps the pond receded from the forefront of his mind as his attention was directed to other bodies of water while he began drafting his first book, *A Week on the Concord and Merrimack Rivers*. Moreover, from May to December 1843 he worked unhappily as a tutor for William Emerson's children on Staten Island; otherwise, he continued laboring for Waldo Emerson, helped his father in the family's pencil factory, and in late 1844 assisted in the construction of his family's new house on Texas Street at the western edge of Concord village. All these circumstances intervened before the Walden experiment could begin.

The idea of living by the pond—to "withdraw a little from the village, and perceive how it is embosomed in nature"—continued to gestate, however. The suburban Staten Island interlude heightened Thoreau's appreciation of Walden Woods, he writing the Emersons of lying awake at midnight recollecting "those walks in the woods in ancient days—too sacred to be idly remembered." In addition, his stay brought him face-to-face with the fancy modern house that he would parody in *Walden* and sharpened his thinking on the question of what is necessary for human shelter. At the same time, he was well aware of how Emerson himself expressed growing enthusiasm for building and landowning, wishing to emulate William's success on fast-developing Staten Island. Waldo wrote his brother in 1846 of his admiration for "all your operations in road building & rural architecture in which every one of us here has a lively interest. . . . Send us a map of your Road & new house & garden lot! . . . You know I am to be a bit of a builder myself on the peak of my woodlot"— referring to his plans to build a literary retreat on land he had recently bought at Walden Pond. He had said in 1843, "In this country where land is so cheap & the disposition of the people so pacific every thing invites to the arts of domestic architecture & gardening. . . . A noble garden makes the face of the country where you live, of no account; low or high, noble or mean, you have made a beautiful abode worthy of man. It is the fine art which is left for us now that sculpture & painting & religious & civil architecture have become effete & have a second childhood. In this climate what a joy to build! The south side of the house should be almost all window for the advantage of the winter sun." These musings, harbingers of architectural themes that Thoreau would take up in *Walden*, appeared in

"The Young American," a lecture that Emerson first read in Boston in February 1844.[44]

When Emerson arranged Thoreau's employment with William, he stressed his young friend's insistence on having his own chamber, especially "in winter when the evening is the best part of the day for the study, a matter of vital importance to all book reading & book writing men, to be at night the autocrat of a chamber be it never so small—6 feet by 6,—wherein to dream, write, & declaim alone. Henry has always had it, & always must." Emerson's sympathy regarding the need for a private study suggests the sorts of writer conversations that must have transpired between the two men, emphasizing solitude in a tiny space. No less than Thoreau, Emerson later described himself as "being solitary from my youth, wishing always to be social, but by nature and habit always driven to solitude as the only home and workshop for me." These conversations too, along with a heady climate of talk about houses and new building, helped eventually point to the Walden experiment.[45]

Thoreau's move to Walden must also be seen in light of Emerson's friendship with local farmer Edmund Hosmer. For Emerson, whose thought ran along the lines of "Representative Men" who embodied distinctive virtues, Hosmer was a subject of deep interest, typifying the wise ("long-headed") yet homespun philosopher-rustic. Emerson showed him off to visitors, including Hawthorne, and made the Hosmer Farm part of a loop to the woods: out the turnpike past Channing's to Hosmer's, then to Goose Pond and Walden. Natural man and natural scenery were thereby studied together. Hawthorne viewed Hosmer as a mere creation of Emerson, blaming "a circle . . . who look up to him as an oracle; and so he inevitably assumes the oracular manner." But Thoreau greatly admired Hosmer and recorded his pithy sayings in his journal. A desire to emulate him may have informed his Walden experiment, especially as Emerson heaped such praise on this self-reliant farmer who lived at the woods edge only about half a mile from the pond.[46]

From Staten Island, Thoreau wrote his mother wistfully, "Methinks I should be content to sit at the back-door in Concord, under the poplar-tree, henceforth forever." Not long after, he moved back to Massachusetts and once again faced the problem of earning a living. Five years later he would write to Horace Greeley that 1843 marked the beginning of a new phase of his life, during which "I have supported myself solely by the labors of my hands—I have not received one cent from any other source, and this has cost me so little time, say a month in the spring and another in the autumn, doing the coarsest work of all kinds, that I have probably enjoyed more leisure for literary pursuits than any contemporary." He then described his Walden experiment, "earning only what I wanted, and sticking to my proper work." He stated that part of his intention during these years, and especially at Walden, was to demonstrate a new way to live the life of the scholar, not starving in a garret or toadying for a rich patron, but doing "work in the ditch occasionally." In Thoreau's mind, then, his famous experiment in living deliberately began not in 1845 but in 1843 and was part of a larger personal redirection toward simplicity and essentialism in order to pursue intellectual study.[47]

The writer's return to Concord was followed by a serious mishap. On April 30, 1844, he and a young friend, Edward Sherman Hoar, went sailing up Sudbury River. They stopped for lunch near Well Meadow and built a fire on a stump to cook fish. The blaze ignited dry grass nearby, quickly got out of control, and burned hundreds of acres—supposedly three hundred, although this is likely exaggerated—and caused $2000 in damage to forests owned by Wheeler and Hubbard, between Fair Haven Bay and the railroad, north of Well Meadow. Wheeler's daughter dragged in charred firewood all winter and never forgave Thoreau for having to go to school in a smudged dress. Indeed, he was harshly blamed by many townsfolk for this "Burnt Woods" episode, an accident exacerbated by the exceptionally dry weather, and much has been written of the supposed psychological trauma the experience caused him. Local farmers still gossiped about it fifty years later.[48]

The return to Concord saw the quickening of Thoreau's friendship with Ellery Channing, who lived intermittently in the town starting in 1843. This former solitary inhabitant of the prairies was a truly difficult person who in later years became deeply misanthropic and far more of a hermit than Thoreau ever was. Fuller called her brother-in-law Ellery "a great Genius with a little wretched boy trotting beside him." He in part took the place of brother John in Thoreau's life, but the influence was far different: the gentle, kindly, sociable John was replaced by a loner no one understood and quite a few actively disliked. A highlight of their early friendship was the long trip they took in summer 1844 to the Catskills, in New York, partly by railroad. This adventure has gone largely unremarked but may have been of great importance in steering Thoreau to Walden Pond the following summer. In particular, a night spent in the home of sawmiller Ira Scribner at Kaaterskill Falls offered the revelation of a rustic architectural ideal: rough, unplastered, open to nature, clean, and healthful. Thoreau's Walden journal begins, "I lodged at the house of a saw-miller last summer, on the Caatskills mountains. . . . They were a clean & wholesome family inside and out—like their house. The latter was not plastered—only lathed and the inner doors were not hung. The house seemed high placed, airy, and perfumed, fit to entertain a travelling God. . . . Could not man be man in such an abode?"[49]

Thoreau was probably influenced, as well, by Channing's own urge to settle. In summer 1842, Channing wished to try farming and "proposed a partnership of this kind to Henry Thoreau." In April 1843 he hired Thoreau to remodel his newly secured Concord house, Red Lodge, an eighth of a mile east of Emerson's. Henry's tasks included repointing its stone cellar, installing doors, laying flooring, building steps and stairs, and setting doorsills. Thanking him, Channing added, "See then, beloved Thoreau, how greatly convenient a house of one's own will be!" The following year Channing was in New York but eager to return to Concord where "in solitude I passed many a day treading wearily the lone avenues of the silent woods." He asked Emerson to keep an eye out for properties that were inexpensive, fertile, yet rich in poetical values: "That Hallowell place & the Cliff, will never do. . . . It's a pity I can't find any place in Concord to my mind; any place in fact, that can be got for a reasonable sum, yet that holds out a prospect of getting me a livelihood." This sounds like Thoreau's earlier laments. When Alcott moved back to Concord in fall 1844 after the Fruitlands debacle, he boarded at Edmund Hosmer's and similarly looked about for a farmstead: "The Hallowell place nearly opposite the bridge close by the Cliffs is for sale—30 acres cultivated, and wood lot near—$1000." These various quests for rustic and Picturesque retreats in rural districts of Concord were unfolding even as Thoreau made his final decision to build a house and farm the land by Walden.[50]

As transcendentalism crested, many young men who had fallen under its sway undertook back-to-the-land experiments. Thomas Wentworth Higginson recalled how he conceived "a project of going into the cultivation of peaches, thus securing freedom for study and thought by moderate labor of the hands. This was in 1843, two years before Thoreau tried a similar project with beans at Walden Pond; and also before the time when George and Burrill Curtis undertook to be farmers at Concord." The Curtis brothers, who had been students at Brook Farm, lived with Edmund Hosmer "near Mr. Emerson and Walden Pond, where we occupied only a single room, making our own beds, and living in the very simplest and most primitive style." Half the day was spent in "intellectual cultivation." A biographer records, "They read much, and had with them a large number of books. It was their custom . . . to spend much time . . . in the Walden and Lincoln woods. It was while the Curtises were living at Hosmer's that they assisted Thoreau in building his hut at Walden Pond."[51]

What finally made it feasible for Thoreau to erect that "hut" was Emerson's purchase of the Tommy Wyman lot in autumn 1844. Writing to his brother William in October, Emerson explained, "I have lately added an absurdity or two to my usual ones, which I am impatient to tell you of. In one of my solitary wood-walks by Walden Pond, I met two or three men who told me they had come thither to sell & to buy a field, on which they wished me to bid as purchaser. As it was on the shore of the pond, & now for years I had a sort of daily occupancy in it, I bid on it, & bought it, eleven acres for $8.10 per acre." The sale took place on September 21. The eleven-acre tally lasted only briefly, as Emerson almost immediately expanded the area to more than thirteen: "The next day I carried some of my well beloved gossips to the same place & they deciding that the field was not good for anything, if Heartwell Bigelow should cut down his pine-grove, I bought, for 125 dollars more, his pretty wood lot of 3 or 4 acres." The value of the standing timber is apparent: the wood-lot cost thirty or forty dollars per acre, versus eight for the cutover field. "And so [I] am landlord & waterlord of 14 acres, more or less, on the shore of Walden, & can raise my own blackberries." Emerson was not quite sure what to do with the lot, but it formed part of his steady expansion of landholdings, for each of which some purpose seemed inevitably to arise; in telling his brother about it he added that he had plans to build a cottage for sister-in-law Lucy Brown on the triangular "heater piece" of land across from his own residence and to help the impecunious Alcott buy a house and farm. In this same generous and paternal spirit, he no doubt encouraged Thoreau to take up residence on the Wyman Lot, providing justification for an otherwise somewhat frivolous purchase.[52]

It was fortuitous for history that Emerson stumbled upon the auction of the Wyman Lot in one of his frequent walks. Its purchase was tied to his dismay at how the coming of the railroad accelerated the consumption of timber. Joel Britton set up a sawmill near Flint's Pond and did brisk business cutting up chestnut trees to make sleepers for the train tracks. The price of wood rose rapidly, and Emerson, at first on a whim but later in earnest, began to buy forested land—partly for the pride of ownership, partly to enjoy cheap firewood, partly for eventual profit, but partly to preserve the scenic beauties he had come to value so highly. This was fifteen years before Thoreau famously pleaded in his journal that "every town should have a park, or rather a primitive forest, of five hundred or a thousand acres, where a stick should never be cut for fuel, a common possession forever, for instruction and recreation. . . . All Walden Wood might have been preserved for our park forever, with Walden in its midst." Emerson acted out of self-interest, not communal spirit, rescuing the tracts where he most liked to stroll and, as his holdings expanded, establishing himself as the Yankee equivalent of an English squire. Landholding suited his condition as one of the wealthiest Concordians, listed in *The Rich Men of Massachusetts* in 1851 as worth fifty thousand dollars.[53]

As Thoreau helped his parents build their so-called Texas House in late 1844, he must have desired to have, at long last, a dwelling of his own, even as he honed the joinery skills he would apply in building it. An old photograph shows that the place had a wing about the size and shape of the later Walden house, with its own chimney. Undertaking a book on his 1839 rivers trip, he recalled the joys of camping out, and in his Walden dwelling he would remember that "the only house I had been the owner of before . . . was a tent," the one used on that earlier excursion with his departed brother. In order to secure a solitary place to compose this book, his first, Henry finally decided to camp out at length by the shores of Walden, on the cut-over, brambly Wyman Lot. Channing wrote him enthusiastically from New York on March 5, 1845, "I see nothing for you in this earth but that field which I once christened 'Briars'; go out upon that, build yourself a hut, & there begin the grand process of devouring yourself alive." For Thoreau, twenty-seven, the path to Briars had been gradual and roundabout. Emerson later supposed that "perhaps he fell into his way of living, without forecasting it much, but approved it with later wisdom," a "life of labor and study" that he first essayed fully on the scruffy Wyman Lot at Walden Pond.[54]

4

❧

Far Off As I Lived

(1845–1847)

❧

In January 1845, Bronson Alcott bought a house in Concord, which he would name "Hillside" (today's "Wayside"). For three years it provided a stable homeplace. He had returned a year earlier from the seven-month Fruitlands experiment, where he had engaged in an abortive transcendentalist exercise in self-sufficiency in Harvard, Massachusetts. His diary for 1845 is unfortunately lost; one would like to know what reference it made to Thoreau's Walden house, an act of settling down parallel to Alcott's own. We can imagine, though, the conversations that he might have had with Thoreau: would it not be dramatic to make a public demonstration of living a primitive yet intellectual life in deliberate contrast to the bustling agrarian capitalism that surrounded them in Massachusetts?

By moving to the woods, Thoreau could explore the ancient dichotomy between *rus* and *urbe*, but this time, along a model of solitude, not socialism. As Emerson had said, "Will there not after so many *social* ages be now & here one *lonely* age? Tom Wyman at Walden Pond will be the saint & pattern of the time." And what Emerson had defined as Concord versus Boston in his own life at Bush, his native-son disciple could rework more starkly as Walden versus Concord. Thoreau would fulfill the cherished goal articulated four years earlier—"he intends being a farmer"—and, as historian Richard Francis says, would complete the chain of transcendentalist

House-raising. A carefully researched replica of Thoreau's Walden dwelling was built at the Thoreau Institute at Walden Woods, June 2001. Photo, author.

utopias: "The large-scale enterprise of Brook Farm, the 'consociate family' at Fruitlands, and now Thoreau's 'community of one.'" Such things were in the air, no fewer than thirty-three utopian communities being founded nationwide in 1843–45. "Our grand machine of [American] Society must be sadly disjointed & ricketty" to have spawned so many rebellions, Emerson concluded in December 1844—but "success, then, to all the new aspirants; at their *social* plans, sane or fanatics, they cannot do worse, & the hour is big with something better than the establishment."[1]

On May 3, 1845, George and Burrill Curtis went for a woodland walk "to a new pond near us . . . roaming over the hills and along the shore." This may have been Walden. It was about this same time, in early May, that the raising of Thoreau's house frame took place, with his closest friends assisting: Emerson, Channing, Alcott; Edmund Hosmer and his sons John, Edmund, and Andrew; and the Curtises. George Curtis said, "Thoreau lives in the berry-pastures upon a bank over Walden Pond, and in a little house of his own building. One pleasant summer afternoon a small party of us helped him raise it—a bit of life as Arcadian as any at Brook Farm."[2]

The Curtises's domestic experiment provides an important parallel to Thoreau's. After leaving Brook Farm they boarded with Concord farmers (Nathaniel Barrett in summer 1844, Hosmer in

1845) and did hard agricultural labor for half the day, each finding himself "up to his ears in manure and dish-water!" The rest of the time was devoted to intellectual cultivation, or "all the afternoon roaming over the country far and near . . . thrown so directly and almost alone into nature" and seeking "the yellow violet . . . the rhodora and the columbine." At night they hoped for "some Aesthetical tea or Transcendental club or Poet's assembly" at which former Brook Farmers might congregate. But the basic idea was Emersonian solitude: "The lonely life pleases as much as ever. If I sometimes say inwardly that such is not the natural state of man, I contrive to quiet myself by the assurance that such is the best state for bachelors."[3]

Concord's intelligentsia—bachelors and married alike—were turning to the land in April, when Emerson wrote a friend, "Here we are using the finest hours to train our bushes & graft our apple trees. Ellery has just bought his land. Mr. Thoreau is building himself a solitary house by Walden Pond." Allowing Thoreau to live at Walden was a natural extension of the veritable boardinghouse for transcendentalists that the Emersons were running at Bush and furthered Waldo's goal of making Concord hospitable to talented contemporaries: "Hawthorne, Thoreau, & Channing are all within a mile of me." Emerson wanted to help his young writer friend find an isolated place where he could be, as we saw, "the autocrat of a chamber be it never so small—6 feet by 6,—wherein to dream, write, & declaim alone," in order to produce his long-gestating book manuscript. Henry had not been satisfied living at Bush, but now Emerson could offer the Indian-like youth something more congenial and exciting, the chance to live at Walden in a house built of trees cut right on the lot. Given Emerson's enthusiasm for rustic architecture and suburban retirement, one supposes he watched the experiment with interest, especially as his protégé was putting into practice the high-minded exhortations of *Self-Reliance* and *Nature*. Consistently he sympathized with the Young American of the times struggling with questions of "how to feed, clothe, and warm himself," yet being "met by warnings on every hand that this thing and that have owners, and he must go elsewhere. Then he says, 'If I am born in the earth, where is my part? Have the goodness, gentlemen of this world, to show me my wood-lot, where I may fell my wood, my field where to plant my corn, my pleasant ground where to build my cabin.'"[4]

Undergraduates often comment that Thoreau's experiment was only possible given that he was a bachelor, unencumbered; Emerson, who wrote in 1847 of having "a good deal of domestic immoveableness—being fastened down by wife & children by books & studies," could not have gone to Walden. This truism deserves closer appraisal. Emerson did in fact go to Walden on walks and contemplated building a cabin for occasional retreat. Even if he had been entirely free, though, he likely would not have chosen a year-round Walden life for himself. He doubtless regarded Thoreau's experiment as somewhat eccentric, uniquely suited to "a man of original genius & character," as he called him, "a pretty good Sachem himself, master of all woodcraft." If the sojourn would make Henry happy and productive, Waldo welcomed it and would magnanimously assist—indeed, one may wonder to what extent Thoreau undertook the experiment to confirm Emerson's "Sachem" opinion of him. But personally the sage preferred a comfortable study in town. He once called solitude "a sublime mistress, but an intolerable wife," best sampled intermittently. Still, he could fantasize about the hermit life, writing his friend Caroline Sturgis from Nantucket in November 1844, "I could heartily wish that we were both domesticated in neighboring cabins on these long, lonely shores, where the sea obliterates custom, triviality, & time . . . that we might share these great impressions, and read the runes of nature as leisurely & as sincerely as children."[5]

"What really happened at Walden Pond from 1845 to 1847 will never be known," scholar Charles R. Anderson concluded ruefully. *Walden* keeps secrets, revealing its artifice in the memorable sentence, "Thus was my first year's life in the woods completed; and the second year was similar to it." One commentator calls *Walden* "self-dramatizing, self-advertising and deeply duplicitous." Among other devices, Thoreau cloaks his contemporaries in anonymity and says next to nothing about Emerson's crucial role. And yet, with some digging, much of the Walden story can be assembled from external sources, helping us understand the remarkable series of events by which, as biologist Edward O. Wilson has written, "An amateur naturalist perched in a toy house on the edge of a ravaged woodlot became the founding saint of the conservation movement."[6]

The winter of 1844–45 had proved unusually snowy. On March 5, however, George Curtis recorded that cold had finally yielded to "weeks of mild weather" and "a warm southern April[-like] rain." The season was good for working outdoors. Thoreau would famously write, "Near the end of March, 1845, I borrowed an axe and went down to the woods by Walden Pond, nearest to where I intended to build my house, and began to cut down some tall arrowy white pines, still in their youth, for timber." The ax, it is thought, was Alcott's, and this tool may suggest the important role that Thoreau's older friend played in advocating the experiment. The ax symbolizes, as it were, the skills of Alcott, a man not conventionally educated, but enthusiastic (if not highly competent) in mechanical arts, especially building. Alcott's architecture, as we shall see, was frequently ax-hewn and rustic, the ax symbolizing an approach more primitive than that allowed by the modern saw.[7]

Henry fashioned his timbers from trees that grew right behind the site, in the white pine grove formerly belonging to Bigelow, now to Emerson. He would use the woodlot as his "'best' room" when living at the pond, and it endured as a prominent landmark until the Hurricane of 1938 flattened most of its survivors. Their stumps, often mistaken for the "beanfield pines," are still to be seen today, mossy and crumbling. Thoreau's house was well-built, but its primitive foundation consisted merely of buried corner piers of piled-up stones, with an impermanent sand basement, indications that Henry knew his experiment was temporary and that the structure would be moved when he was finished.

Determined to be economical, Thoreau used recycled boards from an Irish shanty along the railroad. Only a few shanties still stood, the occupants having moved on. One James Collins was interested in selling, and after making the purchase Thoreau removed the pieces to the pondside by small cartloads down a woodland path, spreading the boards on the grass to bleach and warp back into proper shape in the sun. Probably this shanty stood at Deep Cut, in the clearing Thoreau called Shanty Field. Collins may have been the last inhabitant of that settlement, for *Walden* famously begins, "When I wrote the following pages, or rather the bulk of them, I lived alone, in the woods, a mile from any neighbor."

The railroad provided boards for building but also linked Thoreau to the village and society. That linkage was key, for he never intended to abandon civilization, but rather sought temporary refuge at the edge of town where he was, scholar Tom Blanding says, "in a balanced position between nature and civilization." British and American writers who promoted the concept of suburban, rustic retirement emphasized that it should be short-term: Wordsworth escaped "the busy world" for just "an allotted interval of ease, / Under my cottage-roof," and an English Picturesque architect writing on "rural retreats" stressed "the Necessity and Advantage of Temporary Retirement." One was expected to maintain ties with friends and relatives and not forsake the "charms of good society." To see Thoreau's sojourn in the context of the larger rustic-retirement phenomenon helps resolve problems that have long troubled readers, including the apparent hypocrisy of the "solitary" author's frequent trips to the village.[8]

Thoreau's retirement was specifically from crowded, noisy conditions in his parents' house. The railroad causeway took him back to that house as often as he wished, and he lingered there until late in the night, as if somewhat hesitant to return to absolute solitude— "staying in a village parlor till the family had all retired." Then he followed the tracks before finding his way by instinct down the cart path in the rear of his Walden house. During the period of construction in 1845, the Texas House awaited him each afternoon: "There were some slight flurries of snow during the days that I worked [at Walden]; but for the most part when I came out on to the railroad, on my way home, its yellow sand heap stretched away gleaming in the hazy atmosphere, and the rails shone in the spring sun, and I heard the lark and pewee and other birds already come to commence another year with us. They were pleasant spring days." Perhaps his recollections were tinged with romance, for Emerson wrote in late April that "the spring is cold & pale."[9]

The ten-by-fifteen-foot bachelor's house that friends helped Thoreau raise at Walden was a rustic place with "no yard! but

Henry's house. Sophia Thoreau sketched it from memory for the wood-engraved frontispiece to *Walden*, 1854. University of Delaware Library, Special Collections.

unfenced Nature reaching up to your very sills." Henry gives many details of its construction, but much goes unexplained, leaving puzzles for those who have tried, in later years, to create exact replicas. The building of one such replica at the Thoreau Institute in nearby Lincoln in 2001 sparked lively debates. Should there be a ridge pole and king and queen posts? Thoreau mentions them, but they seem unnecessary on so small a house. He says nothing about corner braces, but surely there were some. Was the chimney external or internal? Were the eaves wide or narrow?[10]

The builder moved in on July 4, carrying his possessions out Walden Road in a hayrigging—an episode colorfully reenacted one summer in the 1980s in front of reporters' cameras, at the modern house replica by the reservation parking lot. And house it was; he almost never called it a cabin, hut, or shanty. He was proud of its sturdy construction and ascribed to it ambitious cultural and philosophical meanings. His knowledge of trends and issues in contemporary architecture was surprisingly astute, and it seems likely that he intended *Walden*, in part, to carry on a dialogue with the architectural pattern books popular in the day, ones that, like *Walden*, have long prefatory sections on economy, emphasize the desirability of home ownership, print itemized lists of building costs, discuss the proper ways to site a cottage in the Picturesque landscape, and illustrate model homes on their frontispieces.[11]

In the first week of June, Thoreau planted Emerson's field—the level part of Wyman Lot adjoining Walden Road—with white bush beans. Although the Walden house gets most of the attention, the beanfield was an important component of his experiment, as he tried "leading a simple epic country life—in these days of confusion and turmoil." He was at work there an entire month before he moved into the dwelling. Here he at last joined the agriculturists' cohort, "I with other farmers of N.E. devoted to field-labor." But his purposes were simultaneously lofty, biographer Henry S. Salt calling them "agriculture and mysticism combined." Like the Curtises and other Brook Farmers, Thoreau would toil even as he read the classics, reinventing himself as a cultured *agricola laboriosus*. The activity was a natural one—"I have always cultivated a garden"—but at the same time it was probably spurred by Alcott's enthusiastic embrace of subsistence agriculture and vegetarianism at Fruitlands not long before. Dietary restrictions there were so severe that only vegetables that "aspired" skywards were allowed (such as asparagus and grains), whereas those that grew into the earth were shunned (carrots, beets, potatoes). Thoreau was not so fastidious as this, but he saw the value in an earnest transcendental agricultural experiment, marrying philosophy with practicality: "I was determined to know beans." The greatest inspiration was no doubt Emerson, however. Four years earlier, when Waldo and Henry lived together at Bush, they had hoed corn, lettuce, and peas; trundled a wheelbarrow "whole days together"; and hoped for "a better harvest" than fruits and vegetables, a prophetic yearning for transcendental enlightenment through field labor.[12]

In an insightful article, "The Great Bean Field Hoax," historian Robert A. Gross finds "satirical intent" and "Transcendental high jinks" in Thoreau's choice of beans as a crop: "As a symbolic project of self-culture, the bean field inverted agricultural reform for Thoreau's radical, individualistic purposes," an effort made all the more barbed because Concordians "did *not* grow beans" ordinarily. But in fact Thoreau's journal contains a number of references to beans in Concord, and they may have been especially suitable for sterile sites, including Walden Woods (by adding nutrients to the soil, they perhaps improved Emerson's lot for agriculture). There was an "upland beanfield" about half a mile from Thoreau's, west of Deep Cut; this may have been the one on the Back Road, where Abiel Wheeler planted peas on a warm sandy hillside, in a hollow next to the woods. The squatter Hugh Quoil grew beans at Walden and once killed a woodchuck with a hoe in his beanfield, and elsewhere in town, Rice did the same. Alcott planted beans, as did Thoreau "in the garden at Texas."[13]

Beans were not Henry's only crop. He also planted corn, turnips, and potatoes (there is the occasional later journal reference to revisiting "my old potato field"). But beans were the main item, and he spent a long, hot summer hoeing them. He labored on July 4 as Concord fired off its guns in celebration, distantly heard "in my bean-field at the other end of the town." An enormous amount of toil was required—he had seven miles of beanrows, which adds up to nearly 25,000 plants—and the effort exhausted him. By late August he had concluded, "I will not plant beans another summer." The difficulty of farming came as a sobering revelation and may have, in the end, shortened his Walden sojourn. The beanfield location was "lost" for much of the twentieth century—said to be immediately behind the house site—which is surprising, given that Thoreau's journal repeatedly refers to it as being on the highway. Only thus could he have overheard what travelers unflatteringly said to each other about him as he worked: "Beans so late! peas so late!"; "'Does he live there?' asks the black bonnet of the gray coat."[14]

The journal of summer 1845 shows what Thoreau had moved to the pond to accomplish: copious reading of the classics, an immersion in the literature and philosophy of the distant past in a woodland setting he had always associated with ancientness—and, thus inspired, ample writing. "I am naturally no hermit," he firmly declared, but his love of contemplation and study necessarily made him one, as many writers before and since have discovered for themselves. Repeatedly he stressed his relationship to Homer, whose books lay on his table: "In such place as this he wrote or sang." In August, "I sit here at my window like a priest of Isis—and observe the phenomena of 3000 years ago, yet unimpaired. The tantivy of wild pigeons, an ancient race of birds—gives a voice to the air. . . . A fish-hawk dimples the glassy surface of the pond." There were so many books, one confused visitor thought he had stumbled upon a lawyer's office. Channing knew that the real purpose of Thoreau's moving to the pond was to inhabit "a writing-case"—"this wooden inkstand."[15]

Reading, like writing, requires time and solitude. "My residence was more favorable . . . to serious reading, than a university," Thoreau said, and *Walden's* third chapter, after the fundamental "Economy" and "Where I Lived, and What I Lived For," is "Reading," an eloquent argument for study of the classics. Beside the venerable pond he escaped the nineteenth century and was transported to "those eras in history which had most attracted me," with Walden a source of perennial inspiration, a "Castalian Fountain" of "the Golden Age" beside which he could read constantly and deeply.[16]

On August 2, 1845, Emerson reported having "taken a bath in Walden, & a tramp over the hills with Thoreau." He was one of many visitors while Henry lived there. Even before he moved in, "sometimes a rambler in the woods was attracted by the sound of my axe" as he built the place and stopped to say hello. That first July he was interrupted by railroad workmen (whom he calls, after characters in Homer, Lestrigones) and French Canadian woodcutter Alex Therien, who hauled logs for Emerson and others to Britton's lumber camp. By spring of the following year he had seen girls and boys, young men and women, businessmen, ministers, doctors, lawyers, and the aged. The Curtis brothers came to fish and got lost in the woods at night on the way back to Hosmer's. Thoreau says in *Walden* that "many people of every class came this way to the pond," and he gives an entire chapter to "Visitors" and another, in part, to "Winter Visitors." There were fishermen and hunters, poets and philosophers, farmers, travelers from the highway, Abolitionists holding a rally, a simple-minded pauper from the almshouse, landlords or housekeepers come to cut ice, and even runaway slaves. All types made their way there, Channing recalling that Thoreau, "once meeting two scoundrels who had been rude to a young girl near Walden Pond . . . took instant means for their arrest." Another commentator said that in this "case of a terrified girl pursued through the woods by a couple of young ruffians, sons of influential parents, Henry's valiant rescue was most timely." However romantic Walden seemed to the Emerson circle, it stubbornly retained a degree of edge-of-town lawlessness.[17]

The emphasis Thoreau placed on the heavy visitation he received is no accident, for he intended his experiment to be instructive to the public. Brook Farm had deliberately been so, established to demonstrate "a more natural union between intellectual and manual labor than now exists; to combine the thinker and the worker, as far as possible, in the same individual; to guarantee the highest mental freedom." And when Emerson visited Fruitlands he said, "It seemed so high an attainment that I thought, as often before, . . . that these men ought to be maintained in their place by the country for its culture. Young men & young maidens, old men & women, should visit them & be inspired." He could not recreate Fruitlands or Brook Farm in Concord, but he could "maintain" Thoreau's one-man utopia on his much-visited Wyman Lot. Thoreau would lecture extensively on his enterprise, starting off with reference to the many "inquiries . . . made by my townsmen concerning my mode of life." These inquiries were welcome; after all, what would a utopia be without witnesses? Thoreau positioned himself almost as prominently before the public at Walden as he did on the lyceum stage. Both endeavors, which functioned in tandem, were meant to be good-naturedly but provocatively didactic, Thoreau intending "to brag as lustily as chanticleer in the morning . . . if only to wake my neighbors up."[18]

One should not exaggerate the number of visitors Thoreau had, however. He tells us, "for the most part it is as solitary where I live as on the prairies"; no one came at night except pout fishermen in the spring; "when the snow lay deepest no wanderer ventured near my house for a week or fortnight at a time." But with considerable daytime foot traffic coming by from early spring on, he was surely less isolated than the modern suburbanite who lives up a long driveway. Henry Seidel Canby properly observed in 1939 that Thoreau "was never a hermit, except when snows shut him in, or heavy rain, or his own absorption in work. To go and see Henry Thoreau was a Concord recreation." More recently, literary historian Robert Sattelmeyer has argued that "Thoreau's isolation was a virtual and an imaginative rather than an actual one. . . . Walden Pond was not, in short, either a retired or a pristine place; in fact, one could hardly

"My field." Seventy-five years after Thoreau moved there, the former Wyman Lot was largely open and sunny again, thanks to recent cutting of timber. Looking south. Gleason, "Lingering snow at Thoreau's cairn, Concord, Mass.," March 24, 1920, courtesy Concord Free Public Library.

have chosen a more visible and public spot to retire to." This ratifies the earlier observations of scholar Raymond Adams: "The 'hermit of Walden' was a very public hermit."[19]

Thoreau's experiment was made public in part by the highly accessible character of Emerson's Wyman Lot on which he "squatted." He subtitled his book *Life in the Woods*, but this was no primeval forest. Walden Woods as a whole retained only a semiwild character after generations of cutting. Thoreau lived not far from its northern edge and between the highway and the train tracks, both of which were visible from his door. *Life in the Woods?*—actually, it was life on a tract cut over by Wyman, a stump-strewn area larger than eight football fields surrounded by a larger, patchwork forest. In 1845, it was "about 15 years since the land was cleared," and in fact the whole Wyman Lot had been cut over at least that early, Thoreau estimating in his 1860 forest study that the area around his house site was open by 1825. His dwelling was surrounded by young trees of natural regrowth: "There are scores of pitch pine in my field—from one to three inches in diameter." He took interest in the plants that grew about his house, all species favoring sunny, disturbed sites. There were many hickories, but when he undertook his 1860 study he was puzzled by their disappearance: "I remember that there were a great many hickories with R.W.E.'s pitch pines when I lived there, but now there are but few comparatively. . . . Perhaps the fires have done part of it." He took special interest in "my sumack grove." This sun-loving shrub "grew luxuriantly about my house—pushing up through the embankment I had made, and growing 5 or 6 feet the first season. Its broad pinnate tropical leaf was pleasant *though strange* to look upon."[20]

His catalogue of plants anticipates his coming preoccupation with botany: "In my front-yard grow the black-berry and strawberry & the life-everlasting—Johnswort & golden rod—& shruboak and sandcherry & blue-berry and ground-nut." To a correspondent he sent on August 5, 1845, half a dozen sand cherries that "grew within a rod of my lodge. I plucked them all today." Later he augmented his account of those former dooryard plants with their scientific names: "The sand cherry (Prunus depressa. Pursh. Cerasus pumila. Mx) grew about my door and near the end of May enlivened my yard with its umbels arranged cylindrically about its short branches." In the final *Walden* manuscript, he appears to know far more about the subject of plants than he in fact did when living at the pond.[21]

On August 23, 1845, Thoreau carried his fishing rod through the woods to Fair Haven Bay to supplement his scanty fare of vegetables. His route "down this long hill in the rain to fish in the pond" can be traced on a survey he later did of lots and cart paths near the Andromeda Ponds. On his way home he had a famous *Walden* encounter, glimpsing "a woodchuck stealing across my path" and being "strongly tempted to seize and devour him raw; not that I was hungry then, except for that wildness which he represented." In his journal he added, "The wildest most desolate scenes are strangely familiar to me." Again, was he living a *Life in the Woods*? In spite of the extensive cutting, yes—if he walked a little ways off from Briars he could find surprisingly lonely and unfrequented places little spoiled and well worth exploring. Even today, one can visit them and seldom meet another person on the trail. If his immediate environs were an edge-of-town clearing, they at least put him within easy

Footings. Roland Robbins unearthed the stone foundations of Thoreau's house at Walden one hundred years after the transcendentalist lived there. September 2, 1946, from the Roland Wells Robbins Collection of the Thoreau Society. Courtesy of the Thoreau Society, Lincoln, Mass., and the Thoreau Institute at Walden Woods.

striking distance of a convincing degree of the wild, which his imagination could fill out into wilderness.[22]

In the fall he built a chimney, using recycled bricks from a building of the 1790s. A century later, archaeologist Roland Wells Robbins identified the place where Thoreau first dumped the load behind the house, and he found copious fragments when he excavated the cellar hole. Stones to underlie the hearth, still in place when unearthed by Robbins, had been hauled up from the cove shore. Clean white sand for mixing mortar came from the beach on the east end. Having dug what he needed, Thoreau piled his spade and wheelbarrow into the boat along with the cartloads of sand and paddled back across, water lapping at the gunnels.

Shingling also took place in the fall, as the rustic and breezy house of summertime was transformed into a weatherproof abode. At the same time, Emerson was completing a house for his sister-in-law, Lucy Brown, across the street from his own home. Thoreau's help was apparently indispensable, at least with the fencing, in which he specialized. One Wednesday afternoon at five o'clock, Emerson sent a note that, improbably, still survives: "Dear Henry Can you not without injurious delay to the shingling give a quarter or a half hour tomorrow morning to the direction of the Carpenter who builds Mrs Brown's fence? Cutler has sent another man, & will not be here to repeat what you told him so that the new man wants new orders. I suppose he will be on the ground at 7, or a little after & Lidian shall keep your breakfast warm. But do not come to the spoiling of your day. R.W.E."[23]

On October 1, sixty-one-year-old Hugh Quoil (or Coyle) collapsed in the grass beside Walden Road at the foot of Brister's Hill and, just as travelers rushed to his aid, died. The alcoholic Hugh had worked as a ditcher and claimed to have fought at Waterloo; some called him "Colonel." He and his wife had been Thoreau's nearest neighbors, in the old Wyman place above the east shore, but Thoreau mused that he had hardly known him, having spoken to him only once. He walked over to Quoil's ramshackle house later that fall, shortly before it was dismantled. The Colonel's old clothes lay piled on his raised plank bed. Cards and a broken pipe were scattered on the floor, and a black hen wandered aimlessly. Outside, his unhoed garden of corn, beans, and potatoes grew thick with weeds. After the dwelling's demolition, the "Wyman site" with cellar hole and apple trees remained a landmark in Walden Woods, and traces remained well into the twentieth century. An historian of early New England pottery visited the steep slope above the eastern shore: "Where heavy rains had gullied the embankment, I picked up enough pottery wasters to assure the location of Wyman's workshop, and at the top of the slope, near the road, I discovered numbers of very large bricks from his kiln. A cellar hole across the road marks the site of a good-sized house. . . . The shards included pieces of pans, pots, and mugs, with the usual brown and black glazes."[24]

Thoreau's visit to Quoil's empty house occasioned a long outpouring in his journal and got him thinking about other colorful types who had dwelled in Walden Woods—the subjects of a *Walden* chapter, "Former Inhabitants." He catalogued them, south to north along the road: Wyman, Ingraham, Zilpha, Brister, Stratton, Breed, Hilda. He knew he lived at a transitional moment: on the west shore, the railroad and its noise and smoke and hurry screamed of "this restless, nervous, bustling, trivial Nineteenth Century." But along Walden Road on the east, a colonial route, still survived that one last dwelling of a whole loose colony from olden times. Thoreau thought of himself as born "in the very nick of time," and *Walden* resonates richly with the interplay of departing past and inrushing present. His house stands in between, last of the former inhabitants but, being well-built and intelligently sited, a little prototype of the "villas which will one day be built here." Again, he stands as a link between ancient yesterday and frenetic today, primitivism and civilization.[25]

Channing bunked with him for two weeks in the fall, Emerson writing in surprise, "Ellery lives with H. T. at the pond, in these days, in the absence of his wife!" In October, Thoreau went chestnutting to gather food for winter, passing Goose Pond with its muskrat cabins on his way to Flint's. He left his Walden house while its plaster dried, November 12 to December 6. During this general period he worked intermittently for Emerson in town, erecting a fence, building a drain, laying a cellar floor. It is impossible to escape the fact that Thoreau at Walden remained intimately intertwined with Emerson; as historian Harmon Smith points out, of the $13.34 Thoreau claimed was needed to survive the first eight months at Walden, $10.00 was paid him by Emerson.[26]

Solicitous of his young followers, in late autumn 1845, Emerson arranged Monday night gatherings in his library for the literati who were thickly concentrated nearby now that Brook Farm had dissolved. George Curtis attended with his brother, Burrill, and recalled the distinguished roster: the silent Hawthorne; Thoreau come from "the blackberry pastures of Walden Pond"; Alcott, "sublimely meditating impossible summer-houses"; "enthusiastic agriculturist and Brook Farmer" George Bradford; Edmund Hosmer; Channing; and finally the "Olympian host" of this "congress of oracles" who "beamed smiling encouragement upon all parties." The sage no doubt hoped that each participant would share his experiences in back-to-the-land transcendentalism, and Thoreau did talk of "the secrets won from his interviews with Pan in the Walden woods." But the three sessions proved a failure, with long silences that seemed to ask, "Who will now proceed to say the finest thing that has ever been said?"[27]

More enthusiastic than ever about Walden Pond as a place of beauty and utility, Emerson bought a forty-one-acre woodlot abutting the south shore on November 29, 1845. He paid Abel Moore and John Hosmer thirty dollars an acre for this land embracing the rocky "pinnacle" now known as Emerson's Cliff. Thoreau labeled a survey, "RWE's Woodlot by Walden paced with a pocket Compass at the time he bought it," and on the back he drew the plan of a two-seat boat—always he designed his own. Emerson wrote ecstatically to his literary friend Thomas Carlyle in Britain about his purchase of this "new plaything, the best I ever had—a woodlot," located at Walden, "a place to which my feet have for years been accustomed to bring me once or twice in a week at all seasons. My lot to be sure is on the further side of the water, not so familiar to me as the nearer shore." Some of the wood was old growth, but most had been cut a generation before (about 1820–23, Thoreau would find by later ring counts) and was now growing thriftily.[28]

In late fall Henry, "like the wasps," resorted to the northeast corner of the pond, a "fireside" where the sun glanced off a stand of pitch pines and warmed a low pile of stones on the shore. He participated in English poetic tradition; James Thomson, whom he admired, had begun *Winter* (1726) with allusion to "Fair AUTUMN, yellow rob'd! I'll sing of thee, / Of thy last, temper'd, Days, and sunny Calms; / . . . BEHOLD! the well-pois'd *Hornet*, hovering, hangs, / With quivering Pinions, in the genial Blaze." The pond skimmed over on the night of December 12, except a strip from the sandbar to the northwest shore near his house site, and the long winter began. Even in its depths, however, Thoreau was not alone. Woodchoppers were busiest at that season. When a stranger paid a visit in search of a lost hound, Thoreau told him, "Yes they are chopping right up here behind me—how far is it—only a few steps—hark a moment—there dont you hear the sound of their axes."[29]

As frigid weather persisted into early March, Thoreau wondered which was colder, the pond or local springs. He measured the temperature of a bucket of water drawn from the pond (forty-two degrees), finding it colder than a village well or even Boiling Spring, coldest of all sources in summer. On the thirteenth the ice on Walden was still a foot thick, even as a song sparrow was singing. Before the pond melted, the naturalist in his continuing empirical mindset undertook a survey "with compass and chain, and sounding line" of its vertical and horizontal dimensions. He found Walden to measure "a little over 61 1/2 acres, and . . . 102 feet deep in the middle." His string was a "cod-line" with a one-and-a-half-pound stone attached, which he dropped through holes he cut in the ice to take more than a hundred soundings. When he published the resulting map in *Walden*, at least one reader mistook it for a satire on government coastal surveys. But Thoreau was in earnest, and for his efforts, it has been argued that he "may with justice be called the first American limnologist." When compared to modern maps and

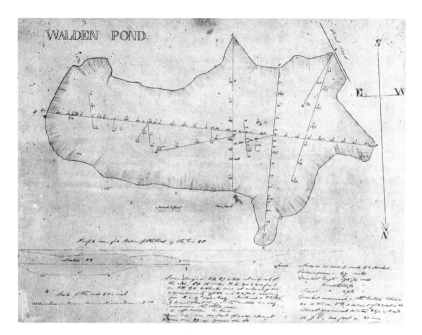

Soundings. Thoreau provided his publisher with a hand-drawn map of his spring 1846 Walden survey. He showed his house near the northerly cove (at bottom). Courtesy Concord Free Public Library.

soundings of the pond, his measurements prove to be remarkably accurate.[30]

Spring, when it finally came, must have been welcome. On the misty morning of March 27 he saw geese from his door, and when he walked down to the shore they rose and circled, twenty-nine of them. Soon purple martins twittered over his clearing and "the Pewee (Phoebe?)" hovered before his door, looking for a nesting place. By April he was getting up early and bathing in the pond. In the first week of May he heard the whippoorwill nightly and, by day, the brown thrasher, veery, wood pewee, chewink, and wood thrush. On the second he caught pouts from the boat in twenty feet of water off the cove, only one of many fishermen there lately. He started his beans (far fewer than the year before), tomatoes, squash, corn, and potatoes in early June, but a frost on the twelfth killed them to the ground. On the twentieth he caught a red chivin in the river, which he measured and described minutely in his journal.[31]

Continuing to work for Emerson, Thoreau about this time built a fence on his mentor's "schoolhouse lot" across the street from

Bush. After a grueling winter lecture schedule, Emerson himself relaxed this spring by visiting his new Walden woodlot. "My spirits rise whenever I enter it. I can spend the entire day there with hatchet and pruning-shears, making paths, without the remorse of wasting time. I fancy the birds know me, and even the trees make little speeches, or hint them." He was glad to escape the noise of the house, his family having grown to include Ellen, seven; Edith, five; and Edward, two—with the numerous Alcott, Channing, and Hosmer children often dropping by. In May, Alcott reported, "Emerson called, and I walked with him to the haunts near Walden Water, and he led me by the wood-paths to the summit of the ledge on which he purposes to build himself a lodge for study and writing. The prospect was commanding for our champion country— Monadnock on the North, Wachusett and the spires of Groton and Sudbury on the West and South West, and near was the Concord River, and close by on the opposite side was Thoreau's cot. It was a fit spot for a poet's lodge. We descended by a hatchet-path to the dell near the railroad, to a spring of water near the railroad, some distance from the hilltop. Here he hopes to ensure retirement and uninterrupted seclusion for writing." On the eighth, "Evening. Emerson came in to consult me on the lodge he intends building on the peak of his woodlot, near Walden Water. He showed me H. Thoreau's design, to which I added another story, as a lookout." Visits to Walden were numerous this summer; in June, "Walked again with Emerson to Walden Water. We talked a good deal. . . . Returning along our little green lane, I felt more vividly than before the rare privilege I enjoy of passing at once from the busy and painstaking toil of the week into the presence, and being admitted to the first thoughts, of this our first great poet—and a friend of mine, too."[32]

Emerson's Walden woodlot—"My Garden," he would call it in a famous poem—had instantly become a central feature of his life, a remoter equivalent to his town garden and, like it, promising the rich transcendentalist rewards that laboring outdoors afforded. He reported to Carlyle on May 14, 1846, "I go thither every afternoon, & cut with my hatchet an Indian path through the thicket all along the bold shore, & open the finest pictures." His children grew accustomed to frequent trips out Walden Road. Part of each excursion was a visit to Railroad Spring at the foot of a pine grove in his woodlot, and they viewed with awe the nearby ruins of the Irish shanty village, now overgrown with mullein and pokeweed. Best of all was his cliff: "At a good distance in from the shore the land rises to a rocky head, perhaps sixty feet above the water. Thereon I think to place a hut, perhaps it will have two stories & be a petty tower, looking out to Monadnoc & other New Hampshire Mountains. There I hope to go with book & pen when good hours come."[33]

How differently we would perceive Thoreau's house at Walden had Emerson erected a companion to it! At this moment the whole Concord transcendental community, with Emerson's encouragement, was involved in dramas of settling down, landscaping, and gardening, in which context Thoreau's efforts must be seen. The previous summer, as Emerson was spending countless hours building sister-in-law Lucy Brown's house, Harriet Martineau had written him from England about her plans for a dwelling near Wordsworth's. Emerson forwarded the letter to Caroline Sturgis, then vacationing in Vermont. She replied that she wished he were there to "go out into the woods" with her and added, "Was Miss Martineau's letter sent to awaken an enthusiasm for cottages? Perhaps I shall have one sometimes, a mile from *some* great man. But there are many things to be considered before one plants his foot upon the ground"—namely, flocks of guests such as those who descended on Bush. "See what a tax you have to pay because you have a house with a neat white fence before it. . . . So do not ask me to build a house of stone or brick & put up a sign, 'Our Home.'" Instead she would live in a "bandbox, until I can finally determine upon some life of my own." She longed to become part of the community Emerson was gathering around him in Concord: "I wish I could have a lodge, for constancy, in your garden—but your garden should be a forest & your house beside a stream, & its tall turret should overlook mountain & valley."[34]

Although Sturgis was not ready to nest near Emerson, Alcott had already done so, and his home improvement activities are amply documented. In May 1846 he "brought a load of trees from the woods—spruce, larch, and pines." Ten days later, "Brought from the Walden Wood some more trees—pine, hemlock, and a few maples and birches—and set them in my yard." In June, "Emerson called and talked an hour in the garden. I told him it seemed good for me to be using the rake on this little spot—as good, or better, than attempting broader reforms in a popular, or in any manner. I seemed to be as worthily employed as any of my contemporaries. . . . My long-stretching bean-rows [are] trim as an air-line." On July 4, "Discoursed with the spirit of my time over the rake and barrow, dressing the alleys of the garden and winding my peas and beans. I cast my silent vote for the emancipation of the human soul, amidst the plants I love." These transcendentalist thoughts closely parallel those of Thoreau at work in his own beanfield that summer.[35]

Rural and rustic architecture fascinated Alcott. He built himself a Coleridgian summer house of willow wands snipped in the meadow in front of his house, and here he sat with Emerson after supper on September 13. He wrote of it in "Thoreauvian" terms: "Worthy place, the arbour, for the reception of the poet as my guest. Happiest of men, to receive so happy a nature as this poet under a canopy made by my own hands." Five days later, "Henry Thoreau came to see me. He was pleased with my summer-house and I took him to the hill top and showed him the site of my purposed 'Lookout.' He climbed a tree and measured the wide horizon with his eye." "My hill-top" and "the pine woods behind my house" provided a Walden-like refuge for Alcott during the 1845-48 period that he lived at Hillside, as they would for Hawthorne when he later bought the place. In their poetical perceptions of rural life and landscape, all these men were more alike than different, and their experiences are best understood in tandem, Thoreau at Walden being no exception.[36]

In fact, the literary hermitage was all the rage then. Author N. P. Willis at his New York farmstead in the 1830s sought a "PLACE TO WRITE" and was "bent on finding some locality (out of doors it must be) with the average attractions of a sentry-box." All rustic dwellings implied the chance to read—"There is no better vindication of a summer-house than the opportunity it affords for the quiet enjoyment of a book," noted an English author—but some persons went further and expressly designed shelters to house a writing desk and library. Architect J. C. Loudon discussed the "summer reading-room," and a colleague recommended for a person of "philosophic and elegant mind . . . one of these delightful little retreats, situated

Backyard replica. Proud creation of Roland Robbins, 1964. From the Roland Wells Robbins Collection of the Thoreau Society. Courtesy of the Thoreau Society, Lincoln, Mass., and the Thoreau Institute at Walden Woods.

on the border of a lake" with "a small garden" and "a library of all that is useful in art and science, and elegant and just in poetry and philosophy."[37]

At Thoreau's Walden retreat, visitors abounded that second summer, as they had during the first. Perhaps it was about this time that Edmund Hosmer brought his children, one recalling how Thoreau sat at his desk, Hosmer in a chair, and the kids on the bed "listening, not always with patience, to the extended discussions on philosophy or Scandinavian mythology." One Concordian remembered, "We boys used to visit him on Saturday afternoons at his house by Walden, and he would show us interesting things in the woods." Channing probably came often, paddling with his friend and beating the sides of the boat for an echo. He is the "Poet" who invites the "Hermit" fishing in the chapter, "Brute Neighbors." Sophia Ford, the teacher whom Emerson had hired to run a schoolhouse in the barn for his children, and Channing's, visited too, along with Louisa and Abbie May Alcott. Ford led "free walks to Walden Pond, and the surrounding fields and woods"—perhaps seeking Thoreau, to whom, infamously, she proposed marriage. On August 1, the antislavery women of Concord gathered at Thoreau's house for their annual celebration of the freeing of the West Indian slaves. Emerson and W. H. Channing were among the speakers.[38]

Political tensions ran high that summer, at the height of the Mexican War. On July 23, Thoreau walked to town to pick up a repaired shoe at the cobbler's and was arrested for failure to pay his poll tax, which he, like Alcott and some other Abolitionists, refused to do on principle. As Odell Shepard points out, Alcott had declined to pay as early as January 1843 and was briefly hauled to jail, so "Thoreau's whole theory and practice of 'civil disobedience' was corroborated if not suggested by the example" of his older friend. Thus did Thoreau spend his famous night in a jail cell, which he made the subject of an 1848 lyceum lecture, the origin of his influential and controversial essay, "Civil Disobedience." After being released, Thoreau hastened to the woods to get his dinner of huckleberries on Fair Haven Hill.[39]

Little is known of Thoreau's second winter. George Hoar recalled, "I used to go down to see him in the winter days in my vacations in his hut near Walden. He was capital company. He was a capital guide in the wood. He liked to take out the boys in his boat." Alcott came during the long evenings. One may ask how many nights Thoreau spent in his house during wintertime—nearly all of them? Or only a few a week? Is Channing in error in recalling, "He bivouacked there, and really lived at home, where he went every day"? Concordian John Shepard Keyes asserted, "He was at Mr. Emerson's and the village nearly every day, often partaking of meals there and at his father's house." Thoreau's mother was quoted as saying "that Henry was by no means so utterly indifferent to the good things of life as he liked to believe himself, and that regularly every week of his self-enforced retirement he came home to eat a deliciously prepared dinner." Countless critics have heaped derision on Thoreau for his "hypocrisy"—"let it be known that Nature Boy went home on weekends to raid the family cookie jar," one writer crowed in 2001—but this misunderstands Thoreau's intentions. He was a hermit of convenience only, living on the edge of town to escape its close-knit sociability long enough to get writing done. But he lived only a half-hour away, and to have failed to visit friends and family in the town he called home would have been thoughtless and contrary to his nature, which, if flinty, was fundamentally responsible and devoted. In *Walden* he makes no attempt to deny his proximity to town, to which he strolled "every day or two": he lives on the very edge of it in order to see its foibles more clearly, fleeing to the woods to better understand civilization, in the manner of the ancient philosophers. A hundred years of scholarship emphasizing Thoreau's sociability has made not the slightest dent in public perceptions, however, and the "pies" and "doughnuts" of past generations have become "cookies" today—or the variant myth that Thoreau "stole pies" from kitchen windowsills.[40]

Emerson's plans for a literary retreat remained alive for a time; he wrote his brother William in November 1846, "You know I am to be a bit of a builder myself on the peak of my woodlot," with Thoreau, presumably, to play architect. But next January he spent $500 for the two-acre Warren lot next to his own property in town, in order to prevent it from being carved up into house and shop lots. He paid Thoreau one dollar for a survey. Soon he planted it with pears and apples following the instructions in A. J. Downing's *Fruits and Fruit Trees of America* and thought he might now have enough land to keep an employee busy year-round. The cost of this, plus plans for a trip to England, put an end to his dream of a woodlot hermitage. Instead, he shifted his gardening activities to the Warren tract and commissioned Alcott to build a summerhouse on the old cornfield at Bush.[41]

In February 1847, Thoreau delivered his first lecture in Concord based on his Walden experiment, "A History of Myself," later part of "Economy" in *Walden*. This was the same month that Frederic Tudor, famed entrepreneur in the international ice trade, exercised his new rights to the harvest on Walden. "A hundred men of Hyperborean extraction" swooped in by train, as Thoreau memorably describes. They erected a ten-thousand-ton pile of ice blocks about one hundred feet square and thirty-five feet high, "a vast blue fort" covered with hay and boards. Tudor was unable to sell most of the ice, however, and the fort went largely unused, not melting completely until September 1848.

Thoreau worked for Emerson that spring, measuring the number of cords of wood cut by Therien over the winter. He visited Alcott in March, who wrote, "Thoreau's is a walking Muse. . . . His special task [is] delineating these yet unspoiled American things, and . . . inspiring us with a sense of their homelier beauties—opening to us the riches of a nation scarcely yet discovered by her own population." As Shepard remarks, Alcott's lofty assessment of Thoreau was prescient, given that his young friend was still "an unknown man" two years away from publishing his first book.[42]

This same month, Alcott spent the evening with Thoreau "at his hermitage on Walden," where Henry read aloud from his manuscript of *A Week*. Alcott praised the author as "Virgil and Gilbert White and Yankee settler all, singing his prose-poems with remembrance of his reading and experiences in the woods and road-paths. . . . The book is purely American, fragrant with the lives of New England woods and streams. . . . Especially am I touched by this soundness, this aboriginal vigour, as if a man had once more come into Nature." Thoreau's voice echoed in his mind as he made his way home at midnight "through the woody snow-paths."[43]

This spring too, Thoreau first commented on the drippy "sand foliage" in the thirty- or forty-foot-high Deep Cut of the railroad, which would later form a famous passage in *Walden*. A full quarter-mile sometimes showed this curious natural effect. As is often the case with Thoreau, the fact of human disturbance in the landscape fueled new observations. In this case, he recognized that "this phenomenon must have been rare before railroads were built since it is not often even now that you meet with a freshly exposed bank of the right materials." He was not the first contemporary to attend to the aesthetics of sandbanks, as road cuts were a favorite subject of English artists of the Picturesque. And in 1849, Emerson would mention his and Channing's interest in "the foliaceous & spongelike formations by spring-thaw in the argillite of the Deep Cut."[44]

In late March, at the end of a cold spring, Emerson recorded that "the snow still lies in our woods." The pond ice finally melted away on April 8. That month Thoreau walked the boundaries of Emerson's woodlot, 130 rods (2145 feet). In addition, he was paid a few dollars by Swiss scientist Louis Agassiz, who had arrived in America in October 1846, to provide him with animal specimens. It was in the context of this project that Thoreau penned one of his most famous passages: "On the 29th of April, as I was fishing from the banks of the river near the Nine-Acre-Corner bridge, standing on the quaking grass and willow roots, where the muskrats burrow," he witnessed "the most ethereal flight" of a merlin. The experience led him to write, "Our village life would stagnate, I think, if it were not for the unexplored forests and meadows which surround it. We need the tonic of wildness,—to wade sometimes in meadows where only the bittern and the meadow-hen lurk, and hear the booming of the snipe."[45]

He listed wildlife about the pond that he supposed Agassiz might want him to collect: "minks, muskrats, frogs, lizards, tortoise, snakes, caddice-worms, leeches, muscles, etc. . . . The funds which you sent me are nearly exhausted." Actually, his catalogue suggests a degree of ignorance; there were probably few if any lizards, caddice-worms, leeches, or mussels to be had. He did find frogs, turtles, and snakes, however. Mammals in the woods nearby included woodchuck, gray and red squirrels, and chipmunks. On rare occasions he detected muskrat, raccoon, rabbit, fox, and flying squirrels. Mink and otter seemed possible.[46]

By May 3 he had mailed four boxes of specimens to Agassiz in Cambridge, among them the following: from the river, pout and perch, plus suckers he had speared; from Heywood's Brook, suckers taken by hand and twelve live red-finned minnows; from Walden, a pickerel that jumped into his boat in fright. He also sent breams and two kinds of tortoise, of which Agassiz was fascinated by the small, rare *Sternothaerus odoratus*. By late May he had arranged to ship a live fox, it seems, and on June 1 he sent a large number of additional specimens freshly caught in river and pond. From the latter source came fifteen pouts, seventeen perch, thirteen shiners, a large land tortoise, and five muddy tortoises. The tortoises were alive, as was a black snake and perhaps the dormouse caught the night before in his Walden cellar. In all of these shipments Agassiz was delighted to find one or two species new to science: a bream with red marks, and a shiner.[47]

Emerson wrote this summer of 1847, "*Young* Concord holds its levee at Walden Pond on 5 July, under guidance of [Concordians] John Brown & Barzillai Frost"—a church outing, or possibly the annual antislavery rally. That same month, Alcott and his four girls—later famous, of course, as the "Little Women"—went to Walden with their visiting friend Frederick L. H. Willis. In Willis's recollections, tinged with romanticism, the hermit called animals by whistling: a woodchuck, two gray squirrels, a crow that would sit on his shoulder. He took the children onto the pond in his boat, playing

Tumbledown-Hall. Alcott and Thoreau erected a rustic summer house for Emerson at Bush. From *Homes of American Authors*, University of Delaware Library.

the flute and talking of Indians, and they gathered pond lilies, a plant that has never occurred at the actual Walden.[48]

For his part, Emerson was not absent from the woods. Like Thoreau and Channing, he loved Heywood's Brook, the stream southwest of Walden where Henry caught the suckers and minnows. Edward Emerson thought his father referred to a walk with his children down the brook in this dreamlike journal passage penned in 1847: "Run boy from the swamp beside the lake to the big hemlock where a chestnut has been chopped down at twelve feet high from the ground then leave the high wood road & take the ox path to the right;—pass one right hand turn, & take the second, & run down a valley with long prairie hay covering it close; an old felled pine-tree lies along the valley, follow it down till the birds do not retreat before you; then till the faint daymoon rides nearer; then till the valley is a ravine with the hills of Nobscot seen at the bottom of it across [Fair Haven] Bay."[49]

To build the summer house in the cornfield at Bush, Alcott, Emerson, and Thoreau "went to the 'island' in the Walden woodlot, & cut down & brought home 20 hemlocks for posts of the arbour" on July 14, laying them out in the stubble. Not until August 12 did Alcott begin construction: "Provided timbers for the platform and laid some of the planks. H. Thoreau assisted me." Next day they laid the rest of the planks "and set the nine upright joists, to form the corners for the nine Muses to this poet's bower. Set a few uprights to see the effect." "I call this my style of building the 'Sylvan,'" Alcott explained, the materials of his architecture literally taken from Walden Woods. During the slow process of construction, Alcott scoured the forest for crooked cedar with the bark on and confidently declared, "Men of taste [have always] preferred the natural curve." Thoreau commented bemusedly of the builder, "Ah, he is a crooked stick himself. He is getting on now so many *knots* an hour." Thoreau's Aunt Maria wrote a friend, "[Henry says Alcott] pulls down as fast as he builds up, (quite characteristic) but it is rather expensive [and] somewhat tedious to poor Henry, to say nothing of endangering life and limbs for if here had not been a comfortable haystack near that he availed himself of by jumping into, when the top rafter was knock'd off, it might have been rather a serious affair. . . . I hope they will find as soft a landing place, one and all, when they drop from the clouds." Yankee townsfolk scratched their heads at Alcott's display of the rustic: "It is odd"; "The strangest thing I ever saw"; "A log cabin"; "A whirligig." The waggish Channing called it "the chapel-of-ease," "this microscopic cathedral of Cologne," "this Tom Thumb of a St. Peter's," an "eternal pancake . . . [not] quite baked," with a "wicker-work skull" and a "head of moss." On his return from England, Emerson dubbed it "Tumbledown-Hall." Visiting Concord in September 1849, Alcott would "repair the thatching a little, and interior, of Emerson's summer-house, standing gracefully on the lawn and embowered now in evergreens set there by Thoreau and myself—the front gable seen from the south door of his house with its rustic lyre emblazoned and latticed window so pretty. . . . I built and endowed it so far with all the opulence of the woods." No less than Thoreau's Walden house, Emerson's summerhouse, likewise of brief duration, exemplifies the rustic-Picturesque interests of the transcendentalists and seems a remarkable though unexamined landmark in the 1840s flowering of intellectual Concord.[50]

Thoreau jotted in his journal, "Left Walden Woods Sept. 6, 1847." Many have asked why he departed. He gives no definite answer in *Walden*, and five years later he wondered "why I left the woods? I do not think that I can tell. I have often wished myself back—I do not know any better how I ever came to go there—Perhaps it is none of my business—even if it is yours. Perhaps I wanted a change." The reader of the journal will notice that

Thoreau, like many highly curious persons, seldom kept to a theme for long. Besides, he had completed the task he went to the pond for, his book *A Week on the Concord and Merrimack Rivers*, and as a bonus he had written the first draft of *Walden*. The proximate reason for his return was the invitation to house-sit for Emerson when the older man went abroad, starting in early October. Emerson especially needed Thoreau's help after launching his ambitious pear-and-apple operation on the Warren Lot. Perhaps as an incentive, Waldo purchased the Walden house from Henry, which suggests another factor—his young disciple rather desperately needed money. His life now directed back toward managing affairs at Emerson's, Henry moved his green-painted desk from the Walden house to the chamber at the head of the stairs at Bush and began yet another phase of his life.[51]

What had Walden Pond meant to Thoreau? By moving there he successfully made a space for reading and writing. For the first time he had a dwelling of his own, self-built, as he recommended for students everywhere. He had enabled himself to remain in intellectual Concord, and to do it at minimal cost. He achieved his dream of being a farmer while replicating the primitive and authentic philosopher's lifestyle he knew about from reading Virgil and Horace. In addition he enjoyed the pleasures of camping out, not only (as in his tent) in summer, but all year long. At Walden he had escaped the village the better to critique it, using, in time-honored poetic fashion, *rus* to comment on *urbe*. He fulfilled Emerson's dreams for him, as an active young writer supported by a generous mentor on an allotment of land—establishing a one-man, middle-state utopia that related to Emerson's ideas of solitude and Alcott's experiences at Fruitlands. He thereby made a vivid public demonstration of his personal philosophy, establishing himself as a living exemplar of the ideas he would expound at the lyceum. To this list must be added, of course, the rich transcendental meanings that fill the pages of *Walden*. The experiment had developed out of numerous converging influences, many of which go unacknowledged in Thoreau's famous book. *Walden* is no straightforward autobiography of a *Life in the Woods*, but a text rife with secrets and artifice, its complex utopian and reformist ideas couched in a seemingly simple story about a man living in the forest.

"Along the ridge." A carriage path linked Walden Road to Thoreau's Cove. Here in the heart of Emerson's Wyman Lot it descended from the beanfield plateau. Looking south. Gleason, "Walden Woods in November, road in foreground," November 17, 1917, courtesy Concord Free Public Library.

What happened to the Walden house once the experiment was over? Before Emerson left town he drafted an agreement with his Scottish gardener Hugh Whelan concerning the Wyman Lot, on September 28: "R.W.E. will rent the cultivable part of the lot, and [Thoreau's] cottage with some addition, to H.W. RWE allows a sum not exceeding $50.00 for the removal & enlargement of the cottage, and $20.00 worth of manure in the Spring;—and Hugh Whelan shall pay for the rent of the land & of this expense 10.00 per annum, the first & second year. Thereafter, the rent to be moderately increased; Hugh engaging to plant apples, pears, peaches, & grapes; and engaging to remove no forest tree from the land. RWE retains the land growing up to woods near the pond, & a road through the field from the Lincoln road & along the ridge."[52]

Emerson was trying to do Whelan a favor, even as he made good use of his Wyman Lot. In November and December, Thoreau wrote him about Whelan's ambitious plans. "Hugh still has his eye on the Walden *agellum*," hoping, for no more than $80, to move the house to the beanfield, buy and haul rocks from Mr. Wetherbee to line the cellar, manure the field, build an addition twice as big as the original dwelling, and dig a well. Thoreau laughed at Hugh's incomprehension of the true costs involved.[53]

One afternoon in November, Thoreau was walking through Conantum, a hilly tract beyond Sudbury River, when he saw a column of smoke rising to the east "over my house that was (as I judged)" at Walden. It was a fire set by the locomotive's spark, such as one that had previously burned Abel Brooks's lot west of Emerson's. Thoreau instantly wondered if his Walden house had been destroyed, rendering the deed of lease to Whelan invalid. It turned out to be John Richardson's young wood, on the southeast of Emerson's Wyman Lot field—burned nearly all over, and up to the fence rails at Walden Road. He wrote encouragingly to Emerson, "So you see that your small lot is comparatively safe for this season, the back fire having been already set for you." Emerson, in Manchester, England, was grieved to hear of it, although his own lot was untouched: "I am glad the Pleasaunce at Walden suffered no more but it is great loss as it is which years will not repair." Along with the ongoing work of lumberjacks, this fire marked another small step in Walden's steady decline. Born "in the very nick of time," Thoreau had lived at the pond in the nick of time, too.[54]

Channing, with his love of the Picturesque, had found special excitement in Thoreau's rustic house. About the time Henry moved away, Ellery wrote a poem, "Walden": "It is not far beyond the Village church, / After we pass the wood that skirts the road, / A Lake,— the blue-eyed Walden." Shortly after came the eulogistic "Walden Hermitage": "On this shore he used to play, / There his boat he hid away, / And where has this man fled to-day? / Mark the small, gray hermitage / Touch yon curved lake's sandy edge." He copied the verse out neatly and walked through the woods to Walden Pond. There, he said, he hung the poem on the walls of Thoreau's now-deserted house. Then he turned north, back toward the highway, the village, and civilization.[55]

5

❦

Viewed from a Hilltop

(1848–1854)

❧

With all the attention historians have given to Thoreau's time at
Walden, the years immediately following have slipped into obscurity.
They are crucial, however, for understanding the development of
Walden and for seeing how appreciation of the pond and woods
remained a shared endeavor of the Concord transcendental com-
munity.

Emerson was, for the time, absent from that crowd. Thoreau
wrote him in England about gardener Hugh Whelan, who by mid-
January 1848 had moved the Walden house to the beanfield. "He
dug his cellar for the new part too near the old house, Irish like,
though I warned him, and it has caved and let one end of the house
down." That is as far as Whelan's tenancy ever got; insolvent, he
soon disappeared from Concord. Thoreau suggested that Emerson
find some other person and "rent him the shanty as it is, and the
land; or you can very easily and simply let nature keep them still,
without great loss. It may be so managed, perhaps, as to be a home
for somebody, who shall in return . . . fix and locate your lot . . . without expense to you in the mean while, and without disturbing its
possible future value." Meanwhile the Walden house sat empty
beside the big new cellar hole meant for its intended frame addition—a hole that can be plainly seen today in the woods near
Walden Street, perhaps the only earthly monument to Whelan.[1]

Artist of the thaw.
Thoreau's *"grotesque* vegetation," the springtime flowing of sand and clay in Deep Cut. Gleason, "Sand Foliage from Deep Cut," March 17, 1900, courtesy Concord Free Public Library.

Thoreau also wrote to Emerson of changes in Walden Woods. Joel Britton's sawmill business failed by February 1848, "but the woods continue to fall before the axes of other men." Eseek Coombs went missing in the forest and was found dead a week later near Goose Pond, his half-empty jug nearby. In April, Frederick Hayden and James Baker of Lincoln were working on their nearby farms when they noticed smoke rising above the treetops, just after the two P.M. train from Charlestown to Fitchburg went by. In half an hour they were on the scene to find Emerson's so-called island piece of woodlot along the railroad at Heywood's Meadow burning, a stiff wind from the north blowing the flames harmlessly toward the wetland. Charles Bartlett and Abel Brooks had seen smoke from the Concord side of Walden Woods and came running; they watched the fire from across the brook. Two acres of the island woods were severely damaged—trees twenty-five feet high were killed—and John Hosmer later estimated the loss at fifty dollars. On his return from England, Emerson successfully demanded the railroad pay damages. He would spend the rest of his life ruing a succession of such fires.[2]

In his journal in spring 1848, Thoreau wrote about the "sand foliage" in Deep Cut. "Few phenomena give me more delight in the spring of the year than to observe the forms which thawing clay and sand assume on flowing down the sides of a deep cut on the rail road through which I walk. . . . Little streams & ripples of lava like clay over flow & interlace one another like some mythological vegetation. . . . Now it is bluish clay now clay mixed with reddish sand—now pure iron sand." The foliage, the meanings of which have been endlessly discussed by scholars, is one of many subjects in *Walden* that actually came to assume greatest importance to Thoreau after he moved away. What became crucial in the final manuscript was mentioned only briefly in the first version of *Walden*, written at the pond: "As I go back and forth over the rail-road through the deep cut I have seen where the clayey sand like lava had flowed down when it thawed and as it streamed it assumed the forms of vegetation."[3]

Emerson returned from England in July 1848. During the remainder of the year he walked constantly with Ellery Channing, enjoying how Concord was "permeable as a park," with rolling terrain and open woods. Channing was struck with the special fitness of the local landscape for the walker and botanist, ringed by meadows and forests that were poor for row crops but rich in wildlife and rustic beauty. For the naturalist ordinarily, "too much farming and gentlemen's estates are in his way." They sauntered together as often as twice a week. Passing the Andromeda Ponds, Emerson proposed that writers attempt as a theme "one of these Spanish slopes of the dry ponds or basins which run from Walden to the river at Fairhaven, in this September dress of colour, under this glowering sky,—the Walden Sierras in September." On another stroll he told Channing, "My woodlot has no price. I could not think of selling it for the money I gave for it. It is full of unknown mysterious values." In October they sauntered to White Pond, "lovely now as Walden once was; we could almost see the sachem in his canoe in a shadowy cove. . . . Ellery, as usual, found the place with excellent judgment 'where your house should be set,' leaving the woodpaths as they were, which no art could make over; and, after leaving the pond [we came to the] rudest woodland landscapes, unknown, undescribed, & hitherto *unwalked* by us Saturday afternoon professors." Walden remained a favorite, Channing hailing "Walden lake! / Like burnished glass to take / With thy daguerreotype / Each cloud, each tree."[4]

In 1849, Thoreau lectured about his Walden experiment, giving "White Beans & Walden Pond" for the Concord Lyceum in January, at the Unitarian Church Vestry. His first book, *A Week on the Concord and Merrimack Rivers*, was published in May, and flopped—the publisher returned to him unsold 706 copies out of 1000—but Channing recognized the volume as the beginning of Thoreau's gradually growing reputation. Thoreau's summertime walks were scorching, it being the hottest season in thirty years, Irish laborers on the railroad working by night instead of day after several died from heat and drinking cold water. On September 3, his former Walden house was moved by the Clark family from the beanfield to their farm north of Concord village, where they would use it, ingloriously, as a corn-storage shed. Following an October trip with Channing to Cape Cod, and still in debt from his book, Thoreau took up surveying as his chief means of earning a living, which he would continue through the next decade, in the process coming to know Walden Woods ever more intimately.[5]

Perhaps the most important development of 1849 was that it marked the start of Thoreau's habit of long, daily walking—it surely being no coincidence that Channing and Emerson were doing the same with zeal. Those two walked constantly, including to Flint's Pond in December, where they admired icicles: "Every day shows a new thing to veteran walkers." About this time Channing moved to Main Street, and within a year the Thoreaus had moved directly across the way, into the Yellow House, bringing Henry and Ellery into even closer contact. Once Thoreau and Channing lived nearby, they could send a note or call up to the window of the other, suggesting a saunter. One message actually survives: "Dear T., how would you like to go up to Holt's point to-day[?]" Thoreau wrote H. G. O. Blake in November, "Within a year my walks have extended themselves, and almost every afternoon, (I read, or write, or make pencils, in the forenoon, and by the last means get a living for my body), I visit some new hill or pond or wood many miles distant. I am astonished at the wonderful retirement through which I move, rarely meeting a man in these excursions, never seeing one similarly engaged, unless it be my companion, when I have one." Walking afforded and symbolized many things: solitude, individualism, immersion in nature, a commitment to the active life. It was pleasurable and produced reverie. At the same time, it was strenuous work, keystone of Thoreau's moral rigor, half-transcendentalist, half-Yankee: "If you would avoid uncleanness, and all the sins, work earnestly." As Channing said of his friend, "All true walking, all virtuous walking, is a *travail*." There was no indolence to Henry in spending half of each weekday sauntering, though few outside the transcendentalist circle understood. Thoreau and friends were helping to pioneer a new approach to the out-of-doors, nature embraced as a friendly realm that offered spiritual, psychological, and physiological benefits. We take these concepts for granted today, making it difficult to appreciate the novelty of what Emerson, Thoreau, Channing, and their English precursors had discovered.[6]

Two misconceptions need to be corrected. First, Thoreau's walks were "solitary" in the sense of his having left village life behind, but he was not necessarily alone; Channing was sometimes a companion. And secondly, open Thoreau's vast journal at random and, chances are, the walk he describes that day went somewhere other than Walden Pond. Walden was just one destination among many, experienced as a component part in a continuous progression through the landscape. It never existed in isolation but was tied to other ponds, hills, swamps, hollows, woods, brooks, and rivers. Our fixation on Walden should not cause us to overlook the totality of Thoreau Country.[7]

Alcott had moved back to Boston, and Thoreau visited in person in May 1849 to deliver a copy of the newly minted *A Week*. Alcott found it "an American book, worthy to stand beside Emerson's Essays on my shelves." He visited Concord in July: "With Emerson. Also see Thoreau a little while. To Walden afterwards, discussing Genesis and the rest." He was there again in August and September: "All day [with Emerson] discussing the endless and infinite theme in the study and while walking . . . [Lorenz] Oken, Goethe, Swedenborg." "Afternoon with Emerson. We walk to Walden and bathe." "To Walden and home by the Village." Another visit came in January 1850: "We conversed all day and late again on the old themes. Toward night we walked to Walden Water and by Thoreau's hermitage, celebrated in some descriptive verses by Ellery Channing which are characteristic of the primeval virtues and sylvan beauty they sing so well. . . . Concord is classic land; for here dwell the poets, the Americans *par excellence* and men of the future, whose names shall render Harvard and Yale, with their professors and halls, one day ridiculous. The names of Emerson and Thoreau and Channing and Hawthorne are associated with the fields and forests and lakes and rivers of this township." Alcott would spend decades eloquently expounding this notion in lectures and publications, until a nation understood.[8]

Thoreau worked hard for Emerson in spring 1850, building a vine arbor in his garden, surveying woodlots, planting hedges. The older man paid him seven dollars for his March survey of "R. W. Emerson's Woodlot and Meadow by Walden Pond—(that part contained within the Lincoln bounds)—the woodlot being a part of what was known in 1746 as Samuel Heywood's 'pasture.'" Thoreau joined brush burners at a controlled burn here by Heywood's Meadow, a vivid experience: "As I was fighting the fire to day in the midst of the roaring & crackling . . . the fire seem[ed] to snort like a wild horse." Taking a break for water at a rill at the westernmost angle of Emerson's lot, he scared up a woodcock.[9]

In May and June, Walden was at its highest in years, within four feet of Hubbard's Pond Hole, and pitch pine pollen skimmed its surface. On one walk, yellow powder of Roman wormwood coated Thoreau's shoes as he crossed the beanfield, "the now neglected garden." October saw him again surveying Emerson's woodlot to resolve a boundary dispute with a neighbor to the east, Charles Bartlett; this matter would linger for years. In November he said that Walden "has been so high over the stones quite into the bushes that walkers have been excluded from it. There has been no accessible shore." He warmed himself at the "fireside" on the northeast corner and studied the reflection of passing railroad cars in the water. From west of Fair Haven Pond on November 21 he "looked on the walden woods eastward across the pond" and "saw suddenly a white cloud rising above their tops now here now there marking the progress of the cars which were rolling toward Boston far below— behind many hills & woods." On a drizzling, misty day, "Mr Emerson's Cliff-hill" seen from the railroad resembled a frowning New Hampshire mountain.

About this time, a new hovel sprouted in Deep Cut near where the railroad workers once had their shantytown. This habitation would be occupied for five years by the Riordan family, Irish immigrants squatting on the right-of-way. The father seems to have made

Dug by Irish hands. This Fitchburg Railroad cut is near Ice Fort Cove. Thoreau's true Deep Cut lies further off. Granite footings at left supported a bridge to the late-nineteenth-century picnic grounds. Looking northwest. Gleason, "Train approaching through the Deep Cut" [*sic*], March 31, 1920, courtesy Concord Free Public Library.

a scanty living by gleaning sticks from the neighboring forest and buying old railroad sleepers at three dollars a hundred, in spite of their being rotten and full of sand. On a raw, drizzling November day, Thoreau encountered four-year-old Johnny Riordan on the railroad causeway. He was touched by the sight of the child walking in all weathers a mile along the tracks to school. Back home, Thoreau wrote an artless poem that sympathized with his hardships: only potatoes and bread to eat, a bed of straw under his father's cot, bitter wind on the causeway, no future but to grow up to "shovel all day / As hard as I can / Down in the Deep Cut / Where the men lived / Who made the rail road."[10]

Alcott continued to dwell in Boston but thought constantly of Concord, longing to return. He voiced his desire for what Emerson had: "If I could plunge into fields and woods from my house every afternoon, Conversation, company, MSS., days, and dreams, would be all the sweeter and the more vigorous for it. Concord woods were more to me than my library, or Emerson even." Henry visited him on his way to read a lecture on "Life in the Woods at Walden" at Medford. Alcott was ecstatic: "A sylvan man accomplished in the virtues of an aboriginal civility, and quite superior to the urbanites of cities, Thoreau is himself a wood, and its inhabitants. There is more in him of sod and shade and sky lights, of the genuine mold and moistures of the green grey earth, than in any person I know. . . . He belongs to the Homeric age, and is older than fields and gardens."[11]

Alcott visited Concord in late April and again enjoyed the pleasures of Walden Woods firsthand. "All the morning was given to conversation in E's study. After dinner we walked to Walden, and in the evening came Thoreau." In June, "These days and nights in Concord with Emerson in study and field, beside Walden Water and woods, are differenced by nameless traits from all days and nights in my calendar of experience. There is nothing like them, nothing comparable. . . . Dined with Thoreau. We had a walk afterward by the Hosmer Cottage, and back by the rail-track. T. tells me that he read his paper on 'Walking' lately at Worcester. He should read this, and the 'Walden' also, everywhere in our towns and cities, for the soundness and rectitude of the sentiments."[12]

In August, Alcott returned to Walden Pond: "With Emerson till dinner. Afternoon, walked with Thoreau, and bathed in the Lake. 'The blue eyed Walden there doth smile / Most tenderly upon its neighbor pines.' Thoreau read me some passages from his paper on 'Walking' as I passed the evening with him." He summarized his opinion of the relative greatness of Emerson, Channing, and Thoreau. The first "was forbidden pure companionship with Nature. He dwelt rather in an intellectual grove, and looked at society from this his retreat through the glass of imagination." Channing stood nearer to nature and came "sometimes . . . into a closer intimacy that makes him passionately one with the heart of things." But "Thoreau has the profoundest passion for the aboriginal in Nature of any man I have known. . . . He has come nearer the primitive simplicity of the antique than any of our poets, and touched the fields and forests and streams of Concord with a classic interest that can never fade."[13]

Alcott recognized that Thoreau drew inspiration from nature more directly than any contemporary. In search of ever more intense experiences, in summer 1851, Thoreau undertook an extraordinary series of walks by moonlight, described with a fullness new to his journal. On a June night he strolled to Walden by railroad and upland wood path. In the Deep Cut the west sandbank was tinged by moonlight even as the east still glowed with the red of sunset. He

Where poets drank. Thoreau came to Brister's Spring on hot summer days after hoeing in his beanfield. Gleason, July 30, 1900, courtesy Concord Free Public Library.

climbed the left bank and approached the pond down Cyrus Hubbard's path. Moonlight shimmered on high water in the cove. To the sounds of crickets, frogs, and the owl he had heard so often when living at the pond, he pushed off from the shore in a boat. Later he climbed the hill through the Wyman Lot and his old beanfield, coming out on Walden Road. One afternoon in July he walked a big circle, down the west side of Sudbury River and up the east, the last part via the railroad, admiring the scalloped southern shore of Walden, but soon feeling his usual revulsion at the Riordan shanty where the occupants drank from a puddle, having no well: "How shiftless—what death in life."

Swedish novelist Fredrika Bremer visited Emerson in late July, the sage announcing his intention "to drive you to one of our beautiful little forest lakes" in his cabriolet. On the way they talked of the intellectual culture of New England and the slavery problem. Emerson pulled aside at the foot of Brister's Hill and said, "Here is a spring famous for its excellent water. May I give you a glass?" For Bremer, who felt strangely drawn to the master in spite of his "icy-alp nature, repulsive and chilling" and anti-Christian stance, this glass signified his character and beliefs, "crystal, pure, fresh, cold."[14]

A famous passage in *Walden* concerns the singing of the telegraph wire, which ran along the railroad line. Again, what we read is, to a considerable extent, what happened to catch Thoreau's eye in the early 1850s, well after he moved away from the pond. He said in August 1851, "I find 3 or 4 ordinary laborers to day putting up the necessary outdoor fixtures for a magnetic telegraph from Boston to Burlington. They carry along a basket full of simple implements— like travelling tinkers—and with a little rude soddering & twisting and straightening of wires the work is done. It is a work which seems to admit of the greatest latitude of ignorance and bungling." Seven years had passed since Samuel F. B. Morse had transmitted "What hath God wrought" on the first telegraph line, which ran along the B & O Railroad between Washington and Baltimore, and since then railroads and telegraphs had undertaken their joint conquest of the continent.

The naturalist carried an umbrella as he walked out Walden Road in September. The pond was at last going down, dead pines leaning about its shores. The next day near the depot on his way to swim in Sudbury River he first noticed the telegraph wire singing: "I heard it vibrating like a harp high over head.—it was as the sound of a far off glorious life a supernal life." On the twelfth he walked to Flint's Pond by the railroad and Emerson's wood path on the south side of the pond. "At the entrance to the Deep Cut I heard the telegraph wire vibrating like an Aeolian Harp. . . . I instantly sat down on a stone at the foot of the telegraph pole—& attended to the communication." Thus began his infatuation with the telegraph line, Emersonian in its emphasis upon sounds and recalling the fact that Alcott built an Aeolian harp into the gables of the Bush summerhouse. For Channing there was no clearer example of his friend's profound "poetic insight" than his ability to transform something so mundane as a barked chestnut pole into an instrument of celestial music.[15]

Thoreau's pond thoughts and *Walden* manuscript—including its passages on the telegraph harp—developed over time, through a long series of encounters. Yes, he lived there for two years; but in the early 1850s, he could say that he had "seen it almost daily for more than twenty years." *Walden* must be viewed against the totality of Thoreau's experiences. Herbert W. Gleason, photographer of

Thoreau Country, commented in 1924 that the Walden experiment "has been perhaps over-emphasized" and "was by no means a hermit's life." "During the rest of his life, in all his voluminous journalizing, there is seldom any reference to this particular association with the pond; but there is frequent comment upon the pond itself, its various seasonal features, and its newly-discovered attractions. Assuredly, Walden pond held a perennial interest."[16]

On another of his 1851 walks, Thoreau passed through George Heywood's cleared lot somewhere near Walden and, to his surprise, found a "pigeon place" where passenger pigeons—today extinct—were trapped. Grain lay strewn on sandy ground; six dead trees were set up for birds to alight on; a brush house nearby was meant to conceal a man who would pull a string, dropping a net over the quarry as they fed. "I was rather startled to find such a thing going now. . . . Several men still take pigeons in Concord every year."

In September, Thoreau was employed to survey the Concord-Lincoln line, originally laid in 1754. Coming up from Sudbury River, he walked from a split stone on James Baker's land to one "by Walden Pond," both set up in 1829. He did a little measuring to satisfy private curiosity, too: "About the middle of Oct. it was 20 ft 6$\frac{1}{2}$ inches from the surface of Walden Pond to the top of the rail of the R.R. at the western extremity of the pond."[17]

Walden's poignant accounts of the destruction of forests derive not so much from 1845–47 as the winter 1851–52 cutting of the eastern and northern shores. George Heywood hired workmen in an arrangement similar to one Thoreau describes—a woodcutter and assistant (paid a dollar daily) felled trees all winter at ten cents each, thirty or forty trees a day. Their tools were one four dollar cross-cut saw, ax, beetle, wedges, and whetstone. In September, Henry walked Emerson's frequent route, Hosmer's-Goose Pond-Walden, and viewed the pond from the hill on the north side with the sawed pine stump atop, scaring up black ducks. The cutting was distressing, but "Walden plainly can never be spoiled by the wood-chopper—for do what you will to the shore there will still remain this crystal well." Maples on the western edge glowed red. Thoreau's lament about the woodchoppers forms part of a familiar Picturesque theme, recalling Wordsworth in the Region of the Lakes: at Ullswater "the axe has here indiscriminately levelled a rich wood of birches and oaks. . . .

Clearcut. Gleason, "Slaughtered Pines Across from Walden," March 29, 1918, courtesy Concord Free Public Library.

Those beautiful woods are gone, which *perfected* its seclusion." Around the lakes "there will, in a short time, scarcely be left an ancient oak," so much "havoc" had been made.[18]

Wood chopping proceeded into January 1852, and Thoreau was appalled: "This winter they are cutting down our woods more seriously than ever—Fair Haven Hill—Walden. . . . Thank God they cannot cut down the clouds." Next day he proposed a solution: "Methinks the town should have more supervision & control over its parks than it has. It concerns us all whether these proprietors—choose to cut down all the woods this winter." He walked across Flint's Pond on the twenty-fourth and came home by Walden. Standing on the ice, he watched railroad cars rattle by, a steam cloud glowing rosy-pink in the sunset sky. Although the cutting pained him, he was somewhat numb to it: "These woods! why do I not feel their being cut more sorely? Does it not affect me nearly? The axe can deprive me of much. Concord is sheared of its pride. I am certainly the less attached to my native town in consequence. . . . I shall go to Walden less frequently." As if in solace for his loss, he was cheered by the telegraph harp in the Deep Cut, almost envying the wretched Riordans who could hear it daily from their shanty door.

A couple of days later he walked out Walden Road and examined lichens in Heywood's woodlot near the town line southeast of the pond, near the area being cleared. By 2 P.M. he had climbed Emerson's Cliff to watch the clouds drifting in the west. When he passed some railroad workers on the tracks, they bowed to him as an old acquaintance, having seen him so often they mistook him for an employee. Clay flowed on the east side of Deep Cut, and the telegraph harp sang in the stillness of the winter's afternoon.

Notwithstanding his attacks on charity in *Walden*, Thoreau's family—who lived near the schoolhouse on Main Street and employed, in 1850, thirteen-year-old Catherine "Rioden" in their kitchen—had given some of Thoreau's old trousers to her brother Johnny. When Thoreau saw him in January 1852 with torn clothes and no coat he was again troubled, and he carried a new cloak to the hovel for Johnny to wear. "I found that the shanty was warmed by the simple social relations of the Irish," he said, but soon turned to his usual condemnation: "Living all winter with an open door for light—& no visible wood pile—The forms of old & young permanently contracted through long shrinking from cold.—& their faces pinched by want—I have seen an old crone sitting on the hill side, there in the middle of January while it was raining & the ground was slowly thawing under her—knitting there." Riordan got his family's water from the ditch by the railroad even when it was a stew of rainwater and sand. Drawing from these experiences, in *Walden* Thoreau condemns "the shanties which every where border our railroads, that last improvement in civilization; where I see in my daily walks human beings living in sties." The Riordans' condition would eventually improve, the family moving into town and for a time, apparently, occupying a cottage adjacent to the Thoreaus.[19]

During one outing Henry managed to find some good in the timber operation at the pond: "Though they are cutting off the woods at Walden it is not all loss. It makes some new & unexpected prospects." As he stood on the partially cleared bank at the east end he looked south into a still-wooded deep dell where a chopper worked, silhouetted against a snowy hillside. The industrious scene reminded him of Maine or New Hampshire, with the logger's team of oxen on the ice chewing cud; a long pine stripped of its branches and chained upon a sled, resting on a stout crossbar and trailing behind. The commotion was bad for the fishermen, one telling Thoreau he had had no luck at Walden that winter because of the woodcutters felling trees onto the ice.

Thoreau crossed the frozen pond on his way to Pine Hill on the twenty-ninth. In March he stood on Walden again and saw that the eastern shore was now entirely laid waste. Woodcutters picked their way along a hillside, dimly seen through the mist. A few chestnuts remained standing, to be cut later in the spring when their bark would more easily peel. During a thaw he observed the oozing of red sand in Deep Cut, making hard work for railroad repairmen. Water flowed in the wooden troughs, and smoke curled up from the Riordan shanty. "The railroad is perhaps our pleasantest and wildest road. It only makes deep cuts into and through the hills—on it are no houses nor foot travellers. The travel on it does not disturb me. The woods are left to hang over it—Though straight it is wild in its accompaniments—all is raw edges."[20]

Dismayed by the felling of so many trees, Thoreau predicted that he would come to the pond less often. In fact, the opposite proved true. In August he wrote a fifth draft of *Walden* and began a series of visits to gather information for his evolving manuscript. For this purpose he hauled a boat to the pond, where it remained until late December.[21]

This process of study began with paddling entirely around the pond. He remarked that the shore was paved with little smooth white stones, except for one or two short sand beaches (his cove and the eastern shore). From the boat the water was dark green; from a hilltop, blue. It had risen steadily since he moved away, and fishermen again were busy in Wyman Meadow—the change in the pond's level the result, Thoreau supposed, of its "deep springs." High water triggered alders to send out long roots and blueberries to bear luscious fruit, but it killed pitch pines.[22]

Gerardia bloomed yellow on the cut-over hillside north of the pond, which Thoreau now called Heywood's Peak, a locale soon to become of great importance to him. The destruction of Walden's forests ironically stimulated his interest in the place by creating a sweeping view from this height, the foremost of the "new & unexpected prospects" now visible, and by triggering a cycle of plant succession that he would follow intently. But this is typical of Thoreau's transformation of all things to pastoral good, discovering, as Channing said, "the beautiful accidents that attend on man's works, instead of a defilement." Heywood's Peak appears frequently in *Walden*, but is unnamed and has therefore been forgotten. "From a hill top near by, where the wood had been recently cut off, there was a pleasing vista southward across the pond, through a wide indentation in the hills which form the shore there, where their opposite sides sloping toward each other suggested a stream flowing out in that direction through a wooded valley, but stream there was none." This illusion can be detected today.[23]

Seeking further information for *Walden*, and perhaps increasingly realizing how much he had overlooked, he paddled again on September 1, a serene evening of the kind Wordsworth loved in the Lakes. He climbed Heywood's Peak for an expansive view of "the beautifully varied shores of Walden—The western indented with deep bays—the bold northern shore—the gracefully sweeping curve of the eastern and above all the beautifully scalloped southern shore—where successive capes overlap each other . . . and suggest unexplored coves between." From here, as he would later say in his chapter "The Ponds," he could see a fish leap anywhere. The cut-over east bank was distressing, but he took hope: "They cannot fatally injure Walden with an axe, for they have done their worst & failed." Next day as he looked over the pond from the denuded eastern shore he saw fish arc into the air; then he climbed Heywood's Peak. These observations, too, were incorporated into "The Ponds," as were others during fall and winter, all with a Wordsworthian tenor, for example when Thoreau stood on the east beach and studied the glassy surface: "When you invert your head, it looks like a thread of finest gossamer."

The twentieth of the month found Thoreau again on Heywood's Peak: "How soothing to sit on a stump on this height overlooking the pond and study the dimpling circles" and hear oars splashing. Ten days later, he accompanied locals on a bee hunt to Baker Farm and, after lunch, to Walden. To find honey-rich hives, the men trapped the insects in a box, marked them with colored pigments, and released them, watching which direction they flew and counting the minutes to their return. "By the roadside at Walden—on the sunny hill side sloping to the pond—we saw a large mass of golden rod &

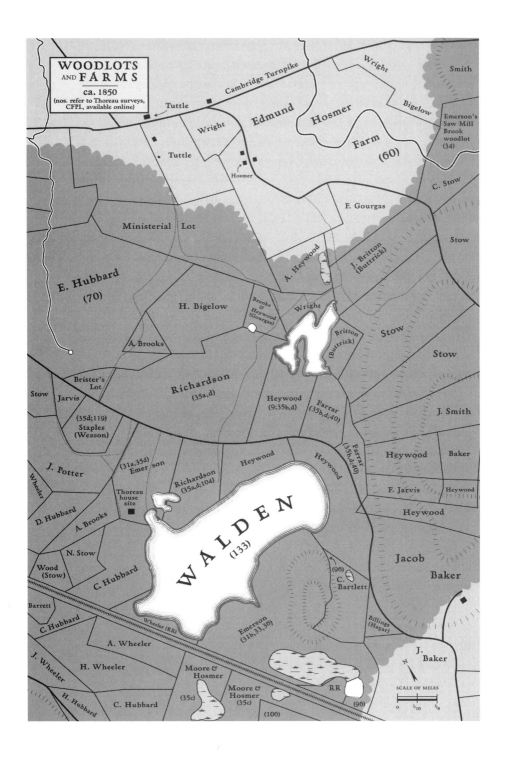

WOODLOTS
AND FARMS
ca. 1850
(nos. refer to Thoreau surveys,
CFPL, available online)

Cambridge Turnpike

Tuttle

Wright

Smith

Edmund

Hosmer

Bigelow

Emerson's
Saw Mill
Brook
woodlot
(34)

Wright

Farm
(60)

C. Stow

Tuttle

Hosmer

F. Gourgas

Stow

Ministerial   Lot

A. Heywood

J. Britton
(Buttrick)

E. Hubbard
(70)

H. Bigelow

Brooks
&
Heywood
(Gourgas)

Wright

Britton
(Buttrick)

Stow

A. Brooks

Stow

Richardson
(35a,d)

Heywood
(9;35b,d)

Farrar
(35b,d;40)

J. Smith

Stow

Brister's
Lot

Jarvis

Farrar
(35b,d;40)

Heywood

Baker

(35d;119)
Staples
(Wesson)

(31a,35d)
Emerson

Richardson
(35a,d;104)

Heywood

Heywood

F. Jarvis

Heywood

J. Potter

Wheeler

Thoreau
house
site

WALDEN
(133)

Heywood

D. Hubbard

A. Brooks

Jacob

N. Stow

(96)
C.
Bartlett

Baker

Wood
(Stow)

C. Hubbard

Barrett

Wheeler (R.R.)

Emerson
(31b,33,30)

Billings
(Hagar)

C. Hubbard

A. Wheeler

J.
Baker

J. Wheeler

H. Wheeler

Moore &
Hosmer

N

SCALE OF MILES

H. Hubbard

C. Hubbard

(35c)

Moore &
Hosmer
(35c)

RR

(96)

0   1/16   1/8

(106)

aster several rods square. . . . Getting out of our wagon we found it to be resounding with the hum of bees." At 1 P.M. they set the box there on a woodpile. Thoreau was fascinated by the process—"I feel the richer for this experience."

Autumn colors from Heywood's Peak caught his eye on October 3, as he continued his intensive studies of the pond for *Walden*. That book would include an account of his chase of a loon five days later. He pursued it in his boat along the north shore. On the twelfth he walked down the railroad and noted the stratification in a bank where sand was mined for brickyards. "Piled up history! I am struck by the slow & delicate process by which the globe was formed," he wrote. (Such mining produced today's pitted terrain southeast of Deep Cut, where an 1895 map shows four acres owned by a brick company.) Afterward, Thoreau paddled on Walden, scaring some ducks, and then dug up ground nuts in the pondside railroad bank with his hands. He prepared this novel dish at home. "I found it better boiled than roasted," he says in *Walden*, pretending that all of this happened when he was living pondside.

The early winter was mild, and Thoreau was astonished still to be able to paddle over Walden on December 5. The increased water level had killed many pitch pines, birches, alders, and aspens. Such fluctuations "make it difficult to walk round" when the water is high but "so much the easier & more agreeable" when low. (Nineteenth-century round-the-pond walking was often done on the stony shore, not on paths, which were steep and narrow on abrupt hillsides. Alternatively, "round the pond" meant taking wood roads well inland.) When dimples appeared on the water Thoreau thought it was raining and quickly grabbed his oars to row to shore, but these turned out to be schools of perch. The pond remained ice-free on December 27, when he paddled across and hauled his boat out for the winter, returning it to town the next day.[24]

As these entries show, Thoreau had recast his life to take daily advantage of walking, investigating natural phenomena for literary purposes. Emerson had other responsibilities: "We remember nature once in a while . . . stopping to look at the sunset across Walden; but we hurry home again to the fracas of the house." Thoreau, however, was reinventing himself as a skilled naturalist with an ever-increasing knowledge of the subject, flora in particular, and the study of nature was rapidly becoming his life's work. Concord was a good place to study plants; of all the species found in eastern America, fully one in five has been recorded there. As botany became Thoreau's overriding interest, Channing remarked that Henry's curiosity came to center on a few types in particular—willows, goldenrods, asters, polygonums, sedges, and grasses. Most of these are notable either for pushing out or blooming very early in the spring or persisting in flower very late in autumn, making them for the poet symbolic of the persistence of the life spirit. All but polygonum could be found at Walden Pond, which for Thoreau increasingly became a place of flowers, the center of some of his most productive investigations.[25]

Alcott spent a morning in 1853 in Emerson's library "at the old game, discussing unreportable things" before walking together to Walden. This occasion may have been when Emerson read to him "from a joint production of Ellery's and his . . . a sort of literary recreation, being transcripts of the friends' walks and conversations in Concord, their speculations and experiences by the fields and woods, along the streams and meadows, seasoned sagely with the pleasantries and learning of both—the whole, judging from the sample read to me, promising an entertainment as elegant and racy as anything in modern literature. Channing's conversation I think far superior to anything of his printed. . . . [He is] the shyest and moodiest of mortals." Alcott enjoyed these outings, such as one he took in August: "All day with Emerson, having the old yet ever-new game of speculation parliamentary; also the ever-Walden walk, with discussions—not unusual—on ways and means," including Alcott's idea of a lecture tour to Cincinnati. Emerson would fund this tour, which ended disastrously, like most of Alcott's ventures thus far. In late summer Channing was indeed writing a book, *Country Walking*, about walks and talks with Emerson and Thoreau. But personal crisis now enveloped Channing, as his long-suffering wife abandoned him; the walking material would not be published until his 1873 biography of Thoreau. He disappeared for a time and probably took few strolls with his friends until 1858.[26]

Emerson continued to enjoy walking around the pond, cutting paths through his woodlot, swimming, and rowing. Once he told his daughter Edith, "I will keep these woods until everything else is gone. It is my camel's hump. When a camel is starving in the desert he eats his own hump." Edward Emerson recalled, "His old pair of skates always hung in his study-closet, and he went to the solitary coves of Walden with his children when he was fifty years old and skated with them, moving steadily forward, as I remember, secure and erect. In summer, but only on the very hot days, he liked to go into Walden, and swam strongly and well." Emerson's disciple Franklin B. Sanborn too recalled "his fondness for swimming in Walden, or skating there in winter. I have so skated with him." Edith remembered, "At four o'clock on Sundays Father came from his study, and called at the foot of the stairs 'four o'clock,' or he whistled for us, and then took us [on] long walks in the woods, showing us pretty flowers he had found in his daily walks. Oftenest we went to Walden and his loved pine grove by the Cove, where Mr. Thoreau had his leave to build his cabin." Thoreau or Channing "used to guide my Father to see rare flowers in hidden places, and then Father took us the next Sunday. In these walks he often crooned his verses lately written, and though he knew nothing of music, and had been emphatically rejected by the singing master." Edward recalled, "He was hard at work in his study until his walking time, except for a half-hour spent in garden and orchard after breakfast. . . . On weekdays he walked alone, but on Sundays he showed us the shrines of the wood-gods." He added, "On Sunday afternoons at four o'clock, when the children came from their Bible-reading in their mother's room he took them all to walk, more often towards Walden, or beyond to the Ledge ('My Garden'), the Cliffs, the old Baker Farm on Fairhaven." Along the way, "He showed us his favorite plants, usually rather humble flowers such as the Lespideza . . . or the little blue Self-heal whose name recommended it. He led us to the vista in his woods beyond Walden that he found and improved with his hatchet . . . and on the shores of frozen Walden on a dull winter's day hallooed for Echo in which he took great delight. . . . Often as he walked he would recite fragments of ballads, old or modern."[27]

Thoreau and Emerson only occasionally walked together, living as they did at opposite ends of the village. Moreover, their relationship had cooled, for complex and much-debated reasons; among other causes, Henry had moved toward botany and ornithology and away from poetry, dashing Emerson's high hopes. Emerson was frus-

trated at Thoreau's apparent preference for pond wading over publication; Thoreau, it has been argued, at Emerson's authoritarian
paternalism that implied condescension. Thoreau's walks continued
to be mostly solitary, as when he sat on Pine Hill in May 1853 and
looked at distant mountains in clear morning light. Days later he
examined frost damage to young oaks in the hollow west of Laurel
Glen, finding an ovenbird's nest before descending to Wyman
Meadow. Climbing Heywood's Peak he disturbed a nighthawk,
which dashed at him "like an imp of darkness—then swept away
high over the pond." In the sunny clearing on the side of the peak he
studied the flower structure of the tufts of pinks. At 5 P.M. he heard
a farmer's horn in the distance, calling hands in from the field to
early tea. As this bucolic sound drifted across Walden Woods—a
reminder that it was in fact an island in the midst of vast reaches of
Massachusetts agriculture—the botanist stooped to examine
hieracium and snapdragon catchfly.[28]

On July days he visited the chestnut behind his old house site
and smooth sumac at Wyman Meadow; passed Cato's cellar hole
and Goose Pond; and studied blooms at Heywood's Peak, this
warm, dry sproutland having become, again, one of his most important botanical locales. In August the heat was furnacelike as he
climbed these steep hills on the north shore, which were cloaked
with shrubs and sweetfern head-high. He was excited to find sickle-
pod, a novel species. "New plants spring up where old woods are cut
off, having formerly grown here perchance—Many such rarer plants
flourish for a few years in such places before they are smothered."

That summer Thoreau was joined by visiting Moncure D.
Conway on a walk to Goose Pond and Baker Farm. Conway recalled
that his host carried a spyglass, microscope, and an old book as plant
press. "His powers of conversation were extraordinary. . . . The
acuteness of his senses was marvellous." A young friend of Edith
Emerson recalled, "Mr. Emerson took my sister and myself into the
woods and fields with his children and talked to us about the birds
and flowers and trees. . . . He took us blue berrying in his 'hay rig-
ging' he sitting up high . . . we sitting in the straw," as Henry and
Sophia Thoreau, Channing, and Conway drove in the carryall.[29]

After Christmas Thoreau walked out Walden Road and around
the pond to see the effects of a fresh snow, enjoying the sight of the

Vista of the ax. "Viewed from a hill top [Walden] is blue in the depths & green in the shallows." Bare Peak, cut in 1840-41, afforded Thoreau views of the pond and even to the steeples of Concord. The peak was bare again in 1918. Looking southwest toward the railroad, Thoreau's Cove at right. Gleason, "Ripples in Walden Pond from Heywood's [*sic*] Peak," April 24, 1918, courtesy Concord Free Public Library.

pure and trackless road leading up Brister's Hill. The new coating kept skaters off the pond. He walked through cut-over sproutlands under "Bartlett's" (Emerson's) Cliff and saw the pitch pine that had been struck by lightning eight years ago, when he lived across the pond. A horned grebe swam in open water—one of only a handful of records of this species ever in Concord. More snow followed, and he carried a two-foot ruler to measure depths in Wheeler's Wood near the railroad and, going around the south side of the pond, on Potter's land along Walden Road. Thus ended another year of intensive investigations.[30]

In January 1854, a year that stands as a landmark for Thoreauvians as marking the publication of *Walden*, Thoreau eyed the snowy landscape from Heywood's Peak. Fishermen were out on the ice. During a February thaw, greenish water filled kettle-hole hollows near Walden Road as he angled across from Deep Cut to Pine Hill. One day he struck the pond ice with an ax to hear it ring, and another time he stood in the middle and viewed "that Indian trail on the hillside about Walden . . . a clear white line unobscured by weeds and twigs. . . . It was quite distinct in many places where you would not have noticed it before." Modern visitors associate today's wide round-the-pond path carved in the 1930s by reservation staff with Thoreau's Indian trail. We should recall, though, that the latter was merely a faint track "in the steep hill-side, alternately rising and falling, approaching and receding from the water's edge," almost imperceptible and only "occasionally trodden by the white man" or "from time to time unwittingly trodden by the present occupants of the land." People seem to have hardly known it was there—Thoreau himself was "surprised to detect" it—for it was merely "a narrow shelf-like path . . . hardly distinguishable close at hand."[31]

During early spring Thoreau completed the seventh and final draft of *Walden*. He wrote the last journal passage to be incorporated into his book on April 27, referring to long-term fluctuations in the height of the pond. In late May he wandered through Hubbard's Close before climbing Heywood's Peak. The sproutland here was covered with pinks; Thoreau counted three hundred open flowers on just one tuft. Two days later he walked out Walden Road to Bear Hill, Lincoln, and noticed gentlemen and ladies sitting in boats at anchor under parasols on the calm afternoon, a glimpse of how suburban Walden Pond really was, or was becoming. In June he walked the same way, studying which plants were blooming at Heywood's Peak and scaring a kingfisher from a branch over the water. Mountain laurel was blooming at Laurel Hillside by the pond—one of a few Thoreauvian locales that cannot be pinpointed today. He then descended to the bathing place at the northwest cove.[32]

He was back at Heywood's Peak on the sixteenth, again to see hawkweed and cornel, and he found a tortoise egg on the hillside sixty feet above the water. Despite the lovely afternoon on the peak, he could not concentrate on the scenery, because fugitive slave Anthony Burns had been arrested in Boston and was to be shipped back to bondage in Virginia. "There is a fine ripple & sparkle on the pond seen through the mist. . . . We walk to lakes to see our serenity reflected in them . . . [but] the remembrance of the baseness of politicians spoils my walks—my thoughts are murder to the state— I endeavor in vain to observe Nature."

Still seething about Burns, he walked to Walden through Deep Cut Woods on June 21 and saw pouts tending their young at Hubbard's Pond Hole. Then he rambled up the connecting, grassy hollows in extensive sproutlands on the Richardson Lot east of Walden Road, near Goose Pond, a wild and strange region hardly explored and just far enough from the highway to seem a thousand miles removed.

The highlight of the summer was the publication of *Walden* in Boston by Ticknor and Fields on August 9, 1854, in an edition of two thousand copies, a dollar each. Ticknor had cared little for the manuscript, but Fields on meeting the author gushed that he carried "a rural fragrance—spicy odors of black birch, hickory buds, and pennyroyal—with him from his native fields into the streets and lanes of Boston." *Walden* would remain in print for five years, garner favorable reviews, and sell moderately well, although nothing like it would when reissued after its author's death. Probably with a sense of accomplishment Thoreau, on the twenty-seventh, walked to Pine Hill by the turnpike and Hubbard's Close, ascending the back of Heywood's Peak to once again study its plants and look down on the surface of Walden Pond. Already Alcott had "read and re-read" *Walden*, deeming it a book "to find readers and fame as years pass by." Emerson wrote his friend George P. Bradford, "All American kind are delighted with 'Walden' as far as they have dared say. The little pond sinks in these very days as tremulous at its human fame," a reference to its decline due to drought.[33]

Thoreau named his book *Walden; or, Life in the Woods*, which he later simplified to *Walden*. The title, of course, places great emphasis upon the pond. His Aunt Maria wrote in 1849, "He is preparing his Book for the press and the title is to be, Waldien (I dont know how to spell it) or life in the Woods. I think the title will take if the Book dont." At times the book resembles a biography of a character named "Walden," curiously synonymous with the author: both are said to live like "a hermit in the woods," and, as Thoreau writes gracefully,

> Of all the characters I have known, perhaps Walden wears best, and best preserves its purity. Many men have been likened to it, but few deserve that honor. Though the woodchoppers have

laid bare first this shore and then that, and the Irish have built their sties by it, and the railroad has infringed on its border, and the ice-men have skimmed it once, it is itself unchanged, the same water which my youthful eyes fell on; all the change is in me. . . .

I cannot come nearer to God and Heaven
Than I live to Walden even.
I am its stony shore,
And the breeze that passes o'er;
In the hollow of my hand
Are its water and its sand.[34]

For Thoreau there were few Walden visits during the rest of the year, as he delivered lectures as far away as Philadelphia; but on December 4 he walked down the railroad and found the isthmus to Wyman Meadow bare. The most important Concord event of late fall was, it would later turn out, the visit of Harvard undergraduate Frank Sanborn, who was introduced to the transcendentalist circle: "The first walk I ever took with Emerson was to Walden, in November, 1854." He took the train on the second and arrived at Emerson's house at 2 P.M. "We sat by the dining room fire and talked awhile. . . . We walked out across the pastures to Walden Pond, and Mr. E spoke of an Englishman, Cholmondely, who had lately come to Concord." Emerson reported, "I asked this man if he saw any difference between our autumn foliage, and that of England. He said no,—but all men who have eyes notice it at once." Sanborn wrote, "We walked on over bare, brown pastures and hills covered with shrub oaks—their leaves all faded, but clinging to the branches—among pine groves too, until we came to the shore of Walden Pond—We stood on the railroad and looked across it." "Then we went along the south shore to Mr. E's woodland, where he has had wood lately cut off—oak and pine. There are no beeches here—few maples, if any—We came back along the east shore of the pond just as the sun was setting behind the hills in the distance. His golden flood of light streamed broad across the still waters and was sifted through the pine branches till our eyes could bear it,—in the East the sky was rose and purple and cool blue—and there the full moon stood just risen above the trees." On the way home Emerson spoke of British thinkers Walter Landor, John Ruskin, and Richard Owen. Emerson's wife Lidian served tea. Before Sanborn departed to catch the train, Emerson gave him a present, a brand-new copy of *Walden*.[35]

6

❦

Walden Wood Was My Forest Walk

(1855–1861)

❦

In his new publication, *Walden*, Thoreau had achieved an extraordinary biography of place, so skillfully that he eventually garnered immortality for "Walden" as book, pond, and back-to-nature idea, all three. As Robert Frost once said of Thoreau's masterpiece, "Think of the success of a man's pulling himself together under one one-word title. Enviable!" The fame of the text and its writer continues almost inexorably to grow; according to scholar Joel Myerson, "Today, *Walden* is arguably the most widely translated and available book by an American author." Researchers have published "well over one hundred articles and sections of books dealing solely with *Walden*," plus full-length monographs, to make a low estimate.[1]

The thirty-seven-year-old Thoreau who held in his hands his first copy of *Walden* differed significantly from the man who had moved to the pond a decade before. The book speaks of a loss of youthful vigor and idealism: the philosophical seeds of virtue planted in the beanfield turned out to have "lost their vitality, and so did not come up"; and "with years I have grown more coarse and indifferent." His interests had shifted toward science; in a larger sense, his brand of transcendentalism had evolved, even as the once-controversial principles of the movement had begun to diffuse powerfully through educated American society.[2]

Thoreau's house site in winter. Looking southeast toward Emerson's Cliff.
Alfred Winslow Hosmer, ca. 1890, courtesy Concord Free Public Library.

When Frank Sanborn moved to Concord in 1855 to teach school,
he briefly stayed on Main Street with Mr. Holbrook, who spoke of
three religious groups in the village—Unitarian, Orthodox, and the
Walden Pond Society. Townsfolk were well aware of the transcendentalists' devotion to peripatetic and their curious elevation of
Walden into a quasi-spiritual realm. Sanborn participated enthusiastically and became close with Thoreau. In April 1858 he moved with
his friend Ellery Channing directly across the street from the
Thoreaus, with whom he dined daily. He would, decades later,
become Henry's biographer and the leading spokesman and historian for the Concord writers, spreading their posthumous fame.[3]

Thoreau continued to walk constantly, both for transcendental
elevation and to study nature. In a January snowstorm in 1855, he and
Channing crossed from the Cliffs by the wood path at their base to
Walden, then home by Brister's Hill and Walden Road, driving snow
stinging their eyes. Days later, Thoreau went out in another snow,
descending into the deepest circular hollow on the Brister's Hill path.
Another time he found Alex Therien cutting down the two largest
chestnuts behind the Walden house site to make posts, the felling of
Concord's forests continuing relentlessly. On one stump Thoreau
counted seventy-five rings. It was so cold, Therien broke his ax on a
knot. The next morning the Thoreaus' thermometer recorded minus
fourteen, but Henry went walking that afternoon as usual.

On a mild mid-February day, Thoreau strolled to Walden by the railroad, looking for animal tracks and setting a trap for mice. Sand flowed in Deep Cut and workmen hammered the rails. In nearby woods he whistled as Channing collected lichens with a knife. Mist hung over the pond as they walked to Spanish Brook. Thoreau stood on Heywood's Peak on March 29 looking over Walden, its surface half-frozen, a huge drift of ice forming a rampart of crumbled fragments against the east end. He inhaled cold wind and felt a strange impulse to swim. He was on the peak again in April, studying a bufflehead duck with his spyglass until a train scared the bird away. Pout fishermen were out in Wyman Meadow, and one wonders what they thought of the strange naturalist who often joined them there.

Emerson remained a regular at the pond, Sanborn observed. "It was for many years Mr. Emerson's custom to pass his mornings in his library, and his afternoons in the open air, walking alone or with a friend across the pastures and through the woods. . . . His favorite walk" was to his Walden holdings "and around this pond." He walked "every day for some hours" and had "composed much of his verse in these walks in field and woodland." As he sauntered he had a distinctive manner "of twirling his walking-stick." During these years Emerson kept his boat in the cove, and he and Thoreau "now and then rowed forth together."[4]

On March 25, Sanborn joined the Emerson family on their Sunday 4 P.M. walk, typical of countless others. "We went through the woods to Walden. We visited 'Fairyland' a beautiful little dell shut in by woods which the children so named. It was cold and blustering, and we were glad to take shelter in Mr. E's dining room when we came back." On May 3, Emerson knocked at Sanborn's schoolhouse door at four, "and we started on our long proposed walk to Baker Farm, whose beauties Ellery Channing has sung, and Thoreau hinted at [in Walden]—We went along the road for a mile perhaps, and then turned into the pasture, following a cart path. In a mile or so more we came to the entrance to Baker Farm. . . . Presently we came to the larger field and the house—an old deserted cabin." Sanborn relished these indoctrinations into peripatetic culture.[5]

Many others enjoyed that culture, too. When Alcott visited in May, he called on Thoreau, Channing, and Emerson and walked with some of these friends to Baker Farm and Fair Haven before catching the seven o'clock train. In July the twenty-five-year-old caricaturist Frank Bellew, summering in Concord, was invited by Emerson "to accompany him in his afternoon rambles through the woods and fields, which I learned was a most distinguished honor." Walden "appeared to be an extinct gravel-pit, filled with the most exquisitely pure water, and was often used by himself and a few others as a bath. I think he claimed that its purity and coldness gave it special tonic properties for this purpose." Emerson invited Bellew "to take a plunge." "But we have no towels," Bellew replied. "Oh, that is of no consequence: we can dry ourselves in the sun. I rarely trouble myself about towels." But Bellew feared getting chilled and declined to swim, which he later regretted, having "so missed an opportunity of something akin to baptism at the hands of the prophet." Emerson showed him trees he had planted at Walden "as an investment for the benefit of his son," calculating that these saplings would be "of considerable value" by the time Eddy turned twenty-one. This scheme would pay far better, he supposed, than his railway shares had done. On the way home he showed Bellew the "shining silver-fish" inside a milkweed pod: "He had a reverential sympathy for everything that was nature. . . . He was exceedingly respectful to all the weeds and insects: nothing was insignificant to him."[6]

In September, Sanborn lay on the grass in the yard reading Tennyson's *Maud* when Channing came outside. Sanborn proposed sailing on Walden. "We went to the village, then to the house where the boat key and oars were, and so on to the pond through the woods. Mr. C talked of Wilkinson, Henry James, and Swedenborg, advising me to read them. He did not like 'Leaves of Grass'—thought it not original. 'Mr. Emerson would praise it for six weeks and then forget it—that was his fashion.' . . . When we got to the pond we first bathed, and I taking the boat key in my teeth, swam out to the boat, unlocked it, and paddled it to the landing place, where we embarked." Sanborn loved boating, either in "Thoreau's green boat or my own clumsy one, which soon gave place to a light skiff, good either for the rivers or for Walden, where it finally went to decay."[7]

That month of September saw the opening of Sleepy Hollow Cemetery in Concord. Like Walden Woods, the scenic locale had long been a favorite retreat of Emerson and his circle—indeed of many townsfolk—and now it had been transformed into a place of utility and beauty combined, with winding paths, plantings, and an artificial pond. Thoreau was hired to survey the grounds in August as the place was laid out. Sleepy Hollow re-created in miniature the delights of Cambridge's Mount Auburn and other cemeteries that had sprung up in cities since the 1830s, an import from the English Picturesque. That such a small town as Concord would have a garden cemetery demonstrates the deep permeation of the idea into contemporary culture and the ambition of the local citizenry. Alcott joined Emerson and his children Ellen and Edward for a walk the following May, "Emerson pointing out to me his family lot still rudely staked on the pine-grove mound, and I for the first time breathing aloud my wish of reclining sometime near my friend's memories . . . thus laid in calm repose not far from that of my benefactor and the friend of whatsoever is imperishable in me." Emerson had chosen the most picturesque spot in the grounds, atop a narrow glacial ridge. Thirty-two years later, Alcott's wish to lie near him would come true. By that time, "Authors' Ridge" was a must-see tourist landmark and Sleepy Hollow an inspiring counterpart to Walden Pond in the gazetteer of American literary shrines.[8]

Thoreau's health was always precarious, in spite of his vigorous lifestyle. For five months in mid-1855 he lay ill and partly confined, struck with the consumption that would eventually kill him. Trips to Walden were few. On June 8 he walked to Goose Pond by Thrush Alley, seeking bird nests. He found a jay's at Ingraham Cellar and a catbird's on Goose Pond peninsula. Four days later, he and Channing examined grasses on Heywood's Peak. Thoreau carried his thermometer to Walden in July: sand between the shimmering rails in Deep Cut was 103 degrees, pondwater eighty. He sat and talked with Therien by the railroad at Walden in October, the woodcutter telling a tall tale about a perch that once leapt into a man's throat. Thoreau took Emerson's path over to Pine Hill for chestnuts. As he came home by the road, the sun reflected brilliantly in the pond.

January 1856 marked the frigid start of the snowiest season since 1803. On the first Thoreau walked to Walden by the railroad, pleased that the snowplow had gone through and track repairers had shoveled paths by the sides of the rails from the depot to the pond.

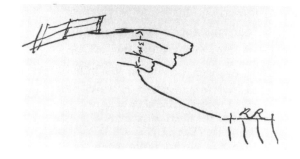

Snowdrift at Deep Cut, January 1856. Thoreau could stand beneath it. His sketch shows double railroad tracks and a fence. Journal (1906) 8:92.

Two intrepid fishermen stood on the ice. In spite of the cold—minus six at eight A.M.—he was back the next day studying rabbit tracks. On the railroad embankment at Heywood's Meadow he scared up snow buntings. On the fourth, fishermen's lines lay frozen in the ice in three coves and the snow was stained with tobacco juice. Huge drifts lined Deep Cut on the sixth, and Thoreau sketched five-foot projections.

Thoreau's strategy as a naturalist was to cultivate a "broad margin to my life" in order to maintain constant flexibility in case some transient phenomenon presented itself and needed investigating. This winter's phenomenon was deep snow. He launched a study of its depth, using a four-foot stick marked in inches, driving it down at every tenth step. He slogged through fields west of the railroad causeway, then crossed the tracks to Stow's Meadow and Trillium Woods, a northerly extension of Walden Woods. Closer to Walden, he traversed the sproutland between the railroad and Andromeda Ponds, then went through Wheeler's Squirrel Wood. He took thirty-four measurements on Walden itself. Heavy snows continued, so that on the twenty-second, Walden Road was filled with snow to the top of the stone wall on the northeast side. He visited Brister's Spring before approaching the pond through the beanfield, observing where fishermen had come away dragging a string of pickerel. "Near my old residence" he discovered squirrel tracks under the pitch pines.[9]

No sooner was the snow off the ground than a locomotive spark set fire to Emerson's woodlot the first week of April. A few days later Walden still had eight inches of dark-green ice. Emerson mistook this for open water, but when Thoreau walked around the pond he found only ice, which trembled when he threw a stone. In May he walked to the pond in the rain, through Deep Cut Woods, the old shanty stubble field, and Hubbard's woodpath by his Pond Hole. Later he walked to Pine Hill and the beech grove via the spring at Heywood's Meadow. He visited Saw Mill Brook with Emerson, who had owned this scenic woodlot with its little waterfall since at least 1850, one of those purchases made to safeguard Concord's places of natural beauty during years of rampant cutting and "improvement." Thoreau impressed his older friend with his knowledge of plants: "He waded into the water. . . . Having found his flowers, he drew out of his breast pocket his diary & read the names of all the plants that should bloom on this day. . . . He thinks he could tell by the flowers what day of the month it is, within two days." When grosbeaks appeared, "he brought [them] nearer with his spy glass, his pockets are full of twine &c also. . . . There came Henry with music-book under his arm, to press flowers in; with telescope in his pocket, to see the birds, & microscope to count stamens; with a diary, jackknife, & twine, in stout shoes, & strong grey trowsers, ready to brave the shrub oaks & smilax, & to climb the tree for a hawk's nest. His strong legs when he wades were no insignificant part of his armour." This is the liveliest picture we have of the naturalist at work. He must have been similarly attired in June as he strolled out Walden Road to Heywood's Peak and Emerson's Cliff, coming home by the railroad.[10]

The publication of *Walden* brought Thoreau a coterie of admirers, foremost among them Daniel Ricketson of New Bedford, Massachusetts, who arrived for a visit. Thoreau was cautious toward this eager follower, a diminutive hypochondriac, but eventually he realized he had found a friend. On a ninety-nine-degree day, Ricketson and Thoreau walked to Walden, "bathed, and crossed the pond . . . in a boat we found upon the shore. Saw the Scarlet Tanager by the aid of Thoreau's glass." Nighthawks skimmed the water. This forms the first record of a post-*Walden* touristic pilgrimage, start of a new era in public appreciation of the place. For Ricketson—as for many since—it must have been thrilling to encounter the scenes that had come alive in the pages of Thoreau's book. The next day he and Henry returned with Emerson and his children, discussing birds and flowers.[11]

Thoreau prefered to visit Walden alone, however, as when he took a solitary swim by Wyman Meadow on July 15: "When I

Back to the woods. Daniel Ricketson sketch, ca. 1855, © New Bedford Whaling Museum.

crossed the entrance to the pond meadow on a stick, a pout ran ashore. . . . Going in to bathe, I caught a pout on the bottom within a couple of rods of the shore. . . . Then, wading into the shallow entrance of the meadow, I saw a school of a thousand little pouts." On the twenty-third, "Saw at Hydropeltis Meadow a small bullfrog in the act of swallowing a young . . . *Rana palustris* [frog]. . . . I wondered what satisfaction it could be to the larger to have that cold slimy fellow, entire, lying head to tail within him! I sprang to make him disgorge, but it was too late to save him. Though I tossed the bullfrog out of the water, the *palustris* was entombed." Wyman Meadow was emerging, as nearby Heywood's Peak once had done, as a prime locale for the study of natural history.

In August, Thoreau studied flowers blooming on Heywood's Peak, perhaps plucking *Desmodium nudiflorum* and *Lespedeza violacea* for his herbarium—specimens that survive today at Harvard, intact down to the minutest veins, dry and faded bits of the great world of nature Thoreau reveled in 150 years ago. Later he and Emerson again walked to Saw Mill Brook, Emerson saying, "I was taken with the aspects of the forest, & thought . . . a walk in the woods [is] one of the secrets for dodging old age." A later outing found Thoreau at Emerson's burned hillside by the railroad and on the west side of Emerson's Cliff. Blackberries were plentiful at the Lincoln bound hollow beyond. Ricketson visited Thoreau again in September and recorded, "Walked with him to Walden Pond and saw the location of the Shanty where he lived alone some two years, bathed and visited the cliff and several other hills to obtain views of the pond and surrounding country."[12]

Thoreau stepped gingerly toward the middle of the pond, one October day, until ice was transparent and he seemed to be "walking on water by faith." His familiar Walden owl hooted in Wheeler's Wood. When Ricketson arrived at Christmas, Thoreau escorted him out the railroad to his Walden house site, where snow lay deep on the boughs of the pines just behind. They crossed the pond and steered toward Baker Farm, where the ancient house in *Walden* was sadly going to ruin. Of Ricketson's latest visit Thoreau would grumble, "I thrive best on solitude." Having a companion "dissipates my days, and often it takes me another week to get over it." Notwithstanding his love of privacy, he joined fishermen around a smoky fire at sundown one December day "hoping to hear a fish story."

Thoreau's spring 1857 journal suggests once more the variety of experiences to be had at Walden. He recorded ice thaw on the pond, as he had its freezing the previous fall. Heywood's Peak was bare of snow by mid-March, when he flushed some partridges there. In April, Willard Farrar and George Heywood hired him to survey lots east of the pond. As Thoreau stood by his compass at the town bound on Walden Road and waited for Farrar to get in position, he saw a black mink glide stealthily across the road. Later he searched for bounds on Farrar's land at Goose Pond. In May, he and Emerson walked to Goose Pond and Saw Mill Brook, the older man declaring, "We will make a book on walking, 'tis certain, & have easy lessons for beginners. 'Walking in ten Lessons.'" Thoreau—always the dean of walkers in Emerson's circle—later circumambulated Walden.[13]

At month's end he and Emerson walked to Flint's Pond. The latter's remarks suggest that an afternoon in the forest remained suspect to townsmen steeped in the work ethic, still requiring apology: "I do not count the hours I spend in the woods, though I forget my affairs there & my books. And, when there, I wander hither & thither; any bird, any plant, any spring, detains me. I do not hurry homewards for I think all affairs may be postponed to this walking.

And it is for this idleness that all my businesses exist." In a poem he
wrote,

> Yet do not I invite
> The wrinkled shopman to my sounding woods,
> Nor bid the unwilling senator
> Ask votes of thrushes in the solitudes.

Enthusiastic about peripatetic, Emerson proposed *"Concord Walks
for a* [writing] *subject"* and strolled regularly with his friends. On an
outing to Saw Mill Brook, he was impressed with Thoreau's burgeoning knowledge of plants. Jacob Bigelow's *Florula Bostoniensis*
(third edition, 1840) went along: "Henry praises Bigelow's descriptions of plants; but knows sixty plants not recorded in his Edition."[14]

After buying the Walden woodlot in 1845, Emerson had walked
the line with Charles Bartlett, from the ridgetop near the Lincoln
line, up the pinnacle, and down a stone wall near a run, not far from
Heywood's Meadow. They came back by "my path along the edge
of the meadow and so up to the wood path which runs parallel to
the bank of Walden, until we came to the stone wall . . .
wherethrough my lot is entered by anyone coming from the Lincoln
road." (Some of these landmarks can still be found today.) About
1850, Bartlett uncovered an old deed that seemed to give him some
of the land Emerson held, and this marked the beginning of serious
trouble.[15]

Actually, relations between the men had already deteriorated
over the matter of some grass Bartlett had cut in Emerson's meadow
in town without first paying Thoreau, as agreed. One day as Waldo
and Henry walked to the woodlot to mark the Lincoln line, they
stopped at Bartlett's to invite him along and resolve the boundary
question. But Thoreau spoiled this by huffily insisting Bartlett pay
him in advance for these surveying services, having failed to do so
for the grass. Bartlett refused to participate. Eventually Bartlett sued
Emerson for the land. In June 1857, Thoreau and Emerson stood in
the woodlot and read aloud Bartlett's deed; they could not tell from
the title description which of the two valleys near Heywood's
Meadow was the one in question. Days later a jury reached a hung

verdict in the matter of Emerson versus Bartlett. It would not be the last court case involving Walden.

For Thoreau, summer brought trips to Cape Cod and Maine. Emerson and Channing walked to Walden in July, the latter remarking on how "very curious" the pond's frogs were and—perhaps they were crossing the beanfield—quipping that farming was "an attempt to outwit God with a hoe." Another time they visited Flint's Pond "in its summer glory, the chestnuts in flower, two fishermen in a boat, thundertops in the sky, and the whole picture a study of all the secrets of landscape." Channing said ecstatically to his friend, "You must come here to see it! It can never be imagined. You must come here to see it, or you have lost your day." For "the greatest scholars," said Emerson, the woods were a fitting retreat at such a season: "Inspired we must forget our books, / To see the landscape's royal looks." A visitor to Concord in autumn recalled how Emerson "drove me from his own house, through the woods, on a bright October afternoon . . . to see Walden Pond, and the ruins, or rather the site of Thoreau's cabin," which points to how Emerson would play a key role in promoting the house site as a place of touristic pilgrimage.[16]

Thoreau had walked around Walden in September with Channing. They sauntered through Deep Cut and went bathing despite the cold water, then passed along the "low path" under "Bartlett's" Cliff and came out into the Walden Road southeast of the pond, where they ate haw fruits. In October, Thoreau climbed Fair Haven Cliffs for an autumn view, then made his way to the high east bank by five P.M. and studied reflections of north-shore shrubs. With her bright belt of color shimmering in the water, Walden was "like an Indian maiden." Thoreau's enthusiastic responses every fall recalled Wordsworth's in the District of the Lakes, the latter writing, "It is in autumn that . . . the atmosphere seems refined, and the sky rendered more crystalline" and that one could observe "clouds gliding in the depths of the lake, or the traveller passing along, an inverted image." Thoreau too relished such inversions.[17]

By late November, following up on his recent surveying in Walden Woods, Thoreau had been hired to measure additional lots for the heirs of John Richardson and other landowners. He walked the Richardson Lot near Goose Pond as three hundred geese soared overhead in an hour. In December he surveyed the frozen Little Goose Pond as well as the Richardson property on Walden. Daniel Ricketson came for another visit and accompanied his friend "on a survey of woodland near Walden Pond." Thoreau measured Goose Pond on Christmas Day for George Heywood, showing its isthmus, island, and half-submerged rock just as they appear today, more than a century having done nothing to alter the outlines of this kettle-hole pond shore.[18]

After all this labor, Thoreau felt almost too familiar with Walden Woods: "I now see it mapped in my mind's eye . . . as so many men's wood-lots; and am aware when I walk there that I am at a given moment passing from such a one's wood-lot to such another's. I fear this particular dry knowledge may affect my imagination and fancy, that it will not be easy to see so much wildness and native vigor there as formerly. No thicket will seem so unexplored now that I know that a stake and stones may be found in it. In these respects those Maine woods differed essentially from ours. There you are never reminded that the wilderness which you are treading is, after all, some villager's familiar wood-lot from which his ancestors have sledded their fuel for generations." It is a revealing passage, suggesting to how great an extent his experiences in Walden Woods were ones of "imagination and fancy," which he could only summon up in conscious compensation for the utilitarian reality of cut-over clearings. "What a history this Concord wilderness which I affect so much may have had!"

Traversing his Walden woodlot one January afternoon in 1858, Emerson came upon Thoreau, who talked of the expansion of willow buds. A few days later Thoreau walked across the frozen lake and visited Goose Pond. "The north side of Walden is a warm walk in sunny weather," perfect for anyone "sick and despairing." Ten-inch-thick Walden ice thundered with "shivering, splintery, screeching cracks," not the usual "dumping of frogs" sound—a good description of the strange noises familiar to modern visitors—but rather "like the cracking of crockery." The surface was heaved a foot high over the bar at Hubbard's Pond Hole, and in February pushed up onto the shore "near where my house was." At Goose Pond he

"Scalloped southern shore," owned by Emerson. Gleason, January 29, 1918. Railroad Bay in foreground. Little Cove is the indentation just in front of the conical hill at center. To the left of that hill is Deep Cove. The east end of the pond lies in the distance. Courtesy Concord Free Public Library.

cut some big blueberry bushes on the water's edge to count their growth rings (42). For Thoreau this was about the start, in Walden Woods at least, of a new method of understanding the history of the forests, ring counts.[19]

By early April he had made three trips to survey the boundaries of Emerson's woodlot, for payment of three dollars; the southwest edge of its pinnacle had been cut that winter. He visited a recently discovered yew bush at Fair Haven Hill and then climbed Emerson's Cliff. When he and Waldo explored Walden, the latter recorded "the creeper *vesey vesey vesey*," a black-and-white warbler. Emerson enjoyed birds and loved to recite to his children,

> In Walden wood the chickadee
> Runs round the pine & maple tree,
> Intent on insect slaughter:
> O tufted entomologist!
> Devour as many as you list,
> Then drink in Walden Water.[20]

In early May, Wyman Meadow was crowded with fishermen catching pout. "We are, as usual at this season, interested especially in flowers and birds," Ellen Emerson wrote, "and Mr. Thoreau is in great demand." Bees hummed in the apple trees at Bush; dog-tooth violets, jack-in-the-pulpit, bellwort, hepaticas, and bloodroots flourished in Edith's wild garden, so that "Mr. Thoreau was moved to admiration"; and Eddy stalked the grounds for his growing collection of birds' eggs and eventually undertook an overnight foray to the woods. Ellen told a correspondent,

> Eddy and Storrow and Johnny Jackson and Ned Bartlett camped out in Walden Woods. They went on Friday and stuck their stakes into the ground and in the afternoon James carried down in the hayrigging the boat, the provisions, the buffaloes blankets and comforters as well as the young heroes themselves supplied with two coarse sheets, a sail, and sewing materials. They spent the afternoon in sewing their sheets into a tent and pitching it. . . . They made a fire gypsy-fashion and cooked their supper and then went out in the boat. When it was entirely dark and still they fired the gun and enjoyed the tremendous crashes of Echo, and then they holloed and had a wonderfully clear return, and so they continued till the moon rose which was full, and that was most beautiful. About mid-night they retired to their tent, but were out on the pond again before sun-rise. At twelve Edie and I went up and dined with them in state. After dinner we went out on the pond, Edie and I to row and Storrow to steer, the other boys remaining behind in pursuit of eggs, but they only found a fine large snake which they saved for Storrow. The going on the pond was delightful. Such a color! Such big waves that rocked the boat boisterously. Next time you come here I hope our boat will be up there and we can go out.

That May saw, too, another early example of a stranger making his way to Walden on a Thoreauvian pilgrimage. In 1953 a first edition of *Walden* was discovered with the inscription, "Walden Pond— 24 May, 1858 1.50 PM—I gratefully acknowledge the Divine Mercy that has permitted me to see for myself this pure gem of the lonely woods. Written, with my heels in the water, (to make sure of my position) at Thoreau's dipping place; a fresh SW wind blowing and the mimic waves sometimes wetting my pants—Wm Pedder." There is no way of knowing how common such visits were or whether Thoreau ever happened to encounter one of these devotees, but he might have, having succeeded in adding Walden Pond to Concord's classic sites just as the railroad allowed tourism to grow in this suburban town, a pleasant day trip west of Boston.[21]

Thoreau took Emerson into the woods in May and June for wildflowers and birds, as he had done for the past few years, showing off his burgeoning knowledge of natural history. Emerson was struck by his generosity: "My naturalist has perfect magnanimity, he has no secrets, he will show you where his rare plants are, where the rare birds breed, carry you to the heron's haunt, or even to his most prized botanical swamp, confiding, I doubt not, that you can never find it again, yet willing to take his risks." Demonstrating his usual zeal even in a morass, in June Thoreau waded into Wyman Meadow and investigated holes in the bottom. "I thrust my arm into the first. . . . I felt something soft, like a gelatinous mass of spawn, but, feeling a little further, felt the horns of a pout. I deliberately took hold of her by the head and lifted her out of the hole and the water, having run my arm in two thirds of its length. . . . Pouts, then, make their nests in shallow mud-holes or bays, in masses of weedy mud. . . . Where do the Walden pouts breed when they have not access to this meadow?"[22]

During the summer he went bathing in the cove by the railroad; examined water plants in the "bath-place by pond in R. W. E.'s wood," at Little Cove; and botanized at Heywood's Peak and Pout's Nest (another of his names for Wyman's Meadow). In September the naturalist picked highbush blueberries on the south shore of the pond. A few days later he paddled around Walden "for a rarity," studying water plants and fish and gathering more blueberries. He found Pout's Nest to be "a frog's paradise." A dark, cloudy November afternoon saw him on Heywood's Peak with his telescope, watching a school of fish dimple the water.

Thoreau walked onto frozen Pout's Nest and examined fish. One kind measured a little over an inch long, patterned with up-and-down bars: "Are they not a new species?" The next day he caught more of the "exceedingly pretty" fish and brought them home, floating them in a bowl to study them. They were *Pomotis obesus* bream, a type first collected by the scientist Baird at Hingham and Holliston and described by Charles Girard to the Boston Society of Natural History in April 1854. In December, Thoreau went back to Walden with hatchet and rake, bringing home more: "How wild it makes the pond and the township to find a new fish in it! America renews her youth here."

Walks in December brought Thoreau again to Walden, as he sought to record how the pond froze. He enjoyed sitting under pitch pines on the rocky shoreline at the northeast corner, his "fireside," and listening to the ice crack. With the pond so low, he could stroll all around on the stony shore: "What a grand place for a promenade!" He was not alone in frequenting the pond this month. Ellen Emerson described an outing her family took:

> As we crossed the pasture the town clock struck four. We remarked that it was the first time for many a month that the Emerson family had started in season. . . . We got into the Road all locking step and treading in Father's tracks in profound silence. . . . By and by we began to talk and have a good time. . . . When we came to Dandelion Pool all the tall pines in Fairyland, black, and hanging heavy with ice and snow, and as still as everything else, made us stop and see. Then we turned into the unbroken Walden Path . . . and we went into the woods. . . . We went down to the Cove and saw Walden and stood to hear how still it was, and the owl made that noise on the other side of the pond, just once, very faint and far away.[23]

Later Ellen was invited skating. She walked alone to "the path to Walden," where she met children riding home in a sleigh; "On coming in sight of Goose Pond I saw both boys and girls a goodly company," skating and sledding. On another occasion, "a very large deputation went to Goose Pond. . . . The ice was perfect, the cold moderate, the sky cloudless, blue overhead, pink all round, and the sun just setting, the moon high and O so big." Walden retained its fascination for Concord's youngest residents.[24]

On a January afternoon in 1859, Thoreau trudged to Walden in a driving snowstorm, a day that "nobody is in the street, or thinks of

going out far," except for the indefatigable saunterer. Wind whipped across the railroad causeway, and snow hung thick in the pitch pines of Thrush Alley. Another day, Eddy Emerson wished Ellen "could go up to Walden Woods with him, for yesterday when he was coasting down the Walden Road with the boys, the trees were covered wonderfully thick with ice and this morning the sun would be on them. In the afternoon Mother read to us from Foregleams of Immortality, then we went to our hymns and went to walk at quarter past four. We walked up the Walden Road, and the trees were as Eddy had said."[25]

February brought the death of Thoreau's father, the man who had first introduced him to Walden almost forty years before. Putting affairs in order busied Henry, but by the end of March he was back at the pond, studying shelducks with his glass until they were startled by a locomotive whistle. With Channing in April he sought out Little Goose Pond, wind-rippled. A "frosty hollow" afforded shelter on the raw day: "We lie at length on the dry sedge, nourishing spring thoughts, looking for insects, and counting the rings on old stumps."

Emerson described his own typical activities: "I hide in a library, read books, or write them, & skulk in the woods." He brought his family to Walden on Sunday afternoons, his wife Lidian coming occasionally. Ellen recalled that the earliest walks of her childhood went to Walden and back, but as the children grew older they went around the pond and to the Cliffs or Baker Farm. In January 1859, "At four we went to walk and coursed up the Walden Road and Wood path to our Cove" and crossed the ice to Sandy Beach, mostly sliding. In March, "We went to Walden high hill to see the sunset." Eddy tried to throw a stone into the pond; Ellen lay on the ground; Emerson sat on a stump, looking off to blue Wachusett. "We came down the hill and crossed to Mr. Tuttle's." Sometimes friends would go along, Sanborn once writing to Edith (to whom he would propose, disastrously, in 1861), "Rememberest when that eve in May / When from the woodland walk / Thy father took the homeward way / And I with him in talk." He often walked the circuit of Walden with Emerson, out Walden Road to the wood path that led to the forest ledge of Emerson's Cliff; then home by the railroad tracks and through the pine grove above Thoreau's house site. Thirty years later, grown Edward would fondly recall outings with his father to "the large tract on the farther shore running up to a rocky pinnacle from which he could look down on the Pond itself, and on the other side to the Lincoln woods and farms, Nobscot blue in the South away beyond Fairhaven and the river gleaming in the afternoon sun."[26]

Eddy caught amphibians in Walden Woods for his aquarium, which he proudly showed to Thoreau. Two salamanders came from Ripple Lake (Little Goose Pond) and the pool just north of Thoreau's house site; Thoreau had once unearthed some of these creatures while hoeing on his nearby beanfield. Such childhood encounters with Henry were memorable to Eddy, who would, years later, write a memoir that helped humanize the "stoic" public image of the famous naturalist. The boy learned about nature from his father, too; in May, Emerson wrote, blackburnian and other warblers "make much of the beauty & interest of the woods." But his experiences with Thoreau were especially unforgettable, as when the older man taught village boys "at still midnight, in the middle of Walden, to strike the boat with an oar,—and, in another minute, the hills around awoke, cried out, one after another with incredible and startling *crash*."[27]

On a walk to Flint's Pond in May 1857, Thoreau had suggested, as Emerson wrote, "planting acres of barren land by running a furrow every four feet across the field, with a plough, & following it with a planter, supplied with pine seed. . . . He proposes to plant my Wyman lot so." From April 19 to 21, 1859, Thoreau was paid $7.50 to plant the place with pines, but by more conventional methods, setting out young trees by hand, as he had done many times at Emerson's house in town. Two men with a horse and cart assisted him in placing four hundred trees fifteen feet apart diamondwise on two acres. On the twenty-ninth he set one hundred little larches imported by Emerson's friend Samuel Gray Ward from England, somewhat ironic for the reader of Wordsworth, as it was larch plantations that that writer so strenuously deplored as supplanting the native forests of the District of the Lakes. Emerson had his eye on eventual profit for his children, but the enterprise also suited the sentiment he had voiced in the 1840s,

> Go out into Nature and plant trees
> That when the southwind blows
> You shall not be warm in your own limbs
> But in ten thousand limbs & ten million leaves
> Of your blossoming trees of orchard & forest.[28]

Thoreau took time out from planting trees to look for salamanders at Ripple Lake, where he watched the wind on the water, typical of spring: "There is a season for everything. . . . There is a time to watch the ripples on Ripple Lake, to look for arrowheads, to study the rocks and lichens, a time to walk on sandy deserts; and the observer of nature must improve these seasons as much as the farmer his. . . . We must not be governed by rigid rules, as by the almanac, but let the season rule us. . . . Now or never! You must live in the present, launch yourself on every wave, find your eternity in each moment." Emerson too wrote in Wordsworth-like praise of Ripple Lake: "The rippling of the pond under a gusty south wind gives the like delight to the eye, as the fitful play of the same wind on the Aeolian harp to the ear." Sanborn would fondly recall the transcendentalist experience of watching these ripples with Emerson, standing on "the headland whence they are best seen in breezy autumn days," the pond "lying as it does but a little aside from a favorite walk of his and Thoreau's and Channing's." Emerson celebrated the ripples in verse:

> He loved to watch & wake
> When the wing of the southwind whipt the lake
> And the glassy surface in ripples brake
> . . . like the thrill of Aeolian strings
> On which the sudden wind-god rings.[29]

The Emerson family were regulars at Walden in August. Ellen wrote, "Eddy and Ned went out to sail Storrow's boat on Walden, and coming home concluded to camp out, so they and George Staples and Johnny started off at sunset, Edward carrying Adirondack Blanket, eggs pork and frying-pan." On other days, "Father and I went out rowing on Walden"; "This morning he disappeared, and about 10 o'clock he walked back across the yard. . . . He said he had walked to Walden and back." Boston artist Hammatt Billings was dispatched to Concord by Emerson's publisher "to sketch some scenes that might fitly adorn an edition of my poems," Waldo wrote. "I proudly accompanied Mr. B. to several of our best woods and waters, and he looked and looked and departed. Of course my hopes were high of being thus married to Nature in my books, but some time afterward learned that the artist could find nothing that would fit anything in the Poetry which of course humbled me to a degree."[30]

A fish hawk soared over Walden on October 1 as Thoreau looked down from Pine Hill. He was back at that hill two weeks later with H. G. O. Blake, his disciple and friend from Worcester, sitting on a rock and watching the wind on blue water, with brilliantly colored trees around. The wide view across Walden Woods, now extensively cut-over, may have inspired a plea in his journal, similar to ideas expressed when Heywood cleared his land in 1851–52, that every town should have a primitive forest set aside, of five hundred to a thousand acres, where no cutting would be allowed. This park would exist entirely for instruction and recreation. "All Walden Wood might have been preserved for our park forever, with Walden in its midst," Thoreau declared in what has become one of his most famous sayings, eventually marshalled to support the cause of late-twentieth-century land conservation near the pond.

Again, Thoreau in after years expressed little sentimentality for the Walden house site, which by 1860 had been growing up in trees for thirteen summers; but Ricketson wrote a poem, "Walden," that looked ahead prophetically to the cult that would eventually develop around the place: "To Walden pond th' ingenuous youth shall hie, / And mark the spot where stood the hermitage." In March, Thoreau studied ice in Wyman Meadow, meeting on the way home Indians camped on Brister's Hill, where they sought black ash trees for basketmaking. He also stood on the northern shore, then climbed Heywood's Peak to see wind gusting across newly melted water.[31]

Thoreau. Here at thirty-nine, June 18, 1856. Benjamin D. Maxham daguerreotype. From the Thoreau Society Archives. Courtesy of the Thoreau Society, Lincoln, Mass., and the Thoreau Institute at Walden Woods.

One Sunday, Lidian Emerson and her children were returning from church in Wayland, driving the carryall with the horse Dolly. Passing Walden, they saw their woodlot was on fire, smoke pouring skywards. Eddy, fifteen, sprinted to town to sound the alarm. As church bells tolled, he ran back to fight the fire. Those bells would ring again on April 3, when United States marshals tried to arrest Sanborn at his home across the street from the Thoreaus' for his role in the recent John Brown affair. A mob drove the marshals out of town—"Civil Disobedience" sprung fully to life. On April 30, Thoreau returned to Walden and, for payment of $1.50 from Emerson, surveyed the fire-damaged area, drawing a map showing the "edge of the burning," which extended from the railroad along the Walden shore almost to the head of Deep Bay. Fifty-six acres had been swept by flames. In June he revisited, probably to study how the woods were healing. He examined pine pollen drifted across the pond and washed up in the southerly bays. Then he climbed Emerson's Cliff for the view.[32]

That same month he turned his attention to Boiling Spring. He had measured its temperature in March 1846, when Walden Pond was forty-two degrees and Boiling Spring was forty-five, in spite of its being decidedly "the coldest [water] that I know of in summer." Now he again tried the temperatures of various local springs and the pond: the air temperature north of their Main Street house at 2:15 P.M. was eighty-three degrees; the Thoreaus' well after pumping was forty-nine; Boiling Spring, as fifteen years earlier, was forty-five; Brister's Spring, forty-nine; Walden Pond, seventy-one. This was prelude to his carrying the thermometer to eighteen local springs in all. He found that Boiling Spring was the very coldest—perhaps, he thought, because it bursts out higher up a hillside than any other.

A freak lightning strike splintered telegraph posts at Walden Pond in July and triggered an explosion in the operating office at the depot. That month Thoreau waded into Walden's warm, soft sand and measured the water temperature. From a boat he lowered his thermometer to sixty feet (seventy-four degrees). Bullfrogs eyed him from the stony shore. Days later he walked over Emerson's woodlot between railroad and pond, the section lately burned and cut over. It was hot, and he swam on the side of Deep Cove. He measured Walden's temperature again in August, lowering a stoppered bottle of water one hundred feet, leaving it there half an hour, then raising it to take a measure (fifty-three degrees). Walden itself seemed a huge, cold spring. He repeated the experiment one evening as the sun fell below a shelf of clouds and illuminated the east end in a burst of light.

Cousins visited the Emersons, Ellen writing, "After tea Haven and Charles and I went out to row by moonlight on Walden. There was no sign of moon when we reached the shore, but before Charles had bailed the boat a cloud moved on and disclosed her just high enough and shining clear yellow in a light-blue sky, surrounded with dove-colored clouds edged with moonlight, and on the other side a clear straw-colored sunset with little dove-colored clouds and black pines against it. Then all sorts of wonderful lights in the woods, from the moon on one side, the West on the other, and from all reflected in the Pond below. . . . When we reached home the boys came in and sat awhile. Mr Thoreau was here."[33]

Nathaniel Hawthorne and family were back in Concord after years abroad, and the children struck up friendships with the younger Alcotts and Emersons who lived nearby. Abby May Alcott, twenty, cornered Julian Hawthorne, fourteen, along the sidewalk and demanded, "Do you like ladies and gentlemen bathing together?" Julian would remember his astonishment: "For a moment I stared dumb-stricken, visions of orgiastic revels rioting through my brain. I was fresh from England, where naked improprieties were unthinkable." But it was just Abby's way of proposing a swimming party at Walden. Ned Bartlett and other boys came along, and there were six girls: probably Una and Rose Hawthorne, Louisa and Abby Alcott, and Edith and Ellen Emerson. At the cove near the site of Thoreau's house they wrapped cotton sheets around four pines where the girls could slip on throat-to-ankle, dark-blue flannel suits. The boys, nearly beside themselves with anticipation for what the girls would look like, retreated behind bushes to don jerseys and pantaloons. It was worth the wait to see Louisa's raven hair tumbling to her hips (the other girls wore caps), and everyone's feet slipperless except the fastidious Edith. "Don't you think it's much nicer with ladies and gentlemen together?" Abby asked Julian as they paddled into the cove. "At that moment the punt careened violently to starboard: Louisa, swimming at large, had grabbed the gunwale to clamber in. The little craft had been built to hold one, or two at a pinch; it capsized amid shouts, screams and splashings; and I, diving deep beneath the glassy, cool, translucent water, escaped replying to Abbie's inquiry. But I afterward learned that Louisa Alcott, in her struggle to get aboard, had split one leg of her flannel pantaloons from hip to knee, revealing a flash of living white amid the blue! One could but be thankful it hadn't happened to Edith Emerson. Louisa simply laughed in the most impenitent way: Ellen Emerson, always self-controlled, drew her within the protection of the tent for repairs."[34]

Concord Farmers Club met in April 1860 at the home of Charles L. Heywood, who delivered "An Essay on Forest Trees." Heywood and family owned the woodlot at the east end of Walden, and he was a "railroad man," so he understood the economics of cutting. In the discussion that followed, Jacob B. Farmer noted, "We find a succession of different trees grow on the same soil. If we cut off pines, oaks will come up. If we cut off oaks, pines will follow on some soils." Thoreau heard about this discussion and at the Cattle Show in September gave a lecture that summarized his accumulated knowledge on "The Succession of Forest Trees." In October he published it in the *New-York Weekly Tribune*, laying the groundwork for his modern reputation as one of the most innovative nineteenth-century thinkers on the subject of forest ecology.[35]

Thoreau launched a study of succession in Walden Woods, looking for oak seedlings in Warren's Wood east of Deep Cut. Chestnut seedlings there surprised him, as no nut-bearing trees were left standing within a half-mile. He credited the squirrels. He studied the pitch pine woods at Thrush Alley on his way to Laurel Glen. On the twentieth he examined old stumps, starting in low Trillium Woods and moving into Warren's Wood and Ebby Hubbard's Wood, the latter consisting of oaks and pines a century old (Emerson had once encouraged a friend to buy the place and advertise it as "the stateliest park in Massachusetts"). The pine wood east of Hubbard's Close by Brister's Spring he remembered as pasture in 1830. On the twenty-second he examined the plants that first invade bare sand in the Deep Cut: sweet-fern, birches, willows, aspens, white and pitch pines, all still to be found there today. He further studied succession in Stow's big woods by the cut, in the pitch pine wood that he recalled from boyhood as Wheeler's Blackberry Field, and in the former Pigeon Place east of there. He counted ninety-four rings in a pine stump in Hubbard's owl wood by the railroad. Heywood's Meadow, dammed for a century, showed no sign of being invaded by trees: "You may say that it takes a geological change to make a wood-lot there." The hillside west of the southwestern lobe of Heywood's Meadow, cut by Hosmer about 1849, was dotted with stumps showing 109 rings.[36]

He then crossed the tracks to Emerson's woodlot, half of it burned and cut the previous spring, before going over to the southeast part of the lot beyond Deep Cove. He was not merely counting rings, but additionally identifying what species of trees the stumps had been, in order to understand what forest types succeed others. Later he returned, finding that the burned part near the pond had been cut in 1830–35 and again in 1860. Stumps on Heywood's lot at the southeast corner, between Emerson's bound and the east-shore "swimming-place," showed up to 135 rings, and pitch pines cut at the "fireside" on the northeast corner had sprouted in 1775. Another day he walked out the railroad to examine stumps on the south side. He started in the part of Emerson's woodlot logged the previous spring, which he found had also been cut about 1830–32. At day's end he dug up little English cherry trees from the top of Heywood's Peak to transplant in town.

In November he climbed Emerson's Cliff for another study of stumps new and old. Each area, he learned, had been cut twice: oaks on the southwest or railroad side, near the hilltop, 1823 and 1858; chestnuts lower down toward the railroad, 1820 and 1848; oaks on the pond end of the hilltop where piles of stones suggested a former pasture, 1822 and 1859. Evidently if you cut a mixed wood of oak and pine with no pine seedlings, an exclusively oak woodlot results. This instructive outing was Thoreau's last visit to Walden before contracting his final illness. Again, this work was epochal, for, as Edward O. Wilson has written, his "ideas on succession and other properties of living communities pointed straight toward the modern science of ecology." Similarly, late-twentieth-century conservationists fighting to preserve the area would argue, "Walden Woods stands as the specific site where Thoreau developed his theory of forest succession, a cornerstone of modern ecological science."[37]

Thoreau's studies are a reminder that the few areas within Walden Woods that had once been agricultural were rapidly growing back to forest by 1860—for, as we have seen, several of the places he investigated had been open within his memory. This same theme was broached at the Concord Farmers Club meeting earlier that year, as members stated vociferously that there were "more acres growing to wood in Concord than there were eighty years ago," "twice as many acres grown or growing to wood than there were forty years ago," "more [wooded] acres growing by one fourth than ten years ago." One's "grandfather had seen forty acres of rye growing where there are now board logs." The shift from wood fires to coal stoves was a primary factor, they agreed. Indeed, Emerson himself had replaced open fireplaces with stoves a few years before. Cutting in the woods was heavy, and Thoreau kept a list of "Woodlots when cut" that shows the great toll of the ax, especially after 1850. But, contrary to the popular notion that Walden Woods was in severe decline during Thoreau's day, the number of acres growing sapling trees was actually increasing as scattered fields reverted to forest.[38]

As Thoreau counted rings near Boiling Spring, a white cedar railroad sleeper along the tracks caught his eye. A painstaking count of its rings yielded the astonishing total of 250, thirty-one to an inch—the oldest and slowest-growing tree he had yet studied—a tree older, he noted, than the settlement at Jamestown, Virginia. He continued to count rings around Concord in the days that followed, including at Bear Garden and Fair Haven Hills. The last of these expeditions came on December 3, to Nawshawtuct Hill (not Fair Haven, as sometimes said). Following this outing he came down with bronchitis. Channing attributed it to staying out too long in the damp cold peering at stumps—debatable, as no man had endured more raw days without ill effect than Thoreau had. Whatever the cause, his chronic tuberculosis set in, and he virtually abandoned his journal until Christmastime, although he did record Channing's report that Walden froze over on the sixteenth.

Confined much of the winter, Thoreau listened with interest to accounts of the pond, including the fact that no one skated that season, owing to heavy snow cover. On March 11, 1861, Channing brought word that the pond was open, earlier than Thoreau had ever known. "I have not been able to go to the pond the past winter," he noted without pathos in his journal after Channing had gone. A snowstorm hit in early April, closing Walden Road for a full day, to Channing's surprise: "I went to take my usual walk by the Poorhouse . . . and behold the road was not broke out," except for the track of a cow that a young man was driving to Lincoln. The snow was over the walls on both sides of the road, and Channing floundered to Walden through adjacent fields.[39]

When summer 1861 came, Walden was doubtless busy again. In July the Fifth Massachusetts Regiment returned to Concord by train, passing the pond as they entered town, "and from windows and platforms and baggage-cars black faces in soldiers caps were peeping out" to catch a glimpse of familiar scenery after the Bull Run debacle. Channing received a "sketcher's book" in August and made drawings of the cove and other places around the pond. About this time he found a wild pigeon's nest near the shore, with a single egg—a remarkable discovery. One September afternoon at five, Ellen Emerson and friends "started for Walden. It was near enough sunset to be very beautiful. I rowed them round and round while Edith spoke Kilmeny twice, Dorcas once and the White Island twice. Oh it was a beautiful time. The Pond was glass, the sky had every variety of soft little clouds in it, the coves already looked dark." "This morning Haven on Grace and I on Dolly took a morning ride," she wrote of another outing. "We went up the Cliff hill and trotted round the Stump field, and crossed to Walden, the woods all dripping and sprinkling us pretty thoroughly."[40]

A trip by railroad to Minnesota had failed to bolster Thoreau's health. He was still able to go for walks, however, in early September, when Ricketson visited. On the second they strolled from the Thoreau house to the Concord battleground. The next day they visited Mr. Davis's antiquarian collection, germ of today's Concord Museum. On the fourth, they walked to Walden via Emerson's, bathing before sauntering over to Edmund Hosmer's at day's end. When Ricketson said good-bye to Thoreau at the depot, he "seemed improving."[41]

He was not. In what proved to be a bittersweet final phase of a lifetime's exploration of the Concord landscape, Thoreau later that month went for long rides every other day in a wagon loaned by Judge E. Rockwood Hoar, whose dog rode along. Thoreau's sister Sophia went too and reported being taken daily "to some of his familiar haunts, far away in the thick woods or by the ponds, all very new and delightful to me." This must have been emotional. She would later recall with feeling "my last day spent [at Walden] with Henry. . . . While I sat sketching, Henry gathered grapes from a vine, dropping its fruit into the green waters which gently laved its roots." Perhaps he recalled those long-ago boyhood days when the shoreline was still thickly wooded and how "in some of its coves grape vines had run over the trees & formed bowers under which a boat could pass."[42]

Of the few walks that Thoreau mentions in that year of his last decline, 1861, the final was as far as the railroad causeway in November. Then came cold weather, pleurisy, his confinement—nature and Walden a memory now as he looked wanly from his bed to the blowing snow outside the windows. He suffered terribly all winter, although he never grumbled. His lungs were failing, a torment to him day and night; Channing looked back with horror on that "year's campaign of sleepless affliction." When he did doze, he experienced nightmares, "such as that dream he had of being a railroad cut, where they were digging through and laying down the rails,—the place being in his lungs." His bed was brought to the front parlor. As he lay dying, friends tried to cheer him with reports on what was happening outdoors, but he seemed to have lost interest. Only once, Channing recalled, did Thoreau speak to him of nature. Staring at the icy window he whispered, "I cannot see on the outside at all. We thought ourselves great philosophers in those wet days, when we used to go out and sit down by the wall-sides."[43]

"I leave the railroad at Walden Crossing and follow the path to Spanish Brook." The railroad embankment through Heywood's Meadow (to the left) was a favorite route of Thoreau's in Walden Woods. Looking southeast. Photograph by the author, 2001.

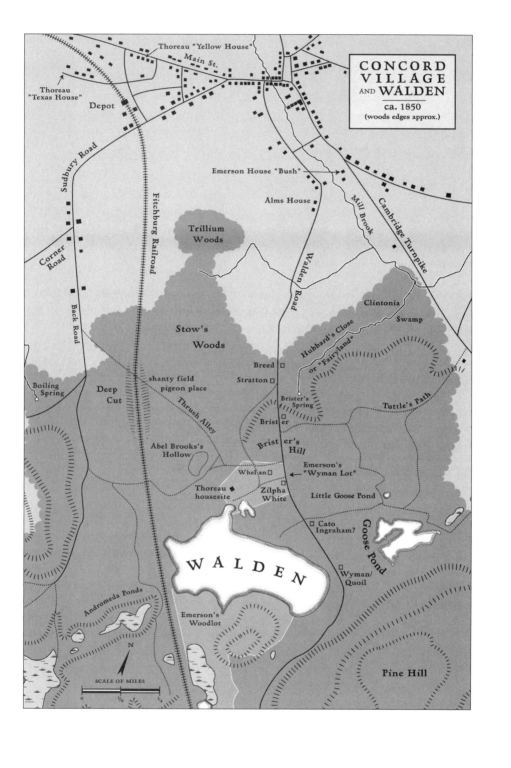

CONCORD
VILLAGE
AND WALDEN
ca. 1850
(woods edges approx.)

Thoreau "Yellow House"
Main St.
Thoreau "Texas House"
Depot
Sudbury Road
Corner Road
Fitchburg Railroad
Back Road
Boiling Spring
Deep Cut
Thrush Alley
Abel Brooks's Hollow
shanty field pigeon place
Stow's Woods
Trillium Woods
Emerson House "Bush"
Alms House
Walden Road
Mill Brook
Cambridge Turnpike
Hubbard's Close or "Fairyland"
Clintonia Swamp
Breed
Stratton
Brister's Spring
Brister
Brister's Hill
Tuttle's Path
Whelan
Thoreau housesite
Zilpha White
Emerson's "Wyman Lot"
Little Goose Pond
Cato Ingraham?
Goose Pond
Wyman/Quoil
Pine Hill
WALDEN
Andromeda Ponds
Emerson's Woodlot
N
SCALE OF MILES
0   1/8   1/4

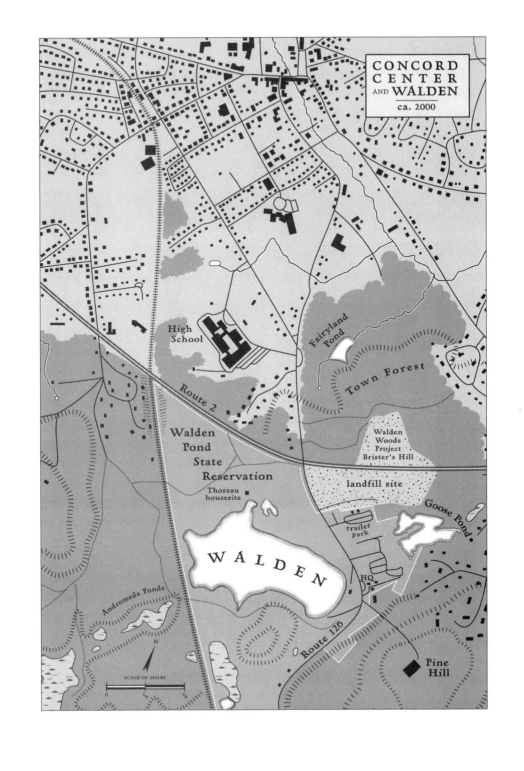

CONCORD
CENTER
AND WALDEN
ca. 2000

High
School

Fairyland
Pond

Town Forest

Route 2

Walden
Pond
State
Reservation

Walden
Woods
Project
Brister's Hill

landfill site

Thoreau
housesite

Goose Pond

trailer
park

WALDEN

HQ

Andromeda Ponds

N

Route 126

Pine
Hill

SCALE OF MILES

0   ½   1

7

❧

All Honest Pilgrims

(1862–1882)

❧

Snow-clad hills around Walden echoed to the laughter of Frank Sanborn's schoolchildren out for a skating party in January 1862. Julian Hawthorne was among them, and his sister Rose skated that day at Goose Pond. Sanborn loved Walden, having published poems to "Walden Woods" and "Walden Water." "Edward and Mary and I rode down to Walden on the sled with James to find some skating," Ellen Emerson wrote on the twenty-ninth, "But finding none went to Goose Pond, which was also covered with snow, so there was nothing for it but to trudge home again." It was a cold spring, snow lying even with the tops of the walls across Walden Road as Emerson slogged to his grove, whistling to the chickadees through his teeth. "Late I found my lukewarm blood / Chilled wading in the snow-choked wood," he would write in "The Titmouse." Walden remained frozen long. Emerson walked across on April 1, 2, 8, and 10: "I fancied it was late in the season to do thus; but Mr. Thoreau told me, this afternoon, that he has known the ice hold to the 18th." Ice was still thick on the seventeenth, when Channing strolled over, but next day Emerson could not quite step onto the surface from "Wyman's cottage landing" at the east end.[1]

These visits to the woods as Thoreau lay dying put Emerson in a reflective mood. He meditated on the value of the forest to him since he first moved to Concord almost thirty years before: "The first care of a man settling in the country should be to open the face of the earth to himself by a little knowledge of nature, or a great deal of knowledge, if he can, of birds, plants, & astronomy, in short, the art of taking a walk. . . . The uses of the woods are many, & some of them for the scholar high & peremptory. When his task . . . requires self-communion & insights: he must leave the house, the streets, & the club, & go to wooded uplands."[2]

Thoreau died on May 6, age forty-four. Louisa May Alcott dropped onto his coffin a wreath of andromeda, one of his favorite swamp plants. Emerson, fifty-nine, delivered a funeral oration (published in August in the *Atlantic Monthly*) that seemed to show their strained relationship and his disappointment that Thoreau had amounted to so little. He borrowed Henry's journals from Sophia Thoreau and spent the summer reading them. His private remarks suggest a deeper sympathy with the man whose direction, after all, he had done much to shape. "He is not long out of mind when I walk, and, as today, row upon the pond. He chose wisely no doubt for himself to be the bachelor of thought & nature." When he spied a loon on Walden he recalled reading in the journal about Thoreau hearing one laugh there. Waldo was eyeing nature through Henry's lens, among the first of a legion of readers who would ultimately do so—an unfolding the scope of which he could hardly have imagined that melancholy summer.[3]

Along with the loss of Thoreau, the Civil War weighed heavily on Emerson's spirits. He welcomed a ragged throng of paroled prisoners, captured at Bull Run, back to Concord in June: "I am sure, that . . . Fairhaven, & Walden Pond, & Nine Acre Corner, & the East Quarter schoolhouse you would have given a month's wages to look upon." Much of the war news was bad, so he sought relief at the pond, refuting those who say "that nature is tedious, & they have had enough of green leaves. Nature & the green leaves are a million fathoms deep." Never, perhaps, had the pond's timelessness and silence seemed more beneficial. When he and Channing boated, they peered down to the bottom where greenish-gray stones lay tumbled and apparently covered with moss or lichen. Channing exclaimed, "There is antiquity. How long they have lain there unchanged!" But nature's balm could not quite push the war from Emerson's mind. On November 1 he found the fall colors in the woods at their height—adding that a wheeling flock of birds reminded him of a troop of cavalry.[4]

Not everyone was gloomy. Concord's young people made happy use of Walden Pond, as Sophia Hawthorne had recorded in her journal that muggy summer. On a "terribly hot" August 4, for example, Una and Rose Hawthorne and Horace Mann bathed there. Four days later, Una, Rose, and Abby Alcott went berrying on the pond. In September, the Rev. Henry Clay Badger and his wife Ada were visiting: "Una and Mr. Badger paddled off in the boat and Ada and I sat on shore and talked." In November, Nathaniel Hawthorne walked to the Concord Bank and then to Walden. These visits were fun, but at the same time memories of Thoreau were palpable. Rose recalled, "Walden woods rustled the name of Thoreau whenever we walked in them." By autumn, admirers were arriving to pay tribute. Unitarian minister Robert Collyer came from the Midwest: "I went in the fall of that year to look at his grave and Walden woods and the pond."[5]

In the rainy year of 1863, at the height of the war—Gettysburg was fought in July—Walden Pond was definitely emerging as a sacred locus identified with the memory of Thoreau. *Walden* was brought back into attention by the legend of his premature, Romantic demise, a theme promoted by his uncommonly articulate family and friends. H. G. O. Blake and Theo Brown visited Walden with Sophia Thoreau; much had changed for them since Blake had sat with Thoreau on the rock on Pine Hill in autumn 1859. Bronson Alcott walked to Walden in September with daughter Abby, seeking tangible connection: "We find the old paths by which I used to visit him from 'Hillside,' but the grounds are much overgrown with shrubbery, and the site of the hermitage is almost obliterated." Channing and Blake may have accompanied Alcott on this sentimental journey, in which nature itself seemed to be erasing the memory of Thoreau from the woods now that his brown, iron-pegged shoes no longer scuffled the trails.[6]

Channing was still reeling from Henry's death, which had made him, Sophia Hawthorne said, "much disordered" with grief. He would prowl the woods and come home muttering bitterly, "I have been trying to find Thoreau." As if to take up the work his companion left behind, he recorded the thawing of Walden ice in April

Ellery Channing.
Rare photograph of
Thoreau's friend, the
strange, mercurial
transcendentalist, ca. 1870s.
Courtesy Concord Free
Public Library.

1863. About this time, Channing penned a biography, published in eight installments in Sanborn's Boston *Commonwealth*, an abortive project that would not see full publication, in book form, for a decade. The biography remains strange and frustrating, maddeningly short on specifics, but it does capture something of the ethereal, erudite, and witty flavor of the conversations that passed between Emerson, Channing, and Thoreau, the "Three Friends" whom the modern environmental movement could regard as a founding triumvirate.[7]

Channing always held a lively interest in the Walden house, where he lived for a time with Henry. It seemed obvious that Thoreau's spirit dwelled most potently at the house site beside the cove. But where was that site, exactly? Bushes had grown tall as the old field reverted to forest. In fall 1863, he and Calvin Greene of Rochester, Michigan, tried "to find the cellar hole, but could not fix it,—but have since. It is in the pathway to the pond. (The place is a bank gently sloping towards the pond,—a hill in some places, but not so marked here.)" Where Thoreau had known a clearing there flourished a "small wood" with "the pond not visible scarcely now." They visited Brister's Spring, where Greene "lay down & took a good, cold drink of water to the memory" of Thoreau, and sought out the Walden house in its new location on the Clark farm. Greene pried off a shingle as a souvenir. The grieving Channing thus found a calling as guide to out-of-town friends who wished to stand on holy ground.[8]

In December 1863, Sophia Thoreau wrote Daniel Ricketson, who had become a valued friend by showing devotion to the dying Henry. She reported walking five or six miles at a stretch, her life now changed following her loss, directed away from the confines of the Yellow House and back to nature, that subject of youthful attention. "I spend much time out of doors, visit Walden very often, and the other day I enticed my good aunt Jennie, who will be 79 years old Christmas day, to accompany me to the pond. It gave her much satisfaction to visit the spot where dear Henry enjoyed so much. I walked up to the north part of the town lately, where his little house now stands, and ate my dinner under its roof, with the mice for company." These places, long unregarded, now came to light as stations on the sacred rounds of the Thoreauvian devotee.[9]

Emerson continued to visit Walden, but at sixty he thought of himself as old. In July, when he rode in a jostling wagon to White Pond with Channing and chatted with picnickers at the cove there, it was his first visit in ten years. As he took the train to Boston in early October, he glimpsed Walden Woods from the window, a familiar whirling blur of water and forest, and "how they reproached him!" for not walking as much as formerly. He would wonder sadly, "And where shall I find the record of my brag of places, favorite spots in the woods & on the river, whither I once went with security for a poetic mood?" But nature continued to offer its pleasures, as often as time and energy allowed; one fall he saw herons and ducks on Goose Pond and, on a fine afternoon, counted fifty geese on Walden. And he said in a poem, "The Miracle,"

> I have trod this path a hundred times
> With idle footsteps, crooning rhymes,
> I know each nest & web-worms tent;
> The fox-hole which the woodchucks rent
> Maple & oak, the old 'divan,'
> Self-planted twice like the banian;
> I know not why I came again
> Unless to learn it ten times ten.

Mill Dam. Thoreau contrasted Concord's busy mercantile district to sylvan Walden Woods. This 1860s view looks west on Main Street toward the dark-shuttered Brick House, home to the Thoreau family in 1823–26. Courtesy Concord Free Public Library.

> To read the sense the woods impart,
> You must bring the throbbing heart . . .
> Wandering yester-morn the brake,
> I reached the margin of the lake,
> And oh! the wonder of the power,
> The deeper secret of the hour!—
> Nature, the supplement of Man,
> His hidden sense interpret can.[10]

That year, 1864, was the third in a row to see a reprinting of *Walden,* its circulation an essential step in spreading Thoreau's fame. Concord itself was more prominent, too, riding the triumph of the Abolitionist cause and confidence in the Union victory, to which its citizens had made such important patriotic and intellectual contributions. Its stature was obvious in the parade of dignitaries at Hawthorne's burial in Sleepy Hollow in May. Longfellow, Lowell, Holmes, Agassiz, Alcott, Emerson, Norton, and Dwight looked on as his body was interred on the glacial ridgetop near the Emerson plot. Within a few years—probably in 1866, certainly by 1868—

Thoreau's body (along with his family) was moved from the town burial ground to lie near the Hawthorne and Alcott plots, and Authors' Ridge was born, another destination for the literary pilgrim. To dig the moldering coffins from the ground and cart them to Sleepy Hollow suggests the deliberateness with which Sophia Thoreau managed the memory of her beloved brother and sought to place him prominently before the public eye.[11]

She was joined in this effort by Thoreau's friends. Blake and Brown made another pilgrimage in September 1864. Channing said, "I showed them Henry's house which still stands [at the Clark farm] and they bought maps of the town on which they wrote many of the localities." This first attempt at plotting the geography of Thoreau Country formed the germ of the map that Blake would publish twenty years later with excerpts from the journals. It would have helped pilgrims such as the group young Concordian George Bartlett encountered when he "took a wagon full of girls to Walden to go swimming" and "found there a large picnic from Watertown who had come to celebrate Mr. Thoreau's birthday."[12]

"Mr. Reynolds came down and took Sunday walk with us," Ellen Emerson wrote in March 1865, "to the [Sawmill Brook] waterfall, and Flint's Pond." Her father's eulogy, Channing's biographical sketches, and the republished *Walden* had their effect in garnering attention for the late Thoreau. In July, Sophia Thoreau prepared Henry's political papers for publication, and his letters were newly published, Alcott praising their wit, moral tone, insights, and style, which showed "the remarkable gifts of the man and the author. Thoreau is sure of living while New England survives and Nature continues to interest mankind." Sophia and her mother watched the growing phenomenon of Thoreau worship with awe and gratitude, the former writing Ricketson in July, "We were much touched the other day to learn that a party of forty ladies and gentlemen, all strangers, came to Walden to celebrate Henry's birthday. A party of young ladies who went to the pond to bathe accidentally discovered the company. They had spread a table on the spot where his little hut formerly stood." Bronson Alcott wrote of an August visitor, James Spooner from Plymouth, who "talks about Thoreau's letters with enthusiasm. Wishes Thoreau's hermitage, now standing in the north part of the town, replaced at Walden as a memorial of Thoreau. I tell him if nothing better is done I can raise a column on the spot, of rude workmanship—some grotesque shaft cut from the woods in the neighborhood, perhaps, and inscribed with his name." Such a monument would have been kin to the rustic summer houses that Alcott fashioned in the 1840s. Though this idea never bore fruit, a permanent, natural-looking memorial would soon arise.[13]

Ricketson was too grieved at Henry's death to feel his former love for Walden Pond. "I could not have joined the party of forty strangers who lately had a picnic on the spot of Henry's hermitage," he told Sophia Thoreau, the first expression of a commonplace lament that the solitary Thoreauvian was getting pushed aside by noisy crowds. But Walden had always been popular, and Thoreau himself cheerfully welcomed visitors when he lived there, especially "all honest pilgrims, who came out to the woods for freedom's sake, and really left the village behind." These words from *Walden* stand as a timeless invitation to the reader to pay a visit, as thousands soon would do.[14]

For Ricketson and others who had known Thoreau, Walden Pond would always be "sacred to H.'s memory. But the master who held the talismanic wand has gone, or only stands fading in the past, half real, half spiritual, still haunting these endeared abodes of poetry and peace." Thoreau might haunt them, but he could not protect them from the greatest alteration Walden had experienced since the railroad cut through: an elaborate picnic ground on the west shore. "Lake Walden" was the brainchild of Charles L. Heywood, employee of the Fitchburg Railroad who formerly lived in Concord and whose family owned (and cut) extensive acreage around the pond. He recalled the place as exceptionally beautiful and unsurpassably convenient by railcar, the perfect destination for urbanites suffering from heat in crowded Boston. He modeled his plans on Harmony Grove on Farm Pond in Framingham, where a railroad spur brought thousands of summertime picnickers from 1850 to 1875.[15]

Emerson must have had advance warning of the development, for in January he acted as trustee in the purchase of sixteen acres on the Walden shores for his daughter, Edith, and her new husband, John Murray Forbes, who lived in Milton, Massachusetts. This "woodlot," acquired for $30 an acre, comprised the Hubbard land

Boating at Lake Walden. Looking west across Ice Fort Cove to the icehouse, swings, and railroad fence, ca. 1868. From the Thoreau Society Archives. Courtesy of the Thoreau Society, Lincoln, Mass., and the Thoreau Institute at Walden Woods.

southwest of the Wyman Lot, including the little basin Thoreau called Hubbard's Pond Hole. Emerson and Forbes now owned the entire shoreline from Wyman Meadow around to the southeast corner, except for the western edge controlled by the railroad. They expected to enjoy some profit from the timber, but the purchase was, it seems certain, primarily meant to create a buffer between the picnic ground and Wyman Lot. Forest fire was always troublesome, and increased visitors meant greater danger. But ownership of the Hubbard lot did not relieve this problem, especially as 1866 was a year of drought. On March 8 a fire swept across Emerson's property, stopping just short of the beanfield pines.[16]

In late April, Channing walked to Walden with Blake and Brown to see the house site. At the shore a big mud turtle splashed into the water. "The Pond getting very low," he noted. "Crost to the Railroad." In the course of this visit they managed to ignite yet another fire that would burn across the Forbes lot, to Emerson's consternation. In May, Emerson walked to Walden with Ellen, Edward, and the former Brook Farm resident Charles King Newcomb to inspect the damage. Thankfully the conflagration had not reached the Wyman Lot to harm his stand of Thoreauvian pines. These incidents were a fact of life at Walden, the environs of which were, Ellen said in the 1870s, "still wooded—more so than in Thoreau's day, but there have been bad wood-fires lately that have taken off some of the best trees."[17]

With the coming of summer, "Lake Walden" debuted on the hillside at Ice Fort Cove. A visitor wrote approvingly of "the boats on the pond, the walks around it, the bathing-houses on its bank, the foot-ball ground adjacent, the dancing-hall, the swings, the see-saws, the pleasant shaded seats, and the beautiful wild-wood walks." Frenzied clearing of brush and trees made the shore accessible for strollers, at a time when the pond happened to be low. Ellen found many "improvements" (as she wryly called them) during the family's Sunday walk in September: "I discovered that there is a regular broad side walk *all round* the pond, even into the deepest cove, the underbrush and trees nearest to the water having been removed for the purpose, and benches set up every two or three rods. As Edie mournfully remarked, 'it looks more like Frog Pond than Walden,'" referring to the skating oval on Boston Common. Channing was disgusted by the changes, which included "a path made around the edge of the pond, and the whole feeling of the place, as described by Mr. Thoreau, destroyed." Surely "privacy and retirement can never again return to this spot, in the summer, hallowed by the genius of Henry."[18]

As memory of Thoreau grew blurred by the passage of years, the Walden that he had known was being dramatically altered, becoming the fulfillment of what Wordsworth had long before predicted for the District of the Lakes if a projected railway sliced through—hoards of "uneducated persons . . . artisans and labourers, and the humbler classes of shopkeepers" brought on holiday "to the shores of Windermere by the cheapest conveyance." Although Wordsworth had celebrated in his poetry the outlook of the common man, he had afterward turned Tory and argued that the rabble were incapable of appreciating serene, poetical nature and would destroy all. Emerson abhorred Wordsworth's conservative politics but must have shared these sentiments as crowds overtook Walden.[19]

The tenth annual Picnic of the Parker Fraternity, a Unitarian festival, was held at Lake Walden in July. Emerson spoke, doing his part to draw attention to the importance of Henry's experiment—the picnic grounds being put to use as a vehicle, even in their first month of operation, for promulgation of the Thoreau movement. Among these Boston Unitarians, Thoreau was well-known already. An eye-witness said, "I heard one person in this party inquiring the way to the Concord [Battle] Monument. But I heard twenty, at least, asking where they could find Thoreau's house on the margin of Walden, or at least the place where it was; and I suppose a hundred actually made the pilgrimage to this shrine. . . . It is at any rate a curious specimen of the progress of hero-worship." Emerson found himself almost chiding the crowd: "He told, in his peculiar and impressive way, of the enjoyment and improvement to be found in communion with nature. He could speak from experience of the eminent attractiveness of the region around them; but he thought that its advantages were better enjoyed by parties smaller than the present one. Positively small parties were much better, and a party of one was best of all. . . . The good general rule was to be alone with nature in your walks." When they arrived at the Thoreau location, the throng found that "the little house by the pond has long since been pulled down, to the regret of all. Its site is plainly visible. . . . A sapling pine grows right in the hollow, and a few bricks from the chimney still remain," probably swept up as souvenirs.[20]

Lidian Emerson was curious to see the changes at Walden. Ellen wrote in August, "Sunday afternoon, Mother went to walk with us, she actually offered to go, and walked all round the Pond, and to the Railroad spring, and up on the Ledge. She was interested in the Picnic Grounds, and not indignant." In September, as the summer excursion season wound down, Alcott met with Charles Sumner, the Abolitionist politician, who "wishes to spend a day or two in Concord presently. Has been reading Thoreau with curiosity, and would like to visit some of his old haunts in wood and field." Such a response must have been increasingly commonplace in these years—a new or renewed encounter with Thoreau's works, coupled with curiosity to see the real places he described. Alcott's always lofty opinion of his departed friend now soared higher: "Thoreau can take no second place on the roll of heroic fame, nor in literature—he of all his contemporaries writing closest to his time and clinging fastest to the truth of life passing about him [and] nearer than any to nature." This theme he would triumphantly reiterate from the lecture platform during coming years, spreading Thoreau's fame across the northern half of the nation.[21]

Their second summer the Lake Walden picnic grounds grew in popularity, "The Naiad Temple of Honor" from Boston among many groups that spilled from the trains in July. Sophia, still mourning the loss of her brother, told Ricketson sadly, "Since arrangements for picnic parties have been made, the pond seldom enjoys a quiet day during the summer months. Associations have rendered the spot so entirely sacred to me, that the music and dancing, swinging and tilting, seemed like profanity almost. An overwhelming sense of my great loss saddened me, and I felt that only the waters sympathized in my bereavement, for there seemed in all that throng no heart nor eye to appreciate the purity and beauty of Nature. The lover of Walden has, indeed, departed." And yet among the strangers were, at times, a handful of reverent pilgrims. In November she told a correspondent, "If you will come to see us I shall be glad to show you some of my dear brother's haunts. Pilgrims from afar often come to visit them. I was spending a day at 'Walden' lately when a gentleman from the West came to the pond to search for Henry[']s house."[22]

Channing deplored the enlargement of the picnic grounds in spring 1868, when "another bathing-house was made, and an extension clapt to the shanty." Many improvements were added, including a separate bath house for women and "a suspension foot bridge" over the railroad cut. In July, seven hundred Sunday school workers and children from Waltham visited for "swimming, boating and swinging." The grounds were fully reserved every weekday through October 1. "The bath houses resounded with scream and splash," but some "drank in the wondrous beauty of the place, and remembered the strange hermit life" of Thoreau, the circle of admirers quietly growing. That month, Emerson reminded Ellen that a letter in his cabinet drawer entitled them "to the use of the Ladies' Bath, at the Pond," in the picnic grounds; "The pic-nicers do not usually arrive till ten, I think, & depart at 5.15 P.M. & on many days do not come at all."[23]

Thoreau's old Walden house at Clark Farm was demolished in June, a serious blow to those who hoped to rebuild the structure at the pond. Channing visited in 1863 with Calvin Greene, then a year later with Blake and Brown, and again in January 1866. But on June 4, 1868, he discovered that the house was "just pulled down" and in "ruins." In October, Daniel Ricketson's children, Walton and Anna, paid a surprise visit to Channing at his house in town and invited him to Walden. "They walked through the Walden woods, and Walton cut a swamp huckleberry stick for a cane, on which he carved the date," a treasured memento. After tea with Sophia they visited what was left of the "granary" that had been "the decaying cabin of Thoreau." The owners used fragments of Thoreau's house to enlarge and repair buildings on their farm, and these scattered and indistinguishable relics have tantalized generations of Thoreauvians with the promise of pieces of the True Cross. Henry Seidel Canby's landmark 1939 biography of Thoreau mentioned that the house "ended by transubstantiation into the fabric of a garage," which he identified as standing "on the estate of Mrs. Willieta Dodge at Concord," formerly the Clark farm. He forgot to add that Mrs. Dodge had later moved from her country estate into Concord village, where she was subsequently plagued by tourists stealing siding off her carport.[24]

The Emerson family found that autumn was a good time to visit Walden, after the crowds had diminished. "Father & I went to the Ledge," Ellen Emerson reported in September 1868, then "to the pic-nic grounds where we found Edward in a boat, and we rowed all over the Pond." A month later, "Edith & I went to church but the boys went to Walden and Goose Ponds, had a bath, traversed all the woods round about and came home with great spoil of red leaves."[25]

A startling expression of the growing adulation of Thoreau was the arrival of Edmond Stuart Hotham in November, trumpeted by the *New York Times* as "Thoreau's Successor—The New Hermit at Walden Pond." Hotham was tall, reserved, and homely looking. A sailor for ten years and throughout the Civil War—Emerson called him "an eccentric naval officer"—he worked as a clerk in a business on Broadway, studying divinity in preparation for stateside missionary work. Thoreau had stressed that *Walden* was "addressed to poor students," of which Hotham was the embodiment, and the $28.12^1/$_2$ Walden house was meant as an example for "the student who wishes for a shelter." Hotham obeyed.[26]

His comments to reporters who interviewed him at Walden suggest his reasons for moving there. He was no mere copyist of Thoreau, Sanborn stressing that "the two men are so wholly unlike in their aims and motives." Hotham's health was poor; he came

"Indented with deep bays." Fires from locomotive sparks kept the western shore bare. Seventy-five years after Thoreau moved to Walden, no path was yet evident along here. Looking north to his cove. Gleason, "Ice breaking up along northwest shore of Walden," March 31, 1920, courtesy Concord Free Public Library.

from a family of invalids and had recently been deathly ill. Outdoor living promised to help, and, indeed, he gained twenty pounds. He was broke and needed to escape the expenses of city life, and he guessed that he could live all winter in the woods for $50, the cost of a month in the city. He wished "to do some work which he could not do elsewhere," studying divinity "alone with Nature." He referred often and cryptically to "this work" without clarification. If he were studying, it is odd that visitors saw "hardly half a dozen books." He intended to model an alternative way of life for poor young men in the city. Nature enthralled him, especially birds—he even emphasized the similarity of his diet to "chicken-feed"—and juncos ate from his hand. A lady in town who sent bread to supplement his austere diet was doubtless offended to hear that he fed the birds with it. At Walden he sought "absolute communion with nature."[27]

Why Walden Pond? He thought he would attract less attention there than anywhere else, since Thoreau had accustomed people to such an enterprise—a serious miscalculation. Hotham impressed those who met him with his quiet politeness; he seemed "by no means a fanatic, or dreamer." He was sane enough to show up in Concord, a place he had never before set foot in, and convince its most famous citizen to let him live Thoreau-like on his Wyman Lot. Lidian Emerson even invited him for mince pie at Christmas.

Hotham's Walden "house," as he called it, was humble. He clawed a hole into the hillside with his hands, "right on a kind of promontory" one hundred yards "in front" of Thoreau's house site. Channing remarked that "Hotham's cabin was by the pond on the bank, in front of Henry's," likely on what Herbert Gleason later called "Thoreau's Point," adjacent to Hubbard's Pond Hole. The house, half the size of Thoreau's, was finished in a week. Earth was heaped against the siding. He spent $13.93, out-economizing Henry: three hundred shingles, $3.00; twenty pounds of nails, $1.30; old boards and a door with a window in it, $6.51; another old window, 50¢; a hired man to finish the place, Hotham's hands being blistered and a snowstorm blowing in, $2.62.[28]

Rumor had it that the scraps from which he built his house came from Thoreau's house at Walden. Sanborn stated that Hotham received them from an Irishman who had acquired remains of the Parkman House where the Thoreaus had lived for a while in town, eventually to be replaced by the Concord Library; but another account, perhaps in wishful thinking, claimed that Thoreau's Walden house "was removed whole, and after having made the pilgrimage of the town, has got back to the pond" with Hotham. It is true that the Walden house at Clark Farm had been dismantled just a few months earlier. Inside his house, Hotham slept on a sailor's mattress on a camp bed, under blankets. He owned a stove, a rude table, two shelves, two stools, a waffle iron, and "a few queerly shaped utensils made from tree branches." Vines decorated the outside of the dwelling, and a "tasty arrangement of forest branches" hung within. He was a vegetarian who ate only two meals a day at a cost of twelve cents. His diet at first consisted of pond water and Graham biscuit, but once he was settled in, he diversified to corn for mush, wheat for bread, dried apples, and lard for frying the mush into "a species of corn-waffle" with no seasoning, his only luxury. He ground corn and wheat in the big coffee mill that had stood for

Coming ashore. Boating at Lake Walden, ca. 1875. From Hudson, "Concord Books," 30, University of Delaware Library.

years in the kitchen of the Middlesex House hotel in Concord—at which Thoreau might have smiled, having always scorned that establishment as a hive of detestable luxury.

Hotham went out of his way to deny that Thoreau had influenced him, by pointing out that he had tried such an experiment before, when very young. But there is no question that he intended deliberately to respond to Thoreau. Indeed his intention seems to have been to outdo Henry; he bragged that he was "much simpler" in diet and household affairs and was living in a dwelling only half the size and less expensive. Thoreau said, "I had not lived there a week before my feet wore a path from my door to the pond-side," but Hotham sniffed that "old hunters tell me [it] was here long before he came and went."[29]

A visitor in April 1869 exclaimed, "A day in Concord can be made a red-letter day in one's life. . . . We walked down to Walden Pond and about the woods that surround it which formed THOREAU'S world of wonder and delight, and was HAWTHORNE'S favorite strolling place, and is EMERSON'S now." That summer, a tourist eyed the pond from woods to the north and heard "the sound of merry voices abroad on its surface, in the numerous gala boats, gay with flags and ribbons," some headed for the "brief strip of sandy beach" at the east end. In a letter to the *Springfield Republican*, Louisa May Alcott joked that a new Concord hotel ought to cater to the abundant "pilgrims to this modern Mecca," serving them Walden water and Thoreauvian wild apples, lodging them on "beds made of Thoreau's pine boughs," and providing telescopes "to watch the soarings of the Oversoul," lassos to "catch untamed hermits"—Hotham—and "photographs of the faces divine which have conferred immortality upon one of the dullest little towns in Massachusetts."[30]

Word was out about Hotham. Alfred Munroe encountered him in mid-April; visiting Concord with a friend, "We made for the pond and woods the first thing" to find the hermit, whom the local innkeeper said "was starving himself on chicken's dough" by the lakeshore. They at last found his house, "not unlike a pile of dirt with a hole in its front . . . built of rough boards and boughs, faced by a small glass window and a glass and wood door, and banked up nearly to the top, except in front, with earth and turf." They screwed up their courage to address him: "'Good morning, Sir. Can you tell us where Mr. Thoreau's hut was situated?'" "'A few paces to the rear of mine'" came the curt reply. They told him that a newspaper had printed a paragraph about him. "'Yes, some jackass saw fit to publish me.'" Already Hotham had been pestered by the *New-York Daily Tribune*, by Sanborn for the *Republican*, and others and was in no mood to be bothered. He complained that "one of the finest groups of trees in the woods" had just been felled; "some avaricious farmer cut them down, thinking that they would be better in tubs and pails to soak old women's feet in."[31]

Hotham and Channing took tea with the Alcotts on April 11. Alcott found the hermit sensible, serious, and unassuming. He visited Walden on the twenty-eighth with an English freethinker, a Mr. Leech, who had known Hotham through philosophical channels in New York. Alcott remarked that Hotham seemed to lack "any light of idealism." Another newspaper article appeared on May 1, in which Hotham announced his eagerness to leave Walden, "so frequent grow the visitors at every point." The hermit fled at last on the eighteenth. He kept in touch with the Emersons, thanking them at Christmas 1871 for their former "house-rent and hospitality" and describing an Adirondack winter: "I have made good the threat . . . that, if I again 'camped,' for sanitary or other purposes, it would be where reporters cease from troubling. I enjoyed a strangely beautiful winter [and] even as I prophesied at the earth-cabin at 'the pond,' my inconsequent name escaped the noble rage of fourpenny tattlers. It was a daily luxury, to live unmolestedly in my own surroundings." He was preaching to a Swedenborgian society in Erie, Pennsylvania, but "ill health threatens a brief career," and thereafter this intriguing Thoreauvian disappears from record.[32]

Hotham's experiences at Walden Pond blended pleasure and disappointment. From *Walden* he expected wild nature, but fire and woodcutters had ravaged the forests. He anticipated isolation but was harassed by visitors coming down busy paths to the picnic grounds and by reporters seeking a story. "As no gossip concerning this immortal town seems to be considered too trivial for the public ear," one wrote, it was not inappropriate to broadcast to tourists the fact that "the new Hermit will grind his meal at noon, precisely." A single generation had passed since Thoreau's tenure at the pond, yet the place was nearly ruined for solitude.[33]

The Thoreauvian hermit was gone, but other disciples continued to come. A. M. Sampson "visited Walden Pond one fine day during the latter part of September 1869. I was alone & wandered along the shore from the place nearest the railroad to the place, as near as I could calculate, where T's house stood, judging from the map in 'Walden.' I climbed a chestnut tree & gathered some nuts." The next year, Emerson drew a map of Walden Woods's historical sites for a visiting reporter. Henry James, twenty-eight, dined at Bush in July 1870 along with English friends, one of whom, Ellen reported, "burst forth in praise of the size, the freedom, the magnificence of America, the gorgeousness of our wild-flowers," especially mountain laurel, pink azalea, and violets. "Harry was charmed with Concord and promised himself that he would come soon & tramp it all over from boundary to boundary."[34]

Emerson had spoken again to the Parker Fraternity at Walden in summer 1869, and April 1870 found him "taking his walk in Walden woods." But the activity on the pond had done much to spoil the place for him, and he wrote his son-in-law Forbes that he was prepared to sell his holdings for $100 an acre if Forbes sold his, too. But, he added, "I am willing to let my land lie, in spite of the Fitchburg R. R. so long as it continues to give me 40 cords of wood every winter." Tourists still wanted to see Walden for themselves, as "they generally inquire for Thoreau's cabin." Among them was thirty-five-year-old humorist Bret Harte, whom Emerson accompanied in October 1871. "They walked by Walden Pond, Harte like all

Westerners growing a little scornful of 'life in the woods' when he found the woods so close to civilization that one could be called in to dinner upon any occasion." In November, Ellen wrote, "Father & I walk to the Pond and see another sunset. I assure him that violet haze & yellow & pink lights are wasted on blackish & brown Walden woods, that they can only be seen to advantage on the palaces of Beacon St. & the new land & reflected in the back-bay. Nevertheless a lemon-coloured half-moon coursing peacefully through Walden's deep-green water was very pretty." Concord resident Simon Brown had walked to Walden on August 20, where 160 tents were set up for a Spiritualist Convention. A crowd gathered under the "Great Roof" and on seats that climbed the hillsides. People drank and smoked but remained orderly. The shores of Walden sheltered the most outrageous kinds of freethinking: "The preaching was shocking. The idea seemed to be that we must not believe anything that we have not seen or heard ourselves."[35]

Spiritualism was a contemporary phenomenon. One night in March 1848, a farm family in western New York had heard rapping sounds that seemed uncannily capable of responding to questions. One of the daughters, Margaret Fox, thirteen, identified the rapper as a Mr. Split-foot, and he would only make the noises when she or sister Katherine, twelve, were present. From these "Rochester Rappings" sprang the Spiritualist movement embraced by millions, a new religion that promised communication with the dead. The Fox sisters toured widely and helped popularize the movement, which flourished until, in 1888, they revealed the rappings to have been a childish hoax meant to spook their parents, achieved by tapping their feet or popping a toe joint. During the heyday, Spiritualist picnics were popular outside major cities, drawing huge crowds, many people attending just for fresh air and exercise. Boston was an early center, with Walden Pond a perfect location for the festive gatherings.

William Dean Howells described a visit to a Spiritualist meeting "in the grove by Walden Pond." Most participants were country folk out "for a day in the woods beside the pretty lake. Their horses were tied to the young pines and oaks; they sat in their buggies and carryalls, which were pushed into cool and breezy spots. . . . Scraps of newspaper that had wrapped lunches blew about the grounds; at one place a man had swung a hammock, and lay in it reading, in his shirt-sleeves; on the pond was a fleet of gay rowboats, which, however, the railroad company would not allow to be hired on Sunday." The floating bathhouses were likewise closed. The meeting convened in "the auditorium in a hollow of the hills beyond the railroad track," under a music stand.[36]

"In the afternoon Father, J[im], & I walked to Walden," Ellen Emerson wrote at six P.M. on July 23, 1872. That night, Bush caught fire and suffered serious damage before the collapse of its slate roof helped extinguish the flames. The letters of condolence that poured in stressed that it was "a historic homestead" that ought to be restored. Emerson and Ellen toured Europe while repairs were undertaken. The same year, Wilson Flagg called attention to Walden in his book, *The Woods and By-Ways of New England*, providing a good measure of how the reputation of the place was steadily growing, ten years after Thoreau's death: "Every student of nature or admirer of poetry . . . should make a visit to Walden Pond" and "seek the spot" where Thoreau lived. But he lamented "the present desecration of that hallowed spot by making it the ground for picnics,— assemblages of people who go there, not for the observation of nature, but for ice-creams and soda-water. . . . A simple excavation now marks the place where stood Thoreau's hut. It is in an open space between two sections of Walden woods. No remnants of the house are to be discovered on the spot. Not a stone marks the place. . . . It has not yet been desecrated by a monument. . . . Young trees of the forest have grown up from its cellar."[37]

That monument, desecration or no, now arrived: the cairn of loose-heaped stones at Thoreau's house site. A quasi-sacred aura hangs about it, owing partly to the fact that the idea, as Herbert Gleason said, "originated with Bronson Alcott, the Concord philosopher, whose axe Thoreau borrowed when he began the construction of his hut, and whom he afterwards described as 'the man of most faith of any alive.'" Alcott was eager to memorialize Thoreau, whom he recalled with reverence and affection as a young man even as he himself inexorably grew old. Opportunity arose in June 1872, when he stopped by Emerson's and invited the visiting Mary Newbury Adams of Dubuque to stroll to Walden with him for the Unitarian picnic. Her daughter later recalled, "She was of course delighted to

Pilgrims at the cairn, 1870s. A sign reads, "Site of Thoreau's Hut." Courtesy Kenneth W. Cameron.

go and when they reached the spot where Thoreau's little house used to stand, mother said it was a pity there was nothing to mark the place, so strangers might know it. 'Well,' said Mr. Alcott, 'a cut stone would hardly be appropriate, would it, for Thoreau?' She suggested building a cairn and then let everyone who loved Thoreau add a stone and said she was going to start it right then. She got a stone and with a little improvised ceremony laid it down in her own name. Then Mr. Alcott got one for himself and one for Mrs. Alcott."[38]

Alcott wrote his own account: "I accompany Mrs. Adams to the Unitarian Picnic at Walden Pond. See several of the young preachers, who express sympathy with the growing Idealism, and the hope of a spiritual Church. Mrs. Adams suggests that visitors to Walden shall bring a stone for Thoreau's monument and begins the pile by laying stones on the site of his hermitage, which I point out to her. The tribute thus rendered to our friend may, as the years pass, become a pile to his memory. The rude stones were a monument more fitting than the costliest carving of the artist. Henry's fame is sure to brighten with years, and this spot be visited by admiring readers of his works."[39]

Unitarian picnickers added stones as well, as did Emerson the next day. The cairn filled a need for a focal point for the Thoreau votaries, adjacent to the picnic ground. The notion of placing rather than taking a memento was an inversion of the usual tourist habit, although there was always some of the latter, too. Sophia Thoreau had remarked that "men and women have come from afar in summer and in winter, to gather a blossom or dried leaf as a memento from the site of the hut. . . . It is really pathetic the way in which regard for [Thoreau's] memory has been manifested," and there is the occasional record of a pilgrim removing a stone from the cairn in lieu of leaving one. In recent years, two clueless visitors were overheard in conversation, "Oh, it's all right to take a stone. That's why they pile them up there—for tourists to take."[40]

Thoreau's cairn derives from a tradition of boulder-stone memorials in Scotland, Wales, and the Lake District. Contemporaries understood these to be "the common monuments which the ancient Britons, like the Northern races generally, erected in honour of their great men." An eighteenth-century traveler in the Hebrides wrote, "These piles may be justly supposed to have been proportional in size to the rank of the person, or to his popularity: the people of a whole district assembled and show their respect to the deceased, and by an active honouring of his memory soon accumulated heaps equal to those that astonish us at this time. But these honours were not merely those of the day; as long as the memory of the deceased existed, not a passenger went by without adding a stone to the heap." "The hero's cairn is erected," Thoreau says in *A Week*, and Alcott too knew such lore. Moreover, cairns found a specialized use in Concord, Thoreau had once reported: "The old select men tell me that before the present split stones were set up in 1829, the bounds were marked by a heap of stones, and it was customary for each select man to add a stone to the heap."[41]

Alcott took Ricketson to Walden in August, and the latter was moved to write a poem, "Thoreau's Cairn": "But in the after years let others come, / As we now come, and reverently place / A monumental stone unto his name." He urged protection of pond and cove: "Then ever-sacred may this spot remain / To nature and her worshippers sincere . . . / O! may not sacrilegious hands disturb /

These haunts." But disturbance was inevitable and impending, and the biggest crowds were yet to arrive.[42]

Thoreau: The Poet-Naturalist, Channing's long-delayed biography, appeared in August 1873. He organized parts as a series of walks to Walden and elsewhere, quoting from the journals of Emerson and Thoreau without identifying the speaker. Channing's language tended toward high Victorian lushness—"the charming Septembrian sunflood." But he did try to let Thoreau do much of the talking, and the book offered the public enticing snippets of the journals, so many, in fact, that Sophia was outraged at his unauthorized appropriations. That same month, Alcott and Mrs. Adams, founders of the cairn, continued to chat about spreading their philosophical visions to larger audiences, an effort that proceeded in tandem with memorializing Thoreau. Alcott wished to establish a "university" or "Concord Academy," an outgrowth of his lecture tours as the "Pilgrim Philosopher," although Adams cautioned that many disciples likely "cannot bodily go to Concord, Mass."[43]

Pilgrims who did make the trek dug for artifacts at Thoreau's hermitage. During this summer a group arrived "determined to find the traces of the hermit home" as souvenirs. They uncovered "pieces of brick and the white dust of mortar, as if a chimney had crumbled just here. This is it, the hermit's cellar, the site of Thoreau's forest home." The Emersons continued to come regularly, Ellen writing in September, "In the afternoon we had a good Sunday afternoon walk, Cousin Sarah went too. . . . To the Cove, of course."[44]

The decade between the publication of Channing's biography and the death of Emerson was to mark the second phase of Thoreau-worship and memorialization. Living recollection increasingly yielded to reminiscence and creative reinterpretation. As Concord developed as a tourist destination, the picnic grounds continued to attract crowds even as Thoreau's cairn, and his reputation, continued to grow rapidly. Concord was growing, too, as evinced by the town library, opened in October 1873, which aimed at dazzling the literary pilgrim as much as serving the needs of locals. The Concord Alcove housed "nearly all the printed works of Concord authors from the time of the settlement . . . to the present." Still today the library functions as a temple to transcendentalism, with

Concord Library.
Stereoview, 1875, courtesy
Concord Free Public
Library.

Thoreau's personal library on display in locked cases and his bust peering out along with those of the other authors. Emerson warranted a life-size statue, enthroned, by Daniel Chester French, in front of which which Henry's published journal resides in a pulpit-like glass case, its pages reverently turned daily.[45]

Alcott attended a town meeting in April 1874 where "new streets are proposed and named." One that cut from Fitchburg Station (Concord Depot) across fields to Walden Street at the foot of Brister's Hill was to be dubbed "Emerson Street," but Emerson demurred and suggested it be named for Thoreau instead. It would be "a compliment of his townsmen associating him henceforth with the village and his route across the fields, when living, to Walden Pond." This typified Emerson's quiet crusade to keep Thoreau's name in memory and enhance his stature. It occurred to Alcott that day that "[Emerson] and Thoreau have given [Concord] a celebrity abroad that no other town of like population enjoys, its Revolutionary fame being almost eclipsed by their literary renown."[46]

Ellen Emerson wrote in July 1874 that Concord and Lexington organized a Sunday school picnic "together at Walden, beginning at 9.30 and lasting till 6. . . . The day was most beautiful and I showed the various glories of the pond not only to strangers, but to many

Concord people who really had never seen it near enough to know anything about it." The usual pilgrims came, too, Calvin Greene returning from Michigan in August to visit the house site: "I now sit writing up this diary of today.—It's a beautiful place! The book, 'Walden' . . . formed an epoch in my life. The cabin is gone, long since moved away but, thank God, they can't move away this foundation, nor the attendant memories." He knew the topography well: "As I sit here facing the pond . . . I notice on my left a grove of those tall 'arrowy' pines such as T. used for his house 29 years ago, last spring. . . . Left the pond passing out by the *'beanfield.'* The grove of trees that T. subsequently planted it to, looked quite sorry from a heartless fire that had run through there a short time ago."[47]

Sophia Thoreau visited the Alcotts in June from her new home in Maine to discuss the disposition of Henry's papers. After her death, she planned to leave the diaries with Blake as a reliable editor in lieu of either Channing or Sanborn, whom she distrusted. Alcott was sure that "Thoreau's character and genius are to win increasing favor as the years pass, and he is an enduring factor in our literature and life. Witness the interest of my correspondent, Mr. Cook, of London, in his genius and works." Later that month he dined at Sanborn's with editor Charles Dudley Warner. "After dinner we ride to Walden and bathe. It is a luxury to bathe in this classic lake. I had not done so for several years, and last with Emerson. After bathing we contribute severally our stone to Thoreau's cairn. The pyramid is insignificant as yet; but could Thoreau's readers add theirs the pile would rise above the treetops to mark the site of his hermitage. The shrubbery is now grown above the cellar, yet its traces are still visible and the path to the lake bears the marks of frequent footsteps. I recall with pleasure the hours spent within his hut, with the hopes and projects of that romantic period in our literature and social history."[48]

That period had slipped away, but perennially unchanging was Walden's popularity with fishermen. In 1875 the town selectmen stocked Walden and White Ponds with desirable species and banned fishing until the fingerlings matured. Policeman Brown shooed anglers away. To the picnic grounds came the Massachusetts Total Abstinence Society, with "dancing in the dance hall, see-sawing, swinging, and boating" plus "rambles round the margin of the lake."

Centennial of Concord Fight. Looking northwest to the Masonic Hall, home of the lyceum where Thoreau lectured. At far right, behind the Great Elm, stands the boardinghouse owned by Thoreau's aunts—Henry's home in 1835–37 (today's Colonial Inn). Courtesy Concord Free Public Library.

There were Spiritualists camping in forty tents in the South Grove, Union Band Concert, American-Hibernian Picnic (five hundred strong). Mr. McDonald of Concord ran the dining tent on the camp ground. The flood of Bostonians was alarming to some, a visitor reporting, "Some of Concord's 'true lovers' are now seriously afraid that it is losing character, and fast becoming like a city suburb. . . . They are outraged at the idea of picnickers daily reveling in Thoreau's haunts at Walden."[49]

The big event was the centennial celebration of April 19, which Edward Emerson helped organize. Nothing had ever done so much to focus national attention on little Concord. Sixty thousand patriots flooded the streets, and a procession of men only wended through town to the Battle Ground, across the newly rebuilt Old North Bridge and past Daniel Chester French's *Minute Man* statue, unveiled as the crowd surged by. Under a gigantic tent, dignitaries gathered on a platform—President Grant and his cabinet, General Burnside, Emerson, James R. Lowell, George Curtis—and addressed the onlookers, who shivered in a cold wind. They carried on even after the grandstand groaned, popped, then collapsed under the weight of their greatness, at which Grant's political enemies among the crowd shouted, "The platform's a rotten one!"[50]

In summer 1876, piped water gushed from two new iron fountains in Sleepy Hollow, and Concord yards were greener than ever before, with "the clicking music of the lawn mower" heard on June mornings. In the 1850s there had been talk, as Thoreau notes with disgust in *Walden*, of bringing Walden water to the town in a pipe, for villagers "to wash their dishes with!—to earn their Walden by the turning of a cock or drawing of a plug!" In time the larger Flint's Pond, by now usually called Sandy Pond, was tapped instead to supply the growing community, and it was this water that sparkled in Sleepy Hollow. "Lake Walden is resorted to much less than usual this season," it was said, but still various groups came. The Universalist Sunday School of Charlestown brought three hundred in five cars; later came Unitarian Societies of Concord and Bedford. Civil War veterans of the First and Twenty-Fourth Regiments had "a jolly time." The "free love, free platform Spiritualists" were back, with a grand ball at the close. Groups of "colored people" arrived. In August there came the ninth annual Brass Bands Picnic; and the Old Folks Picnic, the first held in the region, featured "ancient sacred music."[51]

Tourists who came during the United States centennial year of 1876 found the cairn marked "Site of Thoreau's Hut." Channing brought Emma Lazarus, author of the poem that appears on the Statue of Liberty, and Ellen Emerson and guests "went out and had a picnic on the Pond." Tourists visiting Authors' Ridge in October would have watched grave diggers at work in the Thoreau plot, readying it for the body of Sophia, brought home to lie beside her beloved Henry. E. J. Loomis, who had walked with Thoreau, happened to be in town the day of the funeral, visiting the ridge with "a well-known writer of Washington," likewise "a great admirer." They were "on a pilgrimage to Concord, for the especial purpose of visiting Walden Pond, and the site of Thoreau's cottage." As they stood on the narrow path between the Hawthorne and Thoreau plots, they were startled to see the small cortege approaching, and they watched as the coffin, strewn with autumn leaves, was lowered into the earth.[52]

The Rev. C. A. Cressy stood reverently beside the house site that year. He had recently discovered Thoreau's *The Maine Woods*, telling his wife, "If that man Thoreau is living in the U. S. I'm going to see him." Upon discovering that he was dead, "I could have lain down upon his grave and wept." Now, digging a little behind the cairn, he uncovered a brick, a precious relic that he would later hold proudly in his hand as he lectured on Thoreau in Connecticut and elsewhere. That same year, in October, ornithologist William Brewster drove after dinner from his summer place in Concord "to Walden Pond and visited Thoreau's abiding place, thence to Fairhaven Cliffs."[53]

"One jaunt took me through the woods about Walden Pond,— region hallowed to tramps for all time," recalled Charles Skinner, author of a book about walking, whose visit must have happened about this time. He found two of these tramps bathing and shaving on the shore. "After losing myself delightedly among the woods, I met Ralph Waldo Emerson, and rode into Boston with him. . . . Doubtless I bored the philosopher, yet no sooner had I said, 'I have just been on a pilgrimage to Thoreau's stamping ground,' than he brightened and beamed in the friendliest way." Emerson "showed from the car window where Thoreau's hut had stood. 'More like an Indian,' said he, speaking of the hermit, 'than a white man. He was free and strange. If he found the sky clear when he got up in the morning he might say, 'This is a good day to go to the White Mountains,' and shut his door and trudge off. . . . He used to come up through the woods and call on us without ceremony, and help himself to any axe or spade or bucket that he found on my premises, and would keep it until he was through with it.' A reminiscent twinkle here." The elderly Emerson saw Wachusett in the west but could not remember its name and "shook his head slowly with a shade of sadness in his look. . . . I could but remark the absorbed yet placid air he wore as he looked through the window at the flying landscape."[54]

The appearance of A. H. Japp's English biography in 1877 signaled Thoreau's growing international popularity and inspired Robert Louis Stevenson to write an unsympathetic essay on Henry as "skulker." Actually, Stevenson liked Thoreau more than he let on;

Japp's book was the only reading he brought on his voyage to America, and having perused it he "began to proselytize for Thoreau among his friends." Bronson Alcott, his wife, and daughter Louisa moved into the old Thoreau Yellow House this year, now that Sophia had died and the place had left the family (Sanborn had occupied it for four years). The summer season at the pond was slow, notwithstanding sixteen picnic parties in three weeks in July and the visit of the West End Section of the Boston Paving Department in August: "Lake Walden picnics few and far between."[55]

In August, John Burroughs visited. Inspired by Thoreau and his friend Walt Whitman, he had penned his first nature essays in the gloomy vaults of the Treasury Department in Washington, where he worked as a clerk. Popular acclaim came in the 1870s as public interest in nature and Thoreau surged. This writer who had inherited the mantle of Henry now ventured to Concord for the first time, trying to connect with the spirit of his departed hero, whom he had never met. Sanborn showed him "the home and some of the haunts of Thoreau, and then his grave, and that of Hawthorne." "I like Sanborn all except his lofty coldness and reserve," Burroughs told Whitman. It was the first of three memorable visits. Influenced by Emerson and Thoreau, Burroughs wrote scores of essays, making him one of the key "promoters and interpreters of transcendentalism" from his desk in his rustic New York cottage, Slabsides. Thoreau was lucky to have such eloquent advocates.[56]

Lake Walden dozed, comparatively, in 1878, except that two purse snatchers from Boston were apprehended at the Old Folks Picnic in August. In July, one hundred participants from the Spiritualist National Camp Meeting undertook "the Thoreau Pilgrimage": they "took up their line of march around the Lake to a spot nearly opposite the canvas city, where a simple pile of stones" marked the house site. The ceremony featured readings, music by Dunbar's Band, singing, an improvised poem, and a group photograph. "A large number of stones, suitably named and dated" were added to the cairn, twenty-seven of which were uncovered in Roland Robbins's archaeological dig sixty-eight years later. In August, Alcott, now seventy-eight, took Sanborn to Walden, and, Alcott wrote, "we have a bath and a splendid swim. The water is pure and agreeably cool, the sands soft, and the sun shines brilliantly on the surface. I

Nature's philosopher.
Bronson Alcott built rustic
benches against the
gigantic elms of Orchard
House. Courtesy Concord
Free Public Library.

find I have not lost my early dexterity, and move as rapidly as when on Saturdays we boys had our grand splash in the Mill ponds" in Connecticut.[57]

The town continued its rebuilding. In 1879, Walden Road was widened from Brister's Hill to the Lincoln line, which must have destroyed the picturesque sinuosity Thoreau knew. "Lake Walden seems to be renewing its old-time popularity"; "A picnic at Walden nearly every day this season. The place has not been so well patronized for years." Civil War General Kirkpatrick gave a "thrilling grape[shot] and canister speech" on Independence Day. So popular was Walden once more, there was talk of developing a rival picnic grounds at White Pond. Poor Children's Excursions remained vital; 953 participants came from South Boston in August, "a little rougher army of juveniles than usual." The good safety record was marred when Rose Zego, twenty-two, attending a picnic for Boston Italians, was about to cross the track to catch the train home when she was struck in the head by the outbound locomotive. Fitchburg Railroad was indicted for manslaughter.[58]

"Saturday afternoon Father walked all round the Pond with me, and wasn't at all tired," Ellen Emerson reported in July. The Concord School of Philosophy, long-standing dream of the elderly Alcott, debuted this summer at Orchard House. A kind of running seminar, it brought singular characters to town, Blake and Ricketson among them, and provided fodder for jokesters: "Would you like to come over for a Plato soup?" The students toured Walden, among other "historic spots" of Concord. They added to the growing cairn, which a sketch of August 4 showed ornamented with a cross and signboard. The avid Thoreauvian knew that a visit ought to involve a walk from Concord to the pond—to "come on foot, with staff and scrip," as one self-described student "Pilgrim in Concord" called it. How else to do justice to the man who would "walk every day about half the daylight"? But if the pilgrim expected Thoreauvian solitude, the reality must have been shocking: "I witnessed, and participated in, a . . . radical profanation of these crystal waters, when two hundred of the dirtiest children in Boston, South-enders, were brought down by train on a fresh-air-fund picnic and washed in the lake just in front of the spot where Thoreau's cabin stood, after having been duly swung in the swings, teetered on the see-saws, and fed with a sandwich, a slice of cake, a pint of peanuts, and a lemonade apiece, by a committee of charitable ladies—one of whom was Miss Louisa Alcott."[59]

It seemed sure in summer 1880 that Concord "is getting to be a shrine—a sort of intellectual Mecca." The School of Philosophy again attracted "would-be *literati* of the day, to parade the streets in remarkable garments supposed to be of the latest transcendental style, to disturb the quiet of the Public Library with learned remarks, and to give Mr. Emerson the pleasant surprise of a friendly call." The pond was even more popular than the previous year, with a picnic almost daily, sometimes with as many as thirty-five cars rumbling in. One from Boston's North End brought 1129 kids in sixteen carloads, and their boisterousness "taxed the attention of those in charge to their utmost." By summer's end, 11,000 had come, and the only accident occurred when a youngster dropped a rock on his toes. The downside to picnicking remained the occasional rowdiness: "Rather a rough crowd on our streets, that of the excursionists to Walden from Cambridge on the 11th" of August, the price Concord paid for its new incarnation as a popular summertime destination.[60]

In mid-July the Fish Commissioners opened the waters for those with passes, allowing fishing for bass for the first time since stocking a few years before, and anglers came in large numbers. For the liter-

Emerson family, Bush, 1879. Waldo and Lidian stand against the door. Edward and Ellen are the adults standing at left, Edith at right. Courtesy Concord Free Public Library.

ary pilgrim, the first glance of Walden from the road "will suffice to arouse both admiration and dismay"; Thoreau's pond was still beautiful but "alas! it is no longer consecrated to his memory. The communistic spirit of the age has converted the sylvan solitude into a public picnic-ground; has erected a dancing-hall, a bowling alley, and numerous other abominations among the classic shades; while the very *sanctum sanctorum*, Thoreau's cove, is fulfilling its mission as an excellent place for bathing!" Nonetheless, the Emerson family continued to come—in mid-May and in July, when Ellen again entertained guests and reported, "We rode up to [Fair Haven] cliffs where we beheld unusual glory and as always hated to come home. . . . Next day . . . we had a good walk to Walden Ledge."[61]

The Reading Club of Marlboro, thirty-two strong, rode to Concord in carriages one Saturday. They visited the Old North Bridge and Manse before heading to Emerson's house, where Ellen showed them into the library to greet the sage. They met Alcott at Orchard House and were joined by George Bartlett at the Wayside. He guided them to Sleepy Hollow, where the group gathered at Thoreau's grave and read aloud Emerson's eulogy to his friend. After visiting Bartlett's house they stopped at the library to see manuscripts of Henry and others. "Last of all a visit was paid to Walden Pond, where a vigorous attack was made upon their picnic refreshments and the finest literary feast of the day was enjoyed, the latter upon the site of the hermit home of Thoreau."[62]

When *Early Spring in Massachusetts*, edited by Blake, appeared in 1881, it marked the first publication of extracts from Thoreau's journals, as Sophia had authorized. It included descriptions of the pond new to readers of *Walden*. That same year a fence was erected around the picnic grounds and the usual Poor Children's Excursions were arranged. Some 1200 came from South Cove District and 1400 from the Third and Fourth Police Precincts; in all, 11,080 were ferried to "Walden Lake Grove" in nine excursions, at thirty-four cents a child. The Schubert Choral Union Picnic attracted 2500 participants for music and dancing in August. "The picnics at Walden often bring to the village an undesirable class of visitors," and this year, eight drunks who came on the train ostensibly to the Father Mathew Total Abstinence Society of Salem picnic stayed on to Concord Depot. "Getting loaded up" in town, they staggered out Walden Street past the Poor Farm, where they harangued the staff. Further on they broke down fences and yanked up young maple trees. Atop Brister's Hill, five police officers managed to apprehend them and load them into a wagon, but not without two shots being fired into the air and one man beaten with a club "until the blood flowed freely."[63]

Walt Whitman, sixty-two, visited Concord on September 17, 1881, staying at Sanborn's. An illustrious group gathered for tea—those two, plus Bronson Alcott, Louisa May Alcott, and Emerson. Bronson was struck by Whitman's "ruff of beard and open-bosom collar, folded shirt-cuffs—he standing full six feet in his skirtless blue coat, supporting himself with his staff and stooping a little." They talked of Margaret Fuller and Thoreau, the conversation ranging back to heady days of 1840s transcendentalism. Whitman studied Emerson intently, concluding that the great man's mind was slipping. Later he was escorted to Sleepy Hollow by a lady driving "spirited white ponies." He trudged up the hill to see Thoreau's grave. "Then to Walden pond, that beautifully embower'd sheet of water, and spent over an hour there." His long stay confirms that Walden was established as a literary shrine of signal importance. "On the spot in the woods where Thoreau had his solitary house is now quite a cairn of stones, to mark the place; I too carried one and deposited on the heap."[64]

Twenty years on, place played a critical role in the memorialization of Thoreau. Sophia had seen that Henry's body was moved to Sleepy Hollow and interred across from the Hawthorne plot, at a time when the writer of *The Scarlet Letter* was known worldwide and Thoreau by far fewer. To the extent that this move was calculated, it was audacious and effective—everyone who came to see Hawthorne also saw Thoreau. They became "the authors," eventually to be joined by the Alcotts and Emerson on the ridgetop. To Victorian tourists, the beauty of the pine-topped hill inspired meditation on the authors' lives and deaths, the Thoreau story being particularly romantic and appealing, the gentle naturalist having died young, his task unfinished. Similar meditations could take place at the Walden house site. The cairn, too, was effective showmanship, encouraging touristic participation and instituting a ritual of memorialization. As the cairn grew larger, it impressed the newcomer with its suggestion of Thoreau's great influence—in part an illusion, as many stones were added out of custom, not devotion. Like Sleepy Hollow, the place inspired reflection—the natural beauty, the gravelike cairn, the cutaway bank behind it that was often taken to be the house site— but the dwelling itself was poignantly missing, as was the virtuous naturalist who built it.

Sanborn published *Henry D. Thoreau* in the prestigious *American Men of Letters* series in 1882; it was the third biography of the naturalist to date, an impressive total in the two decades since his death. Meanwhile, Alcott, eighty-two and daydreaming about the past, penned a poem to Emerson, his friend of nearly half a century. It was a moving tribute to bygone days when they conversed in the study at Bush before walking to Walden Pond:

> Oft I recall those hours so fair and free
> When all the long forenoon we two did toss
> From lip to lip, in lively colloquy,
> Plato, Plotinus, or some schoolman's gloss,

Summer morning. Picnickers gathered at the gateway to Lake Walden, ca. 1868. Swings and the Men's Bathhouse stood along Ice Fort Cove. Courtesy Concord Free Public Library.

Disporting in rapt thought and ecstasy.
Then, by the tilting rail, Millbrook we cross,
And sally through the field to Walden wave,
Plunging within the cove, or swimming o'er.
Through woodpaths wending, he, with gesture quick,
Rhymes deftly in mid-air with circling stick,
Skims the smooth pebble from the leafy shore,
Or deeper ripples raises as we lave—
Nor will his pillow press, though late at night,
Till converse with the stars his eyes invite.

Edward Emerson found his father in "Old Age . . . still walking in the woods . . . [but] Walden woods were so sadly changed by publicity from the green temples that first he knew, that he had little pleasure in going to them." Still, he did occasionally enjoy sauntering around the pond, cutting paths through his woodlot, swimming, and rowing.[65]

On April 2, 1882, Emerson walked with Ellen as far as Walden, his last visit. He got drenched during an evening stroll on the nineteenth, developed pneumonia, and died on the twenty-seventh—like Thoreau twenty years before, passing from nature into eternity just as spring blushed across the landscape. First Parish Church was decked with pine boughs from the grove above Thoreau's house site. Alcott and "thousands" followed the procession to Sleepy Hollow, where Emerson's grandchildren filed by and tossed bouquets onto his coffin. The outpouring of feeling suggested the extent to which Emerson had effected a profound transformation in American life. Burroughs, among others, was shaken and felt that literature could never be as vital again. Drawing inspiration in large part from Walden and its woods, the sage had preached a new gospel of nature-worship—mystical and poetic. Walden and Concord became monuments to his memory and influence.[66]

Life went on at Walden Pond. Business was up during that drought summer. The Hutchinson Family, a singing troupe, entertained the Temperance Celebration in June, and the Rev. Henry Ward Beecher lectured. He spoke again at the pond on the afternoon of July 4, after a baseball game at the fairgrounds, Blue Stockings versus Red Stockings. The American Watch Company Band of Waltham entertained the pondside crowd. Schubert Choral Union attendance hit four thousand in August. Poor Children's Excursions remained popular. As usual at these events, some youngsters had no outbound ticket and walked twenty miles along the tracks from sooty Boston. A boy about fourteen and his sister did not arrive until well into the afternoon, by which time the return train had already departed. "'Well, sis, we shall have to walk home,'" the boy said matter-of-factly, "and they started off down the track."[67]

At the Yellow House in October, Alcott suffered a stroke, ending decades of his journal keeping. When he dropped his pen, an era in Concord's intellectual life ended. The following August, his family complained to the newspaper that they were "much annoyed by curious sightseers, who stop their carriages before his house and openly stare and comment upon the aged philosopher as he sits on his piazza." He died in Boston three years later, attended by ailing Louisa, whose death followed his by two days. With the founders of transcendentalism gone and the modern world racing in, the history of Concord and Walden entered another epoch, one of continuous and rapid change.[68]

8

꙰

Thoreau's Country

(1883–1921)

꙰

By the first year of the post-Emerson era, it had been more than three decades since Heywood cut the trees on his shore, and one could stand beneath "the great pines on the eastern side" and admire the sweep of blue water. "Thoreau's cove, so long the abode of solitude, is devoted to the very social amusement of over two hundred boys, black and white," one visitor wrote in amazement. "Walden Pond offers fine opportunities for bathing," a newspaperman said. "The water is apt to be chilly. On picnic days, kids from the lower towns occasionally go in without a bathing dress of any description; this causes a general lowering of the circulation, which is usually restored by rapid friction with a policeman's locust."[1]

Pilgrims to Walden are like pilgrims everywhere—they love to stand where their heroes stood, see what they saw. In *Literary Landscapes of the British Isles*, David Daiches tells of how, "rambling round Ullswater," "I came across a clump of daffodils in precisely the spot where Wordsworth and his sister Dorothy had seen them," enhancing his appreciation of Wordsworth's "I Wandered Lonely As a Cloud" and confirming that "topography could assist literary understanding." Wordsworth himself noted and deplored the influx of literary enthusiasts to the Lakes. Washington Irving ventured to Shakespeare's house at Stratford only to find it "covered with names and inscriptions in every language by pilgrims of all nations."

Hudson River tourism was inspired by the novels of James Fenimore Cooper, and a patriotic tour was outlined by Benson Lossing's *Pictorial Field-Book of the Revolution* (1850). But the first exclusively literary pilgrimage in America, starting in the 1860s, was to Concord and Walden Pond.[2]

One of these literary pilgrims was John Burroughs. Meditating on the death of Emerson, he visited Frank Sanborn in June at his house beside Concord River. Edward Emerson was there; he resembled his father and "talked well about Thoreau. Said Channing drove away his family, then drove away his dog. This last act angered Thoreau much." A devoted Burroughs looked hard in town for anything "that recalled Thoreau," twenty years on, but found nothing, although the place seemed "the most pleasing country village I ever saw." After breakfast on the second day, he and a Mr. Gilder walked to Walden, "much talk and loitering by the way. Walden, a clean, bright pond, not very wild. Look in vain for the site of Thoreau's hut. Two boys in a boat row up and ask us the question we have on our tongues to ask them. We sit in the woods and try to talk about immortality; do not get very near together on such a theme."[3]

As an authorized biography of Emerson was underway, the three Emerson children gathered in Concord in April 1885 to examine "the stone Edward has brought to stand at Father's grave." As early as 1863 and again in 1879, Ellen and her siblings had "been talking over the cemetery monument and especially the stone it shall be made of. . . . Posterity, distant posterity, is my chief thought in the matter. I desire that this monument shall last." It ought to be large, too, as some villain had once tried to dig up her father's body. Now, Ellen said, "Poor Edward has tried very hard to get what he wanted, big beryls in their natural bed of quartz; but all in vain; and at last he has given up and brought a big piece of quartz. The result of last night's family council seemed to be a decision to set it up rough and have a bronze plate sunk in it." Once the massive, translucent purple quartz boulder from New Hampshire was installed at Sleepy Hollow—fitting monument to Emerson's love of the Picturesque—Ellen took Lidian to see it. "Her 'Oh' of admiration and affection says all one could desire. I have had the like pleasure with everyone to whom I have showed it except Dr Hedge & Miss Peabody. They were a little doubtful. I think each said 'I don't quite understand the

Et in Arcadia ego.
Emerson's monument in
time was flanked by the
graves of Lidian and Ellen.
Courtesy Concord Free
Public Library.

idea. It isn't evident to me *why* you chose such a stone. Oh yes it is agreeable enough—I don't dislike it, only one wonders why anything so singular was chosen. It does not explain itself.'" The biography, this extraordinary stone, their later efforts to preserve Walden Pond itself—all were deliberate strategies by the Emerson children to insure their father's continuing fame.[4]

Activities at Lake Walden were varied in 1883: the St. John's Literary Institute of East Cambridge Picnic, Marlboro Sunday Schools, Protestant Sunday Schools of Hudson, one thousand attendees at the Harrington Lyceum of Lynn Picnic, "a party of colored people," 3500 at the Catholic Picnic, the Prophetic Convention at which two converts were baptized in the lake at five P.M. At the Catholic Temperance Society picnic from St. Mary's, Boston, "athletic sports" were featured. Unfortunately, nineteen-year-old deaf mute "Dummy" Roberts drowned, "and persistent efforts by varying expedients to recover the body failed," including firing the town cannon from the bank. A week later, on the day of the first of the six Poor Children's events, a boy ran up from the water shouting, "I've found a dead man in the water!" "Dummy" bobbed near the bathhouse, his head resting on the sand. "A boat rowed by, an attendant of the grounds soon appeared, a cord was slipped around one leg of the body, and it was towed to a secluded spot, followed on shore by a crowd of nearly 100 children, and that was poor Dummy's funeral cortege."[5]

This was not the only headline event in the woods that summer. A fire raged on the land of Staples, Fuller, and Emerson in early September and "caused considerable damage." The local newspaper had recently quipped, "Brister's Hill.—A Latin word compounded of Bristers and Hill, meaning fire in the woods." Ellen Emerson wrote Edith of being "severely exercised by fires in the woods. . . . No sooner would John & Eddy & Johnny get home all tired & hungry than a new column of smoke would be seen to rise and off they would start again for another fight. One fire menaced our grove, the other all our acres beyond the Pond. . . . We went down into the garden, the hated column of smoke was in plain sight. . . . [Edward] called out 'Well, John, we'll go to the woods. Harness the horse & I'll give the alarm.' So away they all went with a load of shovels at their feet." The next day Edward had to go to Boston, and "as he passed by the Walden Ledge in the cars . . . he saw the whole back of it in flames and no man there." He nearly canceled his trip, but concluded that his business "was more important than even 'My Garden.'" Two days later the fire had been contained by three men, who watched it day and night. "Only an acre or two of ours is burned, but almost the whole region from Mr Baker's to the Pond is burned."[6]

Walden's first British edition appeared in 1884, and H. G. O. Blake continued his publication of extracts from the journal with *Summer*, which included a map of Thoreau Country, as some may have already begun calling it. Within a few years Cummings E. Davis, local antiquarian, had nailed five-pointed tin stars to trees along the path from Walden Road to guide pilgrims.

Concord continued its transformation: suburban houses rose all around, yet the occasional cattle drive still thundered down the middle of Main Street. In summer, "barge loads of sight seers drive into town almost every day." To the Lake Walden picnic grounds came the New England Grocers, Colored Odd Fellows, and the usual poor children—forty car loads of them one Tuesday in July. The Fish Commissioners opened the waters in August. The next month, Ellen Emerson "proposed Walden & tea in the boat and away we went with Cousin Sarah. Boats alas! all beached. But we took tea in our pasture, ran down afterward to see sunset colours on the pond, then rode home in moonlight."[7]

The following year a new dance hall or pavilion rose at Ice Fort Cove, as well as a pagoda-shaped telegraph office. Seven boats were added to the fleet. Picnickers included a crowd from Harvard Street Baptist Church in June and two thousand day-trippers from Lynn near the end of August, at which event "one lady of color undertook to dispense spirituous beverages to the thirsty multitude. But finally concluded to walk over to the lockup with Officer Haskell." George Bartlett's influential guidebook described the place, now in its heyday: "Lake Walden, as it is now called, has become one of the most popular summer resorts in the neighborhood of Boston. . . . The grounds are furnished with seats, swings, dining-hall, dancing-hall, speaking-room with seats, boats for excursions over the lake, bath houses, etc., and is now to be provided with base ball grounds."[8]

More improvements came in 1886, including a new depot. It was a drought summer—a fire again burned over a large section of Walden Woods—and in the warm weather, "picnics at Lake Walden are larger and more frequent than ever before." Ten thousand attended the Grocers' Picnic. Later came the Children's Temperance Union and Wells Memorial events, and Ellen Emerson accompanied George Bartlett to a Poor Children's Picnic. At a temperance gathering, seven hundred listened to "the singing of the song, 'Beware,' by the three daughters of Mrs. Kraetzer of Concord." The Fish Commissioners again allowed angling from August to October. Police watched for spirituous liquors: "Officer Haskell's rough-on-beer trap is doing great service in Walden woods." Haskell swooped down on picnickers who pillaged G. F. Wheeler's vineyard near the railroad, but one culprit "made tracks for the pond" and escaped. A highlight of Ellen's summer was the picnic she organized in September: "We took the 4.23 train to the Pond. There were six of us—one boat-load—afloat soon after five. The most brilliant cloud show began about that time all over the heavens. We had our tea, then sunset, yellow glow, rose glow, fading west, bright moonlight, long row, echoes, and when it was already dark stopped the 7.17 train for Concord."[9]

Back-to-nature formed a powerful impulse in this decade. Living in New York in 1886, newspaperman Philip Hubert grew "very tired of city life, of late hours and long hours, of nervous strain." He delved into Edmund Morris's simple-living guide of 1864, *Ten Acres Enough*, and was inspired to try his own experiment. Resigning his job, he moved to coastal Long Island, where he survived on five hundred dollars a year by gardening, beekeeping, raising chickens and goats, and fishing from a boat. His cottage shelves grew heavy with simple-living tracts, including Robert Roosevelt's satirical answer to Morris, *Five Acres Too Much*. And, of course, there was *Walden*: "I have read the famous hermit of Walden Pond with persistency and admiration."[10]

Another follower of Thoreau was Fred Hosmer, thirty-five, a Concord photographer whose prints were popular with tourists. In summer 1884 it was said that he "finds a good sale for his fine views of Concord scenery among the many visitors in town." A carpenter's son and descendant of early settlers, he was described by a Thoreauvian friend as "a bachelor; a salesman in a little variety shop in Concord; an amateur photographer, and better informed about Thoreau's haunts than any man living or dead. *W. E. Channing not excepted*. Fred is also a botanist; an early riser; a member of that high caste erstwhile known as the 'Sunday Walkers'" and a man who "makes his own clothes, and this from a desire to be independent of 'sweating shops.' . . . [I] *admire* Thoreau; Fred *lives* him!" As his photographs of scenery appeared in Margaret Sidney's *Old Concord* in 1888 and subsequent publications, this stalwart would play a key role in the growth of interest in his hero Thoreau.[11]

Meanwhile, *Winter* in 1887 marked the third installment in Blake's issuance of excerpts from the journal. In January the picnic grounds hosted the Winter Conference of Unitarians, which Ellen Emerson attended, but in general that year saw the beginning of a slow, fatal decline in tourism to Lake Walden. The middle-class clientele was dwindling, no doubt as a result of the expansion of summer travel in more distant locales. But there was no slackening of

Thoreauvian pilgrims. English biographer Henry S. Salt corresponded in 1889 with Edward Sherman Hoar, Thoreau's boating companion on the day of the infamous 1844 "Burnt Woods" fire. Hoar, who came from Concord's wealthiest and most illustrious family yet deliberately chose a quiet life devoted to nature, retained his affection for his mentor Thoreau. He wished Salt "all success in calling the attention of this age of millionaires" to the life of the lowly naturalist and marveled how, "after 25 years, pilgrims still visit his grave, to gather or to leave a flower."[12]

If pilgrims were numerous, the Concord habit of peripatetic had largely sputtered out. Ellen Emerson, who organized "Pond teas" for her friends in 1889, lamented the changes in Walden Woods as she went "to view our burnt wood-lot."

> There was a fire this spring on the [south] side of Walden where all our woodland is, that is the wood we depend on for fuel, and Edward says it is very thoroughly burnt up, and we are to see today whether the summer has charmed life back into any part of it. Fires in the woods are very sad. Our old wood-paths where we used to walk are growing up with young trees. Father, Mr. Channing and Mr. Thoreau seem to have no successors to keep them open. Father used to talk about the School of Walkers, said he was a professor of Walking, and used to watch to see whether anyone else valued it, and said he found but one man who might be said to belong to the school—perhaps merit a degree—and that was an elderly Mr. Pulsifer.[13]

Interest in walking and in Thoreau remained high in contemporary Britain, however. In 1890, homesick twenty-five-year-old Irish poet William Butler Yeats roamed the boulevards of London. Pushing through crowded Fleet Street, "I heard a little tinkle of water and saw a fountain in a shop-window which balanced a little ball upon its jet, and began to remember lake water." It took him back to his "ambition, formed in Sligo in my teens, of living in imitation of Thoreau on Innisfree, a little island in Lough Gill." At home in suburban Bedford Park he wrote the best-known poem of his long career, "The Lake Isle of Innisfree":

I will arise and go now, and go to Innisfree,
And a small cabin build there, of clay and wattles made:
Nine bean-rows will I have there, a hive for the honey-bee,
And live alone in the bee-loud glade.

Yeats explained how his father had once "read to me some passage out of *Walden*, and I planned to live some day in a cottage on a little island called Innisfree. . . . I should live, as Thoreau lived, seeking wisdom. . . . I was twenty-two or three before I gave up the dream." The shop window fountain may have launched "Innisfree," but already his friend Katharine Tynan had written a poem, "Thoreau at Walden," in 1885, and Yeats had confessed to her his wish "to go away and live alone on that Island—an old day dream of my own."[14]

During these same years, a homeopathic doctor in Ann Arbor, Michigan, named Samuel Arthur Jones contracted an incurable passion for Thoreau. In late 1889 he lectured on "Thoreau: A Glimpse," and mailed copies to Daniel Ricketson and others. Soon he was corresponding with Fred Hosmer in Concord and the English reformer Henry S. Salt, who published a Thoreau biography in 1890. As Fritz Oehlschlaeger and George Hendrick have written, these three men launched what Jones called the "Thoreau Revival" and did more than anyone else to insure that Thoreau's reputation endured and grew. Thoreau studies entered a new phase, increasingly analytical and scholarly. Also extraordinary is the degree to which the reformist and liberal-minded concerns of Salt and Jones, bolstered in part by their readings of Thoreau, would ultimately become twentieth-century orthodoxies—free-thinking and candid expression, vegetarianism, animal rights, sexual liberation, socialism, environmentalism, world peace.[15]

In August 1890, Dr. Jones traveled to Boston with Michigan Civil War veterans and, bursting with enthusiasm, visited Concord. The scholar Raymond Adams told how Jones hired a tour guide, who pointed out only Emerson and Hawthorne sites. "Finally Jones could stand it no longer and burst out—'I don't care a damn about all these places. Show me something connected with your greatest man, Henry Thoreau.' . . . One would misrepresent Doctor Jones if he omitted his damns. He was as outspoken as Thoreau and used more expletives." Escaping the guide, Jones climbed the ridge to Thoreau's grave in Sleepy Hollow to "stand a pious pilgrim there in the solemn silence of a summer's night, shadows below and starlight above." Another highlight was the house site by Walden, as he wrote to Salt: "I am glad that the leaves reached you unbroken. They grew just in front of where his chimney stood, and are the only approach to a memento that the nearly-filled cellar afforded. As I sat there, oh, how I wished that you were beside me! It is by far the most delightful visit of my life, and it keeps coming back to me in flashes of radiance just like sun-bursts through rifts in the clouds." He avidly interviewed everyone he could find who knew Thoreau, including Sanborn, both at his home and at Concord Library. But Jones was the kind of man who thrived on having an enemy to vex, and Sanborn filled the bill, Jones deciding that he was a scoundrel for having defamed the characters of Thoreau's parents in his biography, among other sins. The feisty Jones returned to Michigan on fire with passion to elevate Thoreau and, in the process, reduce Emerson and spite the detestable Sanborn.[16]

On this Concord trip Dr. Jones was introduced to Fred Hosmer by Eliza Hosmer, Fred's cousin and the daughter of Thoreau's old friend Edmund Hosmer. After he went home, they became regular correspondents. "I envy you the rare pleasure of reading Walden 'on the spot,'" Jones wrote to Fred. "That visit of mine has spoiled me for this life; that is if I have to live it in this no-god no-devil of a Michigan. . . . Perhaps, if I am good, when I die I shall go to Concord!" He fondly recalled the places his new friend had taken him, including the Edmund Hosmer house and Baker Farm, and he proposed they together create a book "on Thoreau's Home and haunts that will beat all yet done in that line," with Fred's photographs illustrating Thoreau's words. Jones would never forget his outings with Hosmer, gushing to Salt, "You can afford to come to America if only to look for a moment into Fred's clear grey eyes— after that, a tramp through 'Thoreau's country' with him for guide is enough to make one's memory radiant forever."[17]

Dr. Jones wrote to Fred Hosmer in February 1891 about his idea of editing an American edition of Salt's Thoreau biography, "and I propose to fill it with Concord scenery in photographs" in an effort "to put the reader 'on the spot.'" In particular he wanted to know "the site of the Bean Field at Walden, Dr. [Edward] Emerson can

Parade on the Mill Dam. Tourist crowds grew ever larger. View east from upstairs in the Brick House, a childhood home of Thoreau, in 1894; at right, the opening to Walden Road. Courtesy Concord Free Public Library.

locate it." In August he published an article in *Lippincott's*, "Thoreau and His Biographers," blasting Sanborn's *Life*: that book "began the era of personal misrepresentation" by slighting Thoreau's parents. Jones's essay forged a sympathetic approach that influences us to this day, marking the beginning of critical reinterpretation of Thoreau and his vast rise in esteem even as Emerson inexorably waned.[18]

Jones received a letter from Thoreau's old friend Blake complaining that the attack against Sanborn and Emerson was "harsh" and "aggressive." Jones replied, "Your kind letter of the 6th instant reached me in the cool of the evening and I read it while sitting within a few feet of some young pine trees that began their life in the cellar of Thoreau's hut at Walden," souvenirs of his trip to Concord the year before. He went on to say, patronizingly, that Blake had fallen under the spell of Emerson's personality as a youth and was therefore biased. Sanborn had done nothing to contribute to the cause but "eke out a miserable existence by writing lying biographies!" Blake was aghast at these remarks. Dr. Jones, true to his nature, had carried his convictions to the acid extreme, as more than a few of Thoreau's twentieth-century followers would do. But of all the prickly characters attracted to Thoreau, Jones had, perhaps, the greatest gift for invective. He once told an opponent, "You don't have enough calcium in that backbone of yours to whitewash the bald spot on the top of your head."[19]

Sanborn and Channing were about to grow closer. Thoreau's friend, now elderly, moved in with Sanborn in September 1891, bringing with him his library of five thousand books. His room at the northwest corner, below the attic, overlooked Concord River meadows where he and Thoreau had paddled often. He remained a strange, reclusive man who, according to one observer, "does not seem to care for nature now; he has long ceased to walk out at all; all he does is to take the morning train for Boston, go to the Public Library, and call for a large number of books . . . and sit there with his back to the rest of the people, and make notes all day." One wonders what his thoughts were as the train sped past Walden Pond, scene of so many delights in what must have seemed a previous lifetime.[20]

So prominent had Thoreau become, his name was now carved among literary greats on the walls of that very Boston Public Library. A few weeks after Channing's move to Sanborn's, thirteen of the Emerson family walked to Fairyland and Walden on an autumn afternoon—even baby Raymond, who would one day inherit much of his grandfather's land in Walden Woods, went along. *Autumn*, published in 1892, a year that would have seen Thoreau's seventy-fifth birthday, marked the fourth and final volume in Blake's series of extracts. A livery driver bragged of taking a thousand visitors in a month to Sleepy Hollow. Jones continued his researches this year, writing to Hosmer, "Fred, I wish you would watch for a good chance and SHOOT Channing—with a Kodak, of course. That venerable ancient is a part of the history of Concord and he should not be allowed to 'peg out' without leaving his 'picter.'" Jones, knowing of his reputation for secretiveness, never tried to approach Channing, in spite of his having known Thoreau better than anyone then living. There were questions he wished he could ask, such as where the Thoreaus lived during John and Henry's *A Week* trip: "All these little things are going to have an importance when the people who can give information are dead, and we who are the link between Thoreau's days and the future should attend to them."[21]

As Dr. Jones and Hosmer amassed Thoreauviana, Hosmer told his friend triumphantly, "I had *good* success in *hooking* a portion of the old shanty, have a piece about 3 x 6 and five feet long—rather worm eaten however." Fred sawed the house into pieces to distribute. Henrietta Daniels wrote excitedly, "Oh, little piece of wood! If you only would tell us what you have known! . . . And now, fifty years later, we hold you little less than sacred." She had been corresponding with Blake, too, suggesting to him "a *Thoreau re-union* at Lake Walden, July 4th" of the next summer, 1893. From Minnesota, the Rev. C. A. Cressy voiced his thanks for the "piece of timber from Thoreau's hut. . . . You can appreciate my gratitude at the reception of the relic. As I look upon the mark of his 'axe,' and realize that Thoreau was cutting, hewing, and handling this piece of pine when I was a little over two years of age it seems almost too much to believe that it is now in my possession." Calvin Greene wrote that he was "pleased to learn that you had that piece of the shanty studding with the print of Alcott's ax yet on it! Hold on to it, I conjure you! When it gets old enough it may work miracles like a piece of the 'true cross'!" Landscape architect Arthur A. Shurcliff got two pieces, which he later donated to Concord Library, where they remain. When the designer of the 2001 Thoreau Institute replica of Thoreau's house studied them, an accompanying *Smithsonian* reporter gathered up the powdery fragments that had scattered on the table top and took them home as "precious bits of Americana."[22]

Fire burned across land of Stow and Prichard in Walden Woods in April 1892. The usual little unfortunate incidents occurred at the picnic grounds that summer, as when, on July 4, "a party of toughs from Lake Walden" wandered into Concord looking for a drink and ended up brawling. Sleepy Hollow drew crowds: that month, a thousand persons were estimated to have climbed the hill to Emerson's grave. In October, Edward and Ellen Emerson, with "Mr. Mackintosh who is to design the gravestones" for their various family members, visited the Hill Burying Ground to study slate tombstones. Their brother Waldo's was "to have a flower." At Lake Walden there was the customary temperance picnic that summer. The outing of the Sanitary and Street Cleaning Department of

Boston was spoiled when one Thomas Bowen of Roxbury rocked the boat in which he was rowing until it capsized. Three companions escaped, but Bowen drowned.[23]

Lidian Emerson died in fall 1892, just weeks after turning ninety. In October, ornithologist William Brewster boated with his wife up Sudbury River to Staples's Camp on Fair Haven Bay. Here they lunched before strolling through the woods to Walden. "I think I have never before seen oak woods so richly colored as these—*painted woods*—wine-red the dominant tint. . . . Walden was very beautiful indeed, the water dark blue and ruffled with wind." Goose Pond, as its name suggests, was productive for birdwatching, and Brewster owned twenty-seven acres there to preserve the habitat.[24]

George Hunt Barton came to Walden Woods to study geology. His colleague in the Boston Society of Natural History, Warren Upham, had recently read a paper "on Lake Walden as a type of Glacial Lake"—the first description of the place in terms of glaciation. Barton himself visited in May 1892, photographing "the glacial channel in the sand plain connecting Walden Pond and the Sudbury River" before climbing Fair Haven Cliffs. Back at the railroad, he photographed layers of sand in those cuts once so familiar to Thoreau. Knowledge of New England's glacial history became widespread in this decade; John Muir, who visited in June a year after Barton, owned a dog-eared copy of an 1862 *Walden* in which he wrote, "Walden is a Moraine pond which dates back to the close of the last glacial period when the general New England ice sheet was receding and is fed by currents which ooze through beds of drift."[25]

At Sleepy Hollow, Muir laid flowers on the graves of Thoreau and Emerson. Then "we walked through the woods to Walden Pond. . . . It is only about one and a half or two miles from Concord, a mere saunter, and how people should regard Thoreau as a hermit on account of his little delightful stay here I cannot guess." He told his wife, "I could have enjoyed living here two hundred years or two thousand," further evidence of the significance the pond now had for lovers of nature.[26]

The picnic grounds at Walden saw a Boston Health Department gathering in summer 1893, and a Concord group assembled at Labor Day. Visitors streamed into town by horse, carriage, and bicycle. Among the pilgrims that year was novelist Elbert Hubbard of East

Aurora, New York, who had come in February, reverently plucking a sprig from the pine overhanging Emerson's boulder-stone grave. The visit inspired him to launch a biographical series, *Little Journeys*, which put him on the path to acclaim, capped by his sensationally popular Spanish American War essay, *A Message to Garcia*. Hubbard's arts-and-crafts Roycrofters enterprise, free-thinking and progressive, owed something to Thoreau, whom he admired, and he composed essays in a Thoreau-like cabin. His interest in the transcendentalists was inspired by his secret mistress, Alice Moore. In 1901 she would move with their illegitimate daughter to Concord, where Hubbard visited them often. They were married in 1904 after his scandalous divorce, and about a decade later they went down together on the *Lusitania*.[27]

In August 1893, Dr. Jones learned that Houghton Mifflin was to publish a ten-volume "Riverside" edition of Thoreau's writings, making them even more accessible. This news stimulated him into again suggesting to Fred Hosmer that they "get up an illustrated work called 'Thoreau's Country.' As the pictures alone would not be intelligible to all who see them, I propose a written text gotten up by the guide, the artist, and the friend, and in a sort of dialogue form. For instance, as though Horace Hosmer (guide), you (artist), and I (friend) had made the pilgrimage together, camping out the while and having our talks in the different places pictured." The idea echoed the "walks" format of Channing's Thoreau biography, which in turn owed its ultimate genesis to Emerson.[28]

Among annual visitors to Concord came a cadre of ardent Thoreauvians. In May 1894, Fred Hosmer displayed wildflowers in his Mill Dam shop, and a couple came in and began talking about them. Hosmer knew the blooming times of local plants, as Thoreau had, and reported that the painted cup would bloom tomorrow. "Are you going to Thoreau's painted cup meadow for it?" the woman asked. Fred replied that indeed he was. Here was startling evidence of how thoroughly some visitors had read and absorbed the journals.[29]

The largest forest fire in years raged at Walden in July 1894. A newspaper reported, "The first alarm was rung in at 1:30 Friday calling the department to Walden woods where the fire had been set by an engine of the Fitchburg railroad." Another blaze erupted on

Sandy Pond Road to the east, but the firemen "had all they could handle near Lake Walden." They thought the blaze had been extinguished, but it ignited again on land of Samuel Hoar at the pond. In the meantime it had burned across four hundred acres belonging to Heywood, Hoar, and Tarbell, nearly consuming the Chisholm House at Thoreau and Walden Streets on the edge of town. "The firemen worked hard but it was discouraging, the way the flames would work through the dry earth heaped along the fire line and get past the men. Many of the fighters were utterly prostrated by the heat and smoke." An arsonist was suspected.[30]

Even as Walden Woods looked increasingly singed, Jones called on Hosmer to undertake "that illustrated book on *Thoreau's Country*. Fred, that must be done; and if you can arrange a route that will make a day's walk, or more, if necessary, I will go through Thoreau's books and get the text." Increasingly Jones fretted that Concordians who remembered Thoreau were getting fewer. There were urgent questions he wanted Fred Hosmer to put to elderly Sam Staples, the jailer who had incarcerated Henry during the Walden years: "Will you ask Mr. Staples if he remembers whether Emerson *visited Thoreau while he was in jail*? Ask him too *about time of the day he arrested* Thoreau, and *about what time Emerson called*." Staples did his best to oblige, in spite of the interval of a half-century, and it did indeed provide the last opportunity for any historian to interview him, as a year later he died while vacationing in Florida. Jones worried, "There is no use in dodging the fact that Concord grows poorer as each of its historic citizens goes Beyond, and the last great link of a distinguished chain will disappear when Channing departs to join his contemporaries. I should like to have seen him, but he has soured on humanity and I must not expect to ever see the face he wore among men." He craved "any relics that can be had for love or money," including "a piece of the Walden hut." Fred continued to photograph Thoreauvian scenes. It was a dry year, and perhaps it was at this time that he snapped "Walden Pond from Thoreau Cove," a valuable record, as it showed the seldom-seen sandbar where Thoreau had boiled the kettle of chowder on a childhood visit. In September, Fred received an urgent query from the American Book Company, typical of many that came his way: "We would like very much to get a picture of the house or hut on Walden

Pond which Thoreau built. We sent to a photographer to have him take a picture of the house if it was still standing, but he informs us that it was removed. . . . Can you tell us anything about this?"[31]

Thoreau's writings continued to enjoy a vogue among English social progressives. One of these blithe spirits visited the cairn in May: "Every pious Thoreauite contributes a stone, and I staggered up from the beach with the biggest boulder I could manage to lift. While thus engaged a party of fourteen ladies came by, and each contributed a small stone to the heap; but I fancy their hearts were not much in the place, for they only lamented that they had brought no dough-nuts to eat, and passed on, having now 'done' Walden." The progressive found this particularly offensive given the nature of his connection to Thoreau, as an ardent vegetarian and advocate of healthy eating. He had come here to enjoy a meal in memory of his illustrious forebear, writing in the magazine *Natural Food* that the occasion found "me lying by the deserted spot upon which Henry Thoreau built his now classic hut. . . . [I] sat down to eat a dinner of oranges, bananas, almonds, and figs upon the spot where Thoreau had doubtless many a time boiled his beans."[32]

This visitor found Walden a mixed blessing. Here stood the sacred house site, but here too were obnoxious crowds and "ugly wooden sheds . . . for the accommodation of the numerous parties of summer visitors." He was not the only pilgrim to complain. "You cannot get away from the Walden Fourth-of-July picnic feeling, not even in Thoreau's own cove," said Kate Tryon, an ornithologist and artist summering at the studio of sculptor Daniel Chester French on Sudbury Road. Even the east end was busy, being "where the village boys love dearly to bathe." Another visitor grumbled, "Thank heaven, Thoreau never saw 'Lake Walden' fitted out with vulgar ice-cream booths, and other odious appendages for the delectation of those gregarious beings who come there to mutilate the trees with carved inscriptions of their raw-sounding names."[33]

Theodore Wolfe's response in his influential *Literary Shrines* was more positive, indeed rapturous. "One long-to-be-remembered day we follow the shady foot-paths, once familiar to the sublimated Concord company, through their favorite forest retreats to 'the blue-eyed Walden,'—sung by many a bard, beloved by transcendental saint and seer. After a delightful stroll of a mile or more, we emerge from the wood and see the lovely lakelet." He identified himself as one of many modern "pilgrims . . . to the shrine of a 'stoic greater than Zeno or Xenophanes,'—a man whose 'breath and core was conscience.' We linger till the twilight, for the genius of this shrine seems very near us as we muse in the place where he dwelt incarnate alone with Nature. . . . We bring from the shore a stone—the whitest we can find—for his cairn, and place with it a bright leaf, like those his callers in other days left for visiting cards upon his door-step, and then, through the wondrous half-lights of the summer evening, we walk silently away."[34]

Wolfe found the environs confusing, however. "The hermit would hardly know the place now; his young pines are grown into giants"; the cellar hole "is obliterated and overgrown with the glabrous sumach"; the beanfield "is covered by a growth of pines and dwarf oaks, in places so dense as to be almost impassable." Fortunately, tourist guidebooks were available and directed visitors to the cherished site. Coming from town and ascending Brister's Hill, the first path to the right went directly to the picnic grounds, the second ("at the telegraph-pole") to the pine grove behind Thoreau's house site. "Tourists from the schools and colleges often come in barges by the country road to Thoreau's Cove, near to which the second road after ascending the hill brings them. Leaving their carriages under the tall pines beside this little road, they can follow well-worn paths down to the waterside, past the cairn." Twenty rods further up Walden Road were Thoreau's "orchard" of planted pines "and the ancient cellars of which he writes." Dominating the west shore were the picnic grounds with their swings, bathhouses, and pavilions for dancing and speakers. "Thousands of people are attracted to Walden Pond by the athletic games and other contests of skill, and many city churches bring their children of all ages," although Poor Children's Excursions now preferred "groves nearer to the city." "Many of the old inhabitants regretted the invasion by picnickers of these quiet nooks where the philosophers and poets walked unmolested," one writing, "A dance-house and attendant pumps / Has stirred up all those ancient stumps; / And loud reformers' noisy shout / The woodchucks from their holes bore out."[35]

Emerson's Cliff was popular, its woods having recently been burned off by a locomotive spark, so that bare ledges afforded a spec-

Atop Emerson's Cliff. Looking northwest. Deep Cove appears at left, Thoreau's Cove in the distance toward the right, with Emerson's pine grove behind. Gleason, "Walden, from Emerson's Hill," November 7, 1899, courtesy Concord Free Public Library.

tacular view. Tryon climbed them, along with other high hills around Concord. She and a friend walked out the Back Road and cut across fields to Walden Woods as a train emerged from "the deep Walden sand-cut." They followed wood roads to the highway at the east shore and descended to "the pebbly beach." Then came the scramble up the cliff. The top was bare, except for one tall, straight pine, very different from the overgrown conditions encountered today. "From here everything finds its focus in Walden Pond. Even the far-off New Hampshire hills seem to be conscious of Walden." Another pilgrim followed the railroad "to Emerson's 'Garden,'" alluding to the master's poem about the place. And Theodore Wolfe wrote, "From the summit of the forest ledge which rises from the southern shore, the lakelet seems a foliage-framed patch of the firmament. This rocky eminence affords a wide and enchanting prospect, and was the terminus and object of many excursions of Emerson and the other 'Walden-Pond-Walkers.' . . . [Here] Emerson proposed to erect a lodge or retreat."[36]

On the day Tryon and her companion climbed Emerson's Cliff, she looked east to Pine Hill, which was, along with the valley intervening, "arid and desolate, with its stumps, brush, and woodpiles," a contrast to oak-clad Fair Haven Hill to the west. They crossed over to Pine Hill for a sunset view. Descending, they clambered through pokeweed head-high and richly fruited. That night they read "Autumnal Tints" aloud and happened to encounter Thoreau's fond description of pokeweed—one of those serendipitous resonances Thoreauvians savor. Tryon based her vacation around the Henry theme, visiting his locales and seeking "to discover what bird-neighbors of Thoreau's still live at Walden, forty-odd years since." Wood thrush, brown thrasher, and "huckleberry bird" were gone now, but scarlet tanagers and chickadees remained. Most common of all were black-throated green warblers, which Thoreau apparently missed.[37]

In fall 1895, Tryon organized "An Evening with Thoreau" at the French studio, decked with ferns, pine boughs, pitcher plants, and vines, plus her watercolor sketches of "the favorite haunts of Thoreau." She gave a speech to the crowd of seventy-five, as did guidebook author George B. Bartlett, Sanborn, Fred Hosmer ("a rare and true interpreter of the Naturalist"), Jane Hosmer, and Daniel Ricketson's son Walton. Jane, who remembered Thoreau for "his never ceasing interest in any question they might ask in regard to Natural History, told of visiting him in his shanty at Walden." Fred proudly exhibited "a piece of the shanty still showing the marks of the ax that was returned 'sharper than when I borrowed it.'" Guests were reminded that furniture from Thoreau's house was on display at the local antiquarian museum. Dr. Jones was excited by news of the gathering: "I presume that Thoreau has enough earnest lovers to justify the founding of a Thoreau Club, having its headquarters in Concord." This indication of thriving interest looked ahead a half-century to the establishment there of a national Thoreau Society.[38]

Henry Salt brought out his revised *Life* in 1896, which sold sluggishly but gradually contributed to enhancing the popularity of Thoreau in England. Living far from Concord, Salt benefited from the investigations of Jones and Hosmer, and Dr. Jones, proud of the newly revised *Life*, exulted at "how Thoreau is coming to the front and Emerson going silently to the rear." In turn, Salt marveled to

Jones about the sad life of Thoreau's oldest friend, who hung on as the twentieth century approached: "How terrible must be Channing's death-in-life at Concord, of which you speak! Thirty-four years since Thoreau died, and he still there! If it be true, as Mr. Sanborn once told me, that C. still mourns constantly for his friend, surely it is one of the world's strangest instances of a pathetic though morbid faithfulness."[39]

Visitation to Concord was so heavy by 1896 that "in almost every shop" the tourist could find "some reminder of the hermit—either his picture or a sketch of his hut at Walden. One enterprising tradesman has invested in plates and ink-stands and paper-cutters of Delftware, bearing pictures of the Walden hut or of the cairn of stones that now marks the spot where the hut once stood." Fred Hosmer's photographs had long been part of this touristic tradition, and now he busied himself recording Thoreau locales to be included in a two-volume, Houghton Mifflin *Walden*. "Site of the House at Walden" showed the cutaway bank in back of the present granite posts. "Pines Set Out by Thoreau on His Beanfield" was his title for a May 18 photograph of the neat rows of trees. "Walden, Showing the Sand Bar" revealed boards littering the cove and a big board fence skirting the railroad.[40]

Locomotives roared through Walden Woods at the rate of seventy a day in the drought-stricken spring of 1896, scattering sparks. Disaster struck near the end of the month, when a fire started at midday one Monday "in the woods surrounding Lake Walden." As a column of smoke rose on the horizon, five alarms were rung at Concord. A special train arrived from Waltham with fifty men. But winds were high, making this blaze "one of the fiercest ever known here," jumping Walden and Sandy Pond Roads and burning far to the east, threatening the old Ebby Hubbard land preserved as "The Park" by Edith Forbes. More than a thousand acres were blackened. The most tragic loss was "the stately pines that sheltered the site of Thoreau's hermitage on the shore of Lake Walden."[41]

Sanborn recounted the destruction in a newspaper article, but when he later visited the site he found he needed to qualify his report. Only half a square mile was burned, mostly a tract east of Walden Road, between Goose Pond and The Park; happily, "the hillsides covered with great oaks, chestnuts and pines" at the latter remained undamaged. "The fine large pines" near the cove and house site were untouched, as were "the woods immediately encircling the water." But the fire "did run through a large plantation of white pines, made by Thoreau some 20 rods from his hut, eastward"—the beanfield pines. Probably these "are mostly killed, and this is a serious loss." And woods along the path up Thoreau's Laurel Glen, already devastated by the ax, were scorched.[42]

"It is quite an astonishment how the Thoreau literature has grown in the last ten years," Dr. Jones marveled to Fred Hosmer in 1897, the year that Fred's photographs were published in the two-volume *Walden*. The expansion of interest was evident in several persons who deliberately imitated the Walden experiment. Paul Elmer More, later a noted essayist and philosopher, undertook a two-year escape from "the hideous contention of commerce," publishing the results as "A Hermit's Notes on Thoreau." A classics specialist, More quit his college teaching job in 1897 to live alone in a little red house in Shelburne, New Hampshire, looking out at the Androscoggin River. He read *Walden* in the cathedral aisles of a pine wood out back. Robert Service was led into the forests of Canada by the example of Thoreau, whom he had read in his teens. He decided to become a farmer; "at this period Thoreau was his mentor, *Walden* his bible," a biographer says. "Robert posed as a backwoods philosopher. He would live like Thoreau, in a log cabin on the edge of a lake somewhere in the virgin forest. 'I would fish, hunt, raise a few potatoes.'" He spent 1896–97 in a farmer's "frame shack" in Cowichan Valley, Vancouver Island. In later years he would write poetry in a tiny log house of his own, continuing his Thoreau emulation. Irving Gilbert, a Boston architect, suffered from "dyspepsia and nervous prostration" and, along with his sister, Florence, grew "weary of the awful tension to which the conditions of modern life are subjecting the present generation. To escape from it they have resolved to adopt Thoreau's plan," moving about 1897 to a small farm in Newton, Massachusetts, where they stitched their own clothes and raised their own food. Their hometown newspaper reported the pair's "Primeval Simplicity: Sioux City Man and His Sister Resolve to Become Hermits."[43]

Blake and Ricketson, among the last of Thoreau's intimates, both died in 1898. In February, Jones lectured in Pontiac, Michigan, "giving some account of Thoreau's parentage, surroundings, education, life at Walden Pond, and the purpose of that episode in his life. I assured them that it was not a 'whim' [but] that Thoreau was carrying out a design formed in his under-graduate days, etc. The audience didn't agree with me, and THAT is what I liked; so I fired into them regardless of THEIR opinions." Thus the feisty doctor carried on his campaign of reeducating the public against outmoded ideas of Thoreau and in the process elevating his reputation.[44]

Elsewhere in the Midwest, a new Thoreauvian emerged—Herbert Gleason. A native of Massachusetts, this minister and amateur ornithologist was living in Minnesota when he discovered those portions of the journal published by Blake, and they "aroused a passionate longing to visit the region so intimately described by Thoreau and enjoy a ramble among his beloved haunts." He wrote a review of the two-volume *Walden*, hailing its "ethical message of great significance as a challenge to the restless, wasteful, materialistic life of the nineteenth century." Fred Hosmer's photographs in that book evidently thrilled Gleason, who, like many contemporaries, had been bitten by the Kodak bug. In 1899, at age forty-four, he moved to Boston. From that base he promptly undertook the first of the "frequent pilgrimages to Concord" that would enliven the remainder of his life. In time he would record two thousand photographs of what Dr. Jones had been calling "Thoreau's Country."[45]

Gleason first photographed Walden Pond in early November 1899. He bicycled out Walden Road, then scrambled to the top of Pine Hill and Emerson's Cliff. He also photographed the stony shore on the south side and the north shore in afternoon light. He took a picture from Walden Road looking toward the carriageway down to the pond—the route the Thoreaus took in 1821—depicting the few beanfield pines that yet stood. He also showed a white oak that was still healthy and thriving in 2003. It is, perhaps, a remnant of the oak copse that threw welcome shade on Thoreau as he hoed.

About this time, one A. S. Clark followed Walden Road out of town through "a fertile though somewhat uncultivated meadow," then ascended the Laurel Glen wood road "that shows signs of continued use" through the fire damage of three years earlier, a "desolation" of pine stumps and blackened undergrowth. Tall trees stood on the hilltop, with a view of the lake to be had between them. "The objective point of every visitor to the pond is the site of the little house," which Clark found on a plateau in a small ravine. "A depression indicates the situation of the cellar." A savvy literary tourist, he looked in vain for the chestnut tree that had shaded Thoreau's dwelling and the trees on either side of the path through which the hermit found his way on the darkest nights. Two or three pines nearby and an oak closer to the water looked to have been "sturdy trees" in Henry's time.[46]

An Appalachian Mountain Club guidebook directed visitors: take Walden Road up Brister's Hill and then down a wood road on the right, running alongside "the remnant of Thoreau's 'orchard,'" his beanfield pines recently consumed by fire. "This walk to Walden is a delightful by-walk." It was not without its drawbacks, however. About this time the Town Report complained, "Dump at the foot of Brister's Hill looks and smells bad."[47]

In March 1900, Gleason made a second photographic expedition, walking past the beanfield to the cove. By this time he may have already been contemplating an updated map of Thoreau's Country, one far more complete than Blake's 1884 map in *Summer*, which he was doubtless finding inadequate in his quest to photograph Henry's exact scenes. In pinning down locations, Sanborn, Judge John S. Keyes, Edward Emerson, and the Misses Hosmer were some help; but in general, "It was useless to appeal to residents of Concord. [The sites] might as well have been situated in Siberia or Patagonia." In his earliest investigations he had recourse to Channing, who ought to have been an extraordinary source, having walked frequently with Thoreau and named several of the "Thoreauvian" locations himself—but "his memory was afterwards proved to be sadly at fault."[48]

Dr. Jones carped that Sanborn "adds nothing to our knowledge of Thoreau, yet with Channing on tap in his house one would think that he would be getting points all the time." Sanborn did try to get his guest to reminisce about walks with Emerson and Thoreau but found himself stymied: Channing, who had always been difficult, "will never talk of Thoreau. . . . A wonderful talker, if in the mood, but must be humoured"; "Channing frequently declares that he cannot remember anything [and] he often makes mistakes, generally willful ones." But one day Channing spoke up and asserted that

Heywood's Brook, a lower section of which he and Emerson liked to call Spanish Brook or the Sanguinetto for its reddish sandy bottom, *flowed out of Goose Pond*. Sanborn was sure this was not so, and on September 2, "after my swim in Walden, I walked round the pond in Emerson's woodland on the south side, ascended the craggy ledge . . . then crossed the railroad, and took the lower path toward Baker Farm, to find the Sanguinetto,—forgetting that it was on the upper path, nearer the railroad." He failed to locate the site, but when he went home and told Channing about his adventure, the old man changed his story and gave a highly accurate account of exactly where it lay, a description that still applies:

> The Sanguinetto flows out of the deep swamp which the railroad crosses in Mr. Emerson's woodland,—so deep that in building the road, they thought it almost bottomless, and hauled into it much of the sand and gravel from the 'deep cut' between it and Concord. Now the brook flows only from the S.W. side of the railroad, and runs along a valley at the foot of the ridges where Mr. [Charles F.] Adams has his stable. If you had gone up the railroad, S.E. until you passed the swamp, you would then have come upon the Sanguinetto and the 'mule path' or steep track on both sides of the brook to which Emerson gave that name.[49]

In June 1901, Gleason was back in town, photographing Emerson's Cliff as well as the pond from the railroad. This inaugurated an active phase for his photography at Walden; five further trips would come between September 1901 and October 1904. Many of these photographs are familiar today from frequent publication, though dozens of others have never appeared in print. They offer a memorable record of Walden, albeit one not truly showing the scenery Thoreau knew, as even the earliest were taken nearly forty years after the naturalist's death and more than half a century after he lived at the pond.[50]

Tourism was lively that summer of 1901, it being not uncommon on the streets of Concord for "a party of four women to be assailed by seven or a dozen boys with guide-books and by five or six hackmen." The picnic grounds were on their last legs, however, receiving attention only when Lucy Fields assaulted Laura Allen with a razor at a "colored picnic" in August: "It was very evident that the quarrel was about the attentions of a colored man." On July 31 an innocuous-seeming notice appeared in the newspaper: "A float and spring board have been placed in Sandy Beach at Lake Walden by private enterprise. Those using it are invited to pay toward the expense of building and maintaining it." The raft proved popular with local men and boys who had long been enjoying the east beach, presumably with the blessing of the Heywood family. At this "swimming-place used by the Concord farmers for two hundred years," the float added an element of organization and permanence that pointed prophetically to the future.[51]

In September 1901, the assassination of President McKinley at the World's Fair caused Sanborn to go "into the Walden woods this afternoon for meditation on the national tragedy at Buffalo," using the place for thoughtful introspection as the nineteenth-century transcendentalists had done. "I passed along the paths I used to traverse so often with Emerson, whose figure almost seemed to escort me, and came to the Pond near Thoreau's Cove," where he spent an hour swimming. The pond was silent except for two fishermen in the lee of Emerson's woodlot and boys splashing at the eastern shore. After dressing, he walked to "the partially dilapidated, and now little frequented picnic buildings and benches of the Fitchburg Railroad. They are not yet closed for the season, nor the boats housed," but no one was around. He crossed through open gates to the tracks and the railroad shore, where, "before these fences were built, I was walking with Emerson one day, when he picked up a pebble from the track, cast it into the water a dozen feet below us, and recited this verse,—He smote the lake to please his eye / With the emerald gleam of the broken wave; / He cast in pebbles, well to hear / The moment's music that they gave."

Determined to find the Sanguinetto, Sanborn followed Channing's directions, with success. But there had been many changes. He had to scramble under a wire fence, through young oaks killed by fire, and down overgrown wood roads to the footbridge that once led to Baker Farm. That storied place was now a gentleman's country estate; Mr. Adams forbade trespassing and had let the bridge collapse. Even the Sanguinetto's sand seemed less red than formerly. "In

On the path to Baker Farm. Near Heywood's Brook, historian Brad Dean investigates a boulder that Thoreau labeled "large rock" on an 1857 survey. Photograph by author, 2001.

the evening I told Channing I had found it where he placed it," and in the conversation that ensued, livelier than usual, Channing argued that this brook drained Walden though the Leach Hole: "Unless it did, Walden would rise much higher than it now does and overflow its banks."[52]

In the end, Channing surrendered few memories. On Thanksgiving he caught cold, and he died on December 23, his passing marking the end of transcendentalist Concord, as Walton Ricketson realized when he peeled a death mask from the poet's face the morning of the funeral. Channing's declining years had coincided with a remarkable Thoreau revival, led in part by Salt, who hailed Thoreau's achievements as "the most vigorous protest ever raised against that artificiality in life and literature which is one of the chief dangers of our complex civilisation." For a growing cadre disaffected from modern progress—as symbolized by skyscrapers, electricity, telephones, phonographs, bicycles, and the coming of the automobile—Thoreau pointed to an alternative as the twentieth century began, with Walden Pond a powerful symbol of this nascent revolt.[53]

The pond seemed for the moment to be reverting to its original state of tranquillity with the steady decline of the picnic grounds. As a freight train approached Concord in May 1900, an engineer saw flames spurting from the Lake Walden dance pavilion. Alarms rang in town, and men came running. Thirty boats were pulled to safety, but the sixty-by-eighty-foot pavilion of hard pine was already "a mass of flame." The fire department pumped water from the lake, but the work was exhausting and the flow feeble. A nearby fruit-and-soda stand was engulfed, and much of the railroad station burned. Sparks set fires in the woods. Damage to the picnic buildings was extensive, with the pavilion "a total wreck." When in July the Fitchburg Railroad was taken over by the Boston and Maine, the picnic grounds' days seemed numbered. Disaster struck again in May 1902. As a passenger train roared by late one afternoon on the way to Concord, the occupants felt a blast of heat from the ice house, burning near the tracks. "Picnic Buildings Passing Away," a headline ran. "By a building at a time the picnic grounds are losing their equipment. It would seem as if the lake would soon sing its swan song as a place for picnics." Days later, the bridge over the tracks caught fire too. Ruth Robinson, a young Thoreauvian who would later be Mrs. Ruth Wheeler, noted Concord historian, wandered among the empty bathhouses, boardwalks, and dance halls that survived, taking snapshots in 1903. By the following January all these structures had been demolished. Only granite piers and a cinder bicycle track survive today. Memories of the picnic grounds have faded away, but as late as the 1960s, an old man who frequented the opening day of trout season recalled the place affectionately, telling of how a black employee would row visitors around the pond for a nickel.[54]

Herbert Gleason looked back without nostalgia at Walden's "picnic resort" era, when "every summer thousands of people were brought to its shores to enjoy 'a day off': boating on the pond, swinging in the pines, patronizing the lemonade-stands and bowling-alleys, and then going away and leaving the usual assortment of lunch-boxes, waste paper, peanut-shells, etc.,—the whole a proceeding which would surely have brought sorrow to Thoreau's heart." Swimming continued, however, at the east end. He photographed the "swimming beach at Walden" in May 1903—the month of the Emerson Centennial—showing only the thinnest strip of sand, with men bathing.[55]

As the picnic grounds disappeared, another scourge, far worse, appeared. It aimed, warned the *New-York Tribune*, "To Desecrate Walden Pond." Concord "has of late been greatly stirred by the impending desecration of one of its most famous places of pilgrimage, the site of Thoreau's old hut. . . . Of late years, with the growth in popularity of this author, the Walden retreat has become a favorite haunt of visitors, who come from all over the country in thousands every summer. . . . Now a beef packing concern proposes to erect a large and extensive plant almost on the site of the old hut. . . . The beautiful little cove, situated in the depth of a grove of huge trees, relics of the first grove, is to be cleared away; a spur track from the railroad is to complete this tale of desolation. As if to add an additional horror . . . a huge number of pigs are to be kept by them and to be fattened on the refuse from the factory. Here, then, is the complete tale of the utter ruin impending." The *Chicago Tribune* railed against the "mammoth packing plant for hog products on the shore of Walden pond" with "thousands of hogs . . . fattened ready for killing." Local opposition was intense—although some favored the increased tax revenues—and Lake Walden was eventually dropped, a site in West Concord being proposed instead.[56]

Walden's "surroundings have been much changed by forest fires and the wood cutter," a guidebook cautioned, but devotees still came. Carriages for tours could be caught at Wright Tavern and Town Hall, or the true disciple could walk. "Finding my way to the spot by following the cowpath as directed, I spent one morning at Walden Pond," one said. "The air was laden with the perfume of the pines, and the sun made the waters transparent and as I washed my face in it, I tried to picture Thoreau doing the same." Composer Daniel Gregory Mason came at Thanksgiving, leaving the inn early in the afternoon and walking briskly out the white, sinuous Walden Road, a wintry sun gleaming through the clouds. "A little innocent hero-worship does no one harm at such times," he thought. Ahead a "serried rampart of pines" marked his destination. Turning onto one of the many wood paths, he walked along a ridge between deep hollows, "all covered with low shrubs." At the brow of the hill stood the pine grove; to the left, the house site, "marked now only by a square hollow full of dead leaves," with the cairn nearby topped "by an enormous rock." Mason for an instant felt an urge to live here, "but the next moment I was sane again," free of "fanaticism."[57]

A former student of the School of Philosophy returned in 1905 and found many changes. "The literary pilgrimage business has increased, partly no doubt because trolleys, automobiles, and bicycles have made the town more accessible." Guides and livery teams

Following Henry's footsteps. "H. W. Gleason at Thoreau's Cairn," May 19, 1908, courtesy Concord Free Public Library.

carried tourists pondward. He was surprised to find that "the woods themselves were intact," but "traces of the picnicker were everywhere," and the shores were "trampled and worn in spots." Springboards for diving stood conspicuous. Ominously, "in Walden wood I met an automobile not far from the cairn," these strange new devices being the subject of loud debate in Concord where, as early as 1902, a Mr. Warren of Lincoln had roared through in "The Red Devil" at considerably faster than the speed limit of 10 mph. On June 25, 1905, modernity further asserted itself at the pond when a movie company filmed "a battle and a lynching" there.[58]

Herbert Gleason gave his first Concord slide lecture on Thoreau in June 1903, remarking that his photographs would illustrate a Houghton Mifflin edition of the naturalist's writings. About this time Jones surveyed with pride the revolution in Thoreau studies that he had helped launch, thirteen years before, with "Thoreau: A Glimpse." He wrote Fred Hosmer, "Has it ever occurred to you that the 'Glimpse' is really the beginning of the Thoreau revival? It was the 'Glimpse' that got me the acquaintance with Miss Eliza Hosmer; through her I got to know of you; a desire to see Concord took me there; and from that day you and I have done our duty to Thoreau's memory. . . . This is history, and my dear Fred, we had a hand in it." But their role was about to end. A week later, Hosmer died, a devastating blow to Jones, who had lately lost a son to tuberculosis. As quickly as he had begun his Thoreau studies, Jones abandoned them. His importance would gradually be forgotten until historian Hendrick discovered his voluminous correspondence in an attic in 1974. He and Oehlschlaeger have argued that the collaboration of Jones, Hosmer, and Salt laid the groundwork for the modern critical understanding of Thoreau as more than an Emerson clone or "poet-naturalist," but a complex, socially and politically engaged person whose "retreat to Walden was not the act of a stoic egoist" but an "artistic enactment of withdrawal and return." We understand Thoreau and Walden Pond largely through the lens these men created.[59]

However, the advocacy of Jones and others cannot account entirely for the Thoreau boom. Scholar Lawrence Buell suggests how complex the picture of the transcendentalist's growing fame actually is. Houghton Mifflin, formerly Ticknor and Fields, had first published *Walden*, and later they promoted Thoreau to the point that one is tempted to rename Walden "Houghton Mifflin Pond." To some extent the back-to-nature movement itself, a genre in which Houghton specialized, created Thoreau, and not the other way around: the hermit of Walden assumed the role of a founding father to whom Muir, Burroughs, and Ernest Thompson Seton were heirs.[60]

British enthusiasm lent a huge imprimatur. That enthusiasm makes sense, given how effectively Thoreau himself had adapted Wordsworth for his own uses. Biographer Salt saw him as analogous to England's beloved nature writer Richard Jefferies, and in various ways he resembles Gilbert White and John Ruskin, too. By 1900 there were at least twenty of Thoreau's works in various editions available in Britain. He would be praised by intellectuals there, including Havelock Ellis and W. H. Hudson. William Archer lived in "Walden" cottage in Surrey in 1890–95. Labor Party advocates were great promoters; leader Robert Blatchford slept with a copy of *Walden* under his pillow, and "Walden Clubs" spread widely.[61]

Some American intellectuals embraced Thoreau only after being exposed to foreign writers. Growing up in New Jersey, Van Wyck Brooks heard of Thoreau from a family friend, a teacher named Eliza Kenyon who had studied at Alcott's School of Philosophy in 1879 and walked with Blake to Thoreau's grave and Walden. But Brooks's appreciation really owed to his later reading of Irish writers John Eglinton and George Russell (who signed himself "AE"). It was the former "for whom, in his own youth, Emerson and Thoreau had meant more than any other writers. . . . [He] affected my point of view as, more and more, I came to feel that Emerson, Thoreau and Whitman were creators of our one indigenous tradition of the spirit. But AE especially led me to see what I had not seen in America." Brooks's Pulitzer Prize-winning *The Flowering of New England* would contribute to the Depression-era American renewal of interest in Thoreau.[62]

Thoreau had an impact on the Continent, too. In 1902 doctor and poet Frederick van Eeden penned a foreword to a Dutch *Walden*: "The place where I am writing this is named after Thoreau's stay . . . as an homage and memorial to him who in our time gave us the strongest example of . . . the courage to be sincere and independent." Walden was a utopian community van Eeden founded near Amsterdam, which survived only seven years before going bankrupt, although tourists still flock to the site today.[63]

By a confluence of circumstances, 1901–10 was a boom time for Thoreau. More editions and reprintings of *Walden* appeared (twenty-six) than in the half-century preceding, 1854–1900 (twenty-three). But this was just the beginning—another forty-seven would follow between 1911 and the founding of the Thoreau Society in 1941. A critical moment came in 1906 with the publication of Thoreau's journal by Houghton Mifflin, following on the Centenary Edition of Emerson. The fourteen volumes were richly illustrated with Gleason photographs plus his map of Thoreau Country, still essential today. "He has even succeeded in identifying a number of localities described and named by Thoreau which had previously been unknown to any person now living in Concord." Gleason could not place the beanfield from *Walden* references, so he studied the journal. And, luckily, "on one of my early voyages to Concord I happened to visit the site of the beanfield with Mr. Sanborn, and he told me he distinctly remembered when Thoreau planted the pines for Mr. Emerson." As confirmation, "Dr. Edward Emerson drove me there one day and identified the locality."[64]

The quickening pace of Thoreau publications sent ripples through the world of American letters. In New York in August 1907, Sinclair Lewis labored on *Transatlantic Tales*. During lunch breaks he took an 1899 edition of *Walden* outdoors, jotting on the flyleaf, "Read in noon hours of freedom from the semi-bondage of 'Tales'; on benches in Bryant Park; my Walden 2 feet of bench, my pond a drinking fountain, my forest a few elms and maples, where sparrows twittered." This reading had enormous influence on him. Nor was he the only aspiring author to delve into *Walden* in city parks; in Philadelphia about 1919, novelist Christopher Morley wrote, "I can be as solitary in a city street as ever Thoreau was in Walden. And no Walden sky was ever more blue than the roof of Washington Square this morning. Sitting here reading Thoreau I am entranced by the mellow flavor of the young summer." A generation of writers was being shaped. Robert Frost praised *Walden* in 1915 for "that beautiful passage about the French-Canadian woodchopper. That last alone with some things in Turgenieff must have had a good deal to do with the making of me."[65]

On graduating from Grinnell College in 1910, Iowan James Norman Hall moved to Boston. En route, in Chicago, he bought *Walden* to read on the train. Inspired, he compiled a Thoreau-like list of the value of the items in his lodging at 91 Pinckney Street, and "needless to say, Walden Pond was immediately placed on the itinerary of destinations." He made regular "week-end pilgrimages. . . . In those days I had the Pond pretty much to myself, with the spirit of Thoreau for my only companion. . . . I had such respect for Thoreau's love of privacy that I felt something of an intruder even then, many years after his death. In the mind's eye I would see his solitary figure slipping across back lots on his way to the woods." Later, Hall would team up with Charles Nordhoff to write *Mutiny on the Bounty*. Hall was attracted to Tahiti for Thoreau-like reasons, asking Nordhoff, "Should a man keep his mental faculties at the

Mechanical invaders. The automobile transformed tourism and Concord, as seen looking east on the Mill Dam. The Greek Revival bank was built in Thoreau's youth: "The vitals of the village were the grocery—the bar-room—the post-office—and the Bank." Courtesy Concord Free Public Library.

stretch through all of his waking hours? I don't believe it. The Polynesians have taught me better. . . . The time is coming, I believe, when men will turn back to a simpler, ampler, more wholesome way of living. . . . They will seek wisdom from Henry Thoreau rather than from Henry Ford."[66]

Among the first important twentieth-century critical assessments of Thoreau was that of precocious University of Illinois undergraduate Mark Van Doren, published in 1916. Although ostensibly unsympathetic, Van Doren nonetheless followed Thoreau's example in his own life. In later years he would spend summers writing poetry in a cabin beside a pond in Cornwall, Connecticut, in emulation of the transcendentalist's lifestyle.

The picnic grounds having been abandoned, Thoreau's pond settled into a period of relative quiet, though literary pilgrims continued to come. "Your eye may well catch first a sight of the driftwood on the shore, of which there is much and think it makes the place untidy and wish that the Concord selectmen might have it removed," Winthrop Packard said in 1910. Thoreau too had seen "rotten wood along the shore" and used "driftwood from the pond" as fuel. "The woods grow tall all about," Packard said. "[They] climb the hills and top their summits with half-century old growth that yearly adds to its girth and stature." "Nor," he added, "need these trees again fear the sweep of the woodchopper's axe. The spirit of reverence for its shores . . . should prevent that." He enjoyed the fact that "the same stones [Thoreau knew] pave the wide margins today. You may walk all round it on this crushed granite." Packer's meditations were disturbed when "the first train of the day crashes by the southern margin and stuns the tympanum with a vast avalanche of uproar."[67]

C. T. Ramsey made his "Pilgrimage to the Haunts of Thoreau" in August 1912. Arriving by train, he walked to the library and hotel. At breakfast the second day, the innkeeper insisted that Ramsey wear a coat so as not to offend the ladies. Ramsey checked out in a huff, having come to town determined to stroll on foot, Thoreau-like, with khaki breeches, gray flannel shirt, white tie—and no hat or coat. He clutched binoculars and a Kodak. Gleason's map guided him to Sleepy Hollow and Walden, which he had feared would be "infested with camping parties, bungalows and camp-meetings." He dined on luscious blueberries at the cairn and scared a bittern up from the pond shore, the waters of which were extremely low. "NOTICE! Bathers will wear suitable clothing after 9:00 A.M.," a sign read. He swam naked anyway. "How it thrills me! I give a wild yell. . . . I am regenerated. I lave my sins in the water of Walden!" An Englishman came by to take photographs: "I've been huntin' the cairn all mornin. I say, sir, that mon Thoreau was a queer fellow, but he was a great mon sure." Boys swam at the east end, reached via the "Indian Path by the north shore."

At Brister's Spring "I, of course, drank some of the Pierian water . . . for inspiration's sake." A vireo seemed "the reincarnation of the poet" as it sang, "*Do you see it? Do you understand it? Do you believe it?*" Ramsey knocked at Sanborn's and was cheerfully received: "It was a treat of a lifetime to look into that frank old face as he told the tales of yore. I felt as if I myself were living in the golden days of the grand old Concord School." Sanborn said of Thoreau, "For a long time readers and literary men did not regard him with any seriousness. Now, however, the current feeling seems to have turned the other way; he seems to be the most popular of our Concord authors." But women, he said, rarely cared much. He allowed his guest to rummage among Henry's manuscripts that strewed a tabletop.[68]

Naturalist John Burroughs, seventy-five, received a surprise at his rural home in New York that same year: an automobile from Henry Ford, who sent a note expressing his admiration for the writer. Burroughs nearly killed himself learning to drive—he plowed through the side of his barn—but a friendship was born. In 1913, Ford invited Burroughs on a road trip to Concord to pay homage to the transcendentalists. Town residents watched in surprise as a fleet of Ford cars and trucks roared in on September 1, carrying tents, a field kitchen, even motion-picture cameras. They picked up Sanborn and lunched at the hotel. On this repeat visit Burroughs was still perplexed by Sanborn, "tall, gaunt, deliberate, sharp-featured, stooping; with Emerson's manners and ways. A rather dry, lean nature, but an interesting man. Hates Roosevelt." After lunch "we drive about town, to Walden Pond, to the Emerson house," which they wandered through. Burroughs was deeply impressed.[69]

Sanborn swam in Walden in 1914, a ritual of fifty-five years. As he slipped into the cool water, he thought of long-ago swims with Alcott, Channing, and Charles Dudley Warner—back when he could go a mile without touching bottom—and to boating and skating with Emerson and Moncure Conway. It was another drought year, the sandbar exposed to a length of fifty feet, only the second time he had ever seen it so. If the pond itself seemed eternally unchanging, as self-renewing as Thoreau had known it, the surrounding Walden Woods was greatly altered. A 1915 visitor remarked on fires caused by campers and the locomotive, plus "the gypsy moth has necessitated much cutting; therefore the pond is not as beautiful as in Thoreau's day." That moth had been introduced in the state in 1868-69 but was particularly devastating around 1900. Decades later, writing about Walden Woods, ornithologist Ludlow Griscom would say that "where an area has been constantly (and unnaturally) fire-swept, the humus and the top soil have been completely destroyed" and original conditions will never return. (Still, the fires had produced good habitat for prairie and golden-winged warblers, the region's first colonies appearing here in 1899.) In the 1950s, botanist Richard J. Eaton would confirm that repeated fires had left the place botanically and aesthetically poorer, decimating several species of plants known to Thoreau.[70]

As moth-eaten hardwoods got cut, Walden Woods looked increasingly threadbare. Edward Emerson was painfully aware of the glory they had lost since boyhood excursions when he hunted for salamanders, camped out, and boated with Thoreau. He regretted "these changed days, when the shores of our beautiful pond have been devastated by fire and moths and rude and reckless visitors, when the white sand and whiter stony margin of the cove have been defiled by coke cinders, when even the clear waters have ebbed." Five of the previous ten years had been dry. Whole sections of the woods were clear-cut, and as late as 1932 it was lamented that "Walden has lost very much of its former charm, owing, in part, to the passing of very many of the grand old trees that once skirted its shores."[71]

The ever-increasing popularity of east-shore swimming had apparently led to restrictions being imposed by the Heywood family. But now the policy was changed, so that in July 1917 young people were taking advantage of "the privilege recently granted to bathe in Lake Walden. Two new bath houses are being erected." Policeman Archie Simpson patrolled. The dressing rooms and "sanitiaries" marked the start of building on the eastern shore, pointing the way, however modestly, to its redevelopment for bathing in the 1930s.[72]

The Thoreau Centennial in summer 1917 brought an outpouring of acclaim. "One hundred years from his birth . . . Thoreau has come into his own. . . . He has since his death steadily advanced in popular and critical favor, until now he stands almost side by side" with Emerson. Thirty years before, no one could have imagined this. In May, the Appalachian Mountain Club gathered at Huntington Hall at MIT for a lecture by Edward Emerson and slides by Gleason, author of *Through the Year with Thoreau* and soon to emerge as one of the most important photographers of America's national parks. That same month, Houghton Mifflin published Sanborn's new *Life of Henry David Thoreau*, edited by Francis Allen. But Sanborn had not lived to see the occasion. Getting off the train on a visit to his son in Plainfield, New Jersey, he had been knocked over by a baggage truck and broken his hip. His injury was more serious than first thought, and he died in February, bringing to a close a colorful career, this friend of Thoreau having lived long enough to critique the poetry of

Transcendentalist knicknacks.
An early-twentieth-century
tourist stand in Concord
suggested the form of
Thoreau's Walden house.
"The Little Shop by the
Side of the Road," courtesy
Concord Museum.

Robert Frost. War news and mobilization overshadowed the July date of Thoreau's birthday. A small group huddled at the cairn. A more elaborate ceremony was organized by Edward Emerson in the Town Hall in October, with Gleason again showing slides.[73]

Inspired by these events, Gleason took more Walden photographs in 1918, showing cutting of trees on the north shore. His views from denuded Heywood and Bare Peaks call to mind the many changes these areas had undergone; Channing in 1863 had found Heywood's "almost overgrown." Gleason photographed the sandbar, which made a rare appearance. Fishermen and bathers enjoyed this sunny, exposed part of the shoreline. In 1880, Joseph Hosmer wrote of those who would make "a piscatorial visit to the 'devil's bar,' equipped with all the necessary appliances to allure the finny tribe to destruction." Later the "romantic" area of "Sam Hoar's Point," named for its owner, rang with the laughter of skinny-dipping boys.[74]

During this period, the annual count of "literary pilgrims" to Concord was estimated at thirty thousand. Further attention was drawn to the place by Gleason photographs published in *National Geographic* in February 1920, including one of the snow-covered cairn. He had been "Following Thoreau's Footpaths" for more than fifteen years. In March he photographed the cove, northwest shore, and railroad. About the same time, Edward Emerson sent a correspondent a map clarifying the location of "the bean-field where Thoreau had, in self defense, to 'effect the transmigration' of the wood chuck. . . . When the pines perished in a wood-fire it grew up to birches and scrub oaks, as now seen. Age and disease have destroyed nearly all of the pines which made a screen, in their prime, to the house."[75]

Walden Pond had become "a place of public haunt and even infested with that engaging product of civilization, the rowdy and the rough," the *New York Times* complained in 1921. Its constant unsupervised use worried the aging heirs who still controlled the shoreline. Around 1920 some talked of making Walden a state park. If the land did not come into the public sphere there might be subdivision for houses—Thoreau himself had foreseen "the ornamental grounds of villas which will one day be built here"—or a sanitarium. The slaughterhouse scare remained vivid in memory. The Walden Pond Protective Association, Prescott Keyes, president, met only once, in 1921, but its formation hints at growing concern. "Problems of regulating . . . traffic and preventing forest fires" stood paramount. Gleason recognized that "for many years there has been the wish on the part of a great many people, not only Concord residents but people living far away who have never seen Walden Pond, that the pond and its surroundings could be constituted a perpetual memorial to Emerson and Thoreau, to be maintained as far as possible in its original primitive condition."[76]

At this crucial moment, Edith Emerson Forbes and Edward Emerson stepped forward. They had inherited their father's love of Walden Woods and had watched his efforts to accumulate land to safeguard scenic beauties. Edith had bought Ebby Hubbard's woods to shield them from the ax; Edward promoted his father's historical legacy through writings and lectures; and both shepherded Emerson's papers for posterity. Now they helped orchestrate consensus among Walden landowners to give their holdings to the state. Looking back on this period, nature writer Edwin Way Teale would shudder, "Suppose the area had been made into estates and was protected by private owners?" Walden's twin to the west, White Pond, was privately owned and is now ringed by cottages. Walden too had always been privately controlled, but its future would lie, for good or ill, in the public domain.[77]

9

❧

Walden Breezes

(1922–1959)

❧

"Bill to Make Lake Walden a Reservation," a headline announced in May 1922. Passage of the bill promised to shape the future direction of Walden, "a spot that has strong literary connections with Concord." No longer private, it would come under state control as an eighty-plus-acre park with Middlesex County as trustee. Commissioners would make all management decisions, subject to the terms of the deed of gift from the Emerson, Forbes, Hoar, and Heywood families: "No part of the premises shall be used for games, athletic contests, racing, baseball, football, motion pictures, dancing, camping, hunting, trapping, shooting, making fires in the open, shows, and other amusements such as are often maintained at or near Revere Beach and other similar resorts, it being the sole and exclusive purpose of this conveyance to aid the Commonwealth in preserving the Walden of Emerson and Thoreau, its shores and nearby woodlands for the public who wish to enjoy the Pond, the woods nature, including bathing, boating, fishing and picnicking."[1]

In its reference to preservation, the deed seemed enlightened, meaning to prohibit any future Lake Walden picnic grounds as well as keep the place respectable, not like lowbrow Revere Beach in Boston. Herbert Gleason was delighted with the creation of the reservation, "a change very much for the better," forbidding the "peanut crowd" and limiting activities to those "in harmony with its wood-

August 24, 1924. The new reservation was a swimmers' mecca. "Throw Rubbish in Cans," a sign says. Gleason, "Overlooking swimming beach at Walden Pond," courtesy Concord Free Public Library.

land character." That change had come in the nick of time, as Walden was already "A Community Bathtub" for greater Boston. Gleason pointed to "the advent of automobiles and the greatly increased number of visitors to the pond, many of whom were utterly indifferent to the associations of the place." Swimming was a subject of dispute: "There are those who regret this ever-appreciation of the bathing facilities of the pond, claiming that it is out of harmony with the memorial object of the park; but both Emerson and Thoreau it is quite certain, would have been glad to see this huge and innocent enjoyment on the part of so many people."[2]

Gleason was pleased with improvements undertaken by the state, at the cost of eight thousand dollars per year. Dead trees and limbs were whisked away, and there was talk of reforestation. Two bathhouses were built and larger ones planned. Roadside parking areas were graded; the steep eastern slope was sodded and a path installed; and benches were built at the shore. A police station stood along the highway. At the house site, the cairn was enhanced with a

"Automobiles parked at Walden Pond." Gleason, August 24, 1924, courtesy Concord Free Public Library.

massive boulder bearing a bronze plaque—"But, alas, vandal hands / Have also contributed tomato cans," said a disappointed tourist. Gleason pointed nervously to "A Possible Menace": Boston and Maine Railroad, owner of thirty-seven acres west of the pond, had received offers from developers hoping to build campsites or house lots. Fortunately, in 1928 the strip between railroad and pond became part of Walden Pond State Reservation, which now embraced the entire shoreline.[3]

During a visit in summer 1924, Gleason photographed the Walden Breezes lunch stand, "Home of Hot Dogs," that had sprouted on private land across Walden Road from the reservation. Originally it "bore the appellation in large letters of 'Thoreau's Rest!' This appropriation of Thoreau's name for such a purpose scandalized a good many people." Gleason counted eighty-one cars zipping along Walden Road in ten minutes' time, a situation that troubled reservation staff, who feared that hungry swimmers would be run down while crossing to Walden Breezes. As a response, they began sales of refreshments at the reservation itself, only to be sued in 1930 by the lunch stand owner. In *Granara v. Commissioners of Walden Pond State Reservation*, the plaintiff argued, unsuccessfully, that food sales in the park violated the terms of the 1922 deed of gift.[4]

"As I walked past the outskirts of the village the twilight thrushes sang, and I had a feeling of being drawn into the past," tourist Robert Whitcomb wrote in 1931. "It seemed possible that I might meet the poet-naturalist in the dark, coming into town to have his shoes cobbled. But this feeling was very fragmentary. How otherwise, when the road was brightened with electric lights [and] macadamized." He passed the town dump at the foot of Brister's Hill, from which, the Concord Garden Club complained, trash was always blowing across Walden Street. How disappointing that "the solitude long ago departed from Walden to join Thoreau. The world has worn a path to his door—a concrete path." "I could stretch my imagination to believe that this was the wild spot where Thoreau came to test life out. But at the entrance to the pond property the feeling was shattered. Along the road, brightly lighted and noisy with radios, were two hot-dog stands," Walden Breezes and Jerry's Place. Thankfully "the State had preserved a vestige of the original pond before everything went to hot dogs and garbage."[5]

Far from Concord, in the basement of a Detroit bookstore, a twenty-year-old clerk read *Autumn* in 1919 with fascination. Wade Van Dore was a high school dropout, and Thoreau's call to a life of odd jobs and wandering struck a chord. Two years later he wrote Robert Frost of "my desire to put up a shack in New England and live as the author of *Walden* had." Frost replied, "First about Thoreau. I like him as well as you do. In one book (Walden) he surpasses everything we have had in America. . . . I don't know just what your plan would be. Would it be to camp out for a while . . . and then find a few boards and nails to build a shack of for the winter?" Van Dore moved east, worked for Frost as a handyman, and visited Walden Pond in 1922: "Using my hatchet for a shovel . . . I dug behind the cairn until I found the base of broken bricks and stones Thoreau had described depositing for his fireplace chimney. Extracting a half-brick to keep, I carefully refilled the hole" before filling a match bottle "with Walden water" that he kept for decades. In another homage to Thoreau, three years after Van Dore's pilgrimage—in the spring of 1925—the writer Henry Beston built a

Diving floats. Looking north toward the future Red Cross Beach. Gleason, "Swim beach at Walden Pond," August 24, 1924, courtesy Concord Free Public Library.

twenty-by-sixteen-foot wooden cabin on a Cape Cod beach. He lived there in 1926–27 and wrote a minor classic, *The Outermost House*, beloved as a modern-day *Walden*. The building survived fifty-three years until a nor'easter sent it bobbing out to sea. Van Dore and Beston were among the first of dozens of mid-twentieth-century individualists who would transform their lives by building on Thoreau's example.[6]

Another wave of scholarship and popular interest in Thoreau was about to gain momentum. As scholar Gary Scharnhorst says, the Thoreau known mostly by specialists "would be thoroughly rehabilitated during the economic crisis" of the Depression. "No longer the province of only nature-lovers and scholars, he would at last escape the garret-room where, like an offensive but crazy uncle, he had been so long confined." As if to herald this, President Roosevelt seemed to borrow from a Thoreau journal passage in his 1933 inaugural address when he famously intoned, "The only thing we have to fear is fear itself."[7]

In the new world of radio and transatlantic flight, the living spirit of Thoreau seemed increasingly remote, however. By 1932, the seventieth anniversary of his death, persons who had known him were few. Augusta French, eighty, jotted memories of Concord for her grandchildren in 1926: "I can see Miss Alcott now, breezy and snappy and using a lot of slang—I also see Henry Thoreau with bowed head, on his way to Walden Pond." David Loring, born in 1850, talked of Thoreau until his death in 1938. But these were nearly the last.[8]

The demise of those who had known Thoreau was not necessarily a bane to scholarship, as many of them had scorned him. Years earlier, when Thomas Wentworth Higginson told Judge E. R. Hoar that Thoreau's journals would likely be published, Hoar sputtered, "Henry Thoreau's journals? Pray tell me, who on earth would care to read Henry Thoreau's journals?" John Shepard Keyes, like Hoar a leading Concordian, scoffed at the "cult" of Thoreau and was disbelieving that Sanborn would have bothered to write a "'Life of Thoreau'!!!" When Edward Emerson researched a short biography, he interviewed townsfolk and "found that, while his manifest integrity commanded respect, he was regarded unsympathetically by many." A female friend of Gleason asked an old man by the roadside for the location of what Thoreau called "Spaulding's Farm." "'There never was any such place in Concord, ma'am.' 'But Henry Thoreau says there was, in his journal.' 'Henry Thoreau?'—with an expression of undisguised contempt—'I knew Henry Thoreau ever since he was a boy, and I never had much of an opinion of him. *And I hain't seen nothing since to change my mind!*'"[9]

When Robert Whitcomb visited in 1931, he was told of two persons who remembered Thoreau. He tried to visit Abby Prescott Hosmer but was turned away by a relative who snorted, "I never had much use for that loafer—a man who wouldn't pay his taxes." Frank Pierce, eighty-one, had sold shoes since 1865 in the same shop run by his father in Thoreau's day. " 'Thoreau?' he said. 'Yes, I remember him. We boys liked to run up to him and ask questions about animals and fishes. He was a queer kind of a duck. Always used to wear a gray shirt and tramp through the woods every day.'" Sitting down with an interviewer in 1932, the old man "mentioned the many

A quiet hour. New swim facilities were mirrored at the east end, April 19, 1933. Looking southeast from today's Red Cross Beach. "Sandy Beach Walden Pond," courtesy Concord Free Public Library.

inquiries about Thoreau of late years and seemed a trifle amazed at the great interest in him."[10]

Even as Thoreau attracted a new generation of readers, conditions at Walden were the subject of debate. The place was markedly more touristic and commercial now. John H. Moore spoke bitterly in the newspaper about what had happened in ten years since the takeover. "It was a great injury to Concord when the State acquired its holdings at Walden and opened those grounds to the public. . . . Even the privately owned buildings along Walden Road, near the pond, and far beyond it, for which the state is indirectly responsible, are a disgrace to the town. . . . If Thoreau should return to the pond he made so famous by his example and elegant writings, he would be sick at heart to view the deplorable changes."[11]

Herschel Brickell's response to Walden in 1934, recounted in *North American Review*, shows the worldly-wise cynicism typical of the moment. He "went to Walden . . . although a friend had warned him that it would be a disillusioning experience because of the bathing beaches, hot dog stands, and so on." The house site attracted the young and foolish: "A tall girl in an absolute minimum of bathing suit, placed a long white leg on top of the boulder so that the inscription could not be read." A swimmer dawdled up from the cove and asked idly, "I wonder why they piled so many stones around here. Must be to keep him down."[12]

Thomas Wood's Walden experiences of 1934 were similar. "We stop on Main Street for a Popsicle and drive on to the Pond, where

As seen by Edward Steichen. The master photographer stood near the cairn (lower left). Reprinted with permission of Joanna T. Steichen.

we put newspapers over the windows of the sedan and change our clothes for a swim. State cops in Roxy uniforms stand by to herd the cars in among the pines." Locals avoided the place—"Concord has disowned it"—but not so "the scum from nearby cities." Famous photographer Edward Steichen was careful to avoid modern-day intrusions when he made "repeated trips" in 1934–35, taking pictures for a limited edition of *Walden.* Thoreau's book "had many points of identification for Steichen," an historian notes, and indeed his seminal 1890s photographs of forests near Milwaukee seem imbued with the spirit of Thoreau in Walden Woods. That Steichen and Thoreau should have finally crossed paths at Walden seems appropriate. His photographs, some of them quite stylized and abstracting, are unique in the history of photography at the pond.[13]

Midcentury painters gravitated to Thoreau, including Charles Burchfield, Marsden Hartley, and Edward Hopper. N. C. Wyeth's beloved copy of the journal occupied a shelf in his studio at Chadds Ford, Pennsylvania—"the perfect revealment of the complete Thoreau"—and excitement buzzed in 2002 when it was found to contain an original manuscript page from Thoreau's lecture "Walking." An historian explains that Wyeth "made several pilgrimages to Walden; during one he inscribed a copy of Samuel Arthur Jones's *Thoreau: A Glimpse* 'N. C. Wyeth / Concord, Mass. / 1909,' and a letter of 1913 describes the 'spell of Walden' cast by another visit." Wyeth wrote in 1919, "I have been an enthusiastic student of Thoreau for twelve or fourteen years," and he considered illustrating a book of the naturalist's writings. That September he visited Concord in preparation, sleeping beside Walden in a blanket. When a reporter sat down with Wyeth in his studio in 1932, the artist spoke so enthusiastically of Thoreau, the interviewer was misled into supposing that the two men had known each other. Wyeth visited Walden again in 1935, and a year later there appeared *Men of Concord*, with ten color plates by him and pen-and-ink drawings by his teenage son, Andrew Wyeth, born a century to the day after Henry Thoreau. The elder Wyeth painted two versions of *Walden Pond Revisited* (oil, ca. 1932; tempera, 1942), quasi-religious and enigmatic.[14]

In 1935, Concord purchased the Fairyland area as the Hapgood Wright Town Forest, continuing the work of Edith Emerson Forbes, who had long safeguarded it. This area would remain unspoiled. Up the road at Walden, however, the state had just eradicated the last lingering traces of the wild. "New extensive green lawns stretch almost to the shore of the crystal-clear water. Wide, clean roadways wind beneath the pines to the beach which is 450 feet long and to the 40 by 80 raft with four diving boards. . . . In addition, long white bathhouses for men and women, as well as a building for first aid and personnel headquarters help to make Walden Pond a first-class swimming centre." These changes, undertaken with little sensitivity to the landscape and no concern for what Thoreau or pilgrims might have thought, were permanent alterations. Seven decades later, the smaller bathhouses have been removed and the big central building rendered more aesthetic, but still it looms over the bathing beach and arrests the eye from most points along the Walden shore, a brash intrusion.[15]

Superintendent Fred Hart oversaw these "improvements." He wished to allow as many summertime visitors as possible to enjoy Walden in ease and safety, and so in 1931 he undertook a fateful step: to cut a path around the pond. "This footpath follows what was thought to be the one Thoreau walked. It was started four years ago, and is now complete," said a reporter in 1935. As adjacent hillsides became trampled, quantities of soil began to flow into the once-crystalline pond.

In 1935, ecological prerogatives were a thing of the distant future. Visitor safety was the emphasis. The reservation staff numbered twenty-five, including security officers and fifteen lifeguards—"capable, brawny young men, bronzed by exposure to the sun and wind"—who were proud that there had been no drownings in five years, though that summer alone they had effected eighty-seven rescues. "Every forty-five minutes, day and night, the lake is patrolled with a motorboat." The state chemist announced, "No pollution has yet been found, contrary to rumors."

Crowds were huge: 483,000 swimmers came in summer 1935, it was said, from the Boston suburbs of Waltham, Belmont, Newton, Roxbury, Somerville, and Arlington. "What used to be the Sunday attendance is now the daily crowd, and the number of Sunday visitors has increased enough to cause contemplation of extending the beach and making a new cement raft to replace the present one. This proposed raft would require eighteen thousand cubic yards of cement." Sundays regularly saw 25,000 swimmers, and on the hot day of July 14 the crowd numbered 35,000. Fishing was encouraged, and salmon were stocked with the existing bass, white perch, yellow perch, horned pout, calico bass, and trout.[16]

At the same time, in 1934–35, the "new Concord turnpike" or bypass plowed through the heart of Walden Woods. The divided highway permanently impeded walking, spoiled Brister's Hill, and flooded the landscape with ceaseless roaring. It made Walden Pond convenient by car, swelling the crowds still further. "Kimball's Walden Breezes" trailer park thrived along Walden Road north of the state police barracks, along with the Golden Pheasant Lunchroom. Cars and motorcycles crowded in among the pines. Policing was insufficient, with complaints that "hoodlums and thieves . . . have run rampant on the reservation every summer for many years. . . . Access is

Progress. Two modes of transportation met in Walden Woods when the Concord bypass automobile bridge was constructed over the ninety-year-old Deep Cut of Fitchburg Railroad, August 5, 1934. Looking southeast. "By-pass crosses R. R. at the Cut," courtesy Concord Free Public Library.

gained to cars by breaking windows and forcing locks and even clothing in the bath houses is regularly rifled."[17]

As the Depression dragged on, attention turned nationwide to problems of erosion, soil depletion, and farm abandonment. In Wisconsin, wildlife-management expert Aldo Leopold bought a sand farm in 1935 as a weekend retreat where he could spend time close to nature and try ways of revegetating the landscape. On eighty acres he planted white pines and shrubs, living in a chicken house that had been converted into a cowshed. His experiences at "The Shack" formed the basis for that Thoreauvian classic, *A Sand County Almanac*, accepted for publication in 1948, shortly before Leopold died of a heart attack while fighting a fire that threatened his pines. In recent years, Leopold's fame as conservationist rivals Thoreau's.

Another author who turned his attention to the land during this troubled decade was Joseph Wood Krutch, editor of the *Nation*. He first read *Walden* in 1930. Two years later, as farm prices plunged, he bought an old homestead in Redding, Connecticut. In this escape from New York he studied nature and read Thoreau, which culminated in a 1948 biography. The inspiration of Henry led him to become a nature writer, his popular books selling hundreds of thousands of copies.[18]

Countless others were thrown into a Thoreauvian life by hard circumstances, as millions found themselves unemployed. Midwesterner Myron Wilder recalled, "The Great Depression was a leveler for many men. . . . I absconded the dehumanizing, long lines of desperate men. . . . Turning back to the countryside, I expropriated a one-room dwelling even cruder than Thoreau's cabin on Walden, and situated on the slopes of an idyllic pond. . . . With a small hand-grinder and an inexpensive supply of wheat and corn, I made five dollars stretch" from October to May.[19]

During these grim years, Thoreau studies flowered. Raymond Adams, a young English professor at the University of North Carolina, sent an essay to Henry Salt in England in 1929. Salt in turn gave Adams the twenty-one-year-old revised text of his Thoreau biography, never published. A grateful Adams planned to write a modern version—a passing of the torch between scholarly generations. Adams spent a year in Concord in preparation, only to have historian Henry Seidel Canby beat him to the punch. Adams's widow recalls her husband's frantic attempts to find a publisher: "They told Raymond there was no market for another biography. That cut Raymond to the quick. He was literally ill. He came down with hives. He'd never been that badly hurt. He never did write his biography." Nonetheless, Adams played a critical role in the developing scholarly appreciation of Thoreau. And in 1931 he and Raymond Emerson marked what they thought was Thoreau's cellar hole depression with four granite posts.[20]

Adams spent a day with Herbert Gleason at the Concord Tercentenary in September 1935, a link between Thoreauvians past and present. Adams started a Thoreau newsletter the next year. In time it reported the death of Gleason, who had, at the age of eighty-two in September 1937, taken his last photographs of Concord, concluding a forty-year career of devotion to Thoreau Country. After his death, his glass plates were passed from hand to hand and stored in dank basements. They narrowly survived. Fortunately, seven thousand of them came to the Concord Free Public Library in two accessions, in 1954 and 1997, and form a valuable record of once-rural Thoreauvian landscapes.[21]

In spring 1936, shy student Walter Harding bought a cheap copy of *Walden*. "It was in the middle of the depression then and one dollar was a lot of money for someone trying to earn his way through college." The Massachusetts native had visited Sleepy Hollow and Walden in high school, but they made no impression. He loved birdwatching, though, and Thoreau's bird notes were appealing.

Mobile home. Concord's Tercentenary parade motored along Walden Street near the foot of Brister's Hill, September 14, 1935. Walden house floats appeared in 1950 and 1985 parades, too. "Ripley Gage representing Thoreau and hut at Walden," courtesy Concord Free Public Library.

"More and more he grows upon me," Harding wrote in his diary. Concerning *Walden*, he soon wondered, "How did I live without it?" Thus began the obsession that produced the greatest of twentieth-century Thoreauvian scholars, who, with his infectious enthusiasm, dominated the field for decades and shaped the careers of countless students. His discovery of Adams's newsletter led him to found the Thoreau Society and to undertake doctoral studies under Adams. He numbered his first copy of *Walden* "one" in the catalog of his Thoreau collection, which in time swelled to thirteen thousand items.[22]

Canby's 1939 *Thoreau* culminated the decade's boom in interest. For a generation the book remained the standard biography, until supplanted by Harding's in 1965. Adding to Thoreau's own corpus, it was published by Houghton Mifflin. Editor Paul Brooks had driven around Concord with Canby visiting Thoreau sites. *Thoreau* was something of a publishing sensation, proof of how its subject had become a cottage industry.[23]

In September 1938, Concord lay at the eastern edge of the eye of the great New England hurricane, which flattened countless trees. One casualty was the remnant pines behind Thoreau's house site, survivors of those that had sheltered him. A different kind of storm blew up in December: "Spirit of Thoreau Stirs Concord Gas Station Fight," blared a Boston newspaper. "Henry David Thoreau was said to have a 'stimulating contrariness,' a characteristic that is rampant today in his home town, Concord, where sides are being

New age of asphalt. The intersection of Walden Street and the Concord bypass, top of Brister's Hill, 1930s. A gas station was proposed for the left corner, near the Walden Pond State Reservation sign. Looking north. Courtesy Concord Free Public Library.

taken on whether or not a filling station shall be erected on the site of the author-naturalist's bean field." John Dunn of Watertown had proposed the station, at the corner of Walden Street and the new bypass. It would be the fifth near Concord, "a Colonial-type frame house with a central chimney, and dormer windows. The house will be attractively landscaped and surrounded by a picket fence." In hearings before the Board of Selectmen, Planning Board, and Board of Appeals the fight was lively. Some called it "a great asset to the town," located nowhere near the house site. But local historian Allen French was outraged by this assault on "traditions and standards of beauty" and was "bitterly opposed to the idea of commercializing and disfiguring a Concord beauty spot." The most impressive opponent to the filling station was Gladys Hosmer of the Woman's Club, who inhabited Sanborn's old house on Elm Street, backing up to Concord River. She loved the town's history, and her husband was a ninth-generation Concordian related to Fred Hosmer. A cheeky letter announced her intention "to convert my establishment into a recreational center. . . . The area will be flood-

Home of hotdogs. A lunchstand familiar to generations of swimmers. Edwin Locke, FSA photograph, September 1937, Library of Congress.

lighted by night . . . and a loud speaker will bring you your favorite band. . . . The users of these facilities will be accommodated by the sale of refreshing tonic, hot dogs and ice cream (28 flavors). . . . I believe that these plans offer a really constructive effort to boost Concord into a bigger, better, busier place." In the end came compromise, the gas station being built across the bypass from the beanfield. Only "after years of protest by Thoreauvians" was this eyesore finally removed, in 1975.[24]

As Thoreau's works were reprinted in college literature anthologies and popularized by Canby, his name grew increasingly familiar. E. B. White took advantage by writing an irony-drenched essay based on a 1939 visit to Walden. Best known today as the author of *Charlotte's Web*, White ardently admired Thoreau and had "always wanted to see Walden Pond." After a night at the local inn, "Next morning early I started afoot for Walden, out Main Street and down Thoreau, past the depot and the Minuteman Chevrolet Company." He addressed Henry: "I knew I must be nearing your woodland retreat when the Golden Pheasant lunchroom came into view—Sealtest ice cream, toasted sandwiches, hot frankfurters, waffles, tonics, and lunches. . . . Beyond the Pheasant was a place called Walden Breezes, an oasis whose porch pillars were made of old green shutters sawed into lengths. . . . Behind the Breezes, in a sun-parched clearing, dwelt your philosophical descendants in their trailers, each trailer the size of your hut, but all grouped together. . . . The ground was packed hard under the heel, and the sun came through the clearing to bake the soil and enlarge the wry smell of cramped housekeeping. Cushman's bakery truck had stopped to deliver an early basket of rolls."

White continued exploring. "Leaving the highway I turned off into the woods toward the pond, which was apparent through the foliage. The floor of the forest was strewn with dried old oak leaves and *Transcripts*. From beneath the flattened popcorn wrapper (*granum explosum*) peeped the frail violet. I followed a footpath and descended to the water's edge. . . . In the shallows a man's water-logged shirt undulated gently." On the east shore stood "dressing rooms for swimmers, a float with diving towers, drinking fountains of porcelain, and rowboats for hire." For White, the gulf between expectation and fact, hope and reality was appalling.[25]

Increased 1930s visitation brought new curiosity about the source of the pond's water. There had long been talk of secret underground connections, and some said that a man who drowned in White Pond later popped up in Walden. Others swore that Walden was fed by New Hampshire's Lost River. Superintendent Hart drove to New Hampshire with a bushel box of skewers, each labeled "W. P." He threw them into Lost River, then returned home and waited for them to appear. But "none of the initialed sticks have ever shown up at Walden, which would tend to disprove the belief that this Pond has any connection with Lost River." At the same time, Hart took an interest in the depth of the lake, sending divers down in summer "to see the bottom of the Pond and how it is formed." One winter he put markers on the ice in ten-foot squares and dropped lines to take measurements. These exercises were prelude to a serious study by professional limnologist E. S. Deevey in August 1939. From a rowboat Deevey used a hand winch to lower a lead weight attached to a piano wire. His fifty measurements confirmed the accuracy of Thoreau's soundings.[26]

Glad somebody showed up. Scholars Walter Harding and Raymond Adams, center, lunched at the Colonial Inn during the first meeting of the Thoreau Society, July 1941. From the Thoreau Society Archives. Courtesy of the Thoreau Society, Lincoln, Mass., and the Thoreau Institute at Walden Woods.

To Walt Harding, the time seemed right for a Thoreau Society that would meet every summer in Concord. Nor was he dissuaded by Raymond Adams's saying, "No more than fifteen people are going to show up." Using the mailing list for Adams's newsletter, Harding organized a well-attended "Thoreau Birthday Mecca" in 1941. Participants were to assemble at the cairn, but skies threatened rain, so two hundred squeezed into the D.A.R. Chapter House in Concord. Lunch followed at the Colonial Inn. In the course of the day, speeches were given by Adams, Harding, Odell Shepard, Harry Dana, and Francis Allen. Gleason's colored glass slides were shown. To Harding's delight, the day was a success, and "a 'National Society on Thoreau' is planned."[27]

Shepard was a distinguished participant. As a boy, he had read all of Thoreau's works by the age of twelve. He went on to become a college professor who won a 1937 Pulitzer for his Alcott biography, and later he served as lieutenant governor of Connecticut. His selection of excerpts from the journal remains in print. At Authors' Ridge he "wrestled with his fear and his despairs / Hour after long hour, pleading for some sign" from Waldo and Henry, and he "heard prophetic verses run / Along the waves of Walden's plashy edge." Devoutly Thoreauvian, he spoke his mind. When Harvard professor Perry Miller published Thoreau's "lost" journal volume as *Consciousness in Concord*, Shepard called it "Unconsciousness in Cambridge." The book was fatally marred, he said, by "frequent

Pilgrim trail. The Thoreau Society in Walden Woods. From the Thoreau Society Archives. Courtesy of the Thoreau Society, Lincoln, Mass., and the Thoreau Institute at Walden Woods.

Homage. Raymond Adams, at left, and others placed stones on the cairn, July 1941. From the Thoreau Society Archives. Courtesy of the Thoreau Society, Lincoln, Mass., and the Thoreau Institute at Walden Woods.

inaccuracies of statement, by assertions unproved and unprovable, by confusions and inconsistencies of thought, by the dragging-in of matters wholly adventitious, and by the use and abuse of violent language in a prose style habitually feeble, fumbling, slovenly, and dull."[28]

The Thoreau Society managed a follow-up meeting in Concord in 1942, the year the eight-hundred-ton Liberty Ship S.S. *Henry D. Thoreau* was launched from a West Coast yard and that no fewer than four editions of *Walden* were published, one for just a dollar. At the gathering, bylaws were adopted. Someone proposed that "no cranks or radicals be admitted into the Society." At this, the formidable Harry Dana rose—Henry Wadsworth Longfellow Dana, grandson of two great nineteenth-century writers, who liked to orate from atop the cairn—and condemned the suggestion for excluding Thoreau from his own club. The early society provided a haven for free-thinkers and those who marched to a different drummer. The *Chicago Tribune* wondered, "The Thoreau Cultists—Are They Insane?" Dana had been fired from the faculty at Columbia during World War I for pacifism; Harding was a conscientious objector during World War II. Delightfully odd was Roger Payne, "hobo philosopher" who haunted the New York Public Library. Inspired by *Walden*, he wrote the book *Why Work?* and lived by peddling it. Every summer he hitchhiked to the society meeting and spread out his sleeping bag on the porch of Concord High School. He tantalized Harding with promises of donating his entire estate to the society, which even added an "Inc." to its name to allow it legally to receive the anticipated gift. When Payne was run over by a taxi, the estate arrived in a cardboard box: twenty-four copies of *Why Work?*[29]

Interest in Thoreau remained high in wartime. A doctoral dissertation a year had appeared on Thoreau in the decade leading up to 1944, when an armed forces edition of *Walden* was issued. For infantryman returning home, trailer camping offered an affordable housing option, as soldier James G. Sliman discovered. Discharged from the army at Fort Devens, Massachusetts, he slouched east with his travel trailer looking for a trailer park. At Crosby's Filling Station in Concord, "Harv" Crosby pointed him to Walden Breezes, operated by Malcolm Humphreys. Sliman lived there for a few months before using his entire savings to buy the place. For thirty years the cigar-smoking Jimmy would be a fixture at Walden Pond, expanding and regrading the trailer park at the expense of Thoreauvian topography and working in the refreshment stand and short-order grill fifteen-hour days in summer.[30]

When Paris was liberated, the first book sold in Brentano's bookstore was *Walden*, to an American serviceman. Summer 1945 brought peace as well as the centennial of the Walden experiment. "Almost twice as many old ladies as usual made the pilgrimage to Concord" and ate "a box lunch in the picnic ground that stands as [Thoreau's] monument." They were not alone, Walden being packed with ten thousand swimmers a day that season, Main Beach taking on a Coney Island-like appearance.[31]

Among the crowd of one hundred Thoreauvians who assembled at the cairn at ten A.M. on July 4, a century to the day after Henry moved in, was Lincoln resident Roland Wells Robbins. He felt out of place, knowing nothing about Thoreau and having never visited Walden, but his friend Allen French had invited him. Robbins had attended only a year of high school and had worked as a window cleaner and painter during the Depression, but he published a book of poetry and dreamed of being a writer. Wartime brought a patriotic opportunity to write an historical volume, *The Story of the Minute Man* (1945). In the process he got to know Concord historian French, who presided over the ceremony at the cairn. As speakers read from *Walden*, some began to debate the discrepancies between Thoreau's accounts and the present location of the cairn. Where, exactly, had Henry's dwelling stood? French turned to Robbins and said, "You are the one to settle this issue once and for all."[32]

These words changed the course of Robbins's life. Luckily he had not skipped the ceremony to play tennis, as he had considered doing. He plunged in, filling notebooks with records of library research and probings of the site with steel rod and shovel. His dig, first in a long career as self-taught archaeologist, is recounted in his 1947 book, *Discovery at Walden*. An unforgettable encounter took place at the instant Robbins found proof of the house's location: "On Sunday afternoon, October 28, [1945,] I struck . . . a large quantity of plaster in the first shovelful of dirt. 'Eureka!' I shouted, 'this is it!' . . . Much plaster and a number of large pieces of brick with mortar on them came to light. . . . 'What are you digging for?' inquired a young voice. Looking up startled, I found two army sergeants viewing my labors. . . . [One] seemed unusually interested in what I was doing. . . . 'You mind my asking your name?' I inquired. 'I am Henry David Thoreau, Jr.', he replied." Young Thoreau, a distant relative, was on his way home to California from the war in Europe. He presented his army dogtag as proof of his identity.[33]

From the moment he found the chimney stones, Robbins debated how to mark the site. The day after the discovery, local Thoreauvian Wallace Conant stood and watched as he dug, remarking that "it would prove to be one of the world's greatest shrines." "Let's hope so," said Robbins. At first he hoped to cover the foundations with a grate or glass, allowing them to be seen, but this proved

Marking the Thoreau house site at Walden, March 29, 1948. The two middle posts frame Thoreau's doorway. Note the accuracy of Channing's description of the house site: "It is in the path to the pond." From the Roland Wells Robbins Collection of the Thoreau Society. Courtesy of the Thoreau Society, Lincoln, Mass., and the Thoreau Institute at Walden Woods.

unfeasible. He sought advice from a world-famous authority, expatriate Bauhaus architect Walter Gropius, who lived not far away in Lincoln in an ultra-modernist house of his own design. Would he undertake the project? Gropius expressed admiration for Thoreau but explained that because he had been in the country only eight years, a local should be afforded the honor. Robbins turned to Thomas Mott Shaw, a traditionalist architect who lived on the outskirts of Concord and worked for the Boston firm of Perry, Shaw and Hepburn, renowned for designing Colonial Williamsburg, Virginia. Shaw agreed to help, in 1946 proposing an arrangement of nine granite posts outlining the house site, with a chain running between. Inside, the hearthstone was indicated by an inscribed slab surrounded by boulders, flush with the ground. Concord historian and newspaper editor Ruth Wheeler donated rocks from the local farm where Thoreau had been born. The nine granite posts, funded by a thousand-dollar contribution from the Middlesex County Commissioners, were cut at Fletcher Quarries in Westford.[34]

If Robbins's archaeological explorations celebrated the centennial of Thoreau's move to the pond, so too did Edwin Way Teale's 1946 edition of *Walden*. As a young man Teale had discovered Thoreau during a four-hundred-mile solo rowboat trip from Louisville to the mouth of the Ohio. In a bookstore in a river town he bought a dusty copy of Thoreau's writings to read as he drifted along. Later he took advantage of the end of wartime travel restrictions to visit Concord and shoot more than a thousand photographs for his illustrated *Walden*, which, like his previous publications, aimed to popularize nature for the general public. He kept a diary of his first visit, in September 1945: oak galls and ant lion pits on the trail around the pond; bumblebees buzzing in goldenrod by the cairn; a squadron of military bombers roaring overhead; the "considerable effort" required to find Goose Pond, then "almost dried up, [with] vast stretches of reddish-topped sedges stretched across the marshy lakebed." Writing the *Walden* introduction even as the radio crackled with news of the atomic blast at Bikini Atoll, Teale marveled at the worldwide reach of Thoreau and told of an Australian schoolboy who had named the most important bodies of water in the United States as the Great Lakes, Mississippi River, and Walden Pond.[35]

The messages of Teale's *Walden* resonated with the booming postwar culture of trailer camping, even as magazine cartoonists found humor in long-suffering wives dragged into dark and stormy woods by husbands on Thoreauvian spirit quests. That same year, 1946, schoolteacher Gilbert Byron, who shared Thoreau's birthday, discovered "a modern Walden, in the heart of the Chesapeake Country." He and his wife built a nine-by-twelve cabin on San Domingo Creek near St. Michaels, on Maryland's Eastern Shore, hauling materials in an old Chevrolet. Byron itemized the costs at $133.17. His marriage dissolved, and he was still living alone in the enlarged house when he penned his memoir *Cove Dweller* at age eighty, in 1983—a long-sustained Thoreauvian experiment. After the "Chesapeake Thoreau" died in 1991, his cabin was threatened with demolition, but eventually it was transported to an Audubon Society center for restoration.[36]

Not long before Byron moved to his cove, a young couple in Boston decided to undertake a dramatic Thoreauvian experiment. Vena Angier produced musicals; her husband, Bradford, was an editor. Sick of city life, Bradford proposed that they see "if what Thoreau proved a century ago about returning to nature would still work today. That's it, Vena. Let's put Thoreau to the test." They relocated to Hudson Hope in northern British Columbia, where they fashioned a log house twenty feet by twelve. Roofing paper, heater, and stove pipe drove its cost to $48.16. Here they lived four years, writing articles that allowed them to survive on $10 a week. Temperatures dove to sixty-three below, but life was happy, as they told in *At Home in the Woods: Living the Life of Thoreau Today*.[37]

Walden attracted a devoted following among creative types. The Thoreau Society's first life member was composer Charles Ives. The year 1948 saw the publication of *Walden Two* by psychologist B. F. Skinner, calling for a new kind of utopia. He was faulted for the presumptuousness of his title, but his passion for Thoreau was longstanding. "When I came to Harvard for graduate study [in 1928], I became interested in New England and its history, and I discovered Walden Pond. I had a bicycle and would ride out to the pond to swim" in the cove. "I began to read Thoreau. I took an interest in the site; I used to go out in the late autumn to clean up after the picnickers. . . . When I met the girl I was to marry, I took her on our first date to Walden . . . and on the shores of the Pond she taught me to play chess."[38]

Those shores were increasingly unattractive, however. Eyeing the pond's trash-strewn beaches, a poet decried "mirrored banks profaned from east to west / By thoughtless strangers." "Horses and bicycles on the path around Walden," Teale commented in his diary in 1945. August Derleth complained of papers, bottles, and tin cans when he arrived on a pilgrimage from the Midwest, a hundred years to the month after Thoreau left the pond, to sit cross-legged in meditation on the hearthstone. This Thoreauvian had tried to do for Sauk City, Wisconsin, what Henry did for Concord, penning a book called *Walden West* (1961) and even naming his son "Walden William." On three pilgrimages—in 1938, 1947, and 1965—he recorded incremental degradation as the path grew wider and the shores echoed to the noise of locomotives. On the early morning of his first visit he counted seven trains in seventy-five minutes. On the second there were nine in two hours: two streamliners, two diesel, and five steam, thundering past the still waters.[39]

To those who arrived to admire Robbins's Thoreau memorial, the condition of the cove seemed disgraceful. Robbins watched aghast as an automobile backed over a granite directional marker downhill from the house site, snapping it off. That summer, 1949, saw organized swimming at the cove, and in July, Teale and Harding spent twenty minutes listing the kinds of litter that strewed the ground, assembling what Teale would call in his classic *North With the Spring* "fearful and wonderful evidence of America's high standard of living." They concluded, "Walden lives in all of our dreams as the ideal sanctuary from the cares that infest our days. Unfortunately today's visitor there is in for a rude awakening." At its gathering the Thoreau Society issued a statement "deploring the shameful littered state" of the reservation and calling for a return "to the dignity it deserves as a national shrine." Ruth Wheeler fired off a stern letter to the commissioners, who feebly blamed the public for being so messy and budget shortfalls for limiting litter collection. Finally at New Year's 1950 the authorities bulldozed barriers across incoming roads to keep automobiles out. Permanent good resulted from the protest: the bounds of the reservation were extended to the bypass in 1956, and Raymond Emerson donated the family's remaining holdings south of Walden, greatly enlarging the area protected as parkland.[40]

As birdwatching flourished, thanks in part to a popular series of Audubon Society films, Roger Tory Peterson found himself wealthy and famous, his name synonymous with his Houghton Mifflin guidebooks. In Britain, James Fisher had achieved similar fame with his BBC radio chats about birds. Together they conceived of a book and movie called *Wild America* based on a joint hundred-day expedition across the continent. Near the start of their odyssey, Fisher and Peterson visited Concord, in April 1953. It was an appropriate destination, "the most continuously and consistently bird-watched area in the New World," going back to Thoreau. Their guide was Lincoln resident Paul Brooks, editor at Houghton Mifflin, who had, with office mate and ardent Thoreauvian Francis Allen, accepted

At "Thoreau Farm." Ruth Wheeler, local historian, addressed the Thoreau Society at her home, July 1952. Thoreau was born on this site, in a house that was moved away in 1878 and replaced by this one. From the Thoreau Society Archives. Courtesy of the Thoreau Society, Lincoln, Mass., and the Thoreau Institute at Walden Woods.

Peterson's bestselling *A Field Guide to the Birds* for publication twenty years earlier. But disappointment awaited Peterson and Fisher at Walden. "To me Walden Pond was an anticlimax," Fisher said. "It looked like many an acid pond in Surrey's greensand heath."[41]

The cheery *Wild America* would prove myopic about America's growing environmental ills. These postwar years were marked by a certain complacency, but some Thoreauvians raised their voices in dissent, premonitory of the coming 1960s. Thoreau seemed subversive, and they noted that a Prague edition of *Walden* was impounded by the Russians "pending ideological investigation into its contents." Henry Miller, living in a cabin on the California coast, speculated in a preface to Thoreau's *Life Without Principle* that the author would have denounced the atomic bomb. Joseph Wood Krutch said of Henry, "He was in a sense a prophet of doom. . . . He lived at the beginning of the great era of invention and of industrial expansion. He predicted the failure of a great experiment that was just being tried. We are living at the disillusioned end." And in his essay

"Walden Pond in the Nuclear Age," Winfield Townley Scott was certain that Thoreau "would beat a hasty and permanent retreat from the beach frivolities on the shore of Walden Pond."[42]

During the centennial of *Walden*, E. B. White drafted a meditative essay, "Walden—1954," in a boathouse on his Maine farm, "the same size and shape as [Thoreau's] own domicile on the pond— about ten by fifteen, tight, plainly finished, and at a little distance from my Concord. . . . My house fronts a cove. . . . I find it agreeable to sit here this morning, in a house of correct proportions, and hear across a century of time his flute, his frogs, and his seductive summons to the wildest revels of them all." From an even wilder outpost, an old farmhouse in Jamaica, Vermont, another Thoreauvian book appeared the same year, Scott and Helen Nearing's *Living the Good Life: How to Live Sanely and Simply in a Troubled World*. Scott had helped pioneer American socialism before joining the Communist Party in 1927. Two years later he met Helen Knothe, leaving behind his wife and children and exhausting his savings in moving to Vermont with her in 1932. They undertook maple sugaring, earning only what they needed to survive. *Living the Good Life* helped launch a postwar "homesteading movement," and although Thoreau is mentioned only in passing, the parallel to his Walden woods life in the centennial year was inescapable. Scott was already seventy-one in 1954, but he lived to see the book's reprinting in the 1970s for a new generation. Hippies hailed the work as a bible, and it sold two hundred thousand copies. Fittingly, the Nearings's papers are housed today at the Thoreau Institute at Walden Woods.[43]

Perhaps the most ingenious transmitter of Thoreauvian ideas to late-twentieth-century culture was Jack Kerouac, a native of Lowell, Massachusetts. Writing his novel *On the Road* in Denver in summer 1949, he "rented a small house in the foothills outside of town. He thought of himself as a modern day Thoreau." In the centennial year a re-reading of *Walden* directed him toward the study of Buddhism, which he would help popularize. "He dreamed of visiting Thoreau's hut at Walden Pond and finding a small box full of marijuana, and he was sure that it meant that his faith needed to live in the wilderness to survive." Later he retreated to a lonely cabin at Big Sur. But he and fellow Beats did not obey Henry's strict abstemiousness; Kerouac wallowed in drugs and died of alcoholism, a self-destructiveness contrary to Thoreau.[44]

At Walden Pond itself, Sandy or Main Beach saw thirty-five thousand swimmers on hot weekends in 1952. To serve these crowds, the commissioners had expanded the reservation staff to sixty-seven, a rich source of patronage. But the boom ended with the rainy years 1953–55, when Concord was soaked with up to fifty-three inches of precipitation annually, ten more than the twentieth-century average. Swimming was banned when Walden rose high, flooding the beach and concrete dock. Chairman Thomas B. Brennan (D-Medford), acting in the spirit of the decade, determined to bend nature to human needs. In July 1956 he announced, "We think we know 'the secret' of Walden Pond now. . . . But we don't want to say anything more about it yet. Not until we're more certain." He added, "Knowledge of 'the secret' should make possible control of the pond's water level for the first time." Whatever he supposed the secret was, the solution was inelegant: on August 1 he set up two roaring gasoline motors at Deep Cove to pump four thousand gallons per minute over the ridge top and down into Heywood's Meadow. The deluge erased roads and trout ponds along Heywood's Brook. In fourteen days the lake dropped one foot, enough of a success for Brennan to propose boring a permanent overflow system through the ridge and connecting it to the Andromeda Ponds, sacrificing their bog vegetation. Ruth Wheeler blasted this "attempt to improve on nature," saying it would have been cheaper to install a floating dock that could rise and fall and that pumping would "simply draw in more water from the deep underground springs."[45]

The problem resolved itself, as 1957 was a dry year, and swimming resumed. But Brennan would not let nature's caprices spoil the public's pleasure again. In May the Middlesex County Commissioners announced a "twenty-year program" to transform Walden further. A variety of initiatives were planned, including building "a replica of Henry Thoreau's hermit hut on the shore of Walden Pond . . . at the original site." Brennan said that "construction of the Thoreau hut should be a boon to sightseers. Hundreds come to the pond from all over the world." In the ethos of the 1950s, increased visitation

Red Cross Beach, June 1957. Looking east. Photograph, Save Walden Committee.

Desecration. Photograph, Save Walden Committee.

equaled laudable progress, a reporter adding, "Soon the woods will ring again to anything but solitude."[46]

But the chief goal was a 150 percent enlargement of the swimming beaches. The Red Cross held swim classes for six hundred children annually, a program disrupted when water levels were too high or low. Brennan wanted a huge new beach on the northeast shore, formerly Thoreau's beloved "fireside" but now "the ugliest part of the pond" where trees had fallen and erosion was severe. He awarded a $9,300 contract to a Lincoln construction company for "leveling a section of the hillside for additional parking space [and] construction of a foot road down the slope," allowing ambulance access. A one-hundred-foot-long, $25,000 cinderblock bathhouse was planned. The entire project would cost $54,500.[47]

The commissioners proceeded quickly. By mid-June 1957 their contractors had sawed down 150 trees on an acre and a half, shoved soil far out into the pond, and cut a zigzag road through what remained of the hillside. Bulldozers and a crane churned through shallow water offshore. When the Thoreau Society met in July, its members were horrified. The desecration of the sacred shoreline cast a pall over the meeting, at which the invited speaker, Indian ambassador G. L. Mehta, called Walden "the spot which Gandhi had said he wanted to visit above all others." Ironically, the president's address, prepared well before the bulldozers did their work, was titled "Thoreau and the Preservation of Wildness." One observer noted, "The attack was so brutal and sudden (the entire operation took only fourteen days) that the Thoreau Society alone, in Concord for its annual meeting, was in position to mount a counter-offensive. This group is exquisitely unfitted for massed militancy. It gathers just once a year from all over the country to listen to some 'papers' and then atomizes into bemused solitaries marching off to Walden, each to the sound of a different drum." Nevertheless, the society hastily organized a Save Walden Committee, chaired by Gladys Hosmer, who had defended the beanfield in the gas station imbroglio two decades before. Also on board was Ruth Wheeler, who bitingly commented, "One can only suppose that the pond in its natural state did not attract enough people. Possibly more people will come when we have made it entirely artificial and synthetic. More people, more jobs, to be handed out to deserving hangers-on." They were joined in the fight by architect John E. Nickols, Edwin Way Teale (president of the society in 1957–58), Roland Robbins, and other Thoreauvians, and endorsements were obtained from such luminaries as Shepard, Gropius, Canby, Brooks Atkinson, Kenneth W. Cameron, Van Wyck Brooks, John P. Marquand, Samuel Eliot Morison, Norman T. Newton, and Alvin G. Whitney.[48]

At first Save Walden sought compromise. They offered to acquiesce in the matter of the road and beach so long as the commissioners and Red Cross would desist from building the bathhouse. Neither opponent would agree to this, and a three-year legal battle began. Society members emptied penny jars to pay mounting bills. Professors begged donations from their American literature classes. Edward Waldo Forbes, Emerson's eighty-five-year-old grandson, testified in court. After Save Walden lawyers obtained a temporary injunction to stop the work, the story was carried by the press nationwide. Letters of support poured in for Walden: "Let it remain as it is, nectar and ambrosia for the spirit and mind, and not become a Philistines' Paradise of 'weenie roasts' and 'hot dog stands.'" When the Superior Court vacated the injunction, Save Walden appealed to the Supreme Judicial Court of Massachusetts as *John E. Nickols & Others vs. Commissioners of Middlesex County*, and a public drama ensued.[49]

Gropius toured the devastation and lamented, "the beauty and tranquillity will be lost for all of us." Shepard called the commissioners "ignorant, stupid and unfaithful to a sacred trust." For some Thoreauvians, the rape of Walden was proof that modern technology and society had gone mad. Nickols condemned "bulldozer culture." In his 1958 address to the society, Teale deplored this "artificially-stimulated" generation in a "world spinning the webs of greater complication. . . . You and I want to enjoy Walden Pond. And what happens? We find ourselves fighting to preserve a pond to enjoy. If the world is too much with us now consider the fact that the population of the United States will be 10,000 greater at the end of this meeting than it was at the beginning. . . . Thoreau had his distractions. But he had no power lawnmowers outside his windows, no jet planes above his roof, no ringing telephones, no rock-and-roll radio, no bang-bang-bang westerns on TV."[50]

Not all experts were against the bulldozers, however. "What Side Would Thoreau Take in Walden Pond Row? Some Scholars Claim He Wouldn't Care a Bit," said a Boston newspaper, quoting Perry Miller of Harvard: "I think the beach at Walden does great service to the youngsters of Cambridge and Arlington and Somerville and can't see why Henry Thoreau would have complained about it." As would happen again in later decades, the preser-

Chainsawed. Architect John E. Nickols of *Nickols vs. Commissioners* inspects the damage. Photograph, Save Walden Committee.

vationists were indicted for elitism and snobbery: they were trying to keep out the rabble. Novelist Truman Nelson, on the committee, was so angered by the smears that he kept himself off the witness stand even as his friends were remorselessly grilled. Had he testified, he feared "I would say to hell with the People if they keep waving the bulldozers on to make every wild irregularity in the country, level, accessible and convenient, with plenty of parking and clean rest rooms. And to hell with the Red Cross if they think their pious public service is more important than the preservation, in its wholeness, of this monument to a book. . . . Let Walden alone!" His friend Nickols, who lived just a half-mile from Walden, did testify, only to find himself accused, in essence, of being "a racist and a snob." Countering those charges took quick thinking:

> Prosecutor: You say unauthorized people go in there. By unauthorized people you mean the newer races, don't you?"
>
> Nickols (taken aback): I do mean races. I have seen motorcycle races being held on the path around the pond.

Nickols found his career and personal life wrecked by the enemies he made during the course of these ugly proceedings.[51]

Brennan gave as good as he got, charging, "Did we want children to drown for want of this [road]?" He "personally preferred children to trees." He was a nature lover himself who liked to stroll around the pond, puffing on his cigar. To restore the place to how

Thoreau knew it, "We'd have to cut a lot of trees. [Thoreau's] records show his complaint that wood choppers were always up there." In court he and his allies stressed, "Thoreau never owned an inch of land there and has absolutely nothing to do with Walden now."[52]

Media coverage was widespread—in the *Boston Herald* and *Globe*, *Newsweek*, *Time*, *Saturday Review*, *Christian Science Monitor*, and the *London Times*, plus CBS radio and NBC TV. In the end, the Supreme Judicial Court ruled in May 1960 that the Middlesex County Commission had not acted according to the deed of gift from the Emerson and other families and must immediately "aid the Commonwealth in preserving the Walden of Emerson and Thoreau." Judge Ammi Cutter ordered removal of the new road and replanting of trees. Use of slope material to fill the pond was ruled improper, and the hillside was to be returned to a natural contour. There could be no new bathhouse unless concealed. The protracted court battle had cost Save Walden eleven thousand dollars but was regarded as an important victory for the national historic preservation movement, then gaining momentum.[53]

The Battle of Red Cross Beach marked a turning point in the history of Walden Pond. It demonstrated that the County Commission was indifferent to conservation, and for the first time there was serious talk of forcing a change in management, to the state Department of Natural Resources or even the National Park Service. In the meantime preservationists fumed at how little was done to repair the scars—indeed, the zigzag road is still visible on the hillside today, only reforested in the 1980s and then through the impetus of volunteers. The high cost of the court battles would pale when compared to the millions needed to keep bulldozers at bay in coming decades, for even as this fight was waged, the sound of a larger war could be heard just over the treeline, as the first onslaught of automobile suburbia struck Concord and Lincoln. With shocking suddenness, every Thoreauvian locale was threatened. Naturalists agonized. Ornithologist Ludlow Griscom decried "the continued deterioration of the country . . . near Boston." Botanist Richard J. Eaton followed in Thoreau's footsteps, but without his forebear's sense of leisure and slow time—instead, often just weeks in advance of "the subdivider and his bulldozer."[54]

The contretemps focused attention, too, on the disastrous erosion problem. One critic noted that the destruction of the hillside at Red Cross Beach did nothing to address "the tragically eroded path" just beyond it. Walden's problems were acute, "clusters of rusting beer cans in the clear shallows; long, vicious slashes of erosion in the descending slopes." Erosion had been an issue for years, as a deeply cut "Footpath around Walden Pond" photographed by Fred Hosmer in the late nineteenth century showed. A visitor of 1905 confirmed, "The shores of Walden were trampled and worn in spots." But the coming of crowds after 1930 and the carving of the round-the-pond path made things far worse. Walden is a kettle pond with steep sides of loose sand and gravel thinly covered with humus; break through this layer and yellow sand starts flowing. In 1947, August Derleth found the path "noticeably wider" than on his previous visit nine years earlier. By 1958 critics were blaming the commission for spending "well over ninety percent of the money allotted to Walden" on beach facilities, even as "conservation experts claim that unchecked erosion of the banks and trails has brought the whole area close to ruin."[55]

There was increasing conviction that "every canon of conservation, engineering, and park management had been violated at Walden for years." One person who needed no convincing was Mary Sherwood. Nicknamed "Wildflower Mary," she became the first American woman forester in 1934 and later the sometime-owner of a wildflower nursery, park guide, and plant researcher, supplementing her income by working as a hotel maid. "All I have ever really wanted to do is live in the woods," she said. Sherwood first read *Walden* right out of college, inhabiting a tent beside a river in Connecticut, but a later rereading fully seduced her: "By then I had developed a philosophy of my own, which I was astounded to see paralleled his." From her home in Maine she wrote a letter protesting the Red Cross Beach affair. Impelled by love of Thoreau, she moved to Concord in 1959—living, it is said, in a chicken coop—and her diary records her exultation at her first visit to Emerson's Cliff, a row on the pond, walking on its ice in winter, hunting for arrowheads "in eroded paths." In October 1960 she got word that the commissioners were tackling the erosion problem in a hamfisted way by building wood cribs and dumping gravel. "I'm so mad at myself for

Cribwork combatted severe erosion. Alessandro Macone, photographer, ca. 1960, courtesy Concord Free Public Library.

not getting there at the start of the work—maybe I could have made some kind of noise to stop it." In years to come Sherwood would prove one of Walden's most vocal preservationists.[56]

Even as Save Walden fought the Battle of Red Cross Beach, Concord residents voted 603 to 38 in an October 1958 town meeting to build a new municipal dump just a few hundred yards from Walden. The old dump, on Walden Street closer to town, was being closed to make way for a large regional high school. Among the few dissenters was landowner George Kacavas, who had "built a Thoreau-like cabin on the shore of Goose Pond and . . . become attached to the area as a recreation site." Advocates of the dump promoted it, paradoxically, as a safeguard against commercial intrusions in Walden Woods, part of a proposed " 'green belt' . . . preserved from the hands of industry, business, and real estate development. According to proponents, the new dump area can be easily reforested, once it is filled in." By 1970, the town manager hoped, "technology will have given us another way of getting rid of refuse" and the dump could be returned to trees. Still, the vote suggested how little affection the average Concordian had for the memory of Thoreau. Harding liked to tell of "one dear old lady" who made an annual visit to Sleepy Hollow to lay flowers on the graves of Emerson and Hawthorne—but turning to Thoreau, would shake her fist and say, "None for you, you dirty little atheist." One can imagine her voting an enthusiastic "yes" on the landfill, the construction of which marked a discouraging conclusion to the tumultuous 1950s at Walden.[57]

IO

✣

In These Days of Confusion and Turmoil
(1960–1989)

❧

If Concordians were ambivalent about Thoreau, as evinced in their digging a landfill by Walden Pond, young Americans were about to take him up enthusiastically. In 1960, an icon of an earlier age of radicalism testified to the impact *Walden* had had on him. Upton Sinclair wrote, "I am glad to say that Thoreau was an influence in my life. I lived in a hut too—only mine was a tent! Like him, I learned to stand alone, and speak truth as I saw it." A new folio edition of *Walden* was published, Joseph Wood Krutch noting in its preface, "Within the last few years attacks upon 'conformity' and incitements to its opposite have become so numerous as to constitute a recognizable genre." Novelist James Michener, speaking "In Defense of Beatniks," found Thoreau an early prototype. Another Thoreau enthusiast was the young Massachusetts senator elected president in November. John F. Kennedy's mother, Rose, had lived in West Concord as a child and fondly recalled church picnics to Walden, where she had learned to swim. When raising her own children in Boston, she emphasized physical fitness, including swimming, and drove them all the way to Walden from Hyannis Port on summer Sunday mornings in the 1930s. In later years her son Edward spoke of his affection for Walden Woods "where I spent many weekends as a child. My mother herself grew up not far from Walden. She loved it here and organized family outings to the pond on a regular basis. We all enjoyed picnicking in the familiar and welcoming woods," and they liked "to race between or scale the stately trees." The children would eat sandwiches on forested banks and listen to quotations from Thoreau. When a 1992 Kennedy biographer called Rose distant and uncaring, her surviving offspring fired back in a letter to the *New York Times*, "She took us for walks in our strollers and piled us into the family station wagon to go swimming at Walden Pond."[1]

The early 1960s were a history-minded time, thanks to President Kennedy's rhetoric and the Civil War centennial. The media observed the one hundredth anniversary of Thoreau's death in May 1962, and there was even a little exploitation: the John Hancock Life Insurance Company of Boston ran a full-page color advertisement, "He Heard a Drummer in the Forest," in *Time, Newsweek*, and the *Saturday Evening Post*, showing Thoreau wielding an ax as he built his Walden house: "He lived deep and dreamed deep until he could almost see a universe in a bluebird's eyes." The Thoreau Society organized a gala symposium in New York City, where the lunch menu included Walden Beans and Heywood's Meadow Cranberry Sauce. Thoreau was inducted into New York University's Hall of Fame in the Bronx, for which the society had long campaigned; ironically, the hall was abandoned shortly thereafter and fell into disrepair. Kennedy sent a telegram stressing "Thoreau's pervasive and universal influence on social thinking and political action." For Indian ambassador Braj Kumar Nehru, "There is an unrelenting conflict between the Transcendentalist and the 'Organization man.'" Some struck a note of warning: Thoreau "would be appalled at the progress we have made in a hundred years toward the complete mechanization of man and his life."[2]

The Wilderness Society took advantage of the occasion to draw attention to the Wilderness Bill, introduced in Congress in 1956 but now stalled. That legislation would keep portions of the national forests roadless and unspoiled. The group's motto derived from Thoreau, "In Wildness is the Preservation of the World," and its executive secretary was Howard Zahniser, former president of the Thoreau Society. He and Secretary of the Interior Steward L. Udall organized a celebration in the woods at Dumbarton Oaks, Washington, D. C., where Robert Frost and Justice William O.

Douglas spoke to a crowd of one hundred, including Chief Justice Earl Warren and poets Allen Tate and Robert Lowell. Frost praised *Walden* as literature: "It has everything." Douglas "reported a recent check of the shoreline close to the site of Thoreau's cabin at Walden Pond had disclosed the presence of 116 beer cans, 21 milk bottles, and much other debris, the signs of a 'mass invasion of wilderness areas—a serious problem all over the country.'" The historic Wilderness Act was finally passed in 1964.[3]

The Thoreau Centennial happened to coincide with the publication of a book that triggered an epic change in public opinion about the environment, Rachel Carson's *Silent Spring*, which warned of the dangers of DDT. Carson said, "In this country the pen of Thoreau . . . most truly represented the contemplative observer of the world about us." She kept a copy of *Walden* by her bedside and quoted it to her friend Teale, who would soon be a pallbearer at her funeral, as she was gravely ill with cancer. Paul Brooks edited Carson's book for Houghton Mifflin, chose the title, and defended it against the firestorm it engendered from government and industry. One USDA official said, "The balance of nature is a wonderful thing for people who sit back and write books or want to go out to Walden Pond and live as Thoreau did. But I don't know of a housewife today who will buy the type of wormy apples we had before pesticides."[4]

Meanwhile, in Concord, Mary Sherwood organized a centennial march to Sleepy Hollow, where children strewed Thoreau's grave with wildflowers. Visitors to the cairn at Walden came upon two rainsoaked Thoreauvians who had walked there from Woodstock, New York, carrying a trumpet with which they mournfully played "John Brown's Body." For Sherwood it was a red-letter day. She had confided in her diary two years earlier, "I'm impressed with the futility of my life. . . . Here I am, at age 54—running around a store [in Concord] waiting on people. . . . I've shunned marriage as a trap that would prevent expression of my inner self—yet single & free I have not accomplished a thing." Increasingly she sought refuge in the transcendentalist age, with historic Concord "the center of my universe. . . . I am finding living in the past of a hundred years ago much more pleasant & intriguing [than] the present [with its] arithmetic, commercialism & . . . confusion." She noted that a quarter of Americans were reported to be involved in some kind of crime:

"Who wants to propagate, or save, such a civilization?" But the Thoreau observances poured meaning into her existence—"I knew by the next morning that what I had accomplished May 6th was the crowning glory of my life. . . . *If* there *is* an after life Henry knows what I did & approves."[5]

Sherwood was a friend of Roland Robbins, who, building on his experiences in excavating the Thoreau house site, erected a replica of that dwelling in his backyard in Lincoln. Wade Van Dore and Sherwood helped with the landscaping. Robbins began advertising blueprints and construction materials for sale by spring 1964, the year he was elected president of the Thoreau Society. He would launch a second such campaign around 1980. At the latter date, kits of "The Thoreau-Walden Cabin . . . now available to the discriminating buyer" cost $2400 for drawings and the frame, the other materials to be supplied by the purchaser; the total cost was estimated at $4000 to $6000. Using his own labor, he supervised the erection of one at the Thoreau Lyceum in Concord in 1969 for $3000. In a similar gesture, Edwin Way Teale built a log "writing cabin" at his Connecticut home on the same measurements as Thoreau's, near a pond—his "way of paying homage." He extricated a lichen-covered stone from an old wall along a lane to add to Thoreau's cairn.[6]

On thirty-three wooded acres near Skyline Drive in Virginia, *Washington Post* editor Charles Seib began construction of a weekend cabin in May 1966. "The Woods" or "Walden South" was twenty by sixteen feet, like Henry Beston's, but the primary inspiration was Thoreau, "the most powerful of the influences that brought me here." There was no plumbing, electricity, or telephone, and parking was kept two hundred yards away. Total cost was $1500, which Seib itemized in his book, *The Woods: One Man's Escape to Nature*— far more than Henry had spent, but in line with inflation. Concord house prices had gone from $800 to $50,000 since 1845, Seib calculated, a 6250 percent increase; Thoreau's house today would cost $1758. To create a half-acre Walden, Seib dammed Jonathan Run, and nearby he and his wife planted a seedling white pine from the real Massachusetts pond: "I excuse our small vandalism on the ground that the seedling was struggling for life in the shadow of a trash basket near a picnic table," its roots tangled in a broken bottle.

At The Woods, Seib found a retreat from troubling news of Vietnam, but he worried about "the developers and the bulldozers that surely will come someday," and one "idyllic morning" spent in "kinship with Thoreau . . . was shattered when I turned on the radio to catch the 10 a.m. news. It was a sketchy broadcast, but chilling. Four students were killed yesterday at Kent State University in Ohio." Troubling questions arose, perhaps akin to those Thoreau faced during the John Brown crisis. Seib wrote, "Is it right, I ask myself, to accept this kind of escape when there is so much to be done in the real world? Does any man, today, have a right to run away, even for a little while? Is it a cop-out?"

Seib sold The Woods in 1980, recalling today that it

had drawbacks once the joys and satisfactions of construction were over. It was hot and humid in the summertime. Moreover, it was heavily infested with poison ivy, to which my wife is allergic. It became clear as the years passed (and as the thrills of discovery and creation I had experienced down there faded) that while it served well as a personal retreat it would never become the family getaway that I had fantasized in justifying my investment in it and commitment to it. Also, there was a more subtle change. By writing a book about that place, as I did several years after completing it, I somehow changed it; in a strange way it seemed no longer to belong to me. After the book appeared and I began to receive copies of reviews and letters from readers I started having dreams in which the outside world invaded my hideaway: a supermarket suddenly appeared just a few yards from the cabin; strangers came and turned my bucolic little half-acre pond into a crowded cement swimming pool. Just dreams, to be sure, but after publication of the book symbolically admitted the public, The Woods was never the same to me.[7]

Seib, Teale, Robbins, and others in the loose-knit nationwide community of Thoreauvians were united in their conviction that the hermit of Walden was excitingly relevant to modern life. In a WBZ radio interview in 1962, Walter Harding stressed this point as he summarized his approach to teaching Thoreau:

At home with his hero. Dean of Thoreau scholars, Walter Harding visited the Walden house site every summer. Ca. 1970s, courtesy Walden Pond State Reservation.

I've been amazed at the number of students who have suddenly, upon reading Thoreau, come alive, some to the extent of suddenly just dropping all the college work and taking off for the woods. . . . What he wants you to do is to decide what your great interest is in life and follow it, not follow through in life what your parents want you to do. . . . Don't be a conformist for conformist's sake. Have the courage to do what you really want. . . . I think the most important part of his message, the most important thing he has to say, is his cry for individualism in an age which is becoming more and more devoted to the mass man and to the conformist. That the only way we can get any progress, any new developments, is through the individualist, not through the conformist. And this is what Thoreau stands for, more than anything else.

Harding toured Japan for seven weeks at year's end, 1964, preaching this message to standing-room crowds. His curiosity about Henry was insatiable; he collected every possible memento and tidbit and would eventually even write an article, "And Where

Did Thoreau Part His Hair?" He fervently believed in his idol as a prophet for modern times, and when he published the definitive modern biography, *Days of Henry Thoreau*, a year later, he somewhat startlingly dedicated it to Teale and Martin Luther King, "who although they lead widely disparate lives have both found inspiration in Henry David Thoreau." Talk of the new book lent excitement to the society meeting in July, as did the unveiling of a plaque atop the east shore marking National Historic Landmark status for Walden Pond. A hundred members of the society participated in the cere-mony before walking to the cairn and around Emerson's Wyman Lot. Afterward they adjourned to Robbins's backyard replica.[8]

Environmental consciousness had grown nationwide since *Silent Spring*. For the first time a Pulitzer Prize went to a book about nature—to Teale for *Wandering Through Winter*, fourth in his series of seasonal volumes that had begun fifteen years earlier with *North With the Spring*. The award gave evidence of the historic shift in atti-tudes. Even as public appreciation of the outdoors and Thoreau was making gains, so too was serious scholarship. Harding announced with excitement that a scholarly edition of all of Thoreau's works, including the journal, had been approved, a major "papers project" of the kind only devoted to America's most important political and literary figures. A team of scholars would collaborate with a uni-versity press to produce texts that exactly reproduced Thoreau's words—especially significant for the journal, extensively edited for readability in the 1906 edition. Harding urged patience, warning Thoreauvians that the process might go slowly: "Editing of the new edition is expected to take five years." Thirty-six years after Harding's initial prediction, only fourteen of the proposed thirty vol-umes had appeared, the costs and logistics having proved much more daunting than expected.[9]

"I have been to Walden pond a number of times," Seib recalls, "but I don't consider it a symbol. I think that finding Thoreau's Walden is much more difficult than just going to his pond." For Mary Sherwood, however, Walden was a symbol of profound sig-nificance, and by the mid-1960s she had belatedly found meaning in her life by passionate devotion to the cause of Henry. She glowed when called "Lady Thoreau," and she devotedly tended the bird feeders she had placed beside his grave. By 1965 she had achieved a

Thoreau Lyceum. Visited by Ed Schofield, tireless 1980s crusader for Walden Pond and Woods. Republished with permission of the Globe Newspaper Company, Inc., from the December 13, 1994 issue of the *Boston Globe,* ©1994.

long-standing dream by securing backing to buy a little frame house in Concord and found the Thoreau Lyceum, a kind of on-the-scene counterpart to the Thoreau Society, which met only once a year. Funds were provided by the matriarch of a local family, the Moores, that had grown wealthy in the hotel business (Bob Moore was a cofounder of Sheraton). The lyceum stood next door to the lot where the Thoreau family's Texas House had been; Sherwood hoped to rebuild that house and an adjoining pencil factory. Tourists streamed in, and the lyceum became a place beloved of memory: warm, quirky, intimate. This was perhaps the happiest period in Sherwood's life, but it was not to last. She had antagonized Gladys Hosmer, queen of the Thoreau Society and Concord generally and always lukewarm about the lyceum, and soon was quarreling bitterly with lyceum officials. The board wanted her out. Tensions exploded on the eagerly anticipated Thoreau stamp day.

Lyceum and society supporters had pushed for a Thoreau postage stamp, finally issued by the U. S. Postal Service on the author's birthday in July 1967. Cynics remarked that citizens would, ironically, mail their checks to the IRS with it, licking Thoreau's backside in the process. Artist Leonard Baskin provided a grotesque and tortured ink portrait that many thought was ugly; Gladys Hosmer said it was the first stamp that made you want to spit on both sides. Still, excitement ran high at the lyceum, crowded with celebratory Thoreauvians, who watched in astonishment as Sherwood quarreled angrily with a lyceum officer. "In desperation, yearning with every ounce of me to be rid of this pest, I slapped his face," Sherwood told her diary. Her antagonist shouted, "This is it, Mary. You are fired." By late August she had been evicted, and Anne McGrath, a native Concordian who had met Frank Sanborn as a child, took her place as curator. "I drove to Walden," Sherwood wrote in her diary. "Threw my front door key to the Lyceum into the Pond." Then she turned north, to Maine, ousted from home, job, and true calling.[10]

Mary was back in town by spring, living in her trailer with twenty cats and obsessed with getting back her position at the lyceum. She had found her purpose in life, only to lose it again; at sixty-one, she could hardly start anew. Desperation seized her. "Today I stopped at Thoreau's grave & 'promised Henry' I'd do whatever it takes to get back to my rightful place in the Lyceum," she told her diary. She brooded beside Walden: "While I was at the hut site I made up my mind still further—to go all the way to the Supreme Court if necessary—to get a new law made if none exists to protect founders of non-profit institutions from grabbing Boards." ("Didn't do," she later clarified in the margin.) What options did she have? She could not afford a lawyer. The town had turned against her, having been told that she "walked out" on the lyceum, not that she had been fired. *Time* magazine did not answer her letter. Some bold act seemed appropriate. The recent murder of Martin Luther King had stirred her deeply, and so she conceived of a "one-woman civil rights march" to disrupt the Thoreau Society gathering in July.

In the middle of the society business meeting in First Parish Church, Mary Sherwood appeared in the doorway "dressed in a burlap dress woven with fresh daisies and carrying a lantern in her hand." As Harding remembered with a smile, "She rushed up the aisle and, seizing the lectern, began reading a violent denunciation of all the officers of the Thoreau Lyceum." She may have underestimated her foes, including that force of nature who had turned back the bulldozers at Walden: "Gladys Hosmer, in her memorable formal robin's egg gown, her elbow-length white gloves, and her wide-brimmed garden hat, started dashing up the aisle, shouting, 'Point of order, Mr. Chairman! Point of order!'" Sherwood was soon subdued.[11]

Mary's diary, recently made public, sheds light on this bizarre episode. At 6 A.M. on Henry's 121st birthday she had arrived at his Walden house site. From the supposed beanfield just uphill she gathered shrub oak leaves to stitch to her burlap dress. Torn sneakers symbolized the poor standing up to the rich; the lantern was for the Light of the Lyceum, extinguished since her departure. She had considered carrying a stuffed cowbird, a parasitic species that lays its eggs in other birds' nests. "All these gimmicks to get the Lyceum back" were likely to be futile, she knew. Defeated, Sherwood again left Concord—this time, it seemed, for good.[12]

When Fred Hart retired as superintendent of Walden Pond State Reservation in 1957, Joe Lenox, thirty-one, replaced him, serving twenty-eight years. A World War II navy veteran and Concord fireman, Lenox ran a tight ship, efficiently managing crowds that reached twenty thousand a day on summer weekends. His staff sometimes towed eighty cars off Walden Road and hauled out three pickup loads of trash daily. (Some locals recall these controversial years differently, however, one remembering "autos everywhere" and never any towing.) Eleven lifeguard chairs lined Main Beach, a motorboat patrolling offshore. The beach closed promptly at seven P.M., owing to glare off the water, and was neatly raked at day's end. No bikinis were allowed, and swimming was limited to Main Beach (with classes at Red Cross Beach). Lenox approved of the controversial commissioner Brennan—"he had all good ideas"—and saw a real need for the 1957 beach expansion. The cribwork on eroded paths in the 1960s was installed under Lenox's supervision: "We did it ourselves. We graveled it, seeded it, pumped water onto it from boats." Winter days brought up to four thousand ice skaters, and opening day of fishing season saw anglers lined up around the pond—to the dismay of environmentalists, who watched fragile banks get trampled.[13]

During Lenox's tenure came the driest year of the twentieth century in Massachusetts, 1965, when only twenty-nine inches of precipitation fell, a full fourteen below average. This was the least rain since 1822. The following year was the fourth parched one in a row, and Walden shrank to six feet below "normal." The sandbar stood a foot high and a hundred feet long, and two trucks could drive abreast all around the shoreline. Its waters having dwindled out of the shallow, safely swimmable areas, Walden was closed to bathers from 1966 to 1968. "The pond may be finished as a swimming facility," one commentator mused, but there was talk of using it as a "standby reservoir" for such drought years—reviving an idea older than *Walden*. These were good days for Thoreauvians seeking solitude, including seventeen-year-old Tom Blanding, who paid his first visit to Walden in June 1966 and "practically had the pond (and the sandbar) to myself!"[14]

Of all the historical examples of human interference with the pond, the most shocking for many was the deliberate poisoning of its fish during this drought, in 1968. Fish populations had been manipulated for generations, and the species that now swam in Walden bore scant resemblance to those Thoreau had known. The pickerel he admired were already extinct when the state surveyed in 1905, and Gleason complained in 1924 that catches of all kinds were "very meagre." Gone by the 1960s were eel and fallfish (what Thoreau called roach, or chiven). Henry would have recognized the pumpkinseed sunfish (bream), yellow perch, killifish, bullhead (pout), shiners, and trout, but subsequent introductions were white suckers, smallmouth bass, smelt, bluegill, and new types of trout. Lenox recalls these as "trash fish," and there were few of them at that. Under his oversight, they treated the pond with Rotenone, a poison derived from tropical plants that is used to kill undersized and undesirable types so restocking can take place. Reclamations seldom kill every fish, and in 1971 pumpkinseeds, perch, shiners, and killifish were still present. Two years later Walden was stocked with trout, beginning its modern incarnation as a first-rate put-and-take trout pond.[15]

Every July Thoreau Society members trekked to Walden as part of their annual meeting. In summer 1967, nature writer Hal Borland lectured to the society, and a stone from the town of Thoreau, New Mexico, was added to the cairn. The society arranged for the replacement of the nearby bronze plaque, which had been pelted with stones until illegible. The new version said "Site of Thoreau's House" rather than "Hut," a term Thoreau rarely if ever used, and corrected the spelling of "Merrimack" in the title of the book he had written there—"Merrimac" having long irked Thoreauvians. This plaque was stolen in 1974 but soon recovered. Harding, caught up in the politics of these tumultuous days, had the idea that the society should contribute five hundred dollars to labor activist Cesar Chavez, who had expressed admiration for Thoreau. It was a controversial call that aroused the ire of those members who wished to keep literature and politics separate.

The most ominous issue of the late 1960s, however, was land use, specifically plans underway to widen Route 2 (the Concord bypass) as a commuter artery serving the booming Boston suburbs. In a 1970 proposal, Route 126 (Walden Street) was to be moved farther east of Walden, fulfilling a Department of Public Works plan discussed as early as 1958. A massive cloverleaf would occupy the top of Brister's Hill, and Brister's Spring was to be wiped out, as the new 126 was to be knocked through the town forest to form a straight-away with Thoreau Street in front of the high school. A schematic map published in the Boston *Globe* in 1973 showed the cloverleaf larger than Walden Pond itself, which could only have infuriated opponents, one calling the proposals "a disaster." Fortunately for Walden and environs, these ambitious undertakings were never carried out, but they marked an opening volley in the titanic battles over land use that would define the coming decades in Thoreau Country. Concordians prided themselves on their progressive environmentalist views—this was one of the first communities to ban DDT—and in 1972 the police chief told a visitor, "The town buys up vacant land every year to maintain open spaces . . . [and] about the hardest thing you can do in Concord is get permission to cut a tree down." Another resident said, "Fill up a swamp? We never fill up swamps in Concord. We fight for our swamps!" In the years to come these convictions would be tested.[16]

Walden Pond lost its longtime champion when Gladys Hosmer died in February 1970. The 1860 horse-drawn town hearse that had carried the bodies of Thoreau and Emerson came out of retirement to trundle her to Sleepy Hollow as the bell of First Parish tolled eighty-three times, once for each year of her life. In July, the Thoreau Society meeting descended into near-chaos: the Chavez matter rankled, and the president elected to serve that year was not a society member and failed to show up for the meeting, where he was scheduled to give the keynote lecture. Trouble continued the following year, when a controversial resolution condemned the Vietnam War and racism and called for the society to concern itself with more than "nature walks, slides of pretty scenes . . . and flower arrangements." Admittedly, one resolution proponent remarked, Thoreau "could have gotten more from an afternoon with a woodchuck than most men could from a whole night with Cleopatra," but appreciation of nature suddenly seemed irrelevant amidst world crisis.[17]

Meanwhile Thoreau with his skepticism, antiauthoritarianism, and subversive antiwar stance had become the darling of the counterculture. He had never known so much media attention, and in vain did scholars caution against oversimplifications: "Rutgers Professor Contends Thoreau Was Not a Hippie," said the *New York Times*. One writer concluded that Thoreau "would have no part of LSD were he alive today. . . . Thoreau could turn himself on, needing only that natural sky for a psychedelic." A play by Jerome Lawrence and Robert E. Lee, "The Night Thoreau Spent in Jail," played to sellout crowds on college campuses, and a post office on the Lower East Side was thronged by hippies seeking Thoreau stamps. Folk singer Arlo Guthrie named his cat Thoreau. At Sleepy Hollow, an enthusiast appropriated Henry's gravestone as a souvenir. In answer to a query by Harding, protester Allen Ginsberg explained that he had been drawn to Henry by seeing the impact that the transcendentalist's work had made on Kerouac: "T set first classic US example of war resistance, back to nature, tax refusal. As at the moment I'm living in country without electric on commune using 19th century techne to move water (hydrolic ram) & we're doing organic gardening, & I'm a member of the War Tax Refusal group. I find myself more & more indebted to Thoreau."[18]

In "these days of confusion and turmoil" as potent as any Thoreau had lived through, a whole generation discovered the Concord writer. Poet Anne Cimon recalls, "I first heard Thoreau's name in the late Sixties in association with his book *Walden*, which was popular with the counterculture of the day. I was a teenage flower-child, and my long-haired friends and I dreamed of living a back-to-nature life." In fall 1971, graduate student Wes Mott was trying to link his research with "ways of thinking about the tensions aroused by the war in Vietnam—especially as I was both a lover of American, especially New England, history and culture, yet active in the antiwar movement. The cairn and cabin site seemed like a religious shrine at a time when real belief in anything important seemed to have vanished from our culture." He was inspired to switch his area of focus to Emerson and Thoreau and went on to become a leading scholar of transcendentalism. Renewed attention to Thoreau focused many minds on Walden itself; Superintendent Lenox received letters from as far away as California asking "the going rates for shore lots" beside the pond.[19]

About July 1970, Harding undertook an experiment: to spend three hours at the cairn on a Sunday afternoon, pretending to read while in fact listening intently to visitors' comments. He watched as 225 persons strolled by, "predominantly young people" of college age; "many of the young men were bearded and the girls barefooted, carrying sandals in their hands." Serious pilgrims were among them. Voices dropped to a reverent hush and men removed their hats. "A surprising number of the visitors brought along their own well-thumbed paperback editions of *Walden* and took the time to look up their favorite passages," including five teenagers who leaned against the granite posts and read aloud for half an hour. When another historian repeated the experiment thirty-two years later, few were found to be so informed or enthusiastic. It is harder to overhear conversations today with all the droning airplanes overhead, and many contemporary visitors are immigrants or tourists speaking foreign languages. Although a handful who come are as ardent as those of 1970, they are, it seems, far fewer now than in the heyday of the hippie Thoreauvian.[20]

That heyday was epitomized by the visit of folk musician Pete Seeger ("Where Have All the Flowers Gone?") to Roland Robbins's backyard Thoreau House replica in July 1971. The little dwelling was emerging as a small but vibrant outpost of the Thoreau revival. In September of the following year, a hitchhiker showed up at

Robbins's door; he had come all the way from New Hampshire to see the replica in order to learn how to build his own, where he hoped to live like Henry. Mrs. Robbins fixed him a peanut-butter-and-jelly sandwich. By decade's end the *New York Times* could report, "Hundreds of visitors, including honeymooners, folk singers and chief justices of India's Supreme Court, have spent a night or more in the cabin." The guestbook showed signatures from thirty-seven states and twelve foreign countries. Princeton scholar and former president of the Thoreau Society William Howarth sat pensively in the dwelling's doorway for a photograph published in *National Geographic*.[21]

"We must cut down on the consumption of resources," B. F. Skinner told the society in 1972. "It is quite impossible for our level of affluence to prevail in all parts of the world. Imagine a billion Chinese scooting around in a third of a billion cars on hundreds of millions of miles of super-highways." This year too saw a Walden-like experiment unfold near Hollins College, on the outskirts of Roanoke, Virginia. Annie Dillard had written her Hollins master's thesis on "Walden Pond and Thoreau" (1968). Now twenty-seven, Thoreau's age when he moved to Walden, she undertook an investigation of natural phenomena along a nearby stream. The philosophical book she wrote in a study carrel on the second floor of the college library, *Pilgrim at Tinker Creek*, won a Pulitzer Prize in 1975. That award was further proof of the esteem in which Thoreau's ideas were held in the era of Earth Day. She would later find Robert Richardson's Thoreau biography inspiring—so much so that she and Richardson got married.[22]

The early 1970s were rife with experimentalism, and Superintendent Lenox laughingly recalls some of the Walden Pond hijinks of these strange years. A character nicknamed "The Dancer" would pirouette in the buff by Little Cove, then streak into the woods when threatened with arrest. Over by the house site, some hippies "took the picnic tables and tried to build a hut out of them." Park staff hoisted a Volkswagen out of the pond, somebody having dumped it off the end of the concrete pier: "Water was pouring from the windows, and fish were jumping out." In 1972, *Dealing*, a B-movie about a drug heist, ended with a shootout at Walden Pond, and *The Pentagon Papers and American Democracy* was partly filmed on location there. When some boys were caught skinny-dipping, the learned lyceum members Ruth Wheeler and Anne McGrath were consulted on the question, "Did Thoreau bathe in the nude?"[23]

Some of the liveliest action was happening not at Walden Pond, but across the street at the town dump. Only a quarter of the four thousand Concord families had trash pickup at home; "If you want to meet the other 3000," said resident Marian Thornton, "Come to the dump." For Earth Day in April 1970, Thornton organized one of the first recycling centers in New England at the landfill, starting with newspapers and magazines but quickly expanding to cans, aluminum, glass, leaves, Christmas trees, tires, and plastics. Two years later she had earned $4490 for local conservation projects and planned an organization, REUSIT (Rescue the Environment and Us from being Smothered In Trash). The dump afforded a colorful scene: "Girl Scouts sell cookies; politicians politick. Thoreau would have loved the place."[24]

About this time the Middlesex County Governmental Task Force sounded the first signal that things were about to change in the management, or mismanagement, of Walden Pond State Reservation. They blasted the commissioners for having neglected "serious land use questions" while seeing the place "as a convenient source of temporary jobs, especially in summer, for friends and relatives," as many as two hundred at a time. A new, more enlightened group of commissioners, opposed to the old spoils system and pledged to take matters more seriously, was elected in 1972 as a reform slate: S. Lester Ralph, John Danehy, and future United States senator Paul E. Tsongas. They named a Walden Pond Advisory Council of citizens in April 1973 and announced their intention to restore Walden in time for the Bicentennial.[25]

As environmental awareness had rapidly grown, more and more people awoke to Walden's shortcomings, especially as twenty thousand a day came to swim on weekends in 1973. Its eastern edge was decried as "a study in cement"; the shores were ringed by "raw, foot-broken banks bleeding dirt off into the pond"; and the woods echoed with "the groan of the big trucks on Route 2." When Robbins walked the paths with a Sierra Club group "it was terrible, just like Coney Island . . . people packed into Thoreau's Cove, motorcycles revving up in the water, dogs fighting." Having no admittance fee proved a double curse, maximizing crowds and minimizing revenues. When celebrated anthropologist Loren Eiseley visited in summer 1973, he quipped, "A few refuse receptacles placed along the shore might at least encourage some people to deposit their trash rather than throw it into the Pond." Walden's problems would surely worsen, as visitation was expected to undergo "a phenomenal increase" of 140 percent by 2000, to 1,809,600 visitors per year.[26]

In August the county commissioners met for the first time at Walden and heard recommendations from the advisory council. Tsongas summarized the prevailing opinion: "There are two ways to look at Walden Pond. The first is perhaps the way it has been looked at in the recent past. And that is that you provide for the maximum number of people to have a swimming place. I think on some bodies of water and under some conditions that is perhaps an acceptable approach. At Walden Pond it is not. . . . What's coming out of the committee is a return back to what the Pond used to be, and if the price that has to be paid is that fewer people will be able to use the Pond, and if there should be some exclusion of the rights to Walden Pond, then that simply has to be." Restricted parking and an admissions fee seemed appropriate. Roland Robbins disagreed, calling such restrictions un-Thoreauvian. But there was no mistaking the fact that momentum was at last building to strengthen protection of Concord's much-abused landmark.[27]

The newly visionary Middlesex County Commissioners filed a bill at the Massachusetts State House in April 1974 calling for Walden Pond to come under the management of the State Department of Natural Resources. At a ceremony on the pond's shore the following January 7, Govenor Francis W. Sargent signed the legislation into law, transferring administrative control away from the County Commission and setting the stage for what, it was hoped, would be a major refurbishing of the park in time for Bicentennial crowds. Sargent told the Department of Natural Resources, "You have an important and very difficult task of providing a balance between recreation and preservation." Seated at the table were Paul Tsongas, Roland Robbins, and landscape architect Ken Bassett. Tsongas, then running for Congress, announced, "We have driven away modern-day Thoreaus from Walden Pond. I hope it will again attract people who care what nature and Walden Pond is all about." His campaign

From county to state. Control of Walden Pond State Reservation was transferred to the Department of Natural Resources at a pondside ceremony, January 1975. Left to right: Gilbert Bliss, Paul Tsongas, Arthur Brownell, Ken Bassett, Bruce Jones, Roland Robbins. Courtesy Walden Pond State Reservation.

literature proudly declared, "He saved Walden Pond," and he went on to distinguish himself in Washington for championing environmental causes.[28]

In early spring 1974 an historic public meeting had been convened at Emerson School in Concord to discuss the proposals outlined in the so-called Gardiner Report prepared by the Cambridge landscape architecture firm Richard A. Gardiner and Associates. Four proposals were under consideration, with parking the key determinant of use at 411-acre Walden Pond State Reservation: the options were a 1000-car, a 700-car (the status quo), a 300-car, and a 150-car lot (the "extreme preservation alternative"). The largest lot implied a management plan emphasizing recreation, with the beach tripled in size. The second option meant doubling the beach area and hardening the pond-path borders with wood slabs. The other two plans entailed no beach enlargement; the 150-car lot would allow restoring the pond path "to a natural condition similar to that of Thoreau's time." The handful of citizens present agreed with the advisory council in preferring the 300-car lot, meant to allow one thousand visitors at once. It was a fateful choice, one that would reduce visitation to Walden, but not so drastically that it could become a true natural sanctuary.[29]

The Department of Natural Resources—later the Department of Environmental Management, DEM—looked to the Walden Pond Advisory Council for guidance. The talented group included Bassett, Roland Robbins, Jackie Davison, conservation-minded Lincoln landowner John Quincy Adams, and Jim DeNormandie. The last was a longtime Lincoln resident and state senator who had for years worked to enlarge Walden Pond State Reservation by the purchase of outlying parcels. He played a role in the 1974 deal whereby James G. Sliman agreed to turn the trailer park over to the state for fair market value and a promise that his customers be given life tenancy—including one who was blind and paraplegic. Over the decades, Sliman's Walden Breezes park had grown to considerable size, and sixty-nine home trailer lots now stood on the site, plus a mobile home dealership and several travel trailers. The sale may have averted the construction of a condominium complex. Although the handover took place in 1976, the park was slow to dwindle; twenty-seven years later, one last trailer still remained. But the transfer did mark the end of the famous hot dog stand. No longer could Thoreauvians bait the kids behind the counter by asking them, "Could you tell me where Henry Thoreau lives?" "Well, uh, I guess he doesn't live here any more—we, uh, we don't know him."[30]

The final trailer at Walden Breezes belonged to the elderly Edna Toska, a resident for nineteen years, whose perspective on "the pahk" is a unique one. Whereas the visitor eyes a forlorn expanse of abandoned cement pads punctuated by disused waterpipes and rusting laundry poles, Toska sees an elysium. The red maple trees once carefully pruned by Sliman still blush scarlet every autumn; spring and summer bring carpets of flowers on the lawns of former trailers: lily of the valley, Japanese irises, roses, forsythia, azaleas, rhododendrons, daisies. Every slab is rich with memories for Toska, whose eyes well with tears as she remembers her former neighbors: the

Harveys, Flora Haskett, Sadie and her mother, the man who knew all about mushrooms. Always upbeat, she sees advantages in the dwindling population of Walden Breezes: "There wasn't much privacy before." She stresses that this was a highly regarded trailer park, reserved for adults only and meticulously maintained by Sliman, who would have his residents' grass cut if they didn't do it themselves. Did the nearby landfill bother her? "No, never. The tenants got all kinds of things from it—tables, tricycles, pottery, games. One of the neighbors found the nicest drop-leaf table. It looked like it came from Ethan Allen." She wonders, "Why did the government buy this park? They don't keep it neat and trim. After I'm gone, they're just gonna leave it this way; that's the government. I'd like to see this park kept up, like they do at Walden Pond." For now, she does the job for them, sweeping the empty roads daily and planting flowers. Toska wishes to see Walden Breezes refurbished for trailer camping and affordable housing of the kind she inhabits. Once she is gone, however, every trace of her beloved park will likely be obliterated.[31]

The coming of state control in 1975 brought many benefits to Walden Pond. Streetside parking was eliminated, as were unsightly parking lots (capacity 1000) above Red Cross and Main Beaches; the present, smaller lot was built east of Route 126 at a cost of $180,000 and designed to blend as much as possible into the surrounding woods. A $1 use fee was imposed to help pay for reservation upkeep. But bad ideas were broached, too, with varying degrees of seriousness. At a meeting, one participant suggested establishing another railroad station at the west shore: "We ought to be thinking in terms of public transportation to Walden." "You would open the gates of Hell!" someone shouted. Other heavy-handed proposals of the period, suggested but not implemented, included cutting paths along the ridge tops with overlooks and benches (these to replace the pondside path entirely); slicing a wide trail up Emerson's Cliff and clearing a vista; building a visitor center on the old John Richardson lot west of Walden Street; relandscaping Thoreau's house site and cutting new, non-historical trails there; replacing Robbins's house site posts with a "less cumbersome" arrangement of "granite slabs embedded in the soil"; and removing the cairn. Commissioner Brennan had despised that massive artifact, calling it "a mess, it's

Eyesore. Conservationists decried the shabbiness of the bathhouses, seen here during high water, ca. 1984. The smaller buildings were removed in spring 1985, the larger one refurbished. Courtesy Walden Pond State Reservation.

very unsightly and should be taken out of there." This was finally done in 1975. Unfortunately a busload of forty Japanese students arrived not long after, each person clutching a stone to leave as tribute. Howls of complaint from the Thoreau Society resulted in the cairn's return—in the back of a truck—on July 17, 1978.[32]

The cairn imbroglio was symbolic of the difficulties that DNR experienced in its first years at Walden, as it struggled to find the right approach. One thing the commissioners had done well was to regulate swimming. But with the state takeover, three people drowned in the pond in 1975. Only two deaths had occurred in the previous fifty years. Superintendent Joe Lenox faulted a reduction in after-hours policing. Crime spiked, with an assault and an attempted rape. Two years later, Concord police warned the department that the Walden parking situation in summer was such a mess they could not control it, with droves of swimmers still leaving their cars along

Route 126 and at the nearby high school. Walden Pond advocates fought throughout the 1970s and 1980s to overcome seemingly intractable parking problems, some of which are still thorny today.[33]

In these years of giddy change, free spirits embraced Thoreau. When Robert Pirsig undertook the trek recounted in his 1974 best-seller, *Zen and the Art of Motorcycle Maintenance*, *Walden* went along. Poet Wade Van Dore, whose memoir of Robert Frost was called "Walden Three" (1969), published a 1976 "Declaration of Dependence" on nature, inspired by Thoreau and signed by Roger Tory Peterson and other notables. Among the diverse groups that lauded Henry were homosexuals. Thoreau looked out from the cover of *Mr. Sun* in 1966 as "The Thinking Man's Nudist." "If a man does not keep pace with his companions, perhaps it is because he hears a different drummer," Thoreau famously wrote, and "a different drummer" became a gay catchphrase. A visitor to Walden Pond in summer 1974 might have encountered Paul Monette, later a novelist and AIDS activist, perched on Thoreau's hearth, reading *Walden* and listening to news of Watergate on a portable radio. He did the same in the Blue Hills south of Boston, sitting naked in the woods. For Monette, Thoreau was an inspiring precursor whose interest in the woodchopper Therien was more than platonic. Even Harding weighed in on the question of Thoreau's sexuality. He who had innocently called him "Our American Saint Francis" back in 1943 now proclaimed that Henry "loved to watch boys swimming naked, peering out of the woods at them" in the *Journal of Homosexuality*.[34]

The election of Jimmy Carter in 1976 seemed further proof of the steady advance of conservation, for here was a national leader who vocally supported it. He would tell Harding, "Since I was a child, I have enjoyed Thoreau's works, learned from him, and shared his humor and insight with others. His thoughts about solitude, nature, politics, art and the higher aspirations of the human spirit have been very important to me." The publication of *Woodswoman* the year of Carter's election drew attention to a new type of Thoreauvian, the divorcee who turns to nature for a fresh start. Anne LaBastille built a house on Black Bear Lake in the Adirondacks in 1965. Her inspiration was Henry Beston's *Outermost House*, not *Walden*, which she found dull. But on a long car ride she listened to Thoreau's classic on cassette and was enthralled. In 1985 she would build a second cabin, Thoreau II, on an even more isolated pond, try-ing to escape the roar of motorboats. The dwelling was "almost identical" to Henry's, although some items in her Thoreauvian list reflected changing times: plastic sheeting, fiberglass insulation, pad-lock, building permits (total, $130.75). LaBastille's modern-day Walden Pond has shortcomings: unlike Thoreau, LaBastille is sur-rounded by the noise of A-10 and F-16 military aircraft, commercial jets, seaplanes, fire engines, ATVs, generators, lawn mowers, log splitters, and chainsaws. And pond life is declining, the acidity from air pollution a hundred times greater than it was seventy years ago.[35]

Questions were increasingly raised about the ecological health of Walden, too, as revealed in a series of studies. In August 1979, sci-entist Marjorie Green Winkler extracted a core from the deepest basin. Two and a half feet of sediment contained layers of pollen that told the vegetation history of Walden Woods over six hundred years. European settlement and forest clearing in the seventeenth century had ushered in a decline in tree pollen, an increase in grasses and ragweed; pitch pine was largely replaced by white. Charcoal grew common in the nineteenth century, a pollutant from the rail-road and forest fires. Chestnut pollen disappeared around 1913 with the destruction of these trees by blight—all subtle but telling micro-scopic evidence of human impacts on the land.[36]

Winkler's study found that various aquatic *Isoetes*, or quillwort, plants had dramatically declined since swimming and bank erosion began pouring sediments into the pond. Ominously, extinction of certain types of algae showed the pond becoming more acidic and eutrophic (nutrient-rich, oxygen-poor). A peculiarity of Walden is its near-absence of aquatic plant life, except, as Thoreau said, in "the lit-tle meadows recently overflowed, which do not properly belong to it." In Walden itself there were "only a few small heart-leaves and potamogetons, and perhaps a water-target or two"; "heart leaves— in Walden & water target leaves in the overflown meadow." "I push round the pond close to the shore, with a stick. . . . The weeds are eriocaulon, two or three kinds of potamogeton . . . target-weed, heart-leaf, and a little callitriche. There is but little of any of them, however, in the pond itself. It is truly an ascetic pond." In modern terms it is oligotrophic (literally, "little to eat"), because, botanist Edmund Schofield explains, its waters are filtered through the surrounding sands and gravels and scrubbed of nutrients. While there is little green life at the surface, a band of it exists beneath. *Nitella* algae, some eleven thousand pounds of it, thrive in the clear water, producing quantities of oxygen at depths up to forty feet. Nitella's role in the pond's ecology is mysterious, but it seems to keep the water "ascetic" by absorbing phosphorus, a nutrient that otherwise would contribute to algal blooms. Nitella is not the only submerged plant; in 1967 and 1985, botanists confirmed the rare lake quillwort, *Isoetes macrospora*, found nowhere else in Massachusetts. Long-term declines in *Nitella* and *Isoetes* would seem to signal degradation of water quality at Walden.[37]

At year's end in 1980 came the culmination of an heroic effort by individuals and the Lincoln town government to purchase eighty-seven acres in Adams Woods, so called, southwest of Walden. Charles Francis Adams had bought the land in 1893 as part of his gentleman's estate holdings that included Baker Farm and Pleasant Meadow, and his heirs offered it at a discount. The area was of tremendous Thoreauvian significance, containing or adjoining the Andromeda Ponds, Well Meadow, and Heywood's Brook. The Thoreau Society contributed five thousand dollars from a fund established by the gift of a deceased member, a postman in Philadelphia who loved to read Thoreau. The purchase was made in December, for a little over half of the appraised value of a million dollars. Had the asking price not been reached, this valuable and scenic parcel, rich with historic and literary interest, would likely have faced development in the 1980s real estate boom. Preserved, this is one of the most evocative Thoreauvian landscapes, where one may walk in solitude the same paths Henry knew.[38]

Among the most ascerbic and colorful critics of the new economic boom and of American excess in general was Edward Abbey, who descended the Green River of Utah in November 1980 with a "water-soaked, beer-stained, grease-spotted cheap paperback copy of *Walden*." His strain of civil disobedience, which would lead to the controversial ecoterrorist activities of Earth First!, has been traced to the example of Thoreau. That same month brought the presidential election of anti-environmentalist Ronald Reagan, and public interest in Thoreau seemed to ebb after its 1970s heyday. On-street interviews of fifty people in Concord in 1983 showed that only five could recognize the opening paragraph of "Civil Disobedience." Polls of high school students in 1985 and 1987 revealed that three out of four could not identify Thoreau and that only 43 percent knew that the theme of *Walden* was the simple life. A professor lamented, "Students are more interested in the secrets of America's best-run companies than in the mysteries revealed at Walden Pond."[39]

The shadow of crime fell on Walden during these years, the pond reflecting American culture at large, as it so often has. Joan Webster, a twenty-five-year-old architecture student at Harvard, disappeared from Logan Airport at Thanksgiving 1981. An anonymous typed note said that her body would be found in Walden, and so the place was searched by scuba divers and with grappling hooks, to no avail. Her remains were found nine years later in the town of Hamilton. A hoax involving a missing boy led divers to search the pond again in 1982. This decade saw the start of a grim series of suicides at the reservation, in time including a hanging, a shooting, a poisoning (which the author happened upon just as the police arrived), and several gruesome deaths by train. In the 1990s, someone put official-looking signs up around the pond that announced that nude bathing was now permitted. The culprit, it turned out, was a Peeping Tom. Such episodes seemed all but inevitable, given that some seven hundred thousand people were now crowding in annually.

No one was more concerned about burgeoning visitation than Mary Sherwood, who founded a preservationist Walden Pond Society in 1978, two years later renamed Walden Forever Wild. For four years Sherwood, nearly eighty, carried out a campaign of landscape restoration on the hillside at Red Cross Beach. Friends helped—Robbins supervised regrading, and landscape architect J. Walter Brain and others assisted, too. But day in and day out, the grueling task of planting seedling trees and lugging buckets of water was fundamentally Mary's. She spent months on the sunbaked hillside once scalped by bulldozers, bending her aged body toward the earth in a sacred ritual of healing—like Thoreau thirteen decades earlier in his beanfield a few dozen yards to the northwest, an *agricola laboriosus* engaged in an act of deep significance. She had ample time for meditation, both on the beauty of the pond and the overuse that threatened to spoil it. Increasingly her vision was a dark one:

J. Walter Brain, Thoreauvian.
In May 1982 he volunteered
to help Mary Sherwood re-
vegetate the denuded slope
above Red Cross Beach—
today's "Sherwood Forest."
Collection of Edmund A.
Schofield.

the state was not an ally but an impediment. American society was
stupid and unfeeling. Toiling alone on the denuded hillside, she
watched thousands of laughing, insouciant youth and began to realize that they would, locustlike, eventually destroy her beloved
Walden.

In 1983 the water rose high, forcing swimmers inland, their bare
feet trampling her grape vines and seedling trees. "Swimming
should continue at Walden according to deed requirements," she
had said as recently as 1979, but now she knew she had been wrong:
swimmers were the worst enemies of the place, "trashing the
woods, causing the erosion, polluting the swim end of the pond (we
know that in summer the water at the swim end is far more danger-
ously polluted than the public health reports show), bringing in bad
behavior including muggings, drugs and an endless stream of liquor.
. . . They are a special group from back of Boston, who make the
enjoyment of Walden by others impossible." "Our main goals are to
see swimming prohibited, eroded areas restored, and reforestation
rather than landscaping on the shore," Sherwood proclaimed, placing the swim ban first. In support of an anti-swimming "Walden
Protective Act" that Walden Forever Wild offered to the state legislature, she wrote hundreds of letters that stung friends and foes
alike. Environmentalists who should have been her allies were
wounded by what they called her "poison pen" and deplored the
damage done by her factual inaccuracies. The president of the

Massachusetts Audubon Society was treated to a correspondence that was "the most acrimonious in my life." Another target recalls, "From my perspective she was crazy!" And yet one friend remembers her as "one of the few genuine and sincere followers of Thoreau that I have known."[40]

Sherwood's views seemed extreme to many, but she was far from alone in being troubled by conditions at the pond. A reporter asked in 1979, "Walden Pond: Paradise Lost? . . . Tough, beer-drinking, potsmoking high schoolers . . . roam the park's 411 acres, defying Lenox." Nature writer Ann Zwinger recalls, "My first visit to Walden Pond was shocking. On the cement apron were a *lot* of people, radios blaring, anything but peace and quiet. . . . My feelings were always conflicted, feeling that it was a shrine for those of us who respected Thoreau, but disturbed by what it had become. I recognized all the pressures on it but still cannot reconcile its current use with the sanctity I should have liked to have seen and felt." "Walden Pond rocks to the rhythm of the boombox," another writer complained, and a third was aghast to find the place "a mass of humanity, a stew of frantic motion, boom boxes and squealing children. In fact, what Massachusetts fondly calls the birthplace of environmental consciousness is a giant swimming pool, an over-fished fishing hole, a park masquerading as a contemplative shrine." When a Japanese television documentary on Thoreau was filmed there, its narrator—shown fishing in the pond—reported being "horrified by the noise, the traffic, the planes."[41]

In her campaign for Walden Forever Wild, Sherwood was joined by Ed Schofield, the conservationist and onetime antiwar activist who had attended his first Thoreau Society meeting in 1957, witnessing the Battle of Red Cross Beach firsthand. When he moved to Concord in 1982 he was dismayed by "the denuded and trampled banks of the pond," "the noise from the crowds," and "the bewildering unconcern and crass rationalizing of the state government." In January 1983, Schofield stood up in a Walden Pond Advisory Committee public meeting to charge that "Walden is deteriorating, that it is worse than ever, that a piecemeal approach should not be taken, that Walden is being incompetently managed." He and Sherwood organized "Walden Pond Day" on April 23, inviting David Brower of the Sierra Club, who placed a rock from the Sierra

Bank restoration began below the railroad in 1985. Workers laid fibrous netting to stabilize the soil. Big fieldstones (rear) were employed. Courtesy Walden Pond State Reservation.

Nevada on the cairn. His visit was a reminder of that of John Muir, first president of the club, ninety years before. Zwinger recalls of Brower, "He was an impressive man by any estimates, and one felt that he and Thoreau were communicating on some wave length unavailable to us mortals." Brower's visit was a harbinger of high-profile celebrity visits to come, as defenders of Walden sought to bring the place before the attention of the nation in order to overcome the localistic outlook that, Sherwood and her allies thought, continued to guide reservation policy. Before the decade was out, preservation at Walden would be the subject of headlines nationwide, and activists could boast that Thoreau "is acknowledged by conservationists from John Muir to David Brower as the forefather of the movement to preserve environmental equilibrium and natural influences for future generations."[42]

Sherwood saw only the negative—Walden in chaos, overrun by throngs—but positive signs had begun to appear. Police began patrols on horseback. Years of planning (and bad press) culminated in the removal of the ugly concrete restrooms and swim pier. The bathhouse, which many had expected to be demolished too, remained but was partly shingled to improve its appearance. Wooden bollards were erected along Route 126 to prevent illegal parking. Attention was directed to eroded paths, and a considerable sum was spent rebuilding the one that ran along the railroad sandbank, an area submerged in 1984, when the pond reached its highest level in twenty-eight years. Sherwood was adamantly opposed: "I begged them not to do it as it would facilitate trampling crowds getting around the south side, where the path runs across the middle of fragile glacial slopes." The state ignored this advice, angering her further: "I am frustrated by the bureaucratic wrangling and the apathy of both visitors and much of the surrounding community," she said, and she fretted about the "taxpayer money that was already spent opening up the back path at Walden that has now caused so much erosion. I wake up at night worried about it but nobody seems to be worried about it except me." She was nearly alone in protesting the path, designed to satisfy a universal public desire to walk around the pond.[43]

The decision was made to construct a replica of Thoreau's house, the culmination of an idea long under discussion. Thoreau Society member Wallace Conant had proposed in 1947 using timbers from the ruinous Texas House to build such a replica near the road at the reservation, and there had been further talk in 1957 and 1973 of reconstructing the dwelling at the original site. This new one would stand in a prominent location near the parking lot, notwithstanding protests from the Thoreau Lyceum, which feared that it would detract from their own replica and cause tourists to bypass them. Robbins explained the reasons the copy was not placed by the cove: "It would have been vandalized, souvenir seekers would have done their jobs, and up there in the parking lot, it's built at the same angle as the original house. You can see the sun come in the door, just like he did." Nevertheless, many visitors are confused by having the house on the "wrong" site. It was meant to educate the public about Thoreau and correct rampant misconceptions. "Some talk about him like he's been to reform school, smoked dope, was a drunk, that he stole his mother's pies and sponged off Ralph Waldo

"I have thus a tight shingled and plastered house." Roland Robbins (striped shirt) designed a Walden house replica for the reservation, 1985. Tens of thousands of visitors experience it annually. At right is Mary Sherwood. Courtesy Walden Pond State Reservation.

Emerson, who owned the land," the reservation historian said. His supervisor referred to the long-standing Concord dismissiveness about Thoreau and the park's unfortunate record of putting recreation over reflection: "We're trying to make up for thirty years of animosity and to legitimize ourselves as an historic site." The replica was built by the elderly but enthusiastic Robbins, along with assistants, and dedicated on July 12, 1985. Thoreau impersonator David Barto climbed onto a wagon two years later to reenact Henry's moving his furniture to the dwelling. Undertaking an experiment of his own, a journalist pitched a tent at the pond in an attempt to recreate the night Thoreau moved there. "He lasted two years, two months, two days. I lasted four hours and 20 minutes, minus the calls home from a nearby pay phone." Bullfrogs, fireworks, and strangers walking by kept him awake. "Solitude? Peace of mind? Transcendental euphoria? In 1845 maybe. Today, bring your earplugs and a bottle of sleeping pills."[44]

For years there had been alarming signs that commercial development was about to explode near Walden Pond. From 1974 to 1978,
a 179-room Ramada Inn was planned for a site at the intersection of
Routes 126 and 2, diagonally across from the beanfield. Although
these plans were ultimately abandoned, developers did not lose their
interest in this lucrative lot at the top of Brister's Hill and just seven
hundred yards from the pond. Corporate headquarters were sprout-
ing alongside swarming highways in suburbs nationwide in the
1980s, forming so-called edge cities. This fate seemed inevitable for
Brister's Hill when a new scheme was put forward for the Ramada
Inn site—a 147,000-square-foot Concord Office Park with a 518-car
garage—that passed through a public hearing without opposition.
The location had been greenlighted for development seven times
since 1955. Almost simultaneously, a huge condominium complex,
"Concord Commons II," was proposed for wooded Bear Garden
Hill, west of Walden, near Boiling Spring. The days of Walden
Woods as Thoreau knew it—a relict "great uninhabited tract"—
were numbered.[45]

A group of well-to-do homeowners from Fair Haven Hill and
vicinity, including businessman Vidar Jorgensen, formed a citizen's
group to cry "not in my backyard" to Concord Commons. On
March 14, 1988, three concerned Thoreauvians met with Jorgensen
to discuss a coordinated strategy to fight the twin threats of condos
and corporate headquarters. J. Walter Brain was a landscape architect who had moved to Lincoln in 1971 to immerse himself in
Thoreau Country, to learn every trail Henry had walked, and to
rediscover forgotten Thoreauvian sites such as Thrush Alley and
Epigaea Springs. He was joined by Ed Schofield, the botanist active
in Sherwood's Walden Forever Wild, and Tom Blanding, incoming
president of the Thoreau Society, an independent scholar who eked
by on giving lectures and workshops on transcendentalism and playing jazz trumpet. The meeting convened in Blanding's tiny cottage
on Barrett's Mill Road, where his cats, Sophia and Lidian, prowled
among piles of books and manuscripts. That day, Blanding, Brain,
Jorgensen, and Schofield organized themselves as the Thoreau

HELP SAVE WALDEN WOODS

Public Meeting Monday, November 14, 7:30 PM, Alcott School, Concord

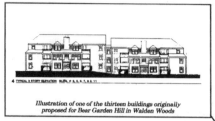

Illustration of one of the thirteen buildings originally proposed for Bear Garden Hill in Walden Woods

Entrance to proposed Concord Office Park on Brister's Hill in Walden Woods, just 700 yards from Walden Pond.

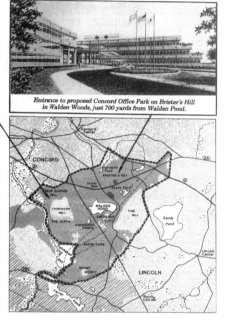

The Source and Symbol of World Conservation

Impact of Traffic and Development on Walden Woods

As Boston expands west, the traffic on 128 escalates, and land values soar, the pressure to develop Walden Woods will only increase. Controlling developments reactively after they are proposed is expensive and inefficient. Now is the time to develop and build a far-reaching and pro-active plan to identify and protect land worthy of preservation.

Of the four great wild tracts identified by Thoreau in Concord, only Walden Woods and Estabrook Woods remain substantially intact. Evenly balanced on the north and south of Concord, and laced together by the river corridors, Walden and Estabrook Woods are the logical foundations of a land preservation plan for Concord. Walden Woods is, of course,

On this ground Thoreau discovered and studied the essential inter-relationships of nature. Walden Woods stands as the specific site where Thoreau developed his theory of forest succession, a cornerstone of modern ecological science. This is also the site of Thoreau's observations concerning the impact of civilization upon the natural world. For conservationists worldwide, Walden Woods is the wellspring of the concept of land conservation. Here, in a landscape that had been settled by Europeans for two centuries, Thoreau saw and forecast the consequences of unbridled development and pleaded eloquently for the protection of the natural world. He is acknowledged by conservationists from John Muir to David Brower as the forefather of the movement to preserve environmental equilibrium and natural influences for future generations.

TCCA advertisement. Concord Journal, November 3, 1988. Courtesy Tom Blanding.

Country Conservation Alliance (TCCA) and, with the help of television reporter Jack Borden and others, began an arduous campaign against seemingly insurmountable odds to, as their first newspaper advertisement said, "Save Walden Woods" from 1980s-style sprawl.[46]

That campaign built on and reacted to previous preservation efforts in Concord. Brain was active in a Friends of Walden Pond group. As a member of the Concord Historical Commission, Blanding had fought for local landmarks and sought to show, as he said in a 1987 editorial, that Walden "is an integral part of Concord's identity, inviolable forever," even though Concord treated the place "as a castoff of the town." The alliance would continue this crusade, even as its very name avoided making reference to Walden, which the controversial Sherwood regarded as her exclusive preserve. Calling the Brister's Hill project "an assault on the human values Thoreau champions" and warning of "massive environmental damage," TCCA arranged public meetings and demanded that impact statements be filed—undaunted by the fact that one Concord offi-cial told Brain, "Walter, it's not even midnight. It's five minutes past midnight." The *Concord Journal* even announced in May, "Walden St. Office Park Goes Up. . . . Construction . . . will begin within the next two weeks." Town politicians called TCCA members naive trouble-makers, and state environmental officials and lobbyists opposed them, pointing to the degraded nature of the Brister's hilltop, an abandoned, litter-strewn sand mine alongside a four-lane highway: "When times are tight we have to be far more selective in the land we protect. . . . Wildlife habitats, endangered species nesting areas and sensitive coastal land are much higher priorities to us"; "You don't spend scarce or nonexistent state funds on this kind of parcel." Still TCCA pressed ahead.[47]

Because Brister's and Bear Garden Hills were unfamiliar place-names to all but a knot of dedicated Thoreauvians, TCCA published materials that reestablished their historical existence within "Walden Woods"—knowing, of course, that this evocative title would garner attention and sympathy and would prove, as Schofield recalls, "a very powerful tool in our public relations campaign." They argued that "Walden Woods is a distinct and coherent natural ecosystem" that had been "increasingly obscured by such manmade divisions as the Concord-Lincoln town line (1754), the railroad (1844), the boundaries of Walden Pond State Reservation (1922 and after), and Route 2 (1934). . . . Walden Woods is a trust for all time, not a com-modity to be exhausted by a few members of a single generation." These were eloquent pleas, but the odds against TCCA remained enormous. The developers were devoid of sentimentalism. Brister's Hill owner, real estate and publishing tycoon Mort Zuckerman, was unmoved by the fact that he also controlled the *Atlantic*, in which Thoreau's essay "Walking" had appeared in 1862. But Blanding was not to be intimidated by Zuckerman, or by official Concord's indif-ference: "There is too much at stake here to bow down to myopic views from people who happen to be sitting in positions of consid-erable power."[48]

In one of its full-page *Concord Journal* advertisements, TCCA loftily called Walden Woods "The Source and Symbol of World Conservation"; "a source of timeless inspiration"; birthplace of *Walden*, "increasingly acknowledged worldwide as one of the most

Tom Blanding at Walden Pond, 1990. Photograph, Ira Wyman.

important works of Western Civilization"; and no less than "among the most important natural, historic and literary sites in the world." But an appeals committee exchange between Blanding and a well-paid lawyer for the condominium concern suggests the difficulties TCCA faced as it urged protection for this somewhat scruffy zone:

> Q: Now, sir, as I understand it, what you say is that some area near Walden, near where Thoreau spent some period of time, stands as a symbolism of man's relationship to nature, is that what you said?
>
> A: That Walden Woods stands as a symbol, yes.
>
> Q: (showing a photograph) Do you recognize that?
>
> A: That is the public beach at Walden Pond.
>
> Q: And is that what you say stands for a symbolism [with] worldwide recognition [of] one of the most important historical literary sites in the western world as a symbolism to man and nature?
>
> A: That is a small piece of the land within Walden Woods.
>
> Q: Okay, now, sir, tell me what about that snow fence surrounding that tree that you find of any significance to western culture or civilization?

A: Since the nature of the symbol does not deal wholly with the materiality of the site, but with its identity, with its inner meaning, then the symbolism of Walden Pond is not determined by any specific physical characteristic that is taken out of context.

Q: What is that a picture of, if you know?

A: That is, I believe, the Walden Breezes Trailer Park.

Q: Trailer Park?

A: Which is being phased out.

Q: Just answer my question. . . . Trailer Park? Is that part of the symbolism now that is important to the culture of western civilization?

A: Yes it is.

Q: Now, sir, what is that a picture of?

A: That is a picture of the Concord landfill.

Q: The landfill from the waste from the Town of Concord goes down and gets dumped in this area that is the symbol of man's relationship to nature, one of the most significant in western civilization, is that your testimony?[49]

A tweedy cohort of Thoreau-inspired intellectuals signed on to the TCCA cause, including poet Robert Bly, editor Paul Brooks, composer John Cage, Annie Dillard, social philosopher Arun Gandhi, Anne LaBastille, Roderick Nash (author of the canonical *Wilderness and the American Mind*), Roger Tory Peterson, photographer Eliot Porter, Paul Tsongas, and Ann Zwinger—in addition to the usual gaggle of Am Lit scholars. The organization scored impressive successes, including the listing of Walden Woods as one of "America's Eleven Most Endangered Historic Places" by the National Trust for Historic Preservation "within a year," as Blanding recalls proudly, "of people denying there *was* a Walden Woods." The alliance slipped into debt—they owed $30,000 to a Boston law firm. But awareness of "Walden Woods" as a threatened landmark was spreading widely, TCCA and its issues becoming the subject of seventy-five newspaper articles in the group's first nine months alone.

Jack Borden, a TCCA member with media expertise, had helped arrange a report in the *Boston Globe*, which led to Blanding and Schofield's being interviewed on CNN in late November 1989.

Walking sticks in hand, they were filmed at the old Brister's Hill sandmine, Schofield remarking, "We're wandering in a wilderness of devastation," and Blanding adding that Thoreau "wanted Walden preserved in its pristine condition." The reporter's voiceover intoned, "Critics say town officials sold out to growth and greed. . . . Opponents of the projects dream of a buyout. But this is prime real estate, worth millions." In Los Angeles, a recording artist happened to walk past the television in his kitchen as the interview aired. He instantly sympathized with the courageous fight TCCA was waging. Thinking that he might be able to help, he picked up the telephone and placed a call to Schofield in Massachusetts. "Hello, I'm trying to reach the group that's trying to protect Walden Woods. I just saw a story on CNN. . . . This is Don Henley."[50]

II

🌿

walden.org

(1990–2003)

🐦

When he heard the name "Don Henley" at the other end of the line, Ed Schofield's first thought was, "Who?" His TCCA companions had the same reaction—but surely they were somewhat exceptional in not knowing the name of the lead singer of the rock-and-roll band the Eagles, which has sold more than one hundred million albums worldwide with a string of popular songs, including "Take It Easy," "Heartache Tonight," and "Hotel California." Like musician Pete Seeger before him, Henley had long admired Henry Thoreau. For one thing, there was more than a little affinity between their personalities. He has described himself as "very tenacious and bull-headed," and he regularly sparred with his detractors in the media, targets of his song, "Dirty Laundry." "It was something I enjoyed, parrying. The critics took it more seriously than I did. It was fun for me. I could put words on paper. I could see if I could be snottier than they are. It's like sword fighting. Touché."[1]

The origins of Henley's Thoreau enthusiasm reached back to childhood in Linden, Texas. His father, C. J., was a farmer and owner of an auto parts store who would tell him, "Someday, son, you will come to appreciate the land." They fished together on Caddo Lake. His mother, a teacher, encouraged him to read. "Growing up, I became best friends with nature, the woods, the lakes, the streams," Henley recalled. "That's why Thoreau has such a resonance for me."

A high school English teacher, Margaret Lovelace, introduced him to Thoreau.[2]

Henley flew to Boston in March 1990 and visited threatened sites in Walden Woods with TCCA members and others. The alliance was thrilled to have Henley's help: "It was just what we were hoping for all along," Tom Blanding asserted at the time. "We wanted to draw someone of national prominence to help us with this. That was our strategy, and it worked." But simultaneously—and, Blanding says, without telling him—Henley was pursuing other, high-profile options. He contacted Senator Edward Kennedy, who offered the services of his staffer, Kathi Anderson, who went along on the initial Walden Woods outing. She and Henley worked together to form the Walden Woods Project in April 1990. Cochaired by Henley, Paul Tsongas (a Democratic presidential primary candidate in 1992), and Michael Kennedy, the Walden Woods Project would attempt to raise enormous sums of money in a matter of months, a thing TCCA seemed incapable of doing. In the rapid course of subsequent developments, Blanding felt pushed aside and voiced anger at what he perceived to be a deliberate effort by the Walden Woods Project "to low-key TCCA." Soon, he says, Henley stopped calling. The two men last spoke in 1991.[3]

Ardently Thoreauvian and committed to a purist approach to raising money, Blanding watched the Walden Woods Project's methods with horror. He had devoted his life to understanding Thoreau as philosopher and to adhering to ideals of near-penniless simplicity and stern integrity. Since 1986 he had been researching and promoting Walden Woods as a symbolic site central to historic Concord. Now his dream of saving Walden Woods "on Thoreau's own terms" had been snatched away, he thought, by interlopers who had no understanding of Henry and who made themselves bedfellows of the local politicians who had long been enemies of historic preservation. From his perspective, TCCA had kept the spotlight on Thoreau, following a high-minded path that relied on "moral force"; the Walden Woods Project enlisted photogenic celebrities and went crassly commercial. According to Blanding, public indignation and a sagging economy had already stopped the developers, Walden Woods had come to life as an inspiring symbol, and money would have soon poured in from schoolchildren, thereby putting moral pressure on government "to pick up the fund-raising ball"—but all of this was spoiled, he felt, when Henley and Anderson broke in with "politics and selfish careerism," cutting deals with powerful interests. "Raising money was not the TCCA strategy, but raising consciousness and bringing massive moral pressure to bear on public officials who had impeded Walden's progress—the very people Henley was now forming a political cabal with."[4]

Blanding thought that Henley, bored with the rock scene, was trying to reinvent himself as the savior of a national treasure, in essence buying cultural sainthood. By grabbing hold of Walden Woods as a vehicle, "He took something that came out of my heart." Jack Borden asked, "Is this about Henry David Thoreau or Henley David Thoreau? Here's a guy who spots a real opportunity. Henry Thoreau! A real American icon! Walden! But once you have saved the land, where do you stop? There's a chance to become the General Motors of Henry Thoreau. You're the great conglomerate here." Outraged by Walden Woods Project press releases detailing their achievements over the years and ignoring TCCA, Blanding in a 2002 interview tried to set the record straight by listing TCCA's successes before Henley ever appeared: they "accomplished the creation of a new national symbol" by drawing attention to Walden Woods, a term heretofore virtually unknown; they brought international moral pressure to bear on feckless government officials; they followed a high-minded, principled route that exemplified how a few individuals could effect extraordinary change "by faithfully adhering to Thoreau's transcendentalist values."[5]

Henley, of course, had an entirely different perspective. The quixotic TCCA was broke when he came along, and he unhesitatingly wrote them a check for $10,000. At great sacrifice in time and energy he took the campaign to save Walden Woods to a level that TCCA could never have attained and began to achieve extraordinary results. Then, apparently out of spleen and jealousy, Blanding turned his back and began to vilify him. "Mr. Blanding seems to me to be living in an intellectual ivory tower and lobbing stones down to the rest of us who are in the arena actually getting the job done. Everything that he wanted for Walden Woods has come true because of our efforts, and I cannot for the life of me see why he cannot find some kind of satisfaction or joy in that." "For its success,

TCCA had to be killed," Blanding has charged; but for his part, TCCA's chief fundraiser Vidar Jorgensen was delighted to have Henley appear on the scene and contribute generously, watching in awe as the Walden Woods Project ultimately raised nearly six hundred times more money than TCCA had. "Far from harming TCCA, Henley went on to actually realize most of the stated objectives that TCCA was not able to accomplish by itself, and making TCCA look far more effective than it would have looked without Henley," he says, adding that the musician "has my full respect, admiration, praise, and support."[6]

Even without internal squabbles, the fight to save Walden Woods promised to be difficult. Henley's personal crusade had hardly begun when he discovered that he had stepped into a hornets' nest of local politics. The Bear Garden condominium project included some relatively low-income units, thanks to delicate negotiations that had lasted months and that aimed to bring Concord into compliance with so-called anti-snob zoning laws. Now Henley, like TCCA before him, was attacked as illiberal for quashing low-income housing in a town in which only 5 percent of homes matched that description. "There are issues of class here," one opponent charged. "If environmentalism is going to be a successful movement, it must include all classes. It can't be meant for well-to-do suburban people to preserve what they have." "Hell, some of the local Thoreauvians would qualify for low-income housing [themselves]," Henley joked—diffusing the crisis by offering to bankroll the construction of affordable housing elsewhere in town.[7]

As the Walden Woods Project began to show its strength and savvy, some locals recoiled with suspicion and resentment. Concord is no stranger to the preservation ethos—35 percent of its twenty-six square miles was already set aside—but its residents have always bristled at outside interference, especially from a California rocker who had never set foot in Walden Woods until March 1990. Adding to the ill will was the fact that Thoreau had long been unpopular with some in the town. One person called him a "kook" and Walden Pond "a mud hole"—and this was an official at the Visitors' Center. Such ugly grumblings hit the newspapers in April 1990, when cantankerous *Boston Globe* writer Alex Beam swung a punch:

This weekend, a curious hodgepodge of Harvard and MIT professors, clerics and aristocrats will join Wampanoag Supreme Medicine Man Slow Turtle at the Walden Earthcare Congress to decry, among other things, the proposed construction of a 139-unit condominium development about three-quarters of a mile from Walden Pond. Those not sated by the weekend jawfest can attend fund-raising concerts next week, to hear ecological authorities such as rock musician Don Henley, actor Don Johnson and sybarite-at-large Carrie Fisher chime in their support for a cause hardly worth fighting for, much less singing for. The Concord residents opposing the condo project . . . jabber about preserving the 'integrity' of Walden Pond, which was long ago despoiled by a dump, summer overcrowding, and the incessant buzz of traffic on Routes 126 and 2. One anti-condo organizer has complained that the offending development will desecrate Bear Garden Hill, 'where Thoreau experienced the moonlight reverie he wrote about in his journals.' Puh-lease.[8]

But Bear Garden Hill was soon saved. The developer, Philip DeNormandie, even sold it at $2 million under the appraised value, perhaps recollecting that his father was the longtime advocate of conservation at Walden, Jim DeNormandie. But Brister's Hill proved more difficult, given the intransigence of Mort Zuckerman. A tycoon worth $400 million, he was in no mood to compromise, having recently retreated from a bruising fight with Jacqueline Kennedy Onassis and other celebrities in New York over a huge skyscraper he wanted to build overlooking Central Park. He had bought the Brister's Hill property in 1984 for $3.1 million, but now he demanded $7.4 million or more, claiming that this represented the total costs incurred. The Walden Woods Project was incensed by this apparent gouging, but forged ahead, convinced that the site was crucial and would set a land-use precedent around Walden Pond for years to come. "We take the long view," Blanding commented for TCCA. "One hundred years from now, Route 2 won't be there. It'll be underground, or there'll be some other kind of transportation. We want to establish the idea of Walden Woods as a unit."[9]

Henley and Zuckerman sparred angrily in the media. The rock star decried the developer's asking such a high price: "The man is filthy stinking rich. He can afford to do better." When the *Wall Street Journal* sided with Zuckerman, Henley fired back that its "purpose in life, its raison d'etre, is to be bootlickers and apologists for big business." Zuckerman scoffed at the idea that the parcel was historic or worth preserving. He said, "Mr. Henley makes millions and millions through his music. He has lots of friends in the entertainment business. I venture to say the entertainment business is in better shape than the real estate business." He complained too about the Walden Woods Project's "inaccurate publicity barrage" and "assault in the media" against him: "Whatever one may think of their ends, their means have been deplorable." Zuckerman finally gave in, faced with an onslaught of bad press. "From day one, we were prepared to try and sell it to [Henley], and he turned it into this issue he tried to demagogue. If that's our definition of a saint, we've got a long way to go in this country."[10]

Saintly or not, the Walden Woods Project overcame all obstacles, impressing observers with a series of purchases (made in partnership with the Trust for Public Land) that safeguarded critical parcels of Thoreau Country. These included 25 acres at Bear Garden Hill, preventing the condominium project, for $3.55 million, in January 1991; 25 acres at nearby Boiling Spring, for $1.25 million, in April 1992; 18.6 acres at Brister's Hill, preventing the office park, for $3.5 million, in May 1993; 18 acres near Pine Hill, for $1.5 million, in July 1994; and 10 acres on Fair Haven Hill, for $900,000, in December 1995. These, plus the purchasing of development rights on other tracts, were splendid achievements, albeit at staggering expense. The Brister's Hill property, for example, cost more than $4 a square foot, a steep price for a gravelly lot. To cover these huge outlays, Henley organized a benefit concert featuring himself, Elton John, Sting, Jimmy Buffett, and other stars that raised more than $1.2 million. A T-shirt garnered nearly $1 million more. A book was published (*Heaven Is Under Our Feet*, a miscellany of environmentalist essays by celebrity friends) and an album released.[11]

Some at first had suspected Henley of caring more for self-promotion than for Walden Woods, but his long hours and obvious passion soon silenced most critics. One interviewer concluded that,

"All Walden Wood might have been preserved . . . with Walden in its midst." At lower right are the Concord dump and (at picture edge) the Zuckerman site. 1988, courtesy Landslides Aerial Photography.

after years of "life in the fast lane," as one of his songs described it, he had yearned for a change. "He sees himself as a messenger from a simpler place and time, caught up in a society on the verge. . . . [Some] see the Walden Woods campaign as an expression of his deepest convictions and desires. Through the fund-raising activities, Henley presents his Thoreauvian beliefs to a wide audience; vindicates his childhood; redeems his celebrity for a good end; wrestles with the developers and other perceived villains he's attacked in music; and proves his effectiveness outside the music world." Another interviewer asked him, "Do you try and do heroic things?" Henley replied, "No, I try to do things that need doing, whether that be making pancakes for my children or preserving Walden Woods. My father had a strong work ethic. If something had to be done, it was done. No arguing, no malingering, no shirking of one's responsibility. You shut up and did the job. That's the way I was brought up."[12]

At every turn Henley was vocal about the cause. "Walden Woods is the cradle of the environmental movement," he told a concert audience on Long Island. "If we can't save that, we can't save anything." As he gained experience, the stubborn and headstrong musician gradually became more cooperative. "I'm trying to be as diplomatic as I possibly can," he said at a press conference announcing victory in the fight for Brister's Hill. "I've learned there's always someone who disagrees." He added, "It certainly has been an education, I'll tell you that. I've learned some about Thoreau and Emerson. I've learned a lot about diplomacy and patience and politics."[13]

As the Walden Woods Project dominated headlines, Mary Sherwood's controversial Walden Forever Wild did not fall silent. Throughout the late 1980s she continued in her campaign to ban swimming at the pond, lecturing everyone who would listen, even teenage lifeguards at the reservation: "Swimming, lifeguards, and beaches ARE desecration in a world-class historical shrine. There should be NO swimming at Walden, those beaches should be returned to forested paths as they were in Thoreau's day. The erosion, fence breaking, and other such damage done all around the Pond, most of it by swimmers out for some exercise, are a disgrace to the State." Unstintingly she spoke her mind, claiming, for example, that the Red Cross manipulated water sampling to make the pond seem cleaner than it was. She insisted that she had seen human feces bobbing in the swimming area. But her opponents, including a columnist in *Sports Illustrated*, reminded her that swimming could never be banned, as the 1922 deed that helped create the reservation specifically sanctioned "bathing."[14]

Sherwood turned eighty-five in 1991, the year she argued forcefully, "At this moment Walden is in its worst condition ever and is only getting worse." She told the *New York Times* that "the world's major problem was overpopulation, and that if she had to do it over again, she'd dedicate her life working to stabilize growth." She even criticized Thoreau, who "didn't go far enough with his Walden Pond experience. He should have gotten more self-reliant by growing his own food and living off the land," not going to his mother's to "pick up roast beef sandwiches and doughnuts and stuff them in his pockets.'" Year after year, her Walden Forever Wild had introduced their "sanctuary bill" in the legislature, only to see it killed. When all her efforts had been defeated, Mary called for a takeover of the reservation by the National Park Service. She was convinced that local management of national treasures will always yield short-sighted exploitation.[15]

When the Walden Woods Project arrived on the scene, Sherwood eyed their efforts with crotchety ambivalence. "The town of Concord thinks Henry David Thoreau was a hippie, and they think Don Henley is one too. I thoroughly dislike his kind of music, but . . . if it takes rock music to bring in the money, I say bring it in." Henley's fund-raising was impressive, but it went only to buy "periphery property" outside the reservation and did nothing to help the pond itself. Henley, she declared, "doesn't know an eroded path when he sees one, or the name of any given tree, or shrub or wildflower, or bug, or bird found at Walden. . . . It would add to Don Henley's stature if he would openly, publicly, recognize the group which is doing the most to save Walden itself. . . . The birds, and wildflowers, and frogs and trees can't eat or breathe money." Well might she have been skeptical of the rock star, who was half her age and seemed to represent the commercial culture she had spent a lifetime heartily detesting. But in the end, Henley's group overwhelmingly prevailed, whereas Sherwood's shoestring operation went broke. Only extreme age prevented the fighter from rallying one more time and renewing her decades-old fight for Henry Thoreau and Walden.[16]

In 1993, the year that pieces of the Berlin Wall were placed on the cairn, a group of divers set out to investigate underwater conditions at Walden. To them, news that a fisherman had lately hooked a trout with a $600 diamond ring in its stomach would not have seemed amusing, but rather evidence that the pond's once-pristine waters now harbored all kinds of junk. It did not take them long to realize that "there is nothing wild about Walden now, nor will there ever be again. It is a large swimming hole, a put-and-take fishing park." Sure enough, underwater trash was copious, and as one diver surveyed the bottom he felt "disappointment, disgust, anger, and *shock.* . . . Walden Pond made White Pond—until then one of the most trashed bodies of still water I had ever seen—look clean." Nonetheless, there was plenty of aquatic life, including a four-foot eel. The divers descended into a world as black as night: "At ninety-three feet, we could see almost nothing—despite the powerful lights we had brought—and the taste of sulfur became almost overpowering. . . . Excepting the filamentous sulfur bacteria suspended in the hydrogen-sulfide broth, Walden Pond is lifeless below 85 feet, where even the tubifex worms can't survive." It was a startling glimpse into the netherworld at the deep floor of the pond.[17]

That same year, *Faith in a Seed*, hailed as Thoreau's final, "lost" manuscript, proved a publishing sensation. Its editor, Brad Dean, thirty-nine, had been made to study *Walden* in high school but only cracked the Cliffs Notes. In 1973 he read the real thing during long hours as a navy mechanic in home port in California. Inspired by Thoreau's uncompromising example, he refused to get a military-style haircut and was court-martialed. His early discharge came after a Thoreauvian two years, two months, and two days of service. Dean's whole life was henceforth directed toward Henry, and today he is a leading scholar. He recalls his first visit to Walden Pond, in summer 1983, with his wife, Debra: "We had driven from Spokane, Washington, anticipating Walden the whole way. When we saw the 'Concord' sign we thought, 'Now we're on sacred ground!' But then there was a dump and a trailer park and a parking lot, and boom-boxes and kids running around shouting for ice cream. So much for Walden Pond! You get besieged with American culture at its very worst. I came all the way across the country for this?" His enthusiasm for Thoreau was undiminished, however. *Faith* took him a decade to complete; *Wild Fruits*, another Dean-edited Thoreau manuscript, came out in 1999. His interests subsequently turned to the beanfield, the location of which he helped reestablish after decades of public confusion about the matter; DEM had even hired a professional archaeobotanist to investigate "beanfield" soils uphill from Thoreau's house site, not realizing that this was the wrong location altogether. Dean's 2001 measurements of the level plateau on Emerson's lot near Walden Road proved extraordinarily close to the beanfield dimensions Thoreau gives in *Walden*.[18]

Sherwood had dreamed of a World Thoreau Center to be housed in the humble lyceum in Concord. Only half of her dream came true. In 1994 the Thoreau Society, which had merged with the lyceum some years earlier, sold the Belknap Street property. At the same time, the Walden Woods Project bought the 1905 gentleman's hunting estate of Alexander Henry Higginson, on the slopes of Pine Hill, for the creation of the kind of center Sherwood and others had envisioned. Ground breaking began the following year for a Thoreau Institute to house both the Walden Woods Project and the Thoreau Society (the latter also opened a somewhat incongruous, but profitable, "Shop at Walden Pond" at reservation headquarters, where fourteen thousand copies of *Walden* would be sold by 2000). Henley gave a concert for Digital Equipment Corporation and in return received half a million dollars' worth of computers and software to create a media center that would spread Thoreau's ideas worldwide. Dean was hired to run the center, www.walden.org streaming Henry across the Internet. By 2001 the site was receiving 1.4 million user hits annually.

But the demise of the lyceum infuriated some of those who had long been involved with it. Blanding, who recalls the lyceum as "a joy to thousands of visitors for a quarter of a century," charged that the Thoreau Society, having been seduced by the wealth and glamour of the very un-Thoreauvian Walden Woods Project, had deliberately destroyed the unpretentious, accessible facility in order to clear the way for a palatial, private study center for scholars only. The *Boston Globe* reported that the institute "has launched the [Thoreau] society into the digital era, but it has also thrown the often eccentric antiquarian literary group into a wrenching internal debate over its future. . . . A small but vocal minority . . . charges that there has been a 'takeover' of their beloved society by academic and corporate interests and that, in adopting modern technology and marketing to further its aims, the society has left Thoreau's values and spirit behind." "Thoreau Would Be Appalled," an editorial headline ran in the *Boston Herald*: "Rolling over and playing dead in this little drama are a handful of so-called Thoreau scholars captivated by the money, the glitz and the nearness to fame of their new benefactors." Journalist Beam wrote, "Hard-core Thoreauvians don't want to move their headquarters to a glitzy edu-tainment center in Lincoln, a town where Thoreau never lived. 'Henry would be horrified,' says Lyceum curator Anne McGrath, one of many Concord residents still on a first-name basis with the sociopathic mooch who left his fabled pondside hermitage twice a week for hot dinners at his mother's house."[19]

But most Thoreauvians cheered the institute and its creator, Henley, by now the undisputed leader of conservation efforts near

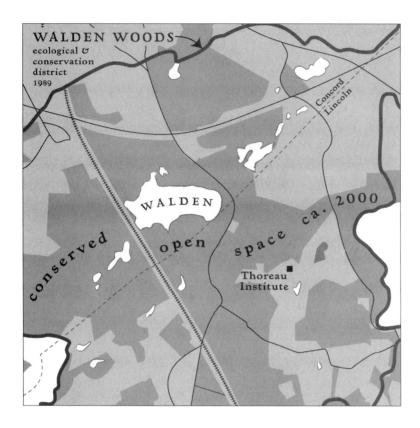

Walden. J. Walter Brain, a TCCA founding member, acknowledges, "Although not our friend, and at odds with our philosophy and vision in saving Walden, Henley proved genuine in his own endeavor to rescue the woods." After Blanding's resignation from TCCA in protest of Henley's increasing sway, the organization began cooperating with the Walden Woods Project regarding the thirty-five-acre town dump, "barely concealed behind a thinning row of dying trees and a flimsy barrier of chicken wire and snow fences papered with blown-away trash." Henley called it "a big, ugly, gaping hole in the ground, and it's right in the middle of Walden Woods." A series of advertisements highlighted "Concord's Trash Dilemma. . . . TCCA is not alone in its belief that the dump has become an embarrassment to the town." Another ad explained "Why It's Time to Close the Concord Landfill." In 1992 townsfolk unhelpfully voted to expand the facility, but two years later they reversed themselves and opted unanimously for closure, convinced that "the dump has been a money-loser in recent years that threatened to expose the town to liability for future pollution." The contentious issue for the next decade would be, what to do with the site now?[20]

Over at the pond, visitors in 1986 had found path restoration underway, as the west shore between Ice Fort and Thoreau's Coves was rebuilt using boulders to stabilize the banks and hillside. Sherwood rightly complained that the results looked artificial. Ten years passed before the rest of the shoreline was rebuilt (1996-98)—more than three thousand feet of it—and in the meantime a new technique had become increasingly popular nationwide, "soil bio-engineering." The method was promoted by the federal govern-ment in erosion-control campaigns of the 1930s, but its recent revival stems from European refinements. At Walden Pond, fascines—bundles of cuttings laid in trenches—were employed. So too was brush layering, the insertion of cuttings into holes in the ground with the shoots sticking out. These cuttings were live, meant to sprout roots and grow, thereby stabilizing and revegetating the banks. Even the stakes that held the fascines in place were living. Thirty thousand native plants were used, of forty-five species. Essential to the success of the million-dollar-plus project, funded by the state, was the use of miles of wire fencing to keep visitors on the path and funnel swimmers to the shoreline at selected points only.

Within five years the results were extraordinary, especially along the heavily damaged north shore—a carpet of blueberry bushes on slopes lately raw; alders and sumacs soaring in a thick, dense screen; grasses and shrubs so lush they required pruning, as had not been the case for decades. Where Walden once showed a bathtub ring of bare dirt all around, there flourished a zone of foliage, astonishing to anyone who recalled the former conditions. For the first time there seemed to be hope for Walden's eroded shores, but only if the "temporary" fences were made permanent and slopes damaged by shortcutters were promptly repaired, all of which would require fur-ther allocations of money.

As this encouraging work was underway, Walden's ringing sym-bolism led to its being chosen by an animal rights group, People for the Ethical Treatment of Animals, for a salvo against sport fishing. (Walden was one of several targets—it was said that the organiza-tion had asked the town of Fishkill, New York, to change its name to Fishsave.) They sent a letter to the Walden Reservation asking for a ban and offering to provide No Fishing signs for free, quoting Thoreau's antifishing remarks in *Walden* and adding that fish feel "fear and pain" when hooked. The group got the attention it sought, a firestorm of criticism erupting across Massachusetts, where leghold trapping of animals had just been defeated in a public referendum—for many hunters and fishermen, worrying evidence that animal rights seemed to be gaining ground. Walden was a shrewd choice; as a ranger said, "This is a very symbolic place. In the '60s a lot of movements got started here. I've gotten so many phone calls. I think they were ingenious." But once again, the venerable wishes of the Emerson family were invoked: "The deed states that the pond would be for fishing and bathing. It's our duty to uphold the intentions of the deed." So fishing continues, as it always has. On the day in 2035 when Concord celebrates its 400th anniversary, someone will surely be fishing at Walden.[21]

On the southeastern flank of Pine Hill, fifteen minutes' walk from Walden Pond, the Thoreau Institute opened with a gala on a sunny, breezy June 5, 1998. There was much to celebrate. The Walden Woods Project had raised more than $17 million and saved ninety-six threatened acres. It had built a state-of-the-art library and media center beside the Higginson estate house. Complaints about the institute's being ostentatious and cloistered (as well as an inappropriate way to spend dollars donated for conservation) were far outnumbered by expressions of praise, including a *Boston Globe* article headlined, "Henley Transcends Critics: Thoreau Center Proves Preservationist's Sincerity." Walden Woods Project efforts had attracted attention from all over the world. Former president Jimmy Carter sent a message that read, "The environmental challenges evident in Thoreau's era pale in comparison with the magnitude of global crises that confront us today. . . . Often they germinate as singular and sometimes 'localized' environmental concerns [such as] the leveling of an historic woodland near Walden Pond."[22]

Henley's political connections were stunningly evident on dedication day. President Bill Clinton and Hillary Rodham Clinton were driven to the top of Pine Hill, from which they strolled down through the woods with Henley, a brief moment of privacy and a good "photo-op." They emerged from the forest onto the grounds of the institute, where assembled dignitaries included famed biolo-

Don Henley triumphant. He walks down from Pine Hill with the Clintons, June 5, 1998. AP/Wide World Photos.

gist Edward O. Wilson, Senators Edward Kennedy and John Kerry, and singer Tony Bennett. (Henley's two original Walden Woods Project cochairs were absent, having both died the year before, Michael Kennedy in a skiing accident and Paul Tsongas of cancer.) The Clintons inserted an original brick from Thoreau's Walden house into the institute's walls. Addressing the crowd, the president said, "Let us hope and pray that Walden Pond will flourish." He mentioned, too, the need for $12 million in additional funds. Other speakers praised Thoreau and Walden Woods. Kerry recalled how Henry had inspired him to spend his own night in jail protesting the Vietnam War. The First Lady remembered her disappointment at the run-down condition of Walden when she made a pilgrimage as a Wellesley student in the 1960s.[23]

The critics were not silent, however. "It's true they have raised money, but I don't know of any consciousness that has been raised," Blanding growled. Several TCCA supporters still regretted having been marginalized, Schofield saying, "I have occasionally felt the sting of being invisible. People left in the dust don't like it." Fundraising efforts for the Walden Woods Project showed little sign of adhering to Thoreauvian simplicity, as Henley fans shelled out money for CDs, T-shirts, drumsticks—even leaves dipped in gold and offered at $8 each. "It's very, very hard to make a true Thoreauvian understand," explained Kathi Anderson. "It's sort of the antithesis of what Thoreau stood for—fancy fund-raisers and other events. But we live in a real world where developers do not give away their property. You have to negotiate with them."[24]

As fundraising progressed, purists worried that Walden Woods was becoming branded as something akin to a commercial product, with Henley's celebrity name elevated above Thoreau's. "People would be at his [benefit] concerts if he were raising money for the In-grown Toenail Foundation," Borden sniffed. "My students believe what I say about Thoreau because Don Henley's told them first," a professor reported—encouraging or alarming? *USA Today* reporter John Larrabee explored how "the man who admonished readers to 'simplify, simplify' has been caught up in the latest trend of 20th-century commerce: cause-related marketing, the strategy of boosting sales, corporate image and a star's drawing power by linking up with a social or environmental crusade." He pointed to corporate sponsorship the Walden Woods Project had received from Reebok, Hard Rock Cafe, and AT&T and reported that organizations that gained publicity from contributions to Henley's group included "liquor companies, a major logging company, the operators of Nevada's newest casino, and Ackerly Communications, Massachusetts' largest billboard company." (These contributions were entirely indirect, Anderson explains, coming as part of a mass donation of magazine advertisement revenues from a Hearst publication.) "I have no apologies to make," said Henley. "We are realists. I think we have struck a very good balance between the integrity of Thoreau's legacy and the harsh realities of charitable fund-raising in this day and age. Walden Woods have tremendous symbolic value. It represents all the battles that are going on in every city and town where Mother Nature is pitted against ignorance and greed." "We try to stick to companies that share our vision of preserving the land," Anderson added. "But you can lose the battle by refusing to take money from anybody at all."[25]

The Walden Woods Project's most vocal critic, Blanding, was interviewed by National Public Radio in August 2002 as "the walking embodiment of Henry David Thoreau." In a conversation later that year he looked back disapprovingly on the past decade: the battle was won, perhaps, but the war was lost.

> Henley saved the trees; he didn't save Walden Woods. Walden Woods is just a political buzzword now. This is not just about *material states*, but a *symbolic message*. The Walden Woods Project has presented Thoreau as an establishment figure, making him conform to their value system by establishing themselves as the authority in this field and effectively blocking others from speaking at all. Saving historic landscapes in Concord and beyond was our vision, establishing a balance between civilization and wilderness, and our idea was catching on. They've bought a handful of parcels, but blocked hopes of saving Walden Woods, saving Concord, and carrying this message to a larger audience. They laughed at TCCA and portrayed us as helpless, but they should be in awe of what we accomplished. They didn't save Walden Woods! *We saved it; they bought it.*

He goes so far as to wish the Brister's Hill development had in fact gone forward: "It would be a much more effective symbol with an office park on it. At least it would be *true*." His views are strikingly at variance with mainstream opinion, summarized by environmental writer John Hanson Mitchell at the time of the institute's opening. Deploring the infighting, he remarked, "They saved the land, so who cares who did it? Thoreau was a pragmatic fellow and I think he would agree. He wouldn't like the glitz and the money and all that, but the fact is the chipmunks and the salamanders and the garter snakes are saved."[26]

Conservation of Thoreau Country in the 1990s was actually more complex than the Blanding-Henley dichotomy would suggest. Many others were involved and found productive ways of bridging the divide between grassroots and glitz. Michael Kellett of the Wilderness Society, for example, was active in both TCCA and the Walden Woods Project as well as in Sherwood's Walden Forever Wild. He sees the rift between Tom and Don as an unfortunate failure of each man to understand the other—ironic, given their many similarities, including passion for music, the environment, and

Thoreau. Looking back, he stresses the quiet effectiveness of Borden, Schofield, Jorgensen, Brain, and other tireless advocates for preservation, and he hails the work of Henley and Anderson, who overcame the skeptics and proved that their commitment to the Walden cause was genuine—more so than Blanding could see. Jayne Gordon, who has worked both for the Walden Woods Project and the Thoreau Society, downplays the schisms as being little different from those that shake cause-oriented nonprofits everywhere. The bigger story at Walden, she says, are the hard-won successes that have arisen from cooperation, not conflict. Jorgensen observes that today, thanks to this cooperation, "There is far, far more good news than bad news at Walden."[27]

The year 1996 was the wettest of the twentieth century, the only one with over sixty inches of precipitation (the average is forty-three). By its usual lag, and owing to a wet 1998 as well, the pond rose very high in 1999. From its new headquarters that year, the Walden Woods Project fought to make headway with local politicians and overcome continuing resentment of them as so-called Hollywood interlopers. It was upsetting when, in April, the Town of Concord approved construction of a cellular telephone tower at the edge of the now-closed landfill. And rather than shut the dump entirely, the town sought to retain a corner for snow removal, composting, and wood chipping. The Walden Woods Project warned of "a profound negative impact on the ecology and aesthetics of the area" from inappropriate uses of the landfill and teamed up with Massachusetts Audubon for a proposed restoration of the site. In addition, they worked with the conservation group Scenic America to name Walden Woods one of twelve "Last Chance Landscapes" nationwide, calling on the town to prohibit any "ugly intrusion on the woods" and to turn the landfill into conservation land—not soccer fields, as some locals wanted. It was an emotional matter, as the dump's "weed-strewn moonscape" lay at the heart of Thoreau Country: "Somewhere under a mountain of garbage is Ripple Lake." By 2002, most of the landfill had been capped with topsoil and was reverting to grassland, but the public works portion of the site remained a point of sharp contention.[28]

A $1.25 million grant to the Walden Woods Project from media conglomerate AOL Time Warner was earmarked for restoration of the landfill and the Zuckerman site on Brister's Hill. As the twenty-first century began, these projects dominated Walden Woods Project energies, along with the challenges of running a research and educational center and raising money for future land acquisition. In 2001, the year a carefully researched replica of Thoreau's Walden house was erected at the institute, Henley could look back with pride on having garnered a phenomenal $23 million for his organization, but needs were still insatiable. "I work on the Walden Woods Project every week," he told a reporter. "This is our 11th year. We are in the process of trying to raise a $28 million endowment fund so the project and institute will be self-sustaining." Henley, who turns sixty in 2007, admits that he faces a "daunting prospect," with so much money to find: "I can't be doing this forever."[29]

❧

Thoreau Society founder Walter Harding was generally protective of Henry's memory and once grew angry when a New York newspaper compared a notorious criminal discovered living in the woods with the gentle hermit of Walden. Ironically, Walt died in April 1996, at the same moment that Thoreau's name was suddenly splashed onto headlines in the least-flattering light imaginable—as a precursor of the infamous Unabomber, a terrorist whose antitechnology manifesto, "Industrial Society and Its Future," had been published the previous year in major newspapers in a controversial attempt to catch the killer. When arrested in Montana, the Unabomber, caked with dirt, turned out to be one Theodore J. Kaczynski, who inhabited a Walden-like cabin near, coincidentally, a town called Lincoln. His dwelling was even smaller than Henry's, just ten by twelve feet. It had no wires or plumbing, but two hundred books were strewn about—including some writings of Thoreau—along with newspaper clippings, fishhooks, notebooks, empty cans, old diplomas, antidepressant pills, three typewriters, five guns, triggers, pipes, explosive chemicals, and a bomb.

Comparisons to Henry were legion. One commentator argued, "Thoreau . . . inspired Kaczynski in more ways than one. Thoreau built a shack in the wilderness and learned to live off the land. So did Kaczynski—he even copied Thoreau's cabin design. Thoreau—in his

"Thoreau defense." The Kaczynski "Unabomber" cabin was hauled off to serve as a courtroom exhibit, 1997. AP/Wide World Photos.

isolation—penned the beloved American classic, *Walden.* . . . In *his* solitude Ted wrote his odious *Manifesto.*" A reporter concluded, "Mr. Kaczynski's cramped residence will be evidence that anyone who lived in it must have been crazy. Some commentators suggested that it sounded like a 'Thoreau defense,' aimed at tapping an American suspicion of people who forsake conveniences and live apart from society. . . . Any parallel between one of the country's most important philosopher-writers and a man whose lawyers say he was a delusional paranoid schizophrenic would clearly be flawed. But as a matter of courtroom tactics, the Thoreau defense has won praise from lawyers."[30]

In fact there was little need to look to Thoreau's house to explain Kaczynski's. Hunters, trappers, and fishermen have long lived in cabins, from Montana to Maine. Kaczynski was a killer, Thoreau so gentle he abandoned his birder's gun for a telescope. And by the late twentieth century a life of isolation was not statistically unusual: the percentage of American households inhabited by only one person soared from 8 percent in 1940 to almost 25 in 1990. There are a great many "Thoreaus" today, with, inevitably, a few Kaczynskis among them.[31]

The supposed link between the Unabomber and Thoreau was not the only bad press that the transcendentalist writer received during the decade. P. J. O'Rourke ridiculed him in *Rolling Stone* as "the worst sort of person in the world, the sanctimonious beatnik," and as for reading beyond the first hundred pages of *Walden*, "I defy any thinking adult without an air-sickness bag to go further." Those who found fault with Thoreauvian escapism could point with dismay to the 1992 tragedy of Chris McCandless, a twenty-four-year-old college graduate from the Washington, D.C., suburbs who inexplicably gave all his money to charity, turned his back on his parents, and disappeared into the Alaskan scrub for a stringent exercise in self-sufficiency: "I now walk into the wild." As Jon Krakauer recounts, McCandless carried several books, including *Walden*, but no map, compass, or ax, and his only food was ten pounds of rice. He shot a moose but did not know how to cure the meat, and on moral grounds he deeply regretted destroying the animal. Afterward he approvingly marked *Walden* passages on vegetarianism. Another section he liked said, "No man ever followed his genius till it misled him. Though the result were bodily weakness"—but McCandless was the unfortunate exception to this dictum. Summer snowmelt raised river levels and trapped him. Without a map, he could not find his way to safety, though the highway lay just twenty miles off. Inside the abandoned bus in which he lived he had scrawled the words, "No longer to be poisoned by civilization he flees, and walks alone upon the land to become *lost in the wild*." Now this statement proved all too true. The young man survived four months before succumbing to starvation, hastened by ingestion of wild potato seeds he did not realize were deadly. It was a quasi-Thoreauvian experiment gone horribly awry.[32]

More benign experiments proliferated, however, as Thoreau-like cabin dwellings appeared in suburban backyards nationwide, a veritable explosion in the construction of so-called tiny houses. An entire literary genre was devoted to them, including *Tiny, Tiny Houses* (1987), *The Tiny Book of Tiny Houses* (1993), and *A Little House of My Own* (2000, with forty-seven designs). Some dwellings were directly suggested by Thoreau at Walden. A poet in upstate New York toured the lyceum replica and was inspired to build a half-size writing shanty in his garden back home, one costlier than Thoreau's: "On nails alone I spent $28." John Hanson Mitchell, a writer and environmentalist, built his tiny house sixteen miles from Walden Pond. "Thoreau went to the woods because he wished to live deliberately. . . . I went there because my wife and I had separated and the woods were the only place I could find affordable housing." Robbins sent him blueprints of his Thoreau replica, but in the end Mitchell built a ten-by-sixteen cabin with Gothic decoration. He has since written a series of books on the history and ecology of this single square mile of territory. "I am not ordinarily given to Thoreauvian fantasies of self-sufficiency," says writer Michael Pollan, but in 1982 he bought an abandoned dairy farm in Cornwall, Connecticut, and eventually erected an architect-designed writing hut outside the main house, fourteen by nine feet. He paid $100 per square foot. "This isn't Thoreau," he explained. "This isn't low-tech. I've got my phone and my computer and my fax. I'm on line here." In California, Jim Yount "has done Mr. Thoreau one smaller, by building his own eight by fifteen foot cabin in the Santa Cruz Mountains." This was the largest building Yount could erect without needing a permit. He prefabricated the house in town from four-by-eight Duratemp panels and later assembled it on site, the whole costing $2000 and more than two hundred hours of his time. Yount designed the house on a computer and has established MiniCabin.com on the Internet, advocating well-built small houses. "Remember, we always want our mini cabins to be structurally sound and safe. If we start building inferior cabins . . . we are inviting government regulation. . . . So, here's to the mighty mini. It's small. It's efficient. It's beautiful. It's paid for! Long may it shelter us, welcome us, protect us, keep us warm, keep us dry, keep us snug, keep us simple!"[33]

So many Americans have embarked on such experiments—or have tried, more generally, to essentialize their lives—that whole organizations are devoted to simple living and the simplicity movement. A torrent of books bear such un-simple titles as *The Simple Living Guide: A Sourcebook for Less Stressful, More Joyful Living*; *Simplicity: Finding Peace by Uncluttering Your Life*; *Voluntary Simplicity: Toward a Way of Life That Is Outwardly Simple, Inwardly Rich*; *Choosing*

Simplicity: Real People Finding Peace and Fulfillment in a Complex World;
and *The Complete Idiot's Guide to Simple Living. Walden* has helped
inspire these movements, which over time have been blended with
a New Age melange of wisdom from Native Americans, Shakers,
Quakers, Buddhists, vegetarians, and environmentalists.

As mainstream religious denominations withered in the late
twentieth century, Thoreau emerged as secular saint and Walden
Woods his shrine. Henley told an interviewer that his youthful discovery of Thoreau happened in mid-1969, when, as a literature
major at North Texas State College, he dropped out in his fourth
year to tend to his dying father. Eye-to-eye for the first time with
"mortality," he experienced

> what you might call an epiphany. . . . I was hungry for some
> sort of spiritual knowledge, because I was trying to make sense
> of my father's illness . . . and the First Baptist Church wasn't
> giving me the answers that I needed. It wasn't nourishing me
> in the way I wanted to be nourished. So somewhere along the
> line I picked up Thoreau. . . . In the '60s it was very popular. It
> was part of the back-to-nature movement. You know, every-
> body was reading *Walden*. . . . I was struggling, again, to make
> sense of my father's illness, and I was also struggling to
> become a songwriter, and I started spending more time in the
> woods, and I started reading Thoreau, and started getting a
> sense of the spirituality that is inherent in nature, and it helped
> me deal with my father's illness.[34]

Henley was not alone. In recent years, and for a wide range of
people, Walden Pond has emerged as an important spiritual center.
In his last publication (1995), Walter Harding called *Walden* "as much
a religious document as any scripture." "I have visited Authors'
Ridge a half-dozen times," a Christian theologian wrote four years
later. "Some of my favorite heretics are buried there." The guestbook in the Thoreau house replica records a quasi-religious awe
among numerous visitors: "A hallowed place," one writes. For
another, "This pond is my savior." A visitor from Denmark in fall
2002 enjoyed "a true religious experience," and a group from France
was recently seen to kneel beside the cairn. E. L. Doctorow, author

of *Ragtime* and *The Book of Daniel*, has said, "Clearly there is a historical luminosity to these woods. They stand transformed by Thoreau's attention into a kind of chapel in which this stubborn Yankee holy man came to his and, as it turns out, our redemptive vision." In 1986, a young cult member reported having broken free of his "dark aura" and recurring visions of being "attacked by nocturnal, mountain-dwelling Entities" by bicycling to Walden, where he studied Thoreau on self-reliance. Walden Pond resonates for Unitarians, who trace their spiritual origins to Concord transcendentalism. A UU minister escorted teenagers on a "pilgrimage to Walden Pond" in 2001: "For them Walden Pond was perhaps the church of choice."[35]

No less spiritual is the response to Walden of former TCCA activist J. Walter Brain, who keeps Thoreauvian peripatetic alive and estimates that he has taken nine thousand lengthy walks in Concord over three decades. In 1998 he studied an elderberry on the edge of Wyman Meadow. "I searched the bush for the pretty longhorn borer beetle it hosts, and readily spotted one which I cautiously helped onto my palm. What beauty of a beetle! . . . [It] shines in the light of day, gaining transcendence in its moment in the sun by way of man's own metaphor. Human consciousness may indeed be thought of metaphorically as that moment in the sun for the whole of creation, from the beetle on my palm back to the light reaching us from the most distant galaxies. . . . The spiritual appears thus immanent to all that exists, a leaf, a pebble, a molecule in it; rendered self-evident in the light that spills from heaven and in every reflection of it, on water, on cloud, on a glossy leaf, on that Walden in the mind." Brain's meditations recall those of the nineteenth-century transcendentalists for whom this pond and meadow were "their temple, the Sainte-Terre" (or Holy Land) to which the pilgrim, to use the Thoreauvian word, forever *saun-ters*. "There is that light of dawn within our minds calling ever at our window. Or, as Thoreau put it, 'Only that day dawns to which we are awake.'"[36]

Mystical responses to Walden take myriad forms. One seeker preserves a bottle of water from his first visit, as from a sacred river or spring. A songwriter who set a transcendentalist poet's words to music in 2001 describes himself as "a regular pilgrim to Walden Pond" and reports, "I had a feeling that I was born to write this piece:

that the spirit of Jones Very had been following me for many years, impelling me toward Walden Pond." Vermont psychotherapist J. Parker Huber leads an annual silent walk around the pond, "performing a ritual done by many pilgrims . . . that had ancient roots in the Tibetan kora and the Hindu pradakshina." At the 2002 meeting of the Thoreau Society, Penobscot Indian elder Arnie Neptune conducted a ceremony at the house site. Not all observers have been happy to see Thoreau appropriated as a secular saint, remade into what one critic sardonically calls "Jeremiah-of-the-Recycling-Bin." But the tide has proved unstoppable, and the turn of the century saw a flurry of children's books about Thoreau, all stressing his moral and spiritual relevance to modern times: *Walking with Henry* (2002), *Henry David's House* (2002), *Henry Builds a Cabin* (2002), and *My Contract with Henry* (2003). The last concerns how "an eighth-grade project on Henry David Thoreau's experimental living at Walden Pond becomes a life-changing experience for a group of outsider students who become budding philosophers, environmental activists, and loyal friends."[37]

To some observers of an unsettled fin-de-siècle culture, "civil disobedience" and disrespect for authority seemed rampant, usually divorced from Thoreau's noble purposes. In urging protection for Walden Woods, TCCA and later the Walden Woods Project repeatedly stressed that "these are the lands where the philosophy of non-violent resistance to unjust laws took shape." This had an ironic result, as 1990s rule breakers at Walden Pond State Reservation defied rangers with recourse to a supposed Thoreauvian principle of do-what-you-will. In a somewhat more considered manner, self-described dissident G. Tod Slone used the example of Thoreau at Walden to challenge governmental power during the 1999 summer that marked the 150th anniversary of "Civil Disobedience." He cussed out a parking lot attendant at the reservation, decrying "the rules" and "Massachusetts with all its . . . corruption and cronyism!" A latter-day Sheriff Sam Staples arrived and hauled Slone to jail, still wearing his wet bathing suit, leaving him shivering in a cell while feeling "nothing but anger for Massachusetts and America"—a latter-day echo of Thoreau's 1859 experience on Heywood's Peak overlooking Walden: "My thoughts are murder to the State." A year later the pugnacious Slone was threatened with arrest if he continued to post notices inside the replica house protesting the treatment he had endured during his personal equivalent of Thoreau's night in jail.[38]

With its immense symbolic value, Walden Pond is a favored site for naturalists seeking to promote their environmentalist ideas. "Every third-grader should be able to identify 100 plants and 100 animals," Concord naturalist Peter Alden believes—not unreasonable, as there are 15,000 species larger than a millimeter in Massachusetts. His Biodiversity Day, an organized count of plants and animals, has received widespread publicity. Initially he was a birder, but one day "he decided to walk around Walden Pond and see what else he could identify—plants, animals, butterflies, trees. He has been identifying species from all over the world ever since," with the goal of educating children, especially, about the natural world. His Biodiversity Day on July 4, 1998, coinciding with "the anniversary of Henry David Thoreau's move into his cabin at Walden Pond," began with coffee and doughnuts at 6 A.M. at the house replica at the reservation. Teams of amateur and professional naturalists succeeded in recording 1905 species "in one day in the two towns flanking Walden Pond." It would have been 1906 if the moose that wandered into Concord Center the next day could have been counted.[39]

Even as Walden's wildlife has been recorded with increasing thoroughness, underwater Walden has proven slow to give up its secrets. A 1998 report noted that "little is known about the pond's ecological features." In 1997–2000 a detailed survey was undertaken by the United States Geological Survey and DEM, which included the fourth bathymetric analysis of the pond since 1846. Thoreau made seventy-five measurements of the pond's depth; Deevey in 1939 took fifty; a 1968 survey "using the latest oceanographic instruments" and, supposedly, a one-man submarine, an unspecified number. The new study, employing seismic reflection and a fathometer, achieved 1700. Two deep basins were previously known, but now a third was discovered between them. Measurements revealed that the deepest part of the pond goes nearly to bedrock.[40]

There were worrying signs of change since the 1939 study, including a shortage of dissolved oxygen by late autumn, the waters having become more eutrophic. The report found "clear, generally good water quality," but it raised a concern, phrased in delicious scientist-ese: "The principal anthropogenic perturbation causing

"From flood to ebb." Thoreau's Cove was at its lowest level in thirty-five years when these schoolchildren visited in October 2002. Looking toward the sandbar. Photo, author.

eutrophication is the hypothesized swimmer input of nutrients." To employ the vernacular, people pee in the pond. Assuming that 80 percent of visitors swim and that half of those engage in "anthropogenic perturbations," then the researchers guessed that they thereby add nineteen pounds of phosphorus to the pond annually, and 639 of nitrogen. The problem is an old one; even in 1945, water tests showed that Walden was among the most polluted in the state with urine. Added nutrients can harm the desirable Nitella plants and encourage the growth of unwanted algae, thereby contributing to the dissolved oxygen deficit.[41]

Concerns about Walden's purity came to a head in the Stinky Sand episode of July 1997. During a period of high water, bathers were driven from Main Beach by a mysterious odor likened to "a musty basement," "a pool of ammonia," or "an open sewer pipe." The source, it turned out, was rotting pollen mixed with the sand, generating harmless bacteria. The beach was soon reopened. Some were led to wonder, though, how robust the health of Walden actually is, and whether it remains as crystalline as formerly. Visibility extends to eighteen feet, but Thoreau could see to twenty-five or thirty. The pond is "unusually clear and pristine for an urban-area lake," scientists say, but at risk of degradation from overuse in summertime and constantly threatened by runoff from the parking lots, underground leakage from the park's septic system, gulls and ducks attracted by litter and feeding, and the risk of a spill resulting from an accident on Route 126. Moving that road well eastward and relocating the restrooms have long been considered, but as of 2002 no final decision had been reached.[42]

The United States Geological Survey reports, released in 1998 and 2001, are "astonishing publications on Walden and have great resonance," says lawyer Steve Ells, who spent twenty-five years working for the Environmental Protection Agency and today advocates for the preservation of Thoreau Country. Even in their dense scientific language "I find much that confirms and would fascinate Henry. For example, the scientists confirm that the irregular contours of the bottom replicate the shape of the giant ice block that formed the pond so long ago. And when I look at the figures showing the phosophorus and oxygen cycles and the pond's recirculation of nutrients as it 'turns over' annually, I remember, 'The phenomena of the year take place every day in a pond on a small scale. Every morning . . . the shallow water is being warmed more rapidly than the deep . . . and every evening it is being cooled more rapidly until the morning. The day is an epitome of the year. The night is the winter, the morning and evening are the spring and fall, and the noon is the summer.'"[43]

Edward O. Wilson, Harvard biologist, conservationist, and two-time Pulitzer Prize winner, began his 2002 book *The Future of Life* with a letter to Thoreau: "Here I am at the site of your cabin on the edge of Walden Pond." Whereas many twentieth-century writers emphasized the latter-day degradation of Walden, Wilson is typical of recent revisionists who, paradoxically, find things better there now than in Thoreau's day. There are more trees, Thoreau having lived "on the edge of a ravaged woodlot" in "scraggly second-growth," Walden Woods then being a "threatened oasis in a mostly treeless terrain." Harding said, "With the return of forests, Concord is much wilder today than it was in Thoreau's day." Another voice in this spirit of revision is scholar Robert Sattelmeyer, who provocatively titled an essay "Depopulation, Deforestation, and the Actual

Walden Pond." A reviewer writes, "If you cherish an image of Walden Pond's pristine and isolated wildness, you had better not read [Sattelmeyer's] instructive dismantling of this pervasive cultural icon."[44]

Our mythologies of Walden, however, owe as much to post-Thoreauvian pilgrimages and various romantic revisions as to any deceptiveness in *Walden*. In general, Thoreau is straightforward about how scruffy Walden was; it is actually our preexisting expectations that cause readers to paint the pond rosy, as a careful re-reading of *Walden* will suggest. Also open to debate is the whole Walden-is-wilder-now argument. There are fewer farm fields and pastures today, it is true, and trees have sprung up. But these dense, immature, and monotonous woodlots are laced with asphalt roads and suburban houses, which hardly qualifies them as "wilder" than in Thoreau's time. And although deer, bear, and moose have reappeared—how Thoreau would have been delighted—the native flora of these deer-nibbled modern woods is less diverse. The abundant wildflowers that kept Emerson and Thoreau spellbound are far fewer. At Walden Pond, conditions are in some ways wilder than in 1850—there are more mature trees—but most indices show degradation. The water is murkier, the gleaming-white stones of the shore have gotten thrown onto the ice and sunk out of sight, exotic plants proliferate (for example, the 2003 outbreak of black swallowwort), chestnut trees have succumbed to blight, many birds are absent, skies are noisy, some trails remain eroded. A view west from Fair Haven Cliffs shows what seems a boundless, primeval forest stretching to the New Hampshire horizon, whereas Thoreau saw a quiltwork of fields. Trees cannot cloak the fact, however, that the Concord population has increased tenfold and all is not well here ecologically.

As early as 1958, Edwin Way Teale fretted in Concord about the exploding United States population. If current rates of visitation hold—and probably they will only increase—the next century will bring seventy million more swimmers and tourists to walk the narrow reservation paths, to bathe in these waters, each one adding fractionally to the burden little Walden must bear. Even one teenager scrambling up a slope can undo hundreds of dollars' worth of bank-stabilization work in an instant, as can often be witnessed, depressingly, on a summer weekend. Can Walden survive such onslaughts? A loving restoration remains possible and would be profoundly inspiring but cannot happen without a far-sighted and determined commitment to reduce human impacts—heaven being under our feet, literally millions of them. All parks now face these problems; more are opting for higher charges, trail closures, elimination of parking lots in favor of shuttle buses, and use of timed tickets. Tree-huggers and some Thoreauvians favor such policies to curb visitation, but state managers and park staff want to welcome the widest possible spectrum of potential users, without encumbrances or inconvenience. Many say it would be undemocratic and un-Thoreauvian to keep out the vast summertime swim crowd for whom this is affordable recreation. And yet it is these crowds that caused a *Boston Globe* reporter in 2003 to call Walden one of "Massachusetts' most disillusioning historic sites," even after two decades' worth of expensive improvements still "hardly a place for spiritual renewal." In a sense, these issues are as old as Wordsworth's diatribe against "uneducated persons . . . artisans and labourers, and the humbler classes of shopkeepers" invading "the shores of Windermere by the cheapest conveyance." Undoubtedly the debate over Walden's future will long continue.[45]

In 2002, a *New York Times* reporter described the illustrious seventy-three-year-old E. O. Wilson "on his hands and knees, pawing in the leaf litter near Walden Pond. . . . Just a dozen yards from the site of Thoreau's cabin Dr. Wilson is delving into the ground with a sense of purpose and pleasure." "This is wilderness," he says of the soil beneath our feet. Half of the planet ought to be set aside for nature, he has argued, but even small parks can contain remarkable diversity of micro-life. At the house site, he observes, "Many of the species you find here are new to science. The basic biology of most of these things is poorly known or not known at all." Wilson has lately emerged as an eloquent commentator on Walden, and the Walden Woods Project has enlisted him frequently in their campaigns. "One of America's sacred places," Walden Pond will be, he argues, "In the long term just as important as Gettysburg and the Mall in Washington" as Americans come to appreciate the vital importance of conservation and the wild.[46]

In the late 1990s a new threat emerged at Walden Woods—the public authority Massport's proposed expansion of Hanscom Field, a little over two miles northeast of the pond. Already it was the second busiest airport in New England, with jet operations having doubled between 1995 and 2000. The Walden Woods Project joined the fierce local opposition to allowing commercial jetliners. Massport's image, already tarnished by the Hanscom fight, was further damaged in 2001 when two jets that took off from different gates at Massport's Logan Airport, Boston, were highjacked by terrorists and used as flying bombs. Walden Pond State Reservation experienced double the expected weekday visitation as shell-shocked citizens sought solace after the September 11th events. It was not the first occasion that Walden had provided a safe haven in a moment of trouble; it was one hundred years almost to the day since Frank Sanborn had "gone into the Walden woods this afternoon for meditation on the national tragedy" after President McKinley was assassinated. Journalists looked to Walden as a symbol, an editor in Pittsburgh contrasting "a still, clear, early Sunday morning" spent "walking our way around the banks of Walden Pond" with the turmoil in New York and suggesting that something akin to the cockerel in *Walden* had now roused America. An Ontario newspaper called for "a Walden-like awakening" worldwide to the realities of the moment, the pond symbolizing the resilience of United States culture: "As for America, nothing changes its spirit. In the words of Thoreau, 'Nations come and go without defiling it. It is a mirror which no stone can crack, whose quicksilver will never wear off, whose gilding Nature continually repairs; no storms, no dust, can dim its surface ever fresh.' . . . Night did fall on a different world. Perhaps day will dawn on another—the world of the pond—Walden Pond. America's Walden Pond."[47]

A year later, one could walk entirely around Walden on the bare shoreline, the water having dropped in response to drought. Grass grew thick in Wyman Meadow, and the sandbar began to appear for the first time since the 1960s. Goose Pond temporarily vanished, its level bed carpeted with emerald grass, and someone cruelly quipped that it would make a nice soccer field for the Town of Concord. As it happened, in early October 2002, that pond and surrounding land, twenty-six acres in all, were acquired by DEM from the town through a land swap. Henley said, "The progress that has been made in the preservation of Walden Woods is attributable, in large part, to

Eagle at Goose Pond. Don Henley addressed the media in Walden Woods, October 2002. Photo, author.

the strength of partnerships between the state and federal governments, the Walden Woods Project, the surrounding communities and local land trusts." He was on hand at a media event on a hillside above Goose Pond, where some black birches had been felled to create a photogenic vista. A television reporter held a microphone close and asked questions: Why would a Texan fight for land conservation in Massachusetts? "Because Walden Woods is a cultural treasure. This is where the environmental movement started"—for the thousandth time stressing, with his quiet forcefulness, the sacredness of this landscape that he and Kathi Anderson have worked so hard to elevate, honor, and protect. Shutters clicked as the star embraced state officials. Participants begged autographs: "Could you sign this to my husband? He's *such* a big fan."[48]

On such an October day as this, Thoreau said, "Walden is a perfect forest mirror," but he would hardly recognize the reflected world that we inhabit 150 years after *Walden*, with its multiplied complexities. "Simplify, simplify," he told his neighbors, but material things have increased manyfold, and expenses have soared; to take but one example, by 2002 the median home price in the hermit's native Concord had reached $620,250, more than 22,000 times the cost of his Walden house. "Mansionization!" says Blanding, who broods on opportunities Concord has lost in the dozen years since he withdrew from the Walden Woods campaign. "Walden Woods is a symbol of us, a symbol of self, an indicator of where we are culturally," he continues to stress. In spite of the millions lately spent around the pond, visitors continue to come "looking for a pristine nature experience and are disappointed. But if Walden is disappointing, that is because Walden is true. It shows where our society stands in relation to nature. Walden Woods is a symbol of equilibrium between nature and society," equilibrium that is now lost in a crowded, hurried twenty-first century. To truly embrace back-to-nature transcendentalism, an act far too radical for any of today's "political and economic interests" to risk, offers a path to renewal, Blanding declares—undaunted by the ridicule he has endured for espousing such "extreme" views. He muses for a moment, then adds, "Thoreau is our philosopher of *balance*. Many people think he is extreme, but that just shows how out of balance things have become. It is not Thoreau who is extreme. We are."[49]

As camera shutters clicked at the press conference in Walden Woods, an autumnal coolness was in the air. Over at Sleepy Hollow, Henry's grave was littered with the usual detritus: pennies, pebbles, pencils, acorns, hand-written messages, to which someone had added a jack-o-lantern. At Walden Breezes Trailer Park—what little remains of it—Edna Toska patiently swept fallen leaves from the silent roadways. And down by Walden Pond, where the water had dropped lower by the day, maples reflected brilliantly in the mirrored surface of the cove. Thoreau once sat here and mused, "Time is but the stream I go a-fishing in. I drink at it; but while I drink I see the sandy bottom and detect how shallow it is. Its thin current slides away, but eternity remains." Queasy thoughts of "swimmer inputs" remind us not to drink today, but still we can gaze at the shimmering reflections and meditate on the passage of the years. Thoreau called the pond "earth's eye; looking into which the beholder measures the depth of his own nature." Many faces have been mirrored here, going back across the generations: Henley, Blanding, Sherwood, Harding, Robbins, Skinner, Teale. Legions of pilgrims. Burroughs, Ford, Muir, and Whitman. Emerson, Alcott, Hawthorne, Channing. Henry taking his morning swim. And John and Cynthia Thoreau the day they brought their children to boil a kettle of chowder on the sandbar, which now begins once more to peek above the water. The current of time flows ceaselessly: afternoon gives way to night, bringing quiet and the blinking of aircraft lights overhead, a cool wind blowing from the west. And early tomorrow, the sun will break above the treetops on Pine Hill, and Walden Pond will awake yet again to morning.

Abbreviations

❦

To avoid overburdening the notes, *Walden* and Thoreau's journal are cited selectively. Some brief accounts from newspapers and *Thoreau Society Bulletins* are listed in the notes but not in the bibliography. The following abbreviations are employed:

CE	*Concord Enterprise*
CF	*Concord Freeman*
CFPL	Concord Free Public Library
CHDT	Thoreau, *Correspondence*
CJ	*Concord Journal*
CLR	Cameron, *Concord Literary Renaissance*
CNW	Channing, notes in his copy of *Walden*, in Sanborn, *Recollections* vol. 2
CPT	R. W. Emerson, *Collected Poems and Translations*
CS	*Concord Saunterer*
DRF	Ricketson and Ricketson, *Daniel Ricketson and His Friends*
ESQ	*Emerson Society Quarterly*, later *ESQ*
FNS	"Field Notes of Surveys made by Henry D. Thoreau since November 1849"
J	Thoreau, *Journal* (Houghton Mifflin, 1906)
JABA	Bronson Alcott, *Journals*
JMN	R. W. Emerson, *Journals and Miscellaneous Notebooks*
LETE	Ellen Emerson, *Letters*
LRWE	R. W. Emerson, *Letters*
PJ	Thoreau, *Journal* (Princeton, 1981-2002)
TMC	Harding, *Thoreau: Man of Concord*
TSB	*Thoreau Society Bulletin*
TMTMR	Oehlschlaeger and Hendrick, *Toward the Making of Thoreau's Modern Reputation*
W	Thoreau, *Walden*, ed. Shanley (Princeton, 1971)
WAE	Thoreau, *Walden: An Annotated Edition*, ed. Harding
WFV	Thoreau, *Walden* first MS version, 1846–47, in Shanley, *Making of 'Walden'*

Notes

❦

Preface and Acknowledgments

1. Sept. 5, 1970, Harding, Walden Pond file (paraphrased). From the Walter Harding Collection of the Thoreau Society, courtesy of the Thoreau Society, Lincoln, Mass., and the Thoreau Institute at Walden Woods.

Chapter 1: In Morning Time

1. *W*, 158.
2. *W*, 89.
3. *W*, 212–14. On Thoreau and fishing, see Sattelmeyer, "True Industry."
4. On fishing at Walden, see Tapply, "Walden."
5. Turner, *Spirit*, 47. Swimmer's Point was called Hoar's Point in the early twentieth century.
6. Colman and Waldron, "Environmental Setting." Kay, "Wall to Wall," 867. Teitell, "Summertime."
7. Beers, "Pilgrim," 77. He refers to the Concord landscape as a whole. Kay, "Wall to Wall," 867. *W*, 175, 179, 197.
8. McGrath, "Curator's Corner." *W*, 86.
9. C., "New England Pilgrimage." See "Thoreau's Pond."
10. *W*, 86.
11. *W*, 150, 152.
12. C., "New England Pilgrimage." Adams, "Emerson's House."
13. Various *TSBs* and *Omni Gazetteer* 10:1481. Ontario: *TSB* 210 (Winter 1995). "Shapiro & Sons." "Walden Pond Apartment Homes." New Jersey's Walden Pond is named for a recreation committee chairman, Alfred S. Walden.
14. Walden Pond Books: *TSB* 195 (Spring 1991).
15. Oates in *W*, ix. ["Teaching Thoreau."] [Anon.,] Review of *Walden*.
16. See www.lsrhs.net. Schiavo, "Class." *TSB* 211 (Spring–Summer 1995).
17. Packard, "Thoreau's Walden." Teale, *Lost Woods*, 273. Tryon, "Day Afield." Kifer, "Bike Trip." "Walden Pond—Different."
18. Whitcomb, "Thoreau 'Country,'" 458. Whicher, *Walden Revisited*, npn.

Boston Globe (July 13, 1983). "Crane Beach." Lloyd, "Visit." Conniff, "Approaching," 88.

19. Munroe, "Concord."

20. *J* 8:56. *PJ* 2:235. *WFV,* 184. *W,* 234, 184.

21. Wolfe, "Walden of Thoreau," 69. Packard, "Thoreau's Walden." Disciple: *TSB* 45 (Fall 1953). Leu, "Trip Summary."

22. Sidney, *Old Concord,* 95. Kay, "Wall to Wall," 867.

Chapter 2: Visited at All Seasons (1821–1834)

1. Thoreau was either four (*W*) or five (*PJ* 2:173), the year 1821 or 1822. The carriage and picnic are supposition. Sanborn reports that Thoreau caught an early glimpse of the pond when once riding by with his grandmother; *Thoreau* (1882), 11.

2. A. W. Hosmer to S. A. Jones, Aug. 8, 1892, *TMTMR,* 162. *W,* 155.

3. *PJ* 2:173–74. *J* 11:358–60. Blancke, "Archaeology."

4. *PJ* 4:287. Ibid., 2:131. *W,* 179. *PJ* 2:137. Wordsworth, *Guide,* 101, 17.

5. *J* 10:219. See Walker, "History." See *W,* 183, and *WAE,* 178. Donahue, pers. comm; see also Blanding, "Historic Walden Woods."

6. Shattuck, *History,* 199. *W,* 86. *PJ* 6:192.

7. Schofield, pers. comm. and "Ecology," 157. Most nineteenth–century references to "Walden Woods" confine them to the immediate vicinity of Walden Pond and refer particularly to the small area of woods just north of it, toward Concord. For Concordians, this was the familiar section of the larger forest south of their village; it was visible from town, and they passed through it, both on the highway to Lincoln and when they visited Walden Pond. In accordance with local custom, H. G. O. Blake placed "Walden Wood" just north of the pond on his 1884 map of Thoreau Country, as Herbert Gleason would later. Thoreau often employed the term "Walden Woods," but he, too, mostly used it to refer to the immediate surroundings of Walden Pond, especially the area just north. It occurs five times in *Walden*— four of them in discussion of Walden Road before it reaches the pond. Living at Walden, Thoreau wrote, "Have I this vast range and circuit in nature—a square mile and more of unfrequented forest for my privacy" (*WFV,* 163). A "square mile and more" implies the area immediately around the pond, not the modern-day definition of Walden Woods as encompassing 4.2 square miles (as in Schofield, "Ecology," 155). And yet in the final version of *Walden,* Thoreau adjusts his language to favor a much broader Walden Woods: "this vast range and circuit, some square miles of unfrequented forest." And in his journal,

he sometimes includes far-flung places within his conception of Walden Woods, such as Goose Pond, Britton's Hollow (toward Flint's Pond), and woods in the direction of Fair Haven Bay. His contemporary Frank Sanborn subscribed, too, to this "great tract" vision of the place (Sanborn, "Thoreau and the Walden Woods"). There is no problem in assuming that "Walden Woods" implied two things, large and small, depending on context.

8. Shattuck, *History*, 200. *W*, 194, 197.

9. Colman and Waldron, "Environmental Setting." Skehan, "Walden Pond."

10. Nov. 6, 1837, *JMN* 5:423. Emerson, "My Garden," *CPT*. Skehan, "Walden Pond."

11. *W*, 292. Colman and Friesz, *Geohydrology*.

12. Rise and fall: *J* 11:344. Emerson, "My Garden," 1866, *CPT*, 179–81. Flint's: *PJ* 8:281. Bartlett, *Concord*, 3d ed., 73. Flint's is geologically dissimilar to Walden, because it was never part of Glacial Lake Sudbury and is not a kettle.

13. *PJ* 5:316–17. Walker, "Concord Mystery."

14. S., "Walden Pond." *W*, 178. Shattuck, *History*, 200. See Cameron, "Thoreau and the Folklore."

15. Horace Hosmer to S. A. Jones, Oct. 6, 1891, Hendrick, *Remembrances*, 40. Jarvis, *Traditions*, 31. G. Moore, "Diary," 1:16, 41, 225. He uses the variant spelling, "Waldron"; cf. John G. Hales map (1830), Blanding, "Walden Woods," 2.

16. *WAE*, 254. Troy, "Pot-Hunting." See Watkins, *Potters*. Foxes: *J* 10:163–64. Potter's wheel: *WFV*, 196. Indian doctor: Marble, *Thoreau*, 118. Wyman assembled two parcels in 1823 (from James Barrett) and 1834 (from Joseph G. Cole and others); see Maynard, "Wyman Lot." Possibly there were two John Wymans, as Minott was only seventeen when John Wyman died; Blanding, pers. comm.

17. *PJ* 2:221. Frank Sanborn in Thoreau, Bibliophile Society *Walden* 2:154. *WAE*, 250.

18. Frank Sanborn in Thoreau, Bibliophile Society *Walden* 2:152–53. *WAE*, 250.

19. Jarvis, "Houses," 98. 1822: *WAE*, 250. Every half-day: *J* 10:438. Layard: *J* 9:213–14. Dead horse: *WFV*, 207; see *WAE*, 309. Tin-hole: *J* 13:396. See also *J* 8:288.

20. *WAE*, 251. Blanding, "Walden Woods," 9 gives a date of March 7, 1836, for the Breed fire. *CE*, July 19, 1894. Edge of wood: *W*, 258. Divisions: *J* 6:390. Road on logs: *PJ* 2:221. Dean, *Wild Fruits*, 109.

21. Hosmer to Jones, March 12, 1891, Hendrick, *Remembrances*, 84, 13–14. *W*, 191, 174.

Chapter 3: Intellectual Grove (1835–1844)

1. Aug. 17, 1851, *JABA*, 253–54. Moldenhauer, "Wordsworth's Guide," 282.
2. Jan. 22, 1837, *JMN* 5:283.
3. *JABA*, 49. Oct. 20, 1835, ibid., 68.
4. July and autumn 1835, *JMN* 5:58, 109. To Caroline Sturgis, Dec. 6, 1839, *LRWE* 7:363.
5. Nov. 1836, *JMN* 5:239. Richardson, *Emerson*, 225. To W. H. Furness, March 12, 1844, *LRWE* 7:592. See *CPT*, 364, and Gregg, "Emerson and Children."
6. May–June 1836, *JMN* 5:166–79.
7. Aug. 12, 1836, *JMN* 5:189. Sept. 11, 1836, *JABA*, 78.
8. Oct. 15, Dec. 10, 1836, *JMN* 5:221, 265–66. Ice-harp: *PJ* 1:16.
9. Wordsworth, *Guide*, 1, 6. Alcott, "Forester," 36. "Walking," April 23, 1851, Dean and Hoag, "Lectures Before," 198. On peripatetic, see Wallace, *Walking*.
10. Downing, *Treatise*, 41. Martineau, *Retrospect* 2:182–83. Harding, *Days*, 49. *W*, 4, 49, 183.
11. Eidson, *Wheeler*, 50–53.
12. August, Oct. 16, 1837, *JMN* 5:352–53, 399.
13. June 29, 1836, *JMN* 5:183–84. Nose: Harding, *Days*, 66.
14. See Buell, "Thoreauvian Pilgrimage," 183. College: to Henry Williams, n.d., *CHDT*, 654.
15. *W*, 11, 13, 15.
16. Emerson, *Later Lectures* 1:18. Blanding, pers. comm.
17. Oct. 13, 1857, *LRWE* 8:535.
18. Alcott, " 'Journal for 1838' (Part One)," 233.
19. To Carlyle, May 14, 1846, Slater, *Correspondence*, 399. Waldo: to Margaret Fuller, May 24, 1838, *LRWE* 2:135. Ca. Nov. 10, 1838, *JMN* 7:143.
20. Jan. 24, 1839, *JABA*, 112. Nov. 27, 1839, *JMN* 7:315. March 13, 1839, *JABA*, 117.
21. April–May 1839, *JABA*, 126–27.
22. May 13, Aug. 3, 1839, *JABA*, 128, 134.
23. April 9, 1840, *JMN* 7:491.
24. Early 1839, *JMN* 7:165. To Elizabeth Hoar, Sept. 12, 1840, *LRWE* 2:330. Curiously, it is Walden itself that, Thoreau says in *Walden*, "one proposes" to call "God's Drop."

25. Beautiful days: to Sarah Ann Clarke, Oct. 9, 1840, *LRWE* 7:418. 1840, *JMN* 7:538–39. See also: to Caroline Sturgis, Dec. 15, 1840, *LRWE* 7:438.

26. Horace Hosmer to S. A. Jones, May 2, 1892, Hendrick, *Remembrances*, 75. To Helen, Jan. 21, 1840, *CHDT,* 37. Frogs: Harding, *Days*, 85. *W,* 81. *PJ* 1:454. *J* 6:91–92. On Thoreau and Gilpin, see Templeman, "Moralist"; Boudreau, "Metaphysical," 368; and Sattelmeyer, *Thoreau's Reading*, 185–87. On the Picturesque, see Buell, *Environmental Imagination*, 408–12, and Conron, *Picturesque*, 289–306. Donahue has discovered that Sarah Hollowell had a life tenancy on the Hollowell Farm and apparently occupied it until her death in 1844, after Thoreau supposedly bought the house; pers. comm.

27. See Moldenhauer, "Wordsworth's Guide"; and Sattelmeyer, "Projected Work."

28. *PJ* 6:83, 117.

29. CNW 2:392.

30. "Winter Walk," 1843, Thoreau, *Natural History Essays*, 60. George Ward to his mother, Feb. 22, 1841, Canby, *Thoreau*, 176.

31. To Caroline Sturgis, June 4, 1841, *LRWE* 7:455. Jan. 1842, *JMN* 8:165.

32. *WAE*, 252. *PJ* 1:328.

33. See Miller, *Fuller*, 74–75. Margaret to Richard Fuller, *TMC,* 153. Vedas: to S. G. Ward, July 28, 1840, *LRWE* 7:398. To Margaret Fuller, June 15 and July 13, 1841, ibid. 2:405, 423.

34. From Fuller, Oct. 18, 1841, *CHDT,* 57; spelling modernized.

35. Aug. 15, 1842, Hawthorne, *American Notebooks*, 335–37.

36. Aug. 18, 1842, Myerson, "Fuller's Journal," 323, 327–28, 332. *CHDT,* 161.

37. Dec. 1849, Bremer, *Homes*, 1:171. Fuller, *Summer*, 58–59.

38. Emerson, *Later Lectures* 1:7–38.

39. 1843, *JMN* 9:13, 23.

40. Aug. 25, 1843, *JMN* 9:7. *CHDT,* 117, 137. To Mrs. John Thoreau, Aug. 6, 1843, ibid., 131.

41. 1844, *JMN* 9:68. Ellen Emerson, *Lidian*, 258; see *J* 12:215. The Deep Cut shantytown must have been about where the modern Route 2 bridge crosses the railroad tracks. Oct. 6, 1843, Hawthorne, *American Notebooks*, 394–96.

42. 1844, *JMN* 9:119. Horace Hosmer to S. A. Jones, May 2, 1892, Hendrick, *Remembrances*, 75. "Musings," 1835, Thoreau, *Early Essays*, 15. Blanding, "Walden Woods," 36. *W,* 192. "Sylvan dell" possibly points to Epigaea Springs on east Fair Haven Hill, recently rediscovered; see Brain, "Epigaea."

43. Wordsworth, *Guide*, 146, 162–63. *W*, 115, 122.

44. To Emersons, July 8, 1843, *CHDT*, 124. Aug. 14, 1843, *PJ* 1:458. To William Emerson, Nov. 27, 1846, *LRWE* 3:362. 1843, *JMN* 9:36–37.

45. To William Emerson, April 3, 1843, *LRWE* 3:162. To George Emerson, Aug. 31, 1872, ibid., 10:90.

46. Aug. 15, 1842, Hawthorne, *American Notebooks*, 336. See to Emersons, July 8, 1843, *CHDT*, 124.

47. To Mrs. John Thoreau, Aug. 6, 1843, *CHDT*, 131. To Horace Greeley, May 19, 1848, ibid., 223–24.

48. "Fire in the Woods." Local farmers: Edwards, "Concord Letter." Schofield, "Burnt."

49. Hudspeth, *Channing*, 44. On Emerson and Channing, see McKee, "Fearful." Sawmiller: *PJ* 2:155; Maynard, "Thoreau's House at Walden."

50. To Caroline Sturgis, Aug. 5, 1842, *LRWE* 7:506. From Channing, ca. April 1843, *CHDT*, 96. To Thoreau, May 1, 1843, Channing, "Selected Letters (Part One)," 189. To Emerson, Dec. 19, 1844, ibid., 217. To Emerson, Dec. 11, 1844, ibid., 213–14. Alcott to Junius Alcott, Oct. 28, 1844, ibid., 215 n. 2.

51. Cooke, *Early Letters*, 69–81.

52. To William Emerson, Oct. 4, 1844, *LRWE* 3:262–63. For purchase from Cyrus Stow, see Middlesex South District Deeds, Book 449, p. 515, cited in "Deed." Chipping squirrels: WFV, 128. See "Emerson's First Purchase."

53. *J* 12:387. On land use, see Foster, *Thoreau's Country*, 210–11. $50,000: Emerson, *Later Lectures* 1:xix.

54. *CHDT*, 161. Myerson, "Emerson's 'Thoreau,'" 40.

Chapter 4: Far Off As I Lived (1845–1847)

1. Francis, *Utopias*, 2. Thirty-three: Richardson, *Thoreau*, 150. To S. G. Ward, Dec. 2, 1844, *LRWE* 7:618.

2. Cooke, *Early Letters*, 216, 95.

3. Ibid., 209, 183, 185, 161, 226.

4. To Anna B. Ward, April 30, 1845, *LRWE* 8:26. Within a mile: to A. H. Clough, July 14, 1852, ibid., 324. To William Emerson, April 3, 1843, ibid. 3:162. "The Conservative," Emerson, *Portable*, 96.

5. To Alexander Ireland, July 31, 1847, *LRWE* 8:120. To W. H. Furness, Aug. 6, 1847, ibid., 121. To John Muir, Feb. 5, 1872, ibid. 10:68. To Caroline Sturgis, Nov. 26, 1844, ibid. 7:616.

6. Anderson, *Magic*, 39. Morse, *Romanticism* 1:150. Wilson, *Future*, xx.

7. March 5, 1845, Cooke, *Early Letters*, 202. *W,* 40. Possibly the ax was Emerson's or Channing's; *WAE,* 38.
8. Blanding, pers. comm. Wordsworth, "Attractions." Malton, *Collection,* i. Downing, "Mistakes," 306.
9. *W,* 174, 170, 41. To Anna B. Ward, April 30, 1845, *LRWE* 8:26.
10. *W,* 128. Maynard, "Thoreau's House at Walden" and "House Revisited."
11. Maynard, "Thoreau's House at Walden." See Gleason, "House Beautiful."
12. *PJ* 2:200–01, 373. Salt, *Life,* 43. *W,* 83. To Caroline Sturgis, June 4, 1841, *LRWE* 7:455.
13. Gross, "Hoax," 495–96, 492. *PJ* 4:381. Ibid. 2:572. *J* 9:289, 303, 363. Emerson: June 1841, *LRWE* 7:455.
14. Potato field: *J* 7:410–11; 10:230. *W,* 160. 25,000: Dean, pers. comm.
15. *W,* 140. *PJ* 2:190. Channing, *Thoreau,* 218. See Sattelmeyer in *PJ* 2:449.
16. Sept. 2, 1842, Myerson, "Fuller's Journal," 332. To Samuel G. Ward, April 30, 1845, *JRWE* 8:23. *W,* 87, 179. Maynard, "Thoreau's House at Walden."
17. To Caroline Sturgis, Aug. 2, 1845, *LRWE* 8:43. Rambler: *W,* 42. Channing, *Thoreau,* 8. Anonymous, 1899, *TMC,* 94; see 106.
18. Ripley to Emerson, Nov. 9, 1840, Francis, *Utopias,* 42. July 8, 1843, *JRWE* 8:433.
19. *WFV,* 164, 264. Canby, *Thoreau,* 218. Sattelmeyer, "Depopulation," 242–43. Raymond Adams, *TSB* 41 (Fall 1952).
20. For citations see Maynard, "Wyman Lot."
21. Thoreau to Benjamin Marston Watson, Aug. 5, 1845, Angelo, "Two Letters." For other citations see Maynard, "Wyman Lot."
22. Maynard, "Down."
23. Cameron, *Companion,* 183–84.
24. See *PJ* 2:401n and 571–72. Watkins, *Potters,* 44. The shards are at Concord Museum.
25. Dec. 5, 1856, *J* 9:160. Restless: *W,* 329.
26. To Caroline Sturgis, Sept. 9, 1845, *LRWE* 8:52. Harding, "Thoreau in Emerson's Account Books," 2. Smith, *My Friend,* 102.
27. Cooke, *Early Letters,* 96–98. See also *Homes of American Authors,* 250–52.
28. Emerson to Carlyle, May 14, 1846, Slater, *Correspondence,* 399. For purchase from Moore and Hosmer see Middlesex South District Deeds, Book 473, p. 351, in "Deed." This "Walden Woodlot" cost $1239.56; see June 17, 1857, *JMN* 12:210. Thoreau, Surveys, no. 31b. Emerson to Carlyle, May 14, 1846, Slater, *Correspondence,* 399. See Cameron, "Emerson's Walden Woodlots."

29. *PJ* 2:190. See also Prudence Ward, Jan. 20, 1846, Canby, *Thoreau*, 216.

30. *W,* 183. *WFV,* 199. Deevey, "Re-examination," 8. Coastal: *TSB* 14 (Jan. 1946). See Maynard, "Cove Names."

31. It was a likely a phoebe that Thoreau saw, but bird books of the day used "pewee" for this species, too.

32. May 6, 1846, Harding, "Emerson's Account Books," 2. Cabot, *Memoir* 2:493. Poet's lodge, lookout: May 3–8, 1846, *JABA,* 178–79. June 28, 1846, ibid., 182.

33. Emerson to Carlyle, May 14, 1846, Slater, *Correspondence,* 399. "In my woodlot, the pokeweed & mullein grow up rankly in the ruins of the shanties of the Irish who built the railroad"; 1848, *JMN* 10:345. Railroad Spring was also called Heywood Spring; Brain, pers. comm.

34. From Caroline Sturgis, August 5, September 1 and 29, 1845, *LRWE* 8:41–42 n. 141, 50 n. 164, 56 n. 191.

35. May 1, and 11, June 5 and 8, July 4, 1846, *JABA,* 178–83.

36. Sept. 13 and 18, 1846, 2 Feb. 1847, *JABA,* 184–88.

37. Willis, *Letters,* 181. Hibberd, *Adornments,* 494. Loudon, *Suburban,* 393. Brown, *Architecture,* 257.

38. Jane Hosmer, Marble, *Thoreau,* 130. Horace R. Hosmer, *TMC,* 143. "Walden Hermitage," Channing, *Thoreau,* 199. See *W,* 174. To Junius Alcott, June 22, 1846, Alcott, "Eighty-Six Letters," 194. Harding, *Days,* 195.

39. *JABA,* 151, n. 5.

40. George F. Hoar, *TMC,* 110. Channing, *Thoreau,* 18. Keyes, *TMC,* 174. Mabel Loomis Todd, ibid., 187. Cookie jar: Zacks, "Fighting," derived from Harding, *Days,* 184. "Pies" in Edward Emerson, *Thoreau Remembered,* 10; "doughnuts" in Canby, *Thoreau,* 216.

41. To William Emerson, Nov. 27, 1846, *LRWE* 3:362.

42. March 9, 1847, Harding, "Thoreau in Emerson's Account Books," 3. March 1847, *JABA,* 193–94; also 213 n. 6.

43. March 16, 1847, *JABA,* 213–14.

44. *PJ* 2:576. *JMN* 11:146.

45. To B. M. Watson, March 26, 1847, *LRWE* 8:112. *WFV,* 206–07.

46. *CHDT,* 180.

47. To and from James Elliot Cabot, May–June 1847, March 8, 1848, *CHDT,* 177–81, 210.

48. To G. P. Bradford, June 29, 1847, *LRWE* 3:403. Willis, *Alcott,* 91–94. Also in *TMC,* 133–35.

49. 1847, *JMN* 10:21.

50. On the Emerson summerhouse, see: July 15, 1847, *JMN* 10:116. July 14,

August 12–13, 1847, *JABA,* 196. Maria Thoreau to Prudence Ward, Sept. 25, 1847, *TMC,* 168. Channing to Emerson, Nov. 1847, Cameron, *Literary Studies,* 190. Maynard, *Architecture.* Emerson suggested "a drawing or a daguerre" of the "picturesque summerhouse"; to George P. Putnam, April 13, 1852, *LRWE* 8:315; see 323. Oct. 18, Nov. 1847, *JABA,* 196. To Margaret Fuller, Aug. 29, 1847, *LRWE* 3:413. To Emerson, Nov. 14, 1847, *CHDT,* 189. See Harding, *Days,* 216–19. To Lidian, Aug. 23, 1847, *LRWE* 3:411. Sept. 28, 1849, *JABA* 215–16.

51. Blanding, "Walden Woods," 5. Jan. 21, 1852, *PJ* 4:275. Canby, *Thoreau,* 243.

52. Harding, "Thoreau in Emerson's Account Books," 3.

53. To Emerson, Nov. 14, Dec. 15, 1847, *CHDT,* 191, 196–97.

54. To Emerson, Nov. 14, Dec. 2, 1847, ibid., 192, 195.

55. Channing, "Walden," 1847, Cameron, *American Renaissance 3.* "Walden Hermitage," Channing, *Thoreau,* 198.

Chapter 5: Viewed from a Hilltop (1848–1854)

1. To Emerson, Jan. 12, 1848, *CHDT,* 204.

2. To Emerson, Feb. 23, 1848, ibid., 208–09. Damages: to S. M. Felton, Aug. 31, 1848, *LRWE* 4:109–10; Cameron, "Emerson's Walden Woodlots," 68. It was probably one acre of the island that Emerson would sell to the railroad for $31 in April 1849; to Emerson, May 21, 1848, *CHDT,* 226. Emerson offered to sell all his land at Walden; Emerson, *Later Lectures* 1:211.

3. *PJ* 2:382–84; see *W,* 304–05. WFV, 204.

4. 1848, *JMN* 10:304. Too much farming: Channing, *Thoreau,* 14. Twice a week: Sept. 1848, *JMN* 10:357; McGill, *Channing.* No price: 1848, *JMN* 11:29. White Pond: Oct. 29, 1848, ibid., 36–37. "Walden Hermitage," Channing, *Thoreau,* 196.

5. Channing, *Thoreau,* 241. Irish: *PJ* 3:252; see *CHDT,* 246.

6. Dec. 14, 1849, *JMN* 11:193. On transcendentalist walks, see Williams, "Emerson Guided." *TSB* 167 (Spring 1984). To Blake, Nov. 20, 1849, *CHDT,* 250–51; punctuation corrected. *W,* 221. Channing, *Thoreau,* 121. On walking, see Simpson, "Walking Muse."

7. Bartlett, *Concord,* 3d ed., 151. Ells, *Seasons* and *Bibliography.* Ells's recent publications on Estabrook Woods, a remarkably unspoiled (but threatened) region north of Concord once beloved of Thoreau, help correct our Walden-centric biases, as do the writings of conservationist J. Walter Brain.

8. May 1849–Jan. 1850, *JABA,* 209–20.

9. FNS, 416; Thoreau, Surveys, no. 33. Harding, "Thoreau in Emerson's Account Books," 2.

10. *J* 7:497. Presumably Riordan took advantage of the campaign of replacing the wooden sleepers at Deep Cut during winter 1851–52.

11. Jan. 18 and 22, 1851, *JABA*, 237–38.

12. April 27, June 8–9, 1851, ibid., 249–50.

13. August 10 and 17, 1851, ibid., 252–54.

14. Bremer, *Homes* 3:370–71, 1:158. They also seem to have visited Little Goose Pond.

15. Channing, *Thoreau*, 191.

16. *W*, 193. Gleason, "Walden Pond."

17. FNS, 483, 485. Alcott "saw Walden with Emerson" the next day; Oct. 18, 1851, *JABA*, 255.

18. Wordsworth, *Guide*, 18, 44.

19. *PJ* 4:336, 342. *W*, 35.

20. *PJ* 4:382; spelling and typos corrected.

21. "Historical Introduction," *PJ* 5:569. See Gleason, "Home Made Boat."

22. *W*, 181.

23. Channing, *Thoreau*, 111. *W*, 86–87.

24. Emerson brought visiting Englishman Arthur Hugh Clough to what may have been Little Goose Pond: "Walk with Emerson to a wood with a prettyish pool"; Clough, Diary, in Salt, *Thoreau*, 72.

25. 1852, *JMN* 13:70. Eaton, *Flora*. Channing, *Thoreau*, 247.

26. May 8, July 1, Aug. 7, 1853, *JABA*, 268–70. Hudspeth, *Channing*, 36.

27. 1862, *JMN* 15:261. Camel: Nelson, "Walden of Emerson," 7. Edward Emerson, *Emerson in Concord*, 157, 172. Sanborn, *Personality of Emerson*, 332. Gregg, "Emerson," 422–29.

28. *W*, 159. Griscom, *Birds*, 40.

29. Conway, "Thoreau." Fenn, "Loring."

30. Lightning: *W*, 132. Griscom, *Birds*, 172.

31. *PJ* 5:394; *W*, 179–80.

32. There was an eighth MS version of *Walden*, the printer's copy, now lost; Blanding, pers. comm.

33. Harding, *Days*, 331. Aug. 1854, *JABA*, 274. To Bradford, Aug. 28, 1854, *LRWE* 4:459–60.

34. Canby, *Thoreau*, 248. *W*, 192–94.

35. Sanborn, *Recollections* 2:321. Nov. 2, 1854, Sanborn, Journal, 9. See Sanborn, *Homes and Haunts*, 67. See also Gregg, "Emerson," 410.

Chapter 6: Walden Wood Was My Forest Walk (1855–1861)

1. Frost, 1954, Ruland, *Interpretations*, 8. Myerson, *Critical*, 5, 8.
2. *W*, 164, 217.
3. *J* 9:331–32. Sanborn, *Recollections* 2:398.
4. Sanborn, *Homes and Haunts*, 66–67. Sanborn, *Personality of Emerson*, 332.
5. March 25 and May 3, 1855, Sanborn, Journal, 20–21, 25.
6. May 14, 1855, *JABA*, 276. Bellew, "Recollections."
7. Sept. 15, 1855, Sanborn, Journal, 28. Sanborn, *Personality of Thoreau*, 275.
8. *J* 13:41. Ibid., 14:109. May 11, 1856, *JABA*, 281–82.
9. Broad margin: *W*, 111.
10. May 21, 1856, *JMN* 14:90–92.
11. June 21–22, 1856, *DRF*, 286–89.
12. Aug. 14, 1856, *JMN* 14:110. Sept. 21, 1856, *DRF*, 296–97.
13. May 2, 1857, *JMN* 14:136–37.
14. Ca. May 30, ca. June 9, 1857, *JMN* 14:145, 148–49. Poem: "Ode, Inscribed to W. H. Channing," 1847, *CPT*, 63.
15. June 17, 1857, *JMN* 12:211.
16. July 26 and Aug. 2, 1857, *JMN* 14:157, 160–61. "Henry D. Thoreau," clipping, Harding, *Sophia Thoreau's Scrapbook*.
17. Wordsworth, *Guide*, 47–48.
18. Dec. 19, 1857, *DRF*, 306.
19. Jan. 1858, *JMN* 14:195–96.
20. May 1, 1858, *JMN* 14:203. MS Poem, 1840–49, *CPT*, 370.
21. To Haven, May 7, 1858, *LETE* 1:142. To Addy, May 31, 1858, ibid., 143. Pedder: *TSB* 45 (Fall 1953).
22. Ca. May 20, 1858, *JMN* 14:147.
23. To Edith, Dec. 6, 1858, *LETE* 1:155.
24. To Edith, Dec. 14–15, 1858, ibid., 158–60.
25. To Edith, Jan. 17, 1859, ibid., 161.
26. 1859, *JMN* 14:249. Ellen Emerson, *Lidian*, 120. At four: to Edith, Jan. 24, 1859, *LETE* 1:165. High hill: to Edith, March 28, 1859, ibid., 179. Poem to Edith Emerson, Sanborn, *Collected Poems*, 32. Sanborn circuit: Sanborn, *Transcendental and Literary*, 142. Edward Emerson, *Emerson in Concord*, 58.
27. Beanfield: *W*, 159. Blackburnian: May 25, 1859, *JMN* 14:284. Edward Emerson, *Thoreau*, 7.

28. Barren Land: May 30, 1857, *JMN* 14:144. To S. G. Ward, April 29, 1859, *LRWE* 8:602. Poem, 1840–49, *CPT*, 410.

29. Spring 1859, *JMN* 14:246. Sanborn, *Transcendental and Literary*, 289. Poem, 1850–59, *CPT*, 429.

30. To Lidian or Edith, Aug. 9, 13, 24, 1859, *LETE* 1:190, 193. To Susan Hillard, March 19, 1872, *LRWE* 10:72.

31. Sanborn skated with Edith Emerson and Alice Jackson in January; Sanborn, *Correspondence*, 18. Ricketson, "Walden," Cameron, *Thoreau Secondary Bibliography Supplement Three*, 87.

32. Ellen Emerson, *Lidian*, 140. Thoreau, Surveys, no. 36. May 17, 1860, payment, Harding, "Thoreau in Emerson's Account Books," 3.

33. To Edith, July 31, 1860, *LETE* 1:215–16.

34. J. Hawthorne, *Memoirs*, 68–71.

35. Kussin, "Farmers."

36. Stateliest park: to Abel Adams, July 2, 1852, *LRWE* 4:299.

37. Wilson, *Future*, xix. "Help Save" (Nov. 3, 1988).

38. Kussin, "Farmers." FNS, 538–40.

39. To Mary Russell Watson, April 3, 1861, Channing, "Selected Letters (Part Three)," 293.

40. July 31, 1861, *LETE* 1:254. To Samuel Gray Ward, Aug. 16, 1861, Channing, "Selected Letters (Part Three)," 299. To Mary Russell Watson, Sept. 3, 1861, ibid., 300. To Edward, Sept. 9, 1861, *LETE* 1:259.

41. Sept. 1861, *DRF*, 320. See *CHDT*, 627.

42. Wagon: to Mary Russell Watson, Oct. 2, 1861, Channing, "Selected Letters (Part Three)," 302. See to Ricketson, Oct. 14, 1861, *CHDT*, 628. Sophia Thoreau to Daniel Ricketson, Dec. 19, 1861, *DRF*, 135. Grapes: Sophia Thoreau to Daniel Ricketson, Aug. 25, 1867, ibid., 172–73. Thoreau described in his journal "the shore of Walden near RR where there are grape vines," and now his last visit was apparently to this western bay. See *PJ* 5:87 and 4:287.

43. Channing, *Thoreau*, 322, typo corrected.

Chapter 7: All Honest Pilgrims (1862–1882)

1. Jan. 17, 1862, Woodson, "Hawthorne," 287. Moran, "Poems." To Emerson, Jan. 29, 1862, *LETE* 1:264. March 3, April 1862, *JMN* 15:241, 249–50. "The Titmouse," 1867, *CPT*, 181.

2. April–May 1862, *JMN* 15:251.

3. To Sophia Ford, May 11, 1862, L. Alcott, *Selected Letters*, 75. June 1862, *JMN* 15:261. To Edward, June 12, 1862, *LRWE* 5:279.

4. Aug.–Nov. 1862, *JMN* 15:205, 281, 290, 293.

5. Woodson, "Hawthorne," 306–18. *TMC*, 88. Collyer, "Thoreau."

6. From Sophia Thoreau, Feb. 7, 1863, *DRF*, 156. Sept. 27, 1863, *JABA*, 358. CNW.

7. To Mary Russell Watson, April 14, 1863, Channing, "Selected Letters (Part Three)," 317. Disordered: May 8, 1862, Woodson, "Hawthorne," 300. Trying to find: K[ing], "Commonwealth Sketches—II," 122.

8. CNW. From Greene, Jan. 3, 1898, Hosmer, Letter File; see also Greene to Fred Hosmer, Nov. 26, 1897, ibid. Sept. 1863, Greene, Diary. See also Blanding, "Walden Woods," 49.

9. From Sophia Thoreau, Dec. 15, 1863, in *DRF*, 159.

10. July 16, 1863, *JMN* 15:355. Oct. 7, 1863, ibid., 365. 1864, ibid., 418. Nov.–Dec. 1864, ibid., 438. "The Miracle," 1860–69, *CPT*, 452.

11. Reburial: *TSB* 208 (Summer 1994). See Blanding, "Beans."

12. To Mary Russell Watson, Sept. 16, 1864, Channing, "Selected Letters (Part Three)," 339. Annie Bartlett to Ned Bartlett, *TSB* 101 (Fall 1967).

13. To Edith, March 27, 1865, *LETE* 1:338. July 28, 1865, *JABA*, 374. From Sophia Thoreau, July 17, 1865, *DRF*, 167. Aug. 8, 1865, *JABA*, 375.

14. To Sophia Thoreau, June 4, 1866, *DRF*, 169. *W*, 154.

15. To Sophia Thoreau, Aug. 4, 1866, *DRF*, 171. On Heywood, see Kussin, "Farmers," 1. Herring, "Halcyon."

16. To John Murray Forbes, Jan. 5, 1866, *LRWE* 5:445–46. To H. G. O. Blake, May 14, 1866, ibid., 463. Fire: CNW.

17. CNW. To H. G. O. Blake, May 14, 1866, *LRWE* 5:463. To Mr. Perry, ca. 1878, in Blanding, "Beans." For Emerson visits to Walden, Goose, and Ripple Ponds (the last "the Eolian Harp of the eye"), see: to Edith, March 21 and April 6, 1866, *LETE* 1:374, 377. 1866 walks suggested Emerson's poem, "My Garden," 1866, *CPT*, 179–81. See: to Edith, June 19, 1866, *LETE* 1:380; 1850–59 poem, *CPT*, 419; 1860–69 poem, ibid., 461; and Gregg, "Emerson," 410.

18. North, "Correspondence." Low water: Blanding, "Walden Woods," 24. To Edith, Sept. 7, 1866, *LETE* 1:400. CNW.

19. Wordsworth, *Guide*, 152, 154.

20. North, "Correspondence." Solitaire, 7.

21. Aug. 8, 1866, *LETE* 1:395. Sept. 16 and 22, 1866, *JABA*, 384.

22. Naiad: Richardson, *Chronicle*, 6. From Sophia Thoreau, Aug. 25, 1867, *DRF*, 172. Sophia Thoreau to Marianne Dunbar. On a cold January day in 1867, Edward Emerson and cousin Will "took a long tramp across the Pond and up onto the Ledge." When Waldo traveled west to Chicago later in the year, he put Edward in charge of cutting in the Walden woodlot. Edward, Edith, and friends went to Fairyland for

early flowers in April, finding cowslips, houstonias, skunk-cabbages, and anemones, two dandelions at Dandelion Pool, and white violets and saxifrage at Brister's Spring. See: to RWE, Jan. 15, 1867, *LETE* 1:423. Cutting: to Edward, Jan. 22, 1867, *LRWE* 9:297. To Haven, April 29, 1867, *LETE* 1:438–39.

23. CNW. "Picnic Excursions." To Ellen, July 4, 1868, *LRWE* 6:23–24.

24. Greene, Diary. See Zimmer, "Hut," 135. CNW. S. A. Jones to A. W. Hosmer, April 25, 1903, *TMTMR*, 389. Oct. 1868: Sanborn, "Channing Table-Talk." Starting in 1866, Channing lived in the west half of the Concord Academy building where John and Henry Thoreau had taught. Canby, *Thoreau*, 217, 472 n. 19. Harding, videotape. The Clarks sold their farm (with its Walden house) to Lewis Flint (1863) who in turn sold it to Daniel Sullivan (1867); Blanding, pers. comm.

25. To Edith, Sept. 17, 1868, *LETE* 1:507. To Haven, Oct. 19, 1868, ibid., 509.

26. Eccentric: to Caroline Tappan, Nov. 4, 1871, *LRWE* 10:53. *W*, 4, 49. Sanborn says that Hotham was from near Malone, New York; that he met Channing in Concord; and that he was, then or later, a protege of Gerrit Smith; Sanborn, "Hermit." Hotham is the Hermit in Channing, *Wanderer*.

27. These and subsequent descriptions are from various sources in Cameron, "Thoreau's Disciple."

28. K[ing], "Commonwealth Sketches—I." Channing, in Robbins, *Discovery*, 28. Gleason, Photographs, 1902.1.

29. K[ing], "Commonwealth Sketches—I." See Sanborn, "Hermit."

30. Munroe, "Concord." Lang, "Walden." [L. Alcott,] "Latest News."

31. Munroe, "Concord."

32. Hotham to Emersons, Dec. 1871, Cameron, "Thoreau's Disciple," 40.

33. [L. Alcott,] "Latest News," 39.

34. A. M. Sampson to Alfred Hosmer, Dec. 17, 1893, Harding, "More Excerpts." Blanding, "Walden Woods," 25. To Edith, July 2, 1870, *LETE* 1:561. See Westerner, "Hawthorne's Haunts."

35. To Edith, April 6, 1870, *LETE* 1:550. To John Murray Forbes, Sept. 27, 1870, *LRWE* 6:133. Generally inquire: Sanborn, "Concord—Old Town." Scharnhorst, *Annotated Bibliography*, 243, 293; and Stewart, *Harte*, 202. Nov. 19, 1871, *LETE* 1:623. Brown, "Journal."

36. Howells, *Undiscovered*, 254–56.

37. To Edward, July 1872, *LETE* 1:676–77. Flagg, *Woods*, 392–96.

38. Gleason, *Through Year*, xxvii. Dawson, "Cairn." Zimmer, "Hut," 136.

39. June 12–13, 1872, *JABA*, 425–26.

40. *TMTMR*, 388. Sophia Thoreau, Dec. 20, 1868, Marble, *Thoreau*, 184–85. *TSB* 124 (Summer 1973).

41. Knight, *English Cyclopaedia*, s.v. *cairn*. Thoreau, *Week*, 345. *PJ* 4:77.

42. Ricketson, "Thoreau's Cairn." Emerson reported on the "lately fire-scorched woods of Walden" to Sarah Ann Clarke, May 31, 1872, *LRWE* 10:79.

43. Channing, *Thoreau*, 183–84. See Channing, Journal, 200. Aug. 9, 1873, *JABA*, 438.

44. R., "Summer Ramble," 203. To Edith, Sept. 2, 1873, *LETE* 2:109.

45. Alcove: Hudson, "Concord Books," 21.

46. April 6, 1874, *JABA*, 447–48.

47. July 20, 1874, *LETE* 2:138–39. Aug. 1874, Greene, Diary. See also Jones, *Unpublished Letters*, 80, 84–85, and Blanding, "Walden Woods," 49–50.

48. June 8 and 28, 1874, *JABA*, 451–52.

49. *CF*, July 10, 1875. Hudson, "Concord Books," 32.

50. The Minuteman statue had been funded by the will of Ebby Hubbard, Thoreau's crochety townsman who owned the old oak woodlot at Brister's Hill.

51. *W,* 192. Various *CF.*

52. McGill, *Channing*, 157, 169. To Edith, July 24, 1876, *LETE* 2:219. For an 1869 visitor, *TSB* 123 (Spring 1973). Loomis, 464.

53. From Rev. C. A. Cressy, Jan. 1897, Hosmer, Letter File. Oct. 24, 1876, Brewster, *October*, 12.

54. Skinner, *Feet*, 57–60.

55. McLynn, *Stevenson*, 164. Sanborn, *Transcendental and Literary*. H[arris], "Hermitage."

56. Ca. Aug. 1877, Barrus, *Burroughs*, 198. Westbrook, "Burroughs."

57. *Banner of Light* (July 27, Aug. 3, 1878), Robbins, *Discovery*, 55–56. Aug. 8, 1878, *JABA*, 491.

58. *CF*, June 19, July 10 and 17, Aug. 21, 1879. Zego: *CF*, Sept. 4, 1879, July 7, 1881.

59. To Edith, July 24, 1879, *LETE* 2:355. Historic spots: July 30, 1879, *JABA*, 502. Drawing, Aug. 4, 1879, *TSB* 151 (Spring 1980). See McGill, *Channing*, 169. Beers, "Pilgrim," 60–61.

60. *CF*, Sept. 2, 1880, and other issues. *Literatti*: King, "Concord," 55.

61. King, "Concord," 55–56. To Edith, May 17, 1880, *LETE* 2:376. To Kit, July 21, 1880, ibid., 389.

62. "Trip to Concord."

63. *CF*, July 14 and 28, 1881.

64. Sept. 17, 1881, *JABA*, 527. Whitman, *Prose* 1:280.

65. Feb. 1882, *JABA*, 532. Edward Emerson, *Emerson in Concord*, 193. 1862, *JMN* 15:261.

66. Rusk, *Emerson*, 506–07. Boughs: *TSB* 182 (Winter 1988). April 30, 1882, *JABA*, 534.

67. *CF*, Aug. 18, 1882.

68. Ibid., Aug. 31, 1883.

Chapter 8: Thoreau's Country (1883–1921)

1. "Concord Social." *CF*, July 20, 1883.

2. Daiches, *Literary*, 7. Irving, *History*, 984.

3. June 27–28, 1883, Burroughs, *Journals*, 96–97.

4. To Haven, June 11–12, 1879, *LETE* 2:345. To Miss Dabney, April 2, 1885, ibid., 547. To Edith, Aug. 24, 1885, ibid., 552.

5. *CF*, July 27, 1883. Cannon: *Annual Reports*, 38. My attention was called to this by Malcolm Ferguson.

6. Considerable damage: *Annual Reports*, 42. Latin: *CF*, Aug. 10, 1883. To Edith, Sept. 4–5, 1883, *LETE* 2:514–15.

7. Stars: *TSB* 30 (Jan. 1950). *CF*, July 11, 1884. To Edith, Sept. 2, 1884, *LETE* 2:533.

8. *CF*, Sept. 4, 1885. Bartlett, *Concord*, 3d ed., 152.

9. *CF*, July 30, August, Sept. 10, 1886. To Edith, Sept. 15, 1886, *LETE* 2:570.

10. Hubert, *Liberty*, 77, 180. Morris, *Ten*. Roosevelt, *Five*.

11. *CF*, July 2, 1886; Aug. 1, 1884. Jones to Salt, June 27, 1897, *TMTMR*, 288.

12. Hoar to Salt, Oct. 2, 1889, Harding, "Edward Hoar."

13. To Haven, July 27, 1889, *LETE* 2:607. Old farmer Abel Brooks told Thoreau that members of the local Walking Society were Stewart, Collier, Channing, Pulsifer, and Emerson; *J* 9: 331.

14. Pierce, *Yeats's*, 7–8. Jeffares, *Yeats*, 30.

15. Jones, "Glimpse." *TMTMR*, 1–2, 6.

16. Harding, "Raymond Adams' Newsletter." Jones, "Thoreau and Biographers." Jones to Salt, Sept. 16, 1890, *TMTMR*, 81.

17. Jones to A. W. Hosmer, Oct. 6, 1890, Jan. 10, Sept. 16, 1891, *TMTMR*, 84–85, 96, 134. High water: Sanborn, "Walden Pond." Jones to Salt, June 27, 1897, *TMTMR*, 288.

18. Jones to A. W. Hosmer, Feb. 23, 1891, *TMTMR*, 102–03. Jones, "Thoreau and Biographers."

19. Jones to Blake, Aug. 9, 1891, *TMTMR*, 128–29. Ibid., 4.

20. Jan. 7, 1893, Burgess, Papers, notes, folder 4 (spelling and punctuation regularized).

21. To Sarah, Nov. 3, 1891, *LETE* 2:638. Livery: McAleer, *Emerson*, 666. Jones to A. W. Hosmer, March 19, 1892, *TMTMR*, 147. The answer to Jones's question: Parkman House, where Concord Library now stands.

22. A. W. Hosmer to Jones, March 25, 1892, *TMTMR*, 149. From Henrietta Daniels, Oct. 18, 1892, Hosmer, Letter File. From Rev. C. A. Cressy, Jan. 1897, ibid. From Greene, Jan. 31, 1898, ibid. Sims, "Building," 106.

23. Fire: to Edith, April 11, 1892, *LETE* 2:646. Tombstones: to Sarah, Oct. 26, 1892, ibid., 2:653. *CE*, July 15, Aug. 19, July 29, 1892.

24. Oct. 14, 1892, Brewster, *October*, 69. Twenty-seven: Richard O'Connor, in Blanding, "Walden Woods," 37–38.

25. Barton, Diary (cited in Schofield, *Bibliography*.) Huber, "Eight Hours," 112, spelling corrected.

26. *CE*, June 8, 1893. To Mrs. Muir, June 13, 1893, Badè, *Muir* 2:268. Muir, *Walden*: *TSB* 179 (Spring 1987). On Muir, see Buell, "Pilgrimage," 176–78; Scharnhorst, *Thoreau: Case Study*, 27; and Huber, "Eight Hours."

27. Capra, "Hubbard."

28. Jones to A. W. Hosmer, Aug. 4, 1893, *TMTMR*, 178.

29. A. W. Hosmer to Jones, May 17, 1894, ibid., 199.

30. *CE*, July 19, 1894.

31. Jones to A. W. Hosmer, May 14 and Oct. 19, 1894, *TMTMR*, 197, 210. Jones to A. W. Hosmer, April 28 and Oct. 3, 1895, ibid., 222, 242. Hosmer, photofile. From N. J. Smith, Sept. 21, 1895, Hosmer, Letter File, box 3, folder 5.

32. Scharnhorst, *Thoreau: Case Study*, 37–39. Waylen, "Visit."

33. Waylen, "Visit." Tryon, "Day" and "High." Burgess, "About Walden."

34. Wolfe, "Walden of Thoreau."

35. Ibid. Bartlett, *Concord*, 16th ed., 21, 170–71.

36. Fire: Sanborn, "Literary Losses." Tryon, "High." Burgess, "About Walden." Wolfe, "Walden," 69.

37. Tryon, "High" and "Day."

38. Local farmers: Edwards, "Letter." Jones to A. W. Hosmer, Oct. 8, 1895, *TMTMR*, 242.

39. Salt, *Thoreau*, xxix. Jones to A. W. Hosmer, Dec. 3, 1896, *TMTMR*, 268. Salt to Jones, July 6, 1896, ibid., 257. Gandhi later read Salt's *Thoreau* with interest and discovered "Civil Disobedience" about 1907 "when I was in the thick of [the] passive resistance struggle. . . . It left a deep impression upon me." Thanks to the Gandhi connection, Thoreau enjoys prestige in India to this day, where his followers take note that India achieved nationhood a hundred years to the day after Thoreau

first delivered his "Civil Disobedience" lecture, Jan. 26, 1848; *TSB* 210 (Winter 1995).

40. Delftware: [Hubert,] "Thoreau's Concord." For "Thoreau's Hut at Walden" cup and saucer, copyright 1896 by Edith A. Buck, see *TSB* 187 (Spring 1989).

41. Seventy: Sanborn, "Literary Losses." *CE,* May 21, 1896. Edith Forbes bought Fairyland from Samuel Hoar on Nov. 27, 1883; Blanding, "Walden Woods," 17.

42. Sanborn, "Thoreau and Walden Woods."

43. Jones to A. W. Hosmer, April 11, 1897, *TMTMR,* 274. More, "Hermit's." Mackay, *Service,* 121, 124–25. "Primeval Simplicity." Influenced by Thoreau as walker was Abbott, *Rambles.*

44. Jones to A. W. Hosmer, ca. Feb. 13, 1898, *TMTMR,* 310.

45. Gleason, *Through Year,* xxviii. Schwie, "Gleason," 156, 151.

46. Clark, "Recent Visit."

47. Bacon, *Walks III,* 187–88. 1894, O'Connor, "Dump."

48. Gleason, "Note to Map of Concord," *J* 14:347. Gleason, *Through Year,* xxxi.

49. Sanborn, "Collection of Materials."

50. Gleason's five trips: Sept. 1901, Feb. 1902, May and Oct. 1903, Oct. 1904.

51. *CE,* Sept. 18, Aug. 21, July 31, 1901. 200: Bartlett, *Concord,* 16th ed., 170.

52. Adds nothing: Jones to A. W. Hosmer, March 19, 1892, *TMTMR,* 147. Never talk: Salt, *Thoreau,* xxi. Sept. 2–15, 1901, Sanborn, "Collection of Materials."

53. Salt, *Thoreau,* 123.

54. "Fire at Lake Walden," *CE,* May 17, 1900. *CE,* May 14 and 21, 1902. Sanborn, *Recollections* 2:394. Lenox, pers. comm.

55. Gleason, *Through Year,* xxvi.

56. "To Desecrate." *Chicago Tribune* (Sept. 18, 1902), *TSB* 110 (Winter 1970). *CE,* Sept. 10, 1902.

57. *Concord: A Few,* 10. Cannon, "Land of Emerson." Mason, "Thanksgiving."

58. Beers, "Pilgrim in Concord," 74–76. *CE,* July 2, 1902. *CE,* June 28, 1905, *TSB* 182 (Winter 1988).

59. Slide lecture: Schwie, "Gleason," 158–59. Jones to A. W. Hosmer, April 30, 1903, *TMTMR,* 390. Ibid., 54.

60. Buell, "Thoreau Enters," 33, 40.

61. Harding, "Thoreau's Fame," 317–18.

62. Brooks, *Autobiography,* 46, 328–29.

63. Harding, "Frederick van Eeden's."

64. Harding, *Centennial Check-List*. Thoreau, *Week*, vii. From Herbert Gleason, March 22 and 26, 1937, Allen, Papers, box 1, folder 3.

65. Mason, "Lewis' Copy." Morley, *Philadelphia*, 4. Frost to Walter Prichard Eaton, July 15, 1915, Ruland, *Interpretations*, 8.

66. Hall, *Island*, 80–81, 113, 320–21. See Friesen, "Companion Spirits."

67. Packard, "Thoreau's." Driftwood: *WFV*, 208; *W*, 54–55.

68. Ramsey, "Pilgrimage."

69. Sept. 1, 1913, Burroughs, *Journals*, 274–75. See Renehan, *Burroughs*. Sanborn, Burroughs, and Ford visited the cairn; caption on photoprint P.O. 921, Henry Ford Museum & Greenfield Village, Michigan.

70. Griscom, *Birds*, 60–61. Sanborn, "Walden Pond." French, *Concord*, 145. Eaton, *Flora*, 9. By contrast, botanist Ed Schofield argues that Walden Woods was always subject to fire, being a droughty sand plain; pers. comm.

71. Edward Emerson, *Thoreau*, 48. Moore, "Walden."

72. *CE*, Aug. 1, 1917.

73. Foerster, "Humanism." Wilson, "Gleason Negatives," 178.

74. CNW. Gleason, Photographs, II.1918.110. J. Hosmer, "Thoreau," 143. K., "Natural Beauty." Romantic: Bartlett, *Concord*, 16th ed., 169. J. Walter Brain thinks the Devil's Bar was the isthmus to Wyman's Meadow, not the cove sandbar; pers. comm.

75. Beers, "Pilgrim," 77. Gleason, "Winter." The cairn would appear again in *National Geographic*, in Nichols, "Literary Landmarks." Edward Emerson to Harry A. McGraw, 1920, from the Raymond Adams Collection of the Thoreau Society, Courtesy of the Thoreau Society, Lincoln, Mass., and the Thoreau Institute at Walden Woods.

76. Park: "Thoreau's Pond." *W*, 180. Sanitarium: Nelson, "Walden of Emerson," 7. Protective Association: *CJ*, Aug. 1, 1963. Problems of regulating: *John E. Nickols*. Gleason, "Walden in Thoreau's Day."

77. Teale, "Week."

Chapter 9: Walden Breezes (1922–1959)

1. *CE*, May 24, 1922. "Deed."

2. Gleason, "Walden Pond in Thoreau's Day."

3. Ibid. Skelding, "Cairn."

4. Gleason, "Walden Pond in Thoreau's Day." Rabinowitz, "Abuse," 23.

5. Whitcomb, "Thoreau 'Country.'" O'Connor, "Dump."

6. Van Dore, *Frost*, 1, 51. Beston, *House*.

7. Gleason, "Walden Pond in Thoreau's Day." Scharnhorst, *Thoreau: Case Study*, 60.

8. A. B. French, Nov. 1926, *TSB* 130 (Winter 1975). Loring: *TSB* 108 (Summer 1969).

9. Gleason, *Through Year*, xvii, n. 1; xxxii. Keyes to Francis Underwood, Nov. 15, 1886, *TSB* 103 (Spring 1968). Edward Emerson, *Thoreau*, 10.

10. Whitcomb, "Thoreau 'Country,'" 459, 461. Pierce, Oct. 22, 1932, *TMC*, 192.

11. Moore, "Walden."

12. Brickell, "Landscape."

13. Wood, "Conquered." Gedrim, *Stiechen*, 31. Stiechen illustrated Thoreau, *Walden* (Boston, 1936).

14. Wyeth, "Thoreau." Wilson, "Wyeth." See Michaelis, *Wyeth*, 227. MS page: Maynard, "Thoreau Manuscript." "Several pilgrimages" and reporter: Podmaniczky, *Wyeth*.

15. Williamson, "Walden."

16. Ibid.

17. "Boys to Face Court." As the automobile reshaped modern life, Walden Pond was not the only literary shrine threatened by road building. A parallel is provided by Gilbert White's Selborne, in England. White's *Natural History and Antiquities of Selborne* (1789) is beloved by Britons the way *Walden* is by Americans, and Selbourne a site of pilgrimage, with the attendant problems of traffic and parking. In the mid-1930s a bypass was proposed, to cut through historic Wakes' Park between the street and the hanger—all sites affectionately described by White. A Selborne Defence League defeated the plan. Rye, *White*, 173.

18. Margolis, *Krutch*.

19. Wilder, "Ex-Hermit."

20. Salt, *Thoreau*, xxviii. Hart, "Woman." When Roland Robbins's granite markers were installed in 1948, the Adams-Emerson posts were moved to mark Thoreau's woodshed.

21. Schwie, "Gleason," 152.

22. Harding, "I Discover."

23. Brooks, *Two Park*, 125. Canby, *Thoreau*, 204.

24. Gas station: *Boston Evening Transcript* (Dec. 21, 1938); *CJ*, Dec. 22, 1938, transcribed by Brad Dean; *TSB* 137 (Fall 1976).

25. "Walden," June 1939, White, *Meat*, 80–87.

26. Williamson, "Walden." Deevey, "Re-examination," 8.

27. Hart, "Woman." "National Society."

28. Obituary, *Hartford Courant* (July 20, 1967), *ESQ* 52 (3d Quarter 1968). Shepard, "The American Scholar" (1932), *ESQ* 13 (4th Quarter 1958): 20. Shepard, "Unconsciousness."

29. Guilfoil, "Cultists." Harding, "Different Drummers." Payne, eighty, died in February 1955.

30. McCaffrey, "Phase-Out."

31. *TSB* 12 (July 1945). Hyman, "Thoreau," 334. Teale, *Lost Woods*, 273.

32. Robbins, *Discovery*, 5. See Linebaugh, "Road."

33. Robbins, *Hidden America*, ch. 2. Robbins, *Discovery*, 24–25.

34. Sidney, *Concord*, 98. "Thoreau Hut Notes #1," Robbins, excavation notebooks.

35. Teale, "Realms of Time." Thoreau/Teale, *Walden*, xx. See Potter, "Kindred." Teale, "Week."

36. Byron, *Cove*, 2.

37. Angier, *At Home*.

38. Skinner, "Walden (One)."

39. Potter, "Sonnet." Teale, "Week." Derleth, *Walden*.

40. Robbins, excavation notebooks. Teale, *North*, 303. *TSB* 28 (July 1949). Harding, Walden Pond file.

41. Brooks, *Two Park*, 71, 68. Peterson, *Wild America*, 30, 418. See Hancock, *Looking*, 19.

42. Harding, *Centennial Check-List*. Winslow, *Miller*, 143–45. Krutch, "Fascination," 300–01. Scott, "Nuclear," 88.

43. White, "Walden—1954," 16–17, 22. Saltmarsh, *Nearing*.

44. Charters, *Kerouac*, 113. McNally, *Angel*, 179, 190–91.

45. K., "Walden's Natural Beauty." Secret: "Replica of Thoreau's Hut." R. R. W. [Ruth Wheeler], *CJ*, Aug. 16, 1956. See Walker, "Walden's Way," 20.

46. "Replica to be Built." "Replica of Thoreau's Hut."

47. "Replica of Thoreau's Hut."

48. Nelson, "Battle," 5. Nelson, "Walden of Emerson," 7. Brady, "Bulldozer."

49. Nelson, "Walden of Emerson," 6–8. Nectar: Aug. 6, 1957, letter, *ESQ* 11 (2d Quarter 1958).

50. Nelson, "Battle," 6. Ignorant: *CJ*, Aug. 8, 1957. Bulldozer culture: Harding, Walden Pond file. Teale, "Realms of Time."

51. Banner, "What Side." Nelson, *ESQ* 13 (4th Quarter 1958): 3. Nelson, "Trial."

52. Nelson, "Battle," 6. Cut a lot: "Walden Pond Fight Mapped." Nelson, "Trial," 33.

53. See Rabinowitz, "Abuse."

54. Griscom, *Birds*, 255. Eaton, *Flora*, xi.

55. Tragically: Nelson, "Walden of Emerson," 7. Clusters: Nelson, "Battle,"

5. Hosmer, Photofile, I.77. Beers, "Pilgrim," 76. Derleth, *Walden*, 16. Motorcycle: Nelson, "Trial," 32. Ninety percent: Nelson, "Walden of Emerson," 7.

56. Nelson, "Trial," 32. Sherwood and Glasheen, "Woman," 46. Oct. 1960, Sherwood, Diary.

57. "History Cited." Harding, *Man of Concord*, vii. See O'Connor, "Dump."

Chapter 10: In These Days of Confusion and Turmoil (1960–1989)

1. Sinclair to Harding, March 26, 1960, *Thoreau Institute*. Thoreau, *Walden*, preface by Krutch, xi. Michener, "Beatniks." Kennedy, speech. Edward Kennedy in Henley, *Heaven*, 42–43. Smith, "Grotesque." Rose Kennedy had lived in West Concord from age seven to thirteen (1897–1904).

2. "He Heard a Drummer." Harding, "Centennial of Thoreau's Death." Nehru, "Thoreau," 119. Harrington, "Living," 99.

3. Harding, "Centennial of Thoreau's Death." See *TSB* 80 (Summer 1962). Simpson, "Short, Desperate," 49.

4. Gartner, *Carson*, 127.

5. Nov. 1960–July 1961, 6 May 1962, Sherwood, Diary.

6. Van Dore, *Frost*, 51. Robbins, "Thoreau–Walden Cabin." Hinds, "Imitating." Zwinger, pers. comm. Teale, *Old Farm*.

7. Seib, *Woods*, 2, 28, 17, 77, 107 (punctuation modified). Seib, pers. comm.

8. "Walden: 1962." Hair: *TSB* 135 (Spring 1976).

9. Harding, "New Edition."

10. Seib, pers. comm. July–Aug. 1967, Sherwood, Diary. Sherwood, "Lyceum History."

11. Harding, "Rambling History," 13.

12. Summer 1968, Sherwood, Diary.

13. In 2002, Lenox made a rare return to the pond, standing on the east beach and reminiscing.

14. Walker, "Walden's Way," 18. "Reservoir at Walden?" Blanding, pers. comm. Lenox (pers. comm.) recalls the sandbar as 180 feet long.

15. Williams, "Then and Now," 18. Gleason, "Walden in Thoreau's Day." On Walden's fish today, see Joyce, "Underwater."

16. Plotkin, "Highway." 1958: "History Cited." Whitman, "Thoreau's Concord."

17. White, "Protest."

18. "Rutgers Professor." LSD: William Laden, 1967, *TSB* 100 (Summer

1967). Guthrie: *TSB* 110 (Winter 1970). Ginsberg to Harding, Aug. 24, 1970, *TSB* 112 (Summer 1970).

19. Cimon, "Discover." Mott, pers. comm. Williams, "Then and Now," 3.
20. Harding, "Report from Walden." Just eight years earlier, it was estimated that only twenty to forty pilgrims came per day; "Walden: 1962."
21. Robbins, *Discovery*, as guestbook, from the Roland Wells Robbins Collection of the Thoreau Society, Courtesy of the Thoreau Society, Lincoln, Mass., and the Thoreau Institute at Walden Woods. Hinds, "Imitating." Howarth, "Following."
22. Skinner, "Walden (One)." Smith, *Dillard*.
23. Lenox, pers. comm. Nude: Whitman, "Thoreau's Concord."
24. Whitman, "Thoreau's Concord."
25. 200: Mahoney, "Debate."
26. Williams, "Then and Now," 5. Christianson, *Fox*, 422–23. *Walden Pond Restoration Study.*
27. Albohn, "Cooling Off."
28. Dudley, "Walden Transferred." *TSB* 130 (Winter 1975). See Adams, "Tsongas."
29. Mahoney, "Debate." See *Walden Pond Restoration.*
30. McCaffrey, "Trailer Park." Condominium: Bassett, pers. comm. Harding, *Thoreau: Studies and Commentaries*, 96. There were fifteen trailers in 1992.
31. Toska, pers. comm.
32. Mahoney, "Debate." Proposals: see "Restoration Proposal." Less cumbersome: *Walden Pond Restoration*, 14. Brennan: Nelson, "Battle," 6.
33. *TSB* 132 (Summer 1975).
34. Van Dore, *Frost*, 290–91. "Thoreau . . . Nudist." Monette, *Becoming*, 261–62, 273. Harding, "Saint Francis." Harding, "Sexuality," 29–30.
35. Harding, "Jimmy Carter." LaBastille, "Fishing."
36. Winkler, "Changes." See also Köster, "Assessment."
37. *W*, 178–79. *PJ* 5:306. *J* 11:160. Colman and Waldron, "Environmental Setting." *Massachusetts . . . Wildlife News.* Winkler, "Changes."
38. Maynard, "Down."
39. Abbey, *Down*, 36. *TSB* 165 (Fall 1983); ibid. 174 (Winter 1986); ibid. 182 (Winter 1988). Sattelmeyer, "Study Nature."
40. "Should continue": Sherwood, "Walden Repair." Sherwood and Glasheen, "Woman," 46. Sherwood, "Renaissance." Sherwood, "Ban Walden Swimmers." McGarrahan, "Groups."
41. Matthews, "Walden Pond." Zwinger, pers. comm. Schnelle, *Valley*, npn. Garner, "Walden." Fahlander, "TV."

42. Schofield, "Henry & Me." Deteriorating: Schofield, Walden Pond Meeting notes. Zwinger, pers. comm. "Help Save Walden Woods" (Nov. 3, 1988).

43. Sherwood and Glasheen, "Woman." Sherwood, Diary.

44. Conant: *TSB* 19 (April 1947). "Thoreau Legacy." Moroney, "Maine."

45. See O'Connor, "Abbreviated."

46. Zuckerman, "Site Right." Schofield, pers comm. "News From Thoreau Country." On Blanding, see Negri, "Emulation." Briefly there was talk of calling TCCA the Walden Woods Preservation Organization or Thoreau Country Preservation Alliance. Schofield warned against the former title as trespassing on Mary Sherwood's turf at Walden Pond; Brain suggested the latter. Schofield, pers. comm.

47. Concord Historical Commission, "Thoreau." "Help Save Walden Woods" (July 7, 1988). Brain, pers. comm. Macone, "Office Park." James Simon and Kelly McClintock, in Tye, "Boost."

48. Schofield, pers. corr. "Support National Historic Landmark Status." Graham, "History."

49. "Help Save Walden Woods" (Nov. 3, 1988). Robert McLaughlin, lawyer for Concord Commons Associates, versus Blanding, in Commonwealth . . . Housing Appeals Committee (testimony abbreviated).

50. "Support National Historic Landmark Status." Hart, "Earth Matters." Schofield, "Henry & Me."

Chapter 11: walden.org (1990–2003)

1. Tenacious: Jaeger, "Woods." Parrying: Canellos, "Mr. Serious."

2. Canellos, "Mr. Serious."

3. "Concord Journal." Blanding, pers. comm.

4. Blanding, pers. comm.

5. Ibid. Knopper, "Battle."

6. Knopper, "Battle." Blanding, pers. comm. Jorgensen, pers. comm. The alliance raised about $40,000 in four years, of which Henley gave $15,000; by contrast, Walden Woods Project has raised about $23 million.

7. Jaeger, "Woods."

8. Gaines, "History." Beam, "If Not Them."

9. Canellos, "Project."

10. Stinking: Canellos, "Mr. Serious." Raison: Jaeger, "Woods." Millions: Canellos, "Project." Inaccurate: Zuckerman, "Site Right." Saint: Knopper, "Battle."

11. See Morse, "Henley."

12. Canellos, "Mr. Serious." Aquilante, "Henley."
13. Robins, "Henley." Canellos, "Henley Vows."
14. Sherwood to Lifesavers. Sullivan, "Keep Walden."
15. Sherwood and Glasheen, "Woman," 47. Rierden, "Perfume."
16. Beam, "Noisy Desperation." Sherwood, "Cooperation."
17. Berlin: Conniff, "Approaching," 86. H-C, "In Walden."
18. Dean, "I Discover." Dean, pers. comm.
19. Blanding, pers. comm. Beam, "Henley Leads."
20. Brain, pers. comm. Daly, "Eyesore." "Concord's Trash Dilemma." "Why It's Time to Close."
21. Monahan, "PETA."
22. *Thoreau Institute*. Allen, "Henley Transcends."
23. "Thoreau Institute Grand Opening."
24. Moroney, "Thoreau Center."
25. Borden: Thomas, "Rumblings." Students: Knopper, "Battle." Larrabee, "Commercialism."
26. Kaufman, "Thoreau." Blanding, pers. comm. Allen, "Henley Transcends."
27. Kellett, Gordon, and Jorgensen, pers. comm.
28. "Brief History." Scenic America. Allen, "Thoreau's Place."
29. Self-sustaining: Johnson, "Life." Daunting: Katz, "Eagles' Henley."
30. "Ted Kaczynski." Graysmith, *Unabomber*, ch. 3.
31. Glaberson, "Cabin Fever."
32. O'Rourke, "Amazon," 68. Krakauer, *Wild*.
33. Walker, *Little House*. Leaux, "Cabin." Mitchell, *Living*. Pollan, *Place*, 5. Kenney, "Chapters." Yount, Mini Cabin.
34. "Ecoview."
35. Mouw, "Women." *WAE,* ix. Doctorow, "Two Waldens." See Buell, "Thoreauvian Pilgrimage." Cult: Laxer, "Ride." McGee, "Naturalism."
36. Brain, "Meaning."
37. *TSB* 193 (Fall 1990). Gann, "Sonnets." Huber, "Eight Hours," 114. McConville, "Thoreau Enthusiasts." Jeremiah: O'Rourke, "Amazon," 68. Locker, *Walking*. Schnur and Fiore, *Henry David's House*. Johnson, *Henry*. Vaupel, *Contract*.
38. "Help Save Walden Woods" (Nov. 3, 1988). Slone, "Thoreau Society." Slone, "Everyday." *J* 6:358.
39. L'Bahy, "Naturalist." Alden, "Biodiversity."
40. Colman and Waldron, "Environmental Setting." Colman and Friesz, *Geohydrology*. *WAE,* 279.
41. Colman and Friesz, *Geohydrology*. Whicher, *Walden Revisited*, npn.

42. Tye, "Odor." *Boston Globe* (July 9, 1997). Colman and Waldron, "Environmental Setting."

43. Ells, pers. comm.

44. Wilson, *Future*, xi–xx. See Conniff, "Approaching," 88. *WAE*, 272. Sattelmeyer, "Depopulation." Robinson, "Emerson," 16.

45. Allen, "Viewing Walden." Wordsworth, *Guide*, 152, 154.

46. Gorman, "Fearsome." Wilson, interview.

47. Sept. 14, 1901, Sanborn, "Collection of Materials." Craig, "Shocked." Riggs, "Walden Revisited."

48. "DEM's Walden Reservation."

49. Blanding, pers. comm.

Bibliography

❧

The following abbreviations are used:

CFPL   Concord Free Public Library
CJ   *Concord Journal*
CLR   Cameron, *Concord Literary Renaissance*
CS   *Concord Saunterer*
ESQ   *Emerson Society Quarterly*, later *ESQ*
HDT   Henry David Thoreau
HL   Henley Library, The Thoreau Institute at Walden Woods
RWE   Ralph Waldo Emerson
SAR   Myerson, Joel, ed. *Studies in the American Renaissance*. Boston:
        Twayne and Charlottesville: University Press of Virginia
TL   Cameron, *Transcendental Log*
TSB   *Thoreau Society Bulletin*
TSBS2   Cameron, *Thoreau Secondary Bibliography Supplement Two*
TWO   Schofield and Baron, *Thoreau's World and Ours*
WPSR   Walden Pond State Reservation
WR   Walden Ringbinder. In Sherwood Papers, C.PAM.162, Item 3,
        CFPL
WWP   Walden Woods Project

Abbey, Edward. *Down the River*. New York: Dutton, 1982.

Abbott, Charles C. *Recent Rambles*. Philadelphia: Lippincott, 1892.

Adams, Raymond. Coll. HL.

———. "Emerson's House at Walden." *TSB* 24 (July 1948).

Adams, Thomas B. "Tsongas and Walden." *Boston Sunday Globe* (Jan. 29, 1984).

Albohn, Phillip. " 'Something More Than Cooling Off' Plan OK'd by Commrs. for Walden." *Minuteman Supplement* (Aug. 23, 1973).

Alcott, Amos Bronson. "Bronson Alcott's 'Journal for 1838' (Part One)." Ed. Larry A. Carlson. *SAR* (1993), 161–244.

———. "The Forester." 1862. In Jones, *Pertaining*, 35–37.

———. *Journals*. Ed. Odell Shepard. Boston: Little, Brown, 1938.

———. "Eighty-Six Letters (1814–1882) of A. Bronson Alcott," Part Two. Ed. Frederick Wagner. SAR (1980), 183–228.

[Alcott, Louisa May.] "Latest News from Concord." *Springfield Republican* (May 4, 1869). In Cameron, "Thoreau's Disciple."

Alcott, Louisa May. *Selected Letters*. Ed. Joel Myerson and Daniel Shealy. Boston: Little, Brown, 1987.

Alden, Peter. "World's First 1000+ Species Biodiversity Day." MS. 1998.

Allen, Francis. Papers. HL.

Allen, Scott. "Henley Transcends Critics." *Boston Globe* (June 5, 1998).

———. "Thoreau's Place." *Boston Globe* (Nov. 23, 1999).

———. "Viewing Walden Pond as Still Life." *Boston Globe* (March 11, 2003).

Anderson, Charles R. *The Magic Circle of Walden*. New York: Holt, Rinehart and Winston, 1968.

Angelo, Ray. "Two Thoreau Letters at Harvard." *TSB* 162 (Winter 1983).

Angier, Vena, and Bradford Angier. *At Home in the Woods: Living the Life of Thoreau Today*. New York: Sheridan House, 1951.

Annual Reports . . . Town of Concord. Boston: Tolman & White, 1884.

[Anon.] Review of Thoreau, *Walden*. www.amazon.com.

Aquilante, Dan. "Henley Cranks It Up." *New York Post* (June 2, 2000).

Bacon, Edwin M. *Walks and Rides in the Country Round About Boston, Part III. Lexington and Concord*. Cambridge: Appalachian Mountain Club, 1900.

Badè, William Frederic. *Life and Letters of John Muir*. 2 vols. Boston and New York: Houghton Mifflin, 1924.

Banner, Earl. "What Side Would Thoreau Take in Walden Pond Row?" *Boston Sunday Globe* (July 21, 1957).

Barrus, Clara. *Life and Letters of John Burroughs*. Boston and New York: Houghton Mifflin, 1925.

Bartlett, George B. *Concord: Historic, Literary and Picturesque*. 3d ed. rev. Boston: Cupples, Upham, 1885.

———. *Concord: Historic, Literary and Picturesque*. 16th ed. rev. Boston: Lothrop, 1895.

Barton, George Hunt. Diary. In Schofield, *Walden Woods Bibliography*.

Bassett, Kenneth. Pers. comm., Feb. 2003.

Baym, Nina. "English Nature, New York Nature, and *Walden's* New England Nature." In Capper and Wright, *Transient and Permanent*, 168–89.

Beam, Alex. "Henley Leads Life of Noisy Desperation." *Boston Globe* (Aug. 5, 1994).

———. "If Not Them, Then Who?" *Boston Globe* (April 18, 1990).

Beers, Henry A. *Four Americans*. New Haven: Yale University Press, 1920. Inc. "A Pilgrim in Concord" (1905).

Bellew, Frank. "Recollections of RWE." *Lippincott's* 34, no. 1 (July 1884): 45–50. In *ESQ* 52 (3d Quarter 1968): 82–84.

Beston, Henry. *The Outermost House*. New York: Doubleday, 1928.

Black's Picturesque Guide to the English Lakes. 2d ed. Edinburgh: Adam and Charles Black, 1844.

Blancke, Shirley. "The Archaeology of Walden Woods." *TWO*, 242–53.

Blanding, Thomas. "Beans, Baked and Half-Baked." *CS* 15, no. 1 (Spring 1980).

———. "Historic Walden Woods." *CS* 20, nos. 1–2 (Dec. 1988).

———. Pers. comm., 2002–03.

———, and Bradley P. Dean. "The Earliest Walden Photographs." *CS* 20, nos. 1–2 (Dec. 1988): 75–85.

Borden, Jack. Pers. comm., March 2003.

Boudreau, Gordon V. "HDT, William Gilpin, and the Metaphysical Ground of the Picturesque." *American Literature* 45, no. 3 (Nov. 1973).

"Boys to Face Court for Walden Thefts." *CJ* (Aug. 10, 1939), transcribed by Brad Dean.

Brady, Fred. " 'Bulldozer Culture' Menaces Walden Pond's Sylvan Shrine." *Boston Herald* (June 30, 1957).

Brain, J. Walter. "In Search of Thoreau's Epigaea Springs." *CJ* (July 18, 2002).

———. "The Lure of Grape Cliff." *Concord Land Conservation Trust Newsletter* (Winter 2003).

———. "The Meaning of Walden." *Lincoln Journal* (July 9, 1998).

———. Pers. comm., 2002–03.

———. "Thoreau's Thrush Alley." *Lincoln Journal* (July 8, 1999).

Bremer, Fredrika. *The Homes of the New World*. 3 vols. London: Hall, Virtue, 1853.

Brewster, William. *October Farm*. Cambridge: Harvard University Press, 1937.

Brickell, Herschel. "The Literary Landscape." *North American Review* 238, no. 4 (Oct. 1934): 376–84.

"Brief History of the WWP." WWP, 2001.

Brooks, Paul. *Two Park Street*. Boston: Houghton Mifflin, 1986.

Brooks, Van Wyck. *Autobiography*. New York: Dutton, 1965.

Brown, Richard. *Domestic Architecture*. 1841; reprint, London: Quaritch, 1852.

Brown, Simon. "Journal." *TSB* 76 (Summer 1961).

Buell, Lawrence. *The Environmental Imagination*. Cambridge and London: Belknap Press of Harvard University Press, 1995.

———. "Henry Thoreau Enters the American Canon." In Sayre, *New Essays on Walden*, 23–52.

———. "The Thoreauvian Pilgrimage: The Structure of an American Cult." *American Literature* 61, no. 2 (May 1989): 175–99.

Burgess, Edward S. Papers. Used by permission of CFPL.

Burgess, Thomas D. "About Walden." *Latin and High School Review* (Feb. 1896). In *TSBS2*, 130–31.

Burroughs, John. *The Heart of Burroughs's Journals*. Ed. Clara Barrus. Boston and New York: Houghton Mifflin, 1928.

Byron, Gilbert. *Cove Dweller*. Trappe, Md.: Unicorn Book Shop, 1983.

C., W. J. "A New England Pilgrimage XXV. Thoreau's Spirit in His Books, Not at Walden Pond." *Boston Herald* (Dec. 2, 1912). In *TSBS2*, 191–92.

Cabot, James Elliot. *A Memoir of RWE*. 2 vols. Boston and New York: Houghton Mifflin, 1888.

Cain, William E., ed. *A Historical Guide to HDT*. New York: Oxford University Press, 2000.

Cameron, Kenneth W. "Emerson's Walden Woodlots and the Fitchburg Railroad." *ESQ* 22 (1st Quarter 1961): 67–68.

———. "Thoreau and the Folklore of Walden Pond." *ESQ* 3 (2d Quarter 1956): 10–12.

———. "Thoreau's Disciple at Walden: Edmond S. Hotham." *ESQ* 26 (1 Quarter 1962): 34–44.

———, ed. *American Renaissance Literary Report 3*. Hartford: Transcendental Books, 1989.

———. *Companion to Thoreau's Correspondence*. Hartford: Transcendental Books, 1964.

———. *Concord Literary Renaissance*. Hartford: Transcendental Books, 1988.

———. *Emerson, Thoreau and Concord in Early Newspapers*. Hartford: Transcendental Books, 1958.

———. *The New England Writers and the Press*. Hartford: Transcendental Books, 1980.

———. *Thoreau Secondary Bibliography Supplement Two*. Hartford: Transcendental Books, 1997.

———. *Thoreau Secondary Bibliography Supplement Three*. Hartford: Transcendental Books, 1999.

———. *Transcendental Climate*. Multivolume. Hartford: Transcendental Books, 1963.

———. *Transcendental Epilogue*. 3 vols. Hartford: Transcendental Books, 1965.

————. *Transcendental Log*. Hartford: Transcendental Books, 1973.

Canby, Henry Seidel. *Thoreau*. Boston: Houghton Mifflin, 1939.

Canellos, Peter S. "Henley Vows to Remain a Presence in Walden Woods Land Acquisitions." *Boston Globe* (April 21, 1993).

————. "Mr. Serious: Don Henley Is Passionate About His Cause—and His Critics." *Boston Globe* (Dec. 14, 1990).

————. "The Lesson of Walden Pond." *Boston Globe* (April 29, 1990).

————. "Walden Project Blocked by Parcel's High Cost." *Boston Globe* (March 10, 1991).

Cannon, Samuel J. "The Land of Emerson and Thoreau." *Brooklyn Times* (Oct. 25, 1902). In *CLR*, 142.

Capper, Charles, and Conrad Edick Wright, eds. *Transient and Permanent*. Boston: Massachusetts Historical Society, 1999.

Capra, Douglas R. "Elbert Hubbard, Concord, and Thoreau," *TSB* 181 (Fall 1987).

Channing, William Ellery. Journal. 1867. In Sanborn, *Literary Studies*.

————. Notes in his copy of *Walden*. In Sanborn, *Recollections*, vol. 2.

————. Pocket Diaries. Manuscript. Houghton Library Ms. bMS Am 800.6, Harvard University.

————. "The Selected Letters of William Ellery Channing the Younger (Part One)." Ed. Francis B. Dedmond. *SAR* (1989), 115–218. "(Part Three)." *SAR* (1991), 257–343.

————. *Thoreau: The Poet-Naturalist*. Boston: Roberts Brothers, 1873.

————. *The Wanderer*. Boston: James R. Osgood, 1871.

Charters, Ann. *Kerouac*. San Francisco: Straight Arrow, 1973.

Christianson, Gale E. *Fox at the Wood's Edge*. New York: Henry Holt, 1990.

Cimon, Anne. "I Discover Thoreau." *TSB* 210 (Winter 1995).

Clark, A. S. "Notes of a Recent Visit to Walden Pond." *New York Times— Saturday Review* (Dec. 23, 1899).

Collyer, Robert. "Henry Thoreau." *Unity* (Aug. 1, 1870). In Blanding, "Historic Walden Woods," 49.

Colman, John A., and Paul J. Friesz. *Geohydrology and Limnology of Walden Pond*. Northborough, Mass.: United States Geological Survey, 2001.

Colman, J. A., and M. C. Waldron. "Walden Pond, Massachusetts: Environmental Setting and Current Investigations." United States Geological Survey Fact Sheet, 1998.

Commonwealth of Massachusetts Department of Community Affairs Housing Appeals Committee (Jan. 19, 1989). TCCA papers, C-PAM 160, used by permission of CFPL.

Concord: A Few of the Things to Be Seen There. Concord: Patriot Press, 1902.

Concord Historical Commission. "Thoreau and Walden: A Neglected Son and Pond." *CJ* (March 12, 1987).

CJ (Aug. 8, 1857). Clipping, WR.

"Concord Journal: Saving Thoreau's Pond: Rock Stars (Who Else?)." *New York Times* (Aug. 14, 1990).

"Concord Social Amusements." Jan. 1884. In *CLR*, 169–70.

"Concord's Trash Dilemma." Advertisement, *CJ* (June 25, 1992).

Conniff, Richard. "Approaching Walden." *Yankee* 57, no. 5 (May 1993): 85–88.

Conron, John. *American Picturesque*. University Park: Penn State University Press, 2000. Inc. "*Walden* as Picturesque Narrative."

Convey, Kevin R. "Why Concord Hates Walden." *Boston Magazine* 81, no. 7 (July 1989): 78–83, 100–05.

Conway, Moncure D. "Thoreau." *Eclectic Magazine* 67 (Aug. 1866): 191–92. In Harding, *Thoreau: Man of Concord*, 38–40.

Cooke, George Willis, ed. *Early Letters of George William Curtis to John S. Dwight: Brook Farm and Concord*. New York and London: Harper & Brothers, 1898.

Craig, John G., Jr. "Shocked into Action." *Pittsburgh Post-Gazette* (Sept. 8, 2002).

"Crane Beach." Oct. 1, 1995. www.tiac.net.

Daiches, David, and John Flower. *Literary Landscapes of the British Isles*. Harmondsworth: Penguin Books, 1979.

Daly, Christopher B. "Removing the Eyesore Near Thoreau's Pond." *Washington Post* (April 16, 1994).

Dawson, James. "A History of the Cairn." *TSB* 232 (Summer 2000).

Dean, Bradley P. "I Discover Thoreau." *TSB* 208 (Summer 1994).

———. Pers. comm., 2002–03.

———, ed. *Faith in a Seed*. Covelo, Cal.: Shearwater, 1993.

———. *Wild Fruits*. New York: Norton, 2000.

Dean, Bradley P., and Ronald Wesley Hoag. "Thoreau's Lectures Before *Walden*: An Annotated Calendar." *SAR* (1995), 127–228.

"Deed of Gift to Commonwealth of Mass. by Forbes and Heywood et al." June 9, 1922. CFPL.

Deevey, E. S., Jr. "A Re-examination of Thoreau's 'Walden.'" *Quarterly Review of Biology* 17, no. 1 (March 1942): 1–11.

"DEM's Walden Reservation Expands." Massachusetts Executive Office of Environmental Affairs press release, Oct. 7, 2002.

Derleth, August. *Walden Pond: Homage to Thoreau*. Iowa City: Prairie Press, 1968.

Doctorow, E. L. *Jack London, Hemingway, and the Constitution.* New York: Random House, 1993. Inc. "Two Waldens," 1990.

Donahue, Brian. Pers. comm., 2002–03.

Downing, Andrew Jackson. "On the Mistakes of Citizens in Country Life." *Horticulturist* 3 (Jan. 1849).

———. *A Treatise on the Theory and Practice of Landscape Gardening.* 2d ed. New York: Wiley and Putnam, 1844.

Dudley, Andrea. "Walden Transferred to State by Gov. in Pondside Ceremonies." 1974. Clipping. Ferguson Papers, folder 6, CFPL.

Eaton, Richard J. *A Flora of Concord.* Cambridge: Museum of Comparative Zoology, 1974.

"Ecoview" TV broadcast, WGMC, Worcester, Mass. (Feb.–March 2000). Coll. Edmund A. Schofield.

Edwards, Kate L. "Concord Letter." *Southbridge [Mass.] Journal* (Dec. 5, 1895). In *TSB* 179 (Spring 1987).

Eidson, John Olin. *Charles Stearns Wheeler.* Athens: University of Georgia Press, 1951.

Ells, Stephen F. *A Bibliography of Biodiversity and Natural History in the Sudbury and Concord River Valley.* Lincoln, Mass.: author, 2002.

———. Pers. comm., 2002–03.

———. *The Seasons in Estabrook Country.* Lincoln, Mass.: author, 1999.

Emerson, Edward Waldo. *Emerson in Concord.* Boston and New York: Houghton Mifflin, 1889.

———. *Henry Thoreau as Remembered by a Young Friend.* 1917; reprint, Concord: Thoreau Foundation, 1968.

Emerson, Ellen Tucker. *Letters.* Ed. Edith E. W. Gregg. 2 vols. Kent State University Press, 1982.

———. *The Life of Lidian Jackson Emerson.* Ed. Delores Bird Carpenter. Boston: Twayne, 1980.

Emerson, Ralph Waldo. *Collected Poems and Translations.* New York: Library of America, 1994.

———. *Journals and Miscellaneous Notebooks.* 16 vols. Cambridge: Harvard University Press, 1960–82.

———. *Later Lectures, 1843–1871.* Ed. Ronald A. Bosco and Joel Myerson. 2 vols. Athens and London: University of Georgia Press, 2001.

———. *Letters.* 6 vols. Ed. Ralph L. Rusk. New York: Columbia University Press, 1939.

———. *The Portable Emerson.* Ed. Mark Van Doren. New York: Viking, 1946.

"Emerson's First Purchase of Walden Land." *TSB* 175 (Spring 1986).

Fahlander, Richard. "Japanese TV Host Takes Modern View of Walden." *TSB* 211 (Spring–Summer 1995).

Fenn, Mary Gail. "Susan Loring on Thoreau." *TSB* 129 (Fall 1974).

Ferguson, Malcolm. Papers. Used by permission of CFPL.

———. Pers. comm., July 2002.

"Fire in the Woods." *Concord Freeman* (May 3, 1844). In *TSB* 32 (July 1950).

Flagg, Wilson. *The Woods and By-Ways of New England*. Boston: James R. Osgood, 1872.

Foerster, Norman. "The Humanism of Thoreau." *Nation* 105 (July 5, 1917): 9–12.

Foster, David. *Thoreau's Country*. Cambridge and London: Harvard University Press, 1999.

Francis, Richard. *Transcendental Utopias*. Ithaca and London: Cornell University Press, 1997.

French, Allen. *Old Concord*. Boston: Little, Brown, 1915.

Friesen, Victor Carl. "Companion Spirits: Henry Thoreau and James Norman Hall." *TSB* 167 (Spring 1984).

Fuller, Margaret. *Summer on the Lakes in 1843*. 1844; reprint, Nieuwkoop: B. de Graaf, 1972.

Gaines, Judith. "History, Past and Present." *Boston Globe* (Oct. 31, 1988).

Gann, Kyle. "Transcendental Sonnets." 2001. www.home.earthlink.net/~kgann.

Garner, Patrick C. "Walden Pond (Psst—It's Not What You Think It Is)." *Wetland Journal* 11, no. 1 (Winter 1999). Reprint, www.patrickgarner.com.

Gartner, Carol B. *Rachel Carson*. New York: Frederick Ungar, 1983.

Gedrim, Ronald J. *Edward Stiechen*. New York: G. K. Hall, 1996.

Glaberson, William. "Cabin Fever: Walden Was Never Like This." *New York Times* (Dec. 7, 1997).

Gleason, Herbert W. "In the Wake of Thoreau's Home Made Boat." *Boston Transcript* (Aug. 5, 1922).

———. Photographs. CFPL.

———. *Thoreau Country*. Ed. Mark Silber. San Francisco: Sierra Club Books, 1975.

———. "Thoreau's House Beautiful." *Boston Transcript* (Jan. 3, 1920).

———. "Walden Pond in Thoreau's Day and Ours." *Boston Transcript* (Dec. 31, 1924).

———. "Winter Rambles in Thoreau's Country." *National Geographic* 37, no. 2 (Feb. 1920): 165–80.

————. *Through the Year with Thoreau*. Boston and New York: Houghton Mifflin, 1917.

Glick, Wendell, ed. *The Recognition of HDT*. Ann Arbor: University of Michigan Press, 1969.

Gordon, Jayne. Pers. comm., Feb. 2003.

Gorman, James. "A Wild, Fearsome World Under Each Fallen Leaf." *New York Times* (Sept. 24, 2002).

Graham, Renee. "History, Past and Present." *Boston Globe* (Oct. 31, 1988).

Graysmith, Robert. *Unabomber*. Washington, D.C.: Regnery, 1997.

Greene, Calvin. Notes and Diary in his copy of *Walden*, 1863, 1874. General Rare Books Division of the Department of Rare Books and Special Collections of the Princeton University Library. Published with permission of the Princeton University Library.

Gregg, Edith Emerson Webster. "Emerson and His Children: Their Childhood Memories." *Harvard Library Bulletin* 28, no. 4 (Oct. 1980): 407–30.

Griscom, Ludlow. *Birds of Concord*. Cambridge: Harvard University Press, 1949.

Gross, Robert A. "The Great Bean Field Hoax: Thoreau and the Agricultural Reformers." *Virginia Quarterly Review* 61, no. 3 (1985): 483–97.

Guestbook, Thoreau house replica, WPSR, 2001–02.

Guilfoil, Kelsey. "The Thoreau Cultists—Are They Insane?" *Chicago Tribune* (Dec. 1, 1946).

H-C, John. "In Walden Pond." *Journal of the Diver's Environmental Survey* (Winter 1993): 12–14. Clipping, WR.

Hall, James Norman. *My Island Home*. Boston: Little, Brown, 1952.

Hancock, Lyn. *Looking for the Wild*. Toronto: Doubleday, 1986.

Harding, Walter. *A Centennial Check-List of the Editions of HDT's Walden*. Charlottesville: University of Virginia Press, 1954.

————. "The Centennial of Thoreau's Death." *TSB* 79 (Spring 1962).

————. *Days of Henry Thoreau*. New York: Knopf, 1965.

————. "Different Drummers." *TSB* 168 (Summer 1984).

————. "Edward Hoar on Thoreau." *TSB* 198 (Winter 1992).

————. "Frederick van Eeden's Walden." *TSB* 14 (Jan. 1946).

————. "Henry Thoreau: Our American Saint Francis." *Our Dumb Animals* (May 1943). Clipping, C.PAM.17, Item B.9, CFPL.

————. "I Discover Thoreau." *TSB* 195 (Spring 1991).

————. "Jimmy Carter on Thoreau." *TSB* 165 (Fall 1983).

————. "More Excerpts from the Alfred Hosmer Letter Files." *TSB* 123 (Spring 1973).

————. "A New Edition of Thoreau." *TSB* 97 (Fall 1966).

————. "A Rambling History of the Thoreau Society." *CS* n.s. 3 (Fall 1995): 5–18.

————. "Raymond Adams' Thoreau Newsletter." *TSB* 178 (Winter 1987).

————. "Report from Walden." *Yankee* (Sept. 1970). In Ferguson Papers, folder 6, CFPL.

————. "Thoreau in Emerson's Account Books." *TSB* 159 (Spring 1982).

————. "Thoreau's Fame Abroad" (1959). In Glick, *Recognition*, 315–23.

————. "Thoreau's Sexuality." *Journal of Homosexuality* 21, no. 3 (1991): 23–45.

————. Videotape, walk around Walden. July 10, 1984. Harding Papers, HL.

————. Walden Pond file. Harding Papers, HL.

————, ed. *Thoreau: Man of Concord*. New York: Holt, Rinehart and Winston, 1960.

————. *Sophia Thoreau's Scrapbook*. Thoreau Society Booklet 20. Geneseo, New York, 1964.

————. *The Thoreau Centennial*. State University of New York Press, 1964.

————, et al., eds. *HDT: Studies and Commentaries*. Rutherford, N.J.: Fairleigh Dickinson University Press, 1972.

Harrington, Donald S. "Living is So Dear." In Harding, *Thoreau Centennial*, 96–105.

H[arris], A[manda] B. "Thoreau's Hermitage." New York *Weekly Post* (Jan. 31, 1877). In *TL*, 296–97

Hart, David. "Chapel Hill Woman [Charlotte Adams] Restores Thoreau to His Pond." *Chapel Hill [N.C.] News* (June 19, 1998).

Hart, Kathy. "Earth Matters." TV broadcast, Cable News Network (Nov. 1989).

Hawthorne, Julian. *Memoirs*. New York: Macmillan, 1938.

Hawthorne, Nathaniel. *American Notebooks*. Ed. Claude M. Simpson. Columbus: Ohio State University Press, 1972.

"He Heard a Drummer in the Forest." *Time* 80, no. 11 (Sept. 14, 1962): 57.

"Help Save Walden Woods." Advertisements. *CJ* (July 7, Nov. 3, 1988).

Hendrick, George, ed. *Remembrances of Concord and the Thoreaus*. Urbana: University of Illinois Press, 1977.

Henley, Don. Pers. comm., Oct. 2002.

—, and Dave Marsh. *Heaven Is Under Our Feet*. Stamford, Ct.: Longmeadow Press, 1991.

Herring, Stephen W. "The Halcyon Days of Framingham's Harmony Grove." *TSB* 215 (Spring 1996).

Hibberd, Shirley. *Rustic Adornments*. London: Groombridge, 1857.

Hinds, Michael deCourcy. "Imitating Thoreau's Cabin, Without the Pond." *New York Times* (May 29, 1980).

"History Cited in Walden Rift." *Christian Science Monitor* (Oct. 25, 1958). Clipping, WWP.

Homes of American Authors. New York: D. Appleton, 1857.

Hosmer, Fred. Thoreau Coll. Letter File, Hosmer Papers, used by permission of CFPL.

———. Photofile, CFPL.

Hosmer, Joseph. "Henry D. Thoreau." "Thoreau Annex," *Concord Freeman* (1880). In Hendrick, *Remembrances*.

Howarth, William. *The Book of Concord*. New York: Viking, 1982.

———. "Following the Tracks of a Different Man: Thoreau." *National Geographic* 159, no. 3 (March 1981): 349–87.

Howells, William D. *The Undiscovered Country*. Boston and New York: Houghton Mifflin, 1880.

Huber, J. Parker. "Eight Hours: John Muir in Concord." *CS* n.s. 8 (2000): 103–25.

Hubert, Philip G., Jr. *Liberty and a Living*. 1889. 2d ed., New York: G. P. Putnam's Sons, 1905.

[———.] "Thoreau's Concord." *New York Tribune* (Sept. 13, 1896). In Scharnhorst, *Thoreau: Case Study*, 25.

Hudson, H. R. "Concord Books." *Harper's New Monthly Magazine* 51, no. 301 (June 1875): 18–32.

Hudspeth, Robert N. *Ellery Channing*. New York: Twayne, 1973.

Hyman, Stanley Edgar. "Henry Thoreau in Our Time." 1963. In Glick, *Recognition*, 334–51.

Irving, Washington. *History, Tales and Sketches*. New York: Library of America, 1983.

Jaeger, Barbara. "Into the Woods: Don Henley Fights to Save Thoreau's Inspiration." *Bergen Record* (Oct. 20, 1991).

Jarvis, Edward. "Houses and People in Concord, 1810 to 1820." MS, 1882. Used by permission of CFPL.

———. *Traditions and Reminiscences of Concord, Massachusetts, 1779–1878*. Ed. Sarah Chapin. Amherst: University of Massachusetts Press, 1993.

Jeffares, A. Norman. *A New Commentary on the Poems of W. B. Yeats*. Stanford: Stanford University Press, 1984.

John E. Nickols & Others vs. Commissioners of Middlesex County. 1960. C.PAM.60 Item C3, CFPL.

Johnson, D. B. *Henry Builds a Cabin.* Boston: Houghton Mifflin, 2002.

Johnson, Dean. "Life in the Serious Lane." *Boston Herald* (Nov. 30, 2001).

Jones, Samuel Arthur. "Thoreau: A Glimpse." *Unitarian* (Jan., Feb., March 1890).

———. "Thoreau and His Biographers." *Lippincott's Monthly Magazine* 48 (Aug. 1891): 224–28. In Oehlschlaeger and Hendrick, *Reputation,* 397–401.

———, ed. *Pertaining to Thoreau.* 1901; reprint, Hartford: Transcendental Books, 1970.

———. *Some Unpublished Letters of Henry D. and Sophia E. Thoreau.* Jamaica, N.Y.: Marion Press, 1899.

Jorgensen, Vidar. Pers. comm., Feb. 2003.

Joyce, Kristina A. "Underwater Walden." *TWO,* 196–98. See also *Concord Magazine* (Sept. 1998), www.concordma.com.

K., S. G. "Walden's Natural Beauty is Still Preserved." *CJ* (July 24, 1952).

Katz, Larry. "The Eagles' Don Henley Soars from WWP Back onto Music Store Shelves." *Boston Herald* (May 23, 2000).

Kaufman, Jill. "HDT." *Morning Edition,* National Public Radio (Aug. 5, 2002).

Kay, Jane Holtz. "Wall to Wall at Walden." *Nation* 246, no. 24 (June 18, 1988): 867–72.

Kellett, Michael. Pers. comm., Jan. 2003.

Kennedy, Edward. Thoreau Institute speech. Aug. 7, 1995. WWP.

Kenney, Michael. "Chapters of a Writer's Hut." *Boston Globe* (April 24, 1997).

Kifer, Ken. "New England Bike Trip, 1993." www.kenkifer.com.

K[ing], E[dward]. "Commonwealth Sketches/Rambles in Concord—I." *Springfield Weekly Republican* (May 1, 1869). In Cameron, "Thoreau's Disciple."

———. "Commonwealth Sketches / Rambles in Concord—II," *Springfield Republican* (May 3, 1869). In Cameron, *New England Writers,* 122.

King, Mary B. "Concord—As a Place of Interest to a Tourist." *Vassar Miscellany* (Nov. 1880): 55–60.

Knight, Charles. *The English Cyclopaedia.* London: Bradbury and Evans, 1859.

Knopper, Steve. "The Battle for Walden Woods." *Rolling Stone* no. 732 (April 18, 1996).

Köster, Dörte. "Paleolimnological Assessment of Human-Induced Impacts on the Nutrient Balance of Walden Pond." *Canadian Journal of Fisheries and Aquatic Sciences*. Submitted.

Krakauer, Jon. *Into the Wild*. Thorndike, Me: G. K. Hall, 1996.

Krutch, Joseph Wood. "The Steady Fascination of Thoreau." 1951. In Glick, *Recognition*, 297–301.

Kussin, Louisa. "The Concord Farmers Club and Thoreau's 'Succession of Forest Trees.'" *TSB* 173 (Fall 1985).

L'Bahy, Rebecca. "Naturalist Wants Children to Know Many Local Species." *Worcester Telegram & Gazette* (Nov. 12, 2001): B4.

LaBastille, Anne. "Fishing in the Sky." In Sayre, *New Essays*, 53–72.

Lang, Thomas. "Walden Pond." *Independent* (April 1, 1869). In *TL*, 187–88.

Larrabee, John. "Commercialism Creeps into Thoreau's Retreat." *USA Today* (July 3, 1995).

Laxer, Mark E. "Take Me for a Ride: Coming of Age in a Destructive Cult." 1994. www.inform.umd.edu.

Leaux, John R. "The Cabin in the Garden." www.campus.houghton.edu/depts/english.

Lenox, Joe. Pers. comm., Oct. 2002.

Leu, Del. "Trip Summary." www.delsjourney.com.

Linebaugh, Donald W. " 'The Road to Ruins and Restoration': Roland W. Robbins, HDT, and the *Discovery at Walden*." *CS* n.s. 2, no. 1 (Fall 1994): 33–62.

Lloyd, Elwood. "A Visit to Walden." 1949. *TSB* 162 (Winter 1983).

Locker, Thomas. *Walking With Henry*. Golden, Co.: Fulcrum, 2002.

Loomis, E. J. *Boston Daily Advertiser* (May 8, 1894). In Sanborn, *Transcendental and Literary*, 464.

Loudon, J. C. *The Suburban Gardener*. London: Longman, 1838.

Mackay, James. *Robert Service*. Edinburgh: Mainstream, 1995.

Macone, John. "Walden St. Office Park Goes Up." *CJ* (May 19, 1988).

Mahoney, Joan. "Walden Pond Debate: Recreation Versus Nature." *Boston Globe* (Feb. 13, 1974).

Malton, James. *A Collection of Designs for Rural Retreats*. London: Carpenter, 1802.

Marble, Annie Russell. *Thoreau: His Home, Friends, and Books*. New York: Crowell, 1902.

Margolis, John D. *Joseph Wood Krutch*. Knoxville: University of Tennessee Press, 1980.

Martineau, Harriet. *Retrospect of Western Travel*. 2 vols. London: Saunders and Otley, 1838.

Mason, Daniel Gregory. "A Thanksgiving Pilgrimage to Thoreau." *Boston*

Evening Transcript (Nov. 26, 1902). In Cameron, *New England Writers*, 290–92.

Mason, Julian. "Sinclair Lewis' Copy of *Walden*." *TSB* 173 (Fall 1985).

Massachusetts Division of Fisheries and Wildlife *News* (1986). In Harding, Walden Pond file, HL.

Matthews, Paul. "Walden Pond: Paradise Lost?" *Lowell Sun* (July 29, 1979).

Maynard, W. Barksdale. *Architecture in the United States, 1800–1850*. New Haven and London: Yale University Press, 2002.

———. "The Cove Names of Walden—Corrected." *TSB* 239 (Spring 2002).

———. " 'Down this Long Hill in the Rain': Rediscovering the Trails of Thoreau in Concord." *Appalachia* 54, no. 1 (June 2002): 90–101.

———. "Emerson's 'Wyman Lot': Forgotten Context for Thoreau's House at Walden." Forthcoming in *CS*, 2004.

———. "Thoreau Manuscript Leaf Found at N. C. Wyeth Studio." *TSB* 243 (Spring 2003): 3.

———. "Thoreau's House at Walden." *Art Bulletin* 81, no. 2 (June 1999): 1–23.

———. "Thoreau's Walden House Revisited." *Vernacular Architecture Newsletter* 93 (Fall 2002): 21–24.

McAleer, John. *RWE*. Boston: Little, Brown, 1984.

McCaffrey, Ed. "Owner, State, Move Phase-Out of Concord Trailer Park." *Concord Free Press* (May 16, 1974). Clipping, Ferguson Papers, folder 6, CFPL.

McConville, Christine. "Thoreau Enthusiasts Walk in Naturalist's Footsteps." *Boston Globe* (July 21, 2002).

McGarrahan, E. Golden. "Groups Spar over Swimming at Walden Pond." *Middlesex News* (Sept. 17, 1987).

McGee, Rev. Michael A. "Naturalism—The Song of Gaia." 2001. www.uucava.org.

McGill, Frederick T., Jr. *Channing of Concord*. New Brunswick: Rutgers University Press, 1967.

McGrath, Anne. "Curator's Corner." *TSB* 205 (Autumn 1993).

McKee, Kathryn B. " 'A Fearful Price I Have Had to Pay for Loving Him' . . . " *SAR* (1994), 251–69.

McLynn, Frank. *Robert Louis Stevenson*. London: Hutchinson, 1993.

McNally, Dennis. *Desolate Angel*. New York: Random House, 1979.

Michaelis, David. *N. C. Wyeth*. New York: Knopf, 1998.

Michener, James A. "In Defense of Beatniks." *Philadelphia Bulletin* (Aug. 7, 1960). In *TSB* 73 (Fall 1960).

Miller, Perry. *Margaret Fuller*. Garden City: Doubleday, 1963.

Mitchell, John Hanson. *Living at the End of Time*. Boston: Houghton Mifflin, 1990.

Moldenhauer, Joseph J. "*Walden* and Wordsworth's Guide to the English Lake District." *SAR* (1990), 261–92.

Monahan, John J. "PETA Has Fishermen Up in Arms." *Worcester Telegram & Gazette* (Feb. 4, 1997).

Monette, Paul. *Becoming a Man*. New York: Harcourt Brace, 1992.

Moore, George. Diary. In Cameron, *Transcendental Epilogue*, vol. 1.

Moore, John H. "Walden Pond." *CJ* (Aug. 11, 1932).

Moran, John Michael, Jr. "More F. B. Sanborn Poems." *ESQ* 43 (2d Quarter 1966): 109–13.

More, Paul Elmer. "A Hermit's Notes on Thoreau." *Atlantic Monthly* 87 (June 1901): 857–64.

Morfit, Spencer Harris. "Walden: Earth's Eye." *Appalachia* n.s. 51, no. 1 (June 1996): 16–39.

Morley, Christopher. *Christopher Morley's Philadelphia*. New York: Fordham University Press, 1990.

Moroney, Tom. "Henley's Thoreau Center Plan Raises Some Eyebrows." *Boston Sunday Globe* (July 3, 1994).

———. "Thoreau Would Have Headed for Maine." *Middlesex News* (July 5, 1987).

Morris, Edmund. *Ten Acres Enough*. New York: James Miller, 1864.

Morse, David. *American Romanticism*. 2 vols. Totowa, N.Y.: Barnes & Noble, 1987.

Morse, Steve. "Don Henley Does It Again." *Boston Globe* (Aug. 27, 1993).

Mott, Wes. Pers. comm., March 2002.

Mouw, Richard J. "The Women at the Concord Tombs." Jan.–Feb. 1999. www.christianitytoday.com.

Munroe, [Alfred.] "Concord." *New York Times* (April 24, 1869). In *TSB* 184 (Summer 1988).

Myerson, Joel. "Emerson's 'Thoreau': A New Edition from Manuscript." *SAR* (1979), 17–55.

———. "Margaret Fuller's 1842 Journal." *Harvard Library Bulletin* 21, no. 3 (July 1973): 320–40.

———, ed. *Critical Essays on HDT's* Walden. Boston: G. K. Hall, 1988.

"National Society on Thoreau Formed in Concord." *Concord Herald* (July 17, 1941).

Negri, Gloria. "Leading a Life of Quiet Emulation." *Boston Globe* (May 21, 1991).

Nehru, Braj Kumar. "HDT: A Tribute." In Harding, *Thoreau Centennial*, 112–19.

Nelson, Truman. "The Battle of Walden Pond." *National Parks* 34, no. 159 (Dec. 1960): 4–6.

———. "Walden on Trial." *Nation* 187, no. 2 (July 19, 1958): 30–33.

———. "The Walden Pond of RWE." *ESQ* 13 (4th Quarter 1958): 6–8.

"News From Thoreau Country" (Summer 1993). TCCA pamphlet, CFPL.

Nichols, William H. "Literary Landmarks of Massachusetts." *National Geographic* 97, no. 3 (March 1950): 279–310.

North [pseudo.]. "Our Boston Correspondence." *National Anti-Slavery Standard* (July 21, 1866). In *TL*, 168.

O'Connor, Richard. "An Abbreviated History of the Development of the Boston Properties Land." TCCA, ca. 1990. Coll. Edmund A. Schofield.

———. "Dump Chronology." TCCA, 1990. Coll. Edmund A. Schofield.

———. Pers. comm., 2002–03.

O'Rourke, P. J. "Up the Amazon." *Rolling Stone* (Nov. 25, 1993): 60–72.

Oehlschlaeger, Fritz, and George Hendrick, eds. *Toward the Making of Thoreau's Modern Reputation*. Urbana: University of Illinois Press, 1979.

Omni Gazetteer of the USA. Multivolume. Detroit: Omnigraphics, 1991.

Packard, Winthrop. "Thoreau's Walden." *Boston Evening Transcript* (Aug. 20, 1910). In *TSBS2*, 187–89.

Peterson, Roger Tory, and James Fisher. *Wild America*. Boston: Houghton Mifflin, 1955.

"Picnic Excursions." *Waltham Free Press* (July 17, 1868). In *TL*, 196.

Pierce, David. *Yeats's Worlds*. New Haven: Yale University Press, 1995.

Plotkin, A. S. "Six-lane Highway to Replace Rte. 2." *Boston Globe* (1973). Clipping, Ferguson Papers, folder 6, CFPL.

Podmaniczky, Christine B. *N. C. Wyeth: Experiment and Invention, 1925–1935*. Chadds Ford, Pa.: Brandywine River Museum, 1995.

Pollan, Michael. *A Place of My Own*. New York: Dell, 1998.

Potter, David. "Sonnet." *Nature Outlook* 1 (Feb. 1943). In Cameron, *Thoreau Secondary Bibliography Supplement Three*, 53.

Potter, Thomas A. "Kindred Spirits: Edwin Way Teale and HDT." *CS* n.s. 9 (2001): 147–55.

"Primeval Simplicity: Sioux City Man and His Sister Resolve to Become Hermits." Clipping, with Cressy to Fred Hosmer, March 15, 1897, Hosmer Papers, CFPL.

R., E. A. "A Summer Ramble to the Hermit-Home of Thoreau." *Boston Journal* (July 3, 1874). In *CLR*, 203.

Rabinowitz, David E. "The Abuse of a Public Trust: A Case History of

Walden Pond." Report for Walden Forever Wild, 1986. Coll. Edmund A. Schofield.

Ramsey, C. T. "A Pilgrimage to the Haunts of Thoreau." 3 parts. *New England Magazine* 50, no. 3 (Nov. 1913): 371–83; no. 4 (Dec. 1913): 434–42; 51, no. 2 (April 1914): 67–71.

Renehan, Edward J., Jr. *John Burroughs*. Post Mills, Vt.: Chelsea Green, 1992.

"Replica to be Built at Thoreau's Pond." *Worcester Evening Gazette* (July 12, 1957). Harding Walden Pond files, HL.

"Replica of Thoreau's Hut to Rise on Shore of Historic Walden Pond." *Boston Traveler* (July 11, 1957). Harding Walden Pond files, HL.

"Reservoir at Walden?" *News-Tribune* (June 7, 1968). Clipping in WR.

"Restoration Proposal." Friends of Walden Pond, Feb. 1975. Ferguson Papers, folder 5, CFPL.

Richardson, Laurence E. *Concord Chronicle 1865–1899*. Concord: author, 1967.

Richardson, Robert D., Jr. *Emerson: The Mind on Fire*. Berkeley: University of California Press, 1995.

———. *Henry Thoreau: A Life of the Mind*. Berkeley: University of California Press, 1986.

Ricketson, Anna, and Walton Ricketson, eds. *Daniel Ricketson and His Friends*. New York: Houghton Mifflin, 1902.

Ricketson, Daniel. "Thoreau's Cairn." Aug. 12, 1872. In *TL*, 262.

———. "Walden." Jan. 17, 1860. *Liberator* (May 23, 1862).

Rierden, Andi. "Wildflowers' Perfume Sweetens a Life Devoted to Nature." *New York Times* (June 9, 1991).

Riggs, Susan. "Walden Revisited." *London [Ontario] Free Press* (May 11, 2002).

Robbins, Roland Wells. Coll. HL.

———. *Discovery at Walden*. Stoneham, Mass.: Barnhead, 1947. Copy used as guestbook. Robbins, Coll.

———. Thoreau hut excavation notebooks. Robbins, Coll.

———. "The Thoreau–Walden Cabin" brochure, n.d. Coll. Donald Linebaugh.

———, and Evan Jones. *Hidden America*. New York: Knopf, 1959.

Robins, Wayne. "Don Henley Goes Straight to the Heart." *Newsday* (April 30, 1990).

Robinson, David M. "Emerson, Thoreau, Fuller, and Transcendentalism." In *American Literary Scholarship* (Durham: Duke University Press, 2000), 3–27.

Roosevelt, Robert B. *Five Acres Too Much*. New York: Harper & Brothers, 1869.

Ruland, Richard, ed. *Twentieth Century Interpretations of Walden*. Englewood Cliffs: Prentice-Hall, 1968.

Rusk, Ralph L. *Life of RWE*. New York: Charles Scribner's Sons, 1949.

"Rutgers Professor Contends Thoreau Was Not a Hippie." *New York Times* (Jan. 4, 1968). In *ESQ 50* (1st Quarter 1968): 97.

Rye, Anthony. *Gilbert White & His Selborne*. London: Kimber, 1970.

S. "Walden Pond." *Middlesex Gazette* (Aug. 11, 1821). In *TSB* 195 (Spring 1991).

Salt, Henry S. *Life of HDT*. Ed. George Hendrick et al. 1908; reprint, Urbana: University of Illinois Press, 1993.

Saltmarsh, John A. *Scott Nearing*. Philadelphia: Temple University Press, 1991.

Sanborn, Franklin B. "Collection of Materials by Franklin Benjamin Sanborn Relating Primarily to W. E. Channing." Sanborn Papers, folder 3, used by permission of CFPL.

———. *Collected Poems of Franklin Benjamin Sanborn of Transcendental Concord*. Ed. John M. Moran. Hartford: Transcendental Books, 1964.

———. "Concord—An Old Town Renewing Its Youth," *Springfield Republican* (Oct. 18, 1871). In Sanborn, *Literary Studies*, 309–10.

———. *Correspondence of Franklin Benjamin Sanborn the Transcendentalist*. Ed. K. W. Cameron. Hartford: Transcendental Books, 1982.

———. "Ellery Channing and His Table-Talk." In Sanborn, *Transcendental and Literary*, 362.

———. *Henry D. Thoreau*. Boston: Houghton Mifflin, 1882.

———. "The Hermit of Walden, Edmond Stuart Hotham." In Sanborn, *Transcendental Horizons*, 7–9.

———. *The Homes and Haunts of Emerson*. In Sanborn, *Transcendental and Literary*.

———. Journal. In Sanborn, *Transcendental and Literary*.

———. *The Life of HDT*. Boston and New York: Houghton Mifflin, 1917.

———. "Literary Losses by Fires in Concord." *Springfield Republican* (May 23, 1896): 12. In Sanborn, *Literary Studies*, 142–43.

———. *Literary Studies and Criticism*. Ed. K. W. Cameron. Hartford: Transcendental Books, 1980.

———. Papers. Used by permission of CFPL.

———. *The Personality of Emerson*. 1903. In Sanborn, *Transcendental and Literary*.

———. *The Personality of Thoreau.* 1901. In Sanborn, *Transcendental and Literary*, 270–91.

———. *Recollections of Seventy Years.* 2 vols. Boston: Richard G. Badger, 1909.

———. "Thoreau and the Walden Woods." *Boston Herald* (May 26, 1896). In Sanborn, *Transcendental and Literary*, 464–65.

———. *Transcendental and Literary New England.* Ed. K. W. Cameron. Hartford: Transcendental Books, 1975.

———. *Transcendental Horizons: Essays and Poetry.* Ed. K. W. Cameron. Hartford: Transcendental Books, 1984.

———. "Walden Pond." *Springfield Republican* (ca. June 1914). In *CLR*, 101.

Sattelmeyer, Robert. "Depopulation, Deforestation, and the Actual Walden Pond." In Schneider, *Thoreau's Sense of Place*, 235–43.

———. "Study Nature and Know Thyself." *ESQ* 31 (3d Quarter 1985): 190–208.

———. "Thoreau's Projected Work on the English Poets." In *SAR* (1980): 239–57.

———. *Thoreau's Reading.* Princeton: Princeton University Press, 1988.

———. " 'The True Industry for Poets': Fishing with Thoreau." *ESQ* 33 (4th Quarter 1987): 189–201.

Sayre, Robert F., ed. *New Essays on* Walden. Cambridge: Cambridge University Press, 1992.

Scenic America. Nov. 1999. www.scenic.org/lcl.

Scharnhorst, Gary. *HDT: A Case Study in Canonization.* Columbia, S.C.: Camden House, 1993.

———. *HDT: An Annotated Bibliography of Comment and Criticism Before 1900.* New York: Garland Publishing, 1992.

Schiavo, Christine. "Class Has Own Golden Pond." *Morning Call* [Allentown, Pa.] (Feb. 9, 1998).

Schneider, Richard J., ed. *Thoreau's Sense of Place.* Iowa City: University of Iowa Press, 2000.

Schnelle, Robert. *Valley Walking.* Pullman: Washington State University Press, 1997.

Schnur, Steven, and Peter M. Fiore. *Henry David's House.* Watertown, Mass.: Charlesbridge, 2002.

Schofield, Edmund A. " 'Burnt Woods': Ecological Insights into Thoreau's Unhappy Encounter with Forest Fire." *Thoreau Research Newsletter* 2, no. 3 (July 1991): 1–8.

———. "The Ecology of Walden Woods." *TWO*, 155–171.

———. "Henry & Me." *Worcester Magazine* (June 3–9, 1998): 10–15.

———. Pers. comm., 2002–03.

———. Walden Pond Advisory Committee Meeting notes, Jan. 18, 1983. Coll. Edmund A. Schofield.

———. *The Walden Woods Bibliography*. 2002. www.walden.org.

———, and Robert C. Baron. *Thoreau's World and Ours*. Golden, Co.: North American Press, 1993.

Schwie, Dale R. "Herbert W. Gleason: A Photographer's Journey to Thoreau's World." *CS* n.s. 7 (1999): 151–65.

Scott, Winfield Townley. "Walden Pond in the Nuclear Age," *New York Times Magazine* (May 6, 1962).

Seib, Charles. Pers. comm., Oct. 2002.

———. *The Woods: One Man's Escape to Nature*. Garden City: Doubleday, 1971.

Shanley, J. Lyndon. *The Making of 'Walden,' with the Text of the First Version*. Chicago: University of Chicago Press, 1957.

"Shapiro & Sons Homes." www.shapiroandsonshomes.com.

Shattuck, Lemuel. *History of the Town of Concord*. Boston: Russell, Odiorne, 1835.

Shepard, Odell. "Unconsciousness in Cambridge: The Editing of Thoreau's 'Lost Journal.'" 1958. Reprint, *ESQ* 52 (3d Quarter 1968): 3–9.

Sherwood, Mary P. "Ban Walden Swimmers." Letter, *CJ* (May 12, 1983).

———. "Cooperation May Help at Walden." Letter, *CJ* (April 16, 1992).

———. Diary. In Sherwood Papers, CFPL.

———. Papers. Used by permission of CFPL.

———. "Renaissance at Walden." *Arnoldia* 46, no. 3 (Summer 1986): 47–60.

———. "Thoreau Lyceum History to 1968." Sherwood Papers, CFPL.

———. To Walden Lifesavers (July 17, 1989). WPSR.

———. "Walden Repair Delayed Nearly Two Decades." *Thoreau Journal Quarterly* (Jan. 1979): 27–32.

———, and Laurie Corliss Glasheen. "A Woman Takes on Walden." *Woman of Power* 20 (Spring 1991): 46–47.

Sidney, Margaret. *Old Concord: Her Highways and Byways*. 1888; rev. ed., Boston: Lothrop, 1892.

Simpson, Jeffrey E. "Thoreau: The Walking Muse." *ESQ* 37 (1st Quarter 1991): 1–33.

Simpson, Lewis P. "The Short, Desperate Life of Henry Thoreau." *ESQ* 42 (1st Quarter 1968): 46–56.

Sims, David. "Building to a Different Drummer." *Smithsonian* 33, no. 1 (April 2002): 101–06.

Skehan, James W. "Walden Pond: Its Geological Setting and the Africa Connection." *TWO*, 222–41.

Skelding, Anthony. "At Thoreau's Cairn." *Boston Herald* (Oct. 17, 1928).

Skinner, B. F. "Walden (One) and Walden Two." *TSB* 122 (Winter 1973).

Skinner, Charles M. *With Feet to the Earth*. Philadelphia and London: Lippincott, 1899.

Slater, Joseph, ed. *The Correspondence of Emerson and Carlyle*. New York and London: Columbia University Press, 1964.

Slone, G. Tod. "Basic, Everyday Rights." *G21*. www.g21.net.

———. "The Thoreau Society & Walden Pond State Reservation Have Proven Irresponsible in Upholding Thoreau's Ideals!" *American Dissident*. www.geocities.com/enmarge.

Smith, Harmon. *My Friend, My Friend*. Amherst: University of Massachusetts Press, 1999.

Smith, Jean Kennedy, et al. "A Grotesque Portrait of Our Parents." *New York Times* (Dec. 3, 1992).

Smith, Linda L. *Annie Dillard*. New York: Twayne, 1991.

Smith, Tim. *Thoreau's Walden*. Charleston: Arcadia, 2002.

Solitaire [pseudo.]. *Waltham Sentinel* (Nov. 30, 1866). In *TSB* 184 (Summer 1988).

Stewart, George R., Jr. *Bret Harte*. Port Washington, N.Y.: Kennikat, 1964.

Sullivan, Robert. "Keep Walden Pond Open." *Sports Illustrated* 67 (Aug. 17, 1987): 86.

"Support National Historic Landmark Status for All of Walden Woods." Advertisement. *CJ* (July 13, 1989).

Tapply, William. "Walden Pond Revisited." *Fins and Feathers* 3, no. 2 (Feb. 1984): 14–20.

["Teaching Thoreau."] www.calliope.org/thoreau/thoroteach.

Teale, Edwin Way. "Henry Thoreau and the Realms of Time." *TSB* 64 (Summer 1958).

———. *The Lost Woods*. New York: Dodd, Mead, 1945.

———. *A Naturalist Buys an Old Farm*. New York: Dodd, Mead, 1974.

———. *North with the Spring*. New York: Dodd, Mead, 1951.

———. "A Week in Concord" (Sept. 1945). Vault A35, E. W. Teale Unit 1 (Series 3, Item 1), CFPL.

"Ted Kaczynski: The Unabomber." 2002. www.crimelibrary.com.

Teitell, Beth. "It's Summertime, and the Livin' Sure Ain't Easy." BostonHerald.com, July 23, 1999. www.teitell.com.

Templeman, William D. "Thoreau, Moralist of the Picturesque." *Proceedings of the Modern Language Association* 47 (1932): 864–89.

Thomas, Bill. "Rumblings Break Serenity at Walden Woods." *Minuteman Chronicle* (April 4, 1992).

Thoreau, Henry David. *Correspondence*. Ed. Walter Harding and Carl Bode. New York: New York University Press, 1958.

———. *Early Essays and Miscellanies*. Ed. Joseph J. Moldenhauer. Princeton: Princeton University Press, 1975.

———. "Field Notes of Surveys made by HDT since November 1849." In Cameron, *Transcendental Climate* 2: 413–549.

———. *The Illuminated Walden*. Ed. Ronald A. Bosco. Ill. John Wawrzonek. New York: Friedman/Fairfax, 2002.

———. *Journal*. Ed. Bradford Torrey and Francis H. Allen. 14 vols. Boston: Houghton Mifflin, 1906.

———. *Journal*. Ed. John C. Broderick et al. 8 vols. Princeton: Princeton University Press, 1981–2002.

———. *Natural History Essays*. Salt Lake: Peregrine Smith, 1980.

———. Surveys. CFPL. www.concordnet.org.

———. *A Week on the Concord and Merrimack Rivers*. Boston and New York: Houghton Mifflin, 1906.

———. *Walden*. 2 vols. Boston: Bibliophile Society, 1909.

———. *Walden*. Boston: Limited Editions Club, 1936.

———. *Walden*. Intro. Edwin Way Teale. New York: Dodd, Mead, 1946.

———. *Walden*. Preface by Joseph Wood Krutch. New York: Libra Coll., 1960.

———. *Walden*. Ed. J. Lyndon Shanley. Princeton: Princeton University Press, 1971.

———. *Walden: An Annotated Edition*. Ed. Walter Harding. Boston and New York: Houghton Mifflin, 1995.

———. *Walden* first MS version. 1846–47. In Shanley, *Making of 'Walden.'*
The Thoreau Institute, June 5, 1998. Pamphlet, WWP.

"Thoreau Institute Grand Opening." *TSB* 224 (Summer 1998).

"Thoreau Legacy: 3 'Walden' Houses" (Dec. 29, 1985). Clipping, WPSR.

Thoreau, Sophia. Letter to Marianne Dunbar. Nov. 29, 1867. In *TSB 33* (Oct. 1952).

"Thoreau . . . The Thinking Man's Nudist." *Mr. Sun* 1, no. 2 (1966).

"Thoreau's Pond." Editorial, *New York Times* (Jan. 30, 1921). In *TSBS2*, 210.

"To Desecrate Walden Pond." *New-York Tribune Illustrated Supplement* (Sept. 21, 1902): 7.

Toska, Edna. Pers. comm., Oct. 2002.

"A Trip to Concord." *Marlboro Advertiser* (June 9, 1880). In Cameron, *Emerson, Thoreau, and Concord in Early Newspapers*, 168–69.

Troy, Jack. "Pot-Hunting at Concord and Walden." *TSB* 101 (Fall 1967).

Tryon, Kate. "A Day Afield." *Boston Advertiser* (Oct. 15, 1895). In Cameron, *New England Writers*, 255–57.

———. "Of High Places About the Historic Town of Concord." *Boston Advertiser* (Dec. 18, 1895). In Cameron, *New England Writers*, 259–62.

Turner, Frederick. *Spirit of Place*. Washington, D.C.: Island Press, 1989.

Tye, Larry. "Walden Pond Offices Get Boost." *Boston Globe* (Dec. 3, 1988).

———. "With Odor Gone, Beach Reopened at Walden Pond." *Boston Globe* (July 9, 1997).

Van Dore, Wade. *Robert Frost and Wade Van Dore: Life of the Hired Man*. Dayton, Ohio: Wright State University, 1986.

Vaupel, Robin. *My Contract with Henry*. New York: Holiday House, 2003.

"Walden: 1962." WBZ radio broadcast, July 20, 1962. Phonographic recording.

"The Walden Decision: Protection Comes at Last to Historic Landscape." *Landscape Architecture* (Fall 1960). Reprint, C.PAM.60, CFPL.

"Walden Pond Apartment Homes." www.waldenpondliving.com.

"Walden Pond—Different Now Than When Thoreau was There." www.epinions.com.

"Walden Pond Fight Mapped." *Boston Herald* (July 18, 1957).

Walden Pond Restoration Study Final Report. Cambridge: Richard A. Gardiner and Associates, June 1974.

Walker, Eugene H. "Concord Mystery: Tracing the Source of Walden Pond's Waters." *Concord Magazine*, www.concordma.com/magazine.

———. "The History Back of the Name Walden." *CS* suppl. 2 (June 1972).

———. "Walden's Way Revealed." *Man and Nature* [Mass. Audubon Society] (Dec. 1971): 11–20.

Walker, Lester. *A Little House of My Own*. New York: Black Dog, 2000.

Wallace, Anne D. *Walking, Literature, and English Culture*. Oxford: Clarendon Press, 1993.

Watkins, Lura Woodside. *Early New England Potters and Their Wares*. 1950; reprint, Hamden, Ct.: Anchor Books, 1968.

Waylen, Hector. "A Visit to Walden Pond," *Natural Food* [Surrey, Eng.] 6 (July 1895), 438–39. In *CLR*, 228–29.

Westbrook, Perry. "John Burroughs and the Transcendentalists." *ESQ* 55 (2d Quarter 1969): 47–55.

A Westerner. "A Day in Hawthorne's Haunts." *Overland Monthly* 4, no. 6 (June 1870): 516–20.

Whicher, George F. *Walden Revisited*. Chicago: Packard, 1945.

Whitcomb, Robert. "The Thoreau 'Country.'" *Bookman* 73, no. 5 (July 1931): 458–61.

White, Charles W. "A Protest Against the Thoreau Society's Annual Meeting." *TSB* 113 (Fall 1970).

White, E. B. *One Man's Meat*. New ed. New York and London: Harper & Brothers, 1944.

———. "Walden—1954." *Yale Review* 44, no. 1 (Sept. 1954): 13–22.

Whitman, Howard. "Thoreau's Concord is Willing to Leave Nature's Work Alone." *New York Times* (Sept. 17, 1972).

Whitman, Walt. *Prose Works 1892*. Ed. Floyd Stovall. 2 vols. New York: New York University Press, 1963.

Whitney, Gordon G., and William C. Davis. "Thoreau and the Forest History of Concord, Massachusetts." *Journal of Forest History* 30, no. 2 (April 1986): 70–81.

"Why It's Time to Close the Concord Landfill." Advertisement. *CJ* (March 31, 1994).

Wilder, Myron. "An Ex-Hermit Looks at Thoreau." *TSB* 129 (Fall 1974).

Williams, Paul O. "Emerson Guided: Walks with Thoreau and Channing." *ESQ* 35 (2d Quarter 1964): 66–68.

Williams, Ted. "Walden, Then and Now." *Massachusetts Wildlife* 24, no. 6 (1973): 2–19.

Williamson, Selma. "Walden Pond." *Concord Herald* (Sept. 5, 1935).

Willis, Frederick L. H. *Alcott Memoirs*. Boston: Richard G. Badger, 1915.

Willis, N. P. *Rural Letters*. New Orleans: Burnett and Bostwick, 1854.

Wilson, Edward O. *The Future of Life*. New York: Knopf, 2002.

———. Interview, Sept. 13, 2001, WWP.

Wilson, Leslie Perrin. "The Herbert Wendell Gleason Negatives in the CFPL: Odyssey of a Collection." *CS* n.s. 7 (1999): 175–92.

———. "N. C. Wyeth, Thoreau, and *Men of Concord*." *CS* n.s. 8 (2000): 65–92.

Winkler, Marjorie Green. "Changes at Walden Pond During the Last 600 Years." *TWO*, 199–211.

Winslow, Kathryn. *Henry Miller*. Los Angeles: Tarcher, 1986.

Wolfe, Theodore F. *Literary Shrines*. Philadelphia: Lippincott, 1897. Inc. "The Walden of Thoreau."

Wood, Thomas. "Conquered, Massachusetts." *Esquire* (July 1934): 76–77, 94.

Woodson, Thomas, et al. "With Hawthorne in Wartime Concord: Sophia Hawthorne's 1862 Diary." *SAR* (1988), 281–359.

Wordsworth, William. *Guide to the Lakes*. 5th ed., 1835. Reprint, Oxford: Oxford University Press, 1970.

———. "When, to the Attractions of a Busy World." 1800–02.

Wyeth, N. C. "Thoreau, His Critics, and the Public" (1919). In Glick, *Recognition*, 227–32.

Yount, Jim. Mini Cabin Website. www.ria.edu/minicabin.

Zacks, Richard. "Fighting the Crowd on Walden Pond." *Mental Floss* 1, no. 2 (2001).

Zimmer, Jeanne M. "A History of Thoreau's Hut and Hut Site." *ESQ* 18, no. 3 (3d Quarter 1972): 134–40.

Zuckerman, Mortimer B. "Get the Site Right." *Newsday* (Oct. 3, 1991).

Zwinger, Ann H. Pers. comm., March 2002.

Index

Page numbers in *italic* refer to illustrations

Tuttle, Mr., 137
Twenty–Year Program, for Walden, 255
Tynan, Katharine, 198

Udall, Steward L., 266
Unabomber, 319, *320*, 321
Union Band Concert, 178
Unitarians, 122, 155, 162–63, 172–74, 179, 196, 324
United States Geological Survey, 326, 328
Universalist Sunday School, 179
Upham, Warren, 203
Urine, in Walden, 326–27, 333
Utopias, 63–64, 73, 91, 221

Van Dore, Wade, 232–33, 268, 286
Van Doren, Mark, 223
Van Eeden, Frederick, 221
Vegetarians, 206, 323
Vegetation history, of Walden, 74–75, 287
Very, Jones, 41, 325
Vietnam War, 269, 277–78, 291, 315
Visitation, at Walden, 4, 6–7, 24–25, 41, 72–74, 174, 230, 255–56, 281, 329–30; visitors to Hotham, 168–70; visitors to Thoreau at Walden, 6, 72–74, 84–85, 160
Visitors' Center, Concord, 304

Wachusett, Mt., 81, 137, 180
Walden, 19, 48, 69, 72, 77, 84, 86, 109, 123; composition and drafts of, 7, 49, 55, 91, 97, 104–5, 108–9, 111–12, 116, 346n.32; as literature, 9–10; pond survey in, 79, *80*, 244, 326; publication of, 115, 117, 127; reprintings and editions, 158, 159, 194, 210–11, 212, 221–22, 236, 246–47, 250, 253, 265; as secretive, 66, 91; significance of, 121
Walden Breezes: trailer park, 238, 247, 283–84, 299, 310, 333; lunch stand, 231–32, 235, *243*, 244
Walden Clubs, England, 221
Walden Cottage, Surrey, 220
Walden Earthcare Congress, 305
Walden Forever Wild, 289–90, 295, 308, 317
Walden, Ontario, 8
Walden Pond: acreage, 5; aerial views, *24*, *307*; attendance, 4; as bottomless, 21; boundstone by, 105; as classic site, 135; as destination for Thoreau, 99; disappointment in, 10–11; housing developments with this name, 9; in Lynn,

Massachusetts, 5; origin of name, 17; other ponds with this name, 8–9, 337n.13; proposed as water supply, 179; prospects of, *19*, 107; as suburban, 116
Walden Pond Advisory Council, 280–81, 283, 291
Walden Pond Day (1983), 291–92
Walden Pond Protective Association, 228
Walden Pond Society: of Mary Sherwood, 289; of nineteenth century, 122
Walden Pond State Reservation, 1, 229–32, 237–38, *242*, 252, 255–62, 274–75, 280–86, *282*, 292–94, 297, 308–9, 311, 313–14, 325–26, 330–32; guestbook, 6–7, *323*
Walden Protective Act, 290, 308
Walden Road (Lincoln Road, Wayland Road): in nineteenth century, 25, *26*, 26–27, 30–31, 50, 70–71, 74, 77, 81, 92–93, 103–4, 107, 114–17, 122, 126–27, 129–31, 136–38, 146, 153, 182, 194, *200*, 207–8, 210, 212–13, 338n.7; in twentieth century, 218, 231, 235, 238, 244, 274, 284, 310. *See also* Route 126; Walden Street
Walden Street, 27, 95, 176, 185, 205, 232, *241*, *242*, 262, 297. *See also* Route 126; Walden Road
Walden Woods: beanfields in, 70–71; boundaries defined, 18, *296*, 297, 299, 338–39n.7; in decline, 93, 161–62, 178, 188, 207, 218, 225–26, 228, 235, 251, 291, 308, 328–30; early accounts, 16–17; as fearsome, 27; forest cover, 74–75, 143–46; as primeval, 16; in relation to town, 85–86; as a term, 18; for walking, 97; as wild, 74–75, 132
Walden Woods Project, 9, 18, 302–19, 325, 331–33
Walker, Eugene H., 21
Walking, 24, 97–98, 111, 128–29, 154, 180, 183; Emerson on, 33, 128–30, 197; Professors of, 97, 197; Walking Society, 352n.13. *See also* Peripatetic; Sauntering
Waltham, Massachusetts, 164, 188, 210, 238
Ward, Samuel G., 138
Warner, Charles Dudley, 177, 225
Warren, Chief Justice Earl, 267
Warren Lot, 86, 91
Warren, Mr., 219
Warren's Wood, 144